Introduction to Mathematical Finance

Discrete Time Models

Stanley R. Pliska

The right of Stanley R. Pliska to be identified as author of this work has been asserted in accordance with the Copyright, Designs and Patents Act 1988.

First published 1997
Reprinted 1997

Blackwell Publishers Inc
350 Main Street, Malden, Massachusetts 02148, USA

Blackwell Publishers Ltd
108 Cowley Road, Oxford OX4 1JF, UK

Library of Congress Cataloging in Publication Data has been applied for

British Library Cataloguing in Publication Data
A CIP catalogue record for this book is available from the British Library

ISBN 1–55786–945–6

Commissioning Editor: Rolf Janke
Desk Editor: Linda Auld
Production Manager/Controller: Lisa Parker
Text Designer Lisa Parker

Typeset in Times on 10/11.5 pt.
by Pure Tech India Ltd., Pondicherry, India
Printed and bound in Great Britain by
MPG Books Ltd, Bodmin, Cornwall

This book is printed on acid-free paper

Contents

Preface

Aims and Audience

This book is designed to serve as a textbook for advanced undergraduate and beginning graduate students who seek a rigorous yet accessible introduction to the modern financial theory of security markets. This is a subject that is taught in both business schools and mathematical science departments, and it is also a subject that is widely and extensively utilized in the financial industry. The derivatives industry has roughly $20 trillion in notional principal outstanding as this book goes to press, and the portfolio management industry is probably even bigger. Mathematics play crucial roles in both these areas. Consequently, financial practitioners (especially 'rocket scientists,' quants, financial engineers, etc.) may find this book useful for their theoretical background.

The full theory of security markets requires knowledge of continuous time stochastic process models, measure theory, mathematical economics, and similar prerequisites which are generally not learned before the advanced graduate level. Hence a proper study of the complete theory of security markets requires several years of graduate study (or equivalent, sink or swim, experience). However, by restricting attention to discrete time models of security prices it is possible to acquire an introduction without making a big investment in the advanced mathematics. In fact, while living in a discrete time world it is possible to learn virtually all of the important financial concepts. The purpose of this book is to provide such an introductory study.

There is still a lot of mathematics in this book. The reader should be comfortable with calculus, linear algebra, and probability theory that is based on calculus (but not necessarily measure theory). Random variables and expected values will be playing important roles. The book will develop important notions concerning discrete time stochastic processes; prior knowledge here will be useful but is not required. Presumably the reader will be interested in finance and thus will come with some rudimentary knowledge of stocks, bonds, options, and financial decision making. The last topic involves utility theory, of course; hopefully the reader will be familiar with this and related topics of introductory microeconomic theory.

Some exposure to linear programming would be advantageous, but those lacking this knowledge can make do with the appendix and independent study.

The aim of this book is to provide a rigorous treatment of the financial theory while maintaining a casual style. There is an emphasis on computational examples, and exercises are provided to check understanding and provide supplemental information. Readers seeking institutional knowledge about securities, derivatives, and portfolio management should look elsewhere, but those seeking a careful introduction to financial engineering will find that this is a useful and comprehensive introduction to the subject.

Brief Summary of This Book

This book consists of seven chapters, each divided into a number of sections. Important equations, fundamental statements, examples, and exercises are labeled with numbers by chapter. For example, equation 2.1 is the first equation in chapter 2.

This summary will point out which subjects are most important, and why (usually because I think something is of fundamental importance rather than a narrow result of limited or temporary consequence). It will also indicate topics that are new, at least in their treatment. Arguably, there are no new results in this book, but, like Monday morning quarterbacking, we can look backwards and see better ways to say and do things. Hopefully, the book will successfully do this, thereby conveying a clear understanding of some fundamental ideas about security markets.

The first two chapters are devoted to single period models. Most of the important concepts in this book are introduced here, making sections 1.1.–1.5 and 2.1–2.3 especially important. Section 2.4 is a modern treatment of the important mean-variance portfolio analysis. Sections 1.6 and 2.5–2.7 are extensions and ventures into significant topics that are a bit out of this book's mainstream.

The rest of this book is devoted to multiperiod models. This builds on the single period results, emphasizing what is new and different. The redundant material is kept concise in order to spare the patience of the stronger reader (but such readers will still find it worthwhile to refer to the first two chapters). Chapter 3 describes the basic elements of securities market models and introduces important notions such as dividend processes and the binomial model. Chapter 4 is devoted to derivatives, including forwards and futures; all the sections here are of fundamental interest. Chapter 5 attends to optimal consumption and investment problems. Sections 5.2 and 5.4 are the most important ones here (of course I might be biased, for the ideas originated from my research in 1982 and 1986), because they deal with the risk neutral computational approach. Sections 5.5–5.8 are extensions and special cases.

Interest rate derivatives have become extremely important in recent years. Chapter 6 is devoted to this subject, covering examples of key derivatives such as caps and swaptions and explaining how discrete time interest rate models are used for derivative valuation.

Chapter 7 provides a brief look at models with infinite sample spaces. This seemingly innocuous extension leads to significant mathematical complications and technicalities, and so this chapter will be most appealing to readers whose interests lean in the direction of abstract mathematics.

Suggested Readings

The aim here is to provide some suggestions for further study, not to give an account of which researchers are responsible for specific results. Most of the references that will be mentioned are books, and some of these have very comprehensive bibliographies of old research. This discussion is for the reader who wishes to learn more mathematical finance, not history.

I will begin with the prerequisites, starting with basic probability theory. Feller (1968, 1971) is a classic still worth reading. I used Olkin, Gleser, and Derman (1980) for teaching probability courses in the 1970s and 80s. More recent texts on basic probability theory include Ross (1976), Karr (1993), and Pitman (1993). All these texts assume the reader knows some calculus, but measure theory is not needed.

This book uses a lot of linear algebra and matrix theory, another subject where the newer books are no better than a classic, namely, Gantmacher (1959). Nevertheless, here are some newer books: Brown (1988), Strang (1988), Brown (1991), and Roman (1992).

Growing out of linear algebra is the subject of linear programming, the problem of maximizing or minimizing a linear objective function subject to some linear constraints. The appendix provides a quick overview of this subject as well as a list of good references. A closely related subject, quadratic programming, involves similar optimization problems, differing only in that the objective function is a quadratic function. Even more general are convex optimization problems, also called nonlinear programming problems, where the objective function is not necessarily quadratic. Such problems arise in finance when a portfolio manager seeks to maximize expected utility. Some good references include Mangasarian (1969), Jeter (1986), Hayhurst (1987), and Bazaraa (1993).

One subject of mathematics that should not be ignored is introductory analysis. This has to do with things like convergence, open and closed sets, functions, and limits. The books by Bartle and Sherbert (1992), Mikusinski and Mikusinski (1993), and Berberian (1994) are popular texts for this area.

Many of the preceding mathematical topics are covered in the introductions to the mathematics that are useful in economics by Chiang (1974) and Ostaszewski (1993). These books are highly recommended, because while giving primary emphasis to the mathematical tools, they also explain how the math is used in economics, thereby providing some economic background for the study of financial markets. In this same category, but focusing more narrowly on the application of optimization theory to economics, is the book by Dixit (1990).

So much for the prerequisites. It is not necessary to be an expert in any of the preceding areas, but you should be familiar with them.

Moving into the area of discrete time stochastic processes (random walks, Bernoulli processes, Markov chains, martingales, etc.), there are several introductory books to choose from: Parzen (1967), Freedman (1971), Hoel, Port, and Stone (1972), Cinlar (1975), Karlin and Taylor (1975, 1981), Taylor and Karlin (1984), and Ross (1985). At a more advanced level (some measure theory may be used) one should be aware of the classics by Doob (1953), Neveu (1975) and Revuz (1984) as well as the more recent books by Durrett (1991) and Williams (1991).

Another mathematical topic that is developed in this book is dynamic programming. This has to do with the optimal control of a stochastic process. In the common situation where the process is Markovian, this topic is called Markov decision theory. Here one can do no better than look at the work by Bertsekas (1976), Denardo (1982), Whittle (1982, 1983), and Puterman (1994).

Finally I come to financial economics. Unfortunately, and with the exception of the many treatments about single period portfolio management problems (the book by Markowitz (1990) is the definitive reference here), there are relatively few books on the theory of security markets. And most of the pages in these books are devoted to continuous time models, which means that much of the financial theory is presented only in the continuous time context.

Dothan (1990) comes the closest in spirit to this book (and, coincidentally, the closest in spirit to Harrison and Pliska (1981)). Presented in a modern fashion in terms of the probabilistic modeling, the first half of the book is devoted to single period and multiperiod models, while the second half is devoted to very general and advanced continuous time models. The emphasis is on arbitrage pricing of options, with little attention to futures, interest rate models, and portfolio management.

Another good book is by Ingersoll (1987). Although the probabilistic modeling is not as modern as Dothan's (1990), Ingersoll's book is more comprehensive and has more of an economic orientation. Somewhat similar is Duffie's (1992) book, although it is very concise and sometimes can be difficult for the average student. Other books containing some treatments of discrete time models, but presented in an older fashion, are Jarrow (1988), Huang and Litzenberger (1988), and Eatwell, Milgate, and Newman (1989).

The books by Duffie (1988) and Merton (1990) contain a huge amount of theory, but all is at an advanced level, in a continuous time context. Meanwhile, three excellent books with a narrower focus, namely, on discrete and continuous time models of derivatives, are by Cox and Rubenstein (1985), Hull (1993), and Jarrow and Turnbull (1996). Also worth looking at is the book by Wilmott, Dewynne, and Howison (1993), which studies option pricing from the partial differential equation perspective, and the one by Dixit and Pindyck (1994), which studies capital investment decisions by firms and thus covers some of the same ground as one would when investing in securities. Finally, the reader should be aware of the lovely, but advanced, survey of optimization problems in finance by Karatzas (1989).

Stanley R. Pliska

Acknowledgments

This book grew out of lecture notes, first organized in a careful fashion for a 1991 PhD class in Japan, while I was a Yamaichi Visiting Professor of Finance at Tsukuba University. I am indebted to Masaaki Kijima for making this experience possible. The work continued in 1992 while I was a Distinguished Visiting Fellow at the London School of Economics (thank you Michael J. P. Selby) and a Visiting Scholar at the University of Warwick (thank you Stewart Hodges).

A preliminary version of the book was tried out in a 1994 PhD class at the University of Illinois at Chicago. The reaction of the students was very useful, especially the feedback from Bill Francis and Rashida Dahodwala.

In January, 1995, I took a close-to-final version to the Program on Financial Mathematics at the Isaac Newton Institute for Mathematical Sciences, University of Cambridge (I am indebted to Chris Rogers for making this rewarding experience possible). There, parts of the book were used for a course, and copies of the whole book were made available to visiting researchers. The feedback I received and the hospitality of the Institute while I was there for six months as a Prudential Distinguished Visiting Fellow were important factors in the final stages of book preparation. In particular, careful comments by Abel Cadenillas and Peter Lakner, two visiting researchers who took copies for 1995–96 courses at their respective universities, were especially helpful. Also, Ruediger Kiesel provided some useful feedback.

1 Single Period Securities Markets

1.1 Model Specifications

Single period models are obviously unrealistic representations of complex, time-varying, random phenomena such as stock and bond prices. But they have the virtues of being mathematically simple as well as being able to illustrate many of the important economic principles associated with even the most complex, continuous time models. Hence single period models are worth studying for introductory purposes.

The following elements of the basic, single period model are specified as data:

- Initial date $t = 0$ and terminal date $t = 1$, with trading and consumption possible at these two dates.
- A finite sample space Ω with $K < \infty$ elements:

$$\Omega = \{\omega_1, \omega_2, \ldots, \omega_K\}$$

  Here each $\omega \in \Omega$ should be thought of as a possible state of the world, the value of which is unknown at time $t = 0$ but which becomes apparent to the investors at time $t = 1$.

- A probability measure P on Ω, with $P(\omega) > 0$ for all $\omega \in \Omega$.
- A *bank account* process $B = \{B_t : t = 0, 1\}$, where $B_0 = 1$ and B_1 is a random variable.[1] The bank account process will be distinguished from the other securities because its time $t = 1$ price $B_1(\omega)$ will be assumed to be strictly positive for all $\omega \in \Omega$. Usually, in fact, $B_1 \geqslant 1$, in which case B_1 should be thought of as the time $t = 1$ value of the bank account when \$1 is deposited at time $t = 0$ and $r \equiv B_1 - 1 \geqslant 0$ should be thought of as the *interest rate*. For many applications the quantities r and B_1 are taken to be deterministic scalars. If necessary for a particular application,

however, B_1 can be a positive random variable with r violating the constraint $r \geqslant 0$.

- A *price process* $S = \{S_t : t = 0, 1\}$, where $S_t = (S_1(t), S_2(t) \ldots, S_N(t)), N < \infty$, and $S_n(t)$ is the time t price of security n. For many applications these N risky securities are stocks. The time $t = 0$ prices are positive scalars that are known to the investors, whereas the time $t = 1$ prices are non-negative random variables whose values become known to the investors only at time $t = 1$. When $N = 1$, it is convenient to simply write S_t for the time t price.

Having specified all the data describing the model, the next step is to define several quantities of interest. A *trading strategy* $H = (H_0, H_1, \ldots, H_N)$ describes an investor's portfolio as carried forward from time $t = 0$ to time $t = 1$. In particular, the scalar H_0 is the number of dollars invested in the savings account, and for $n \geqslant 1$ the scalar H_n is the number of units of security n (for example, shares of stock) held between times 0 and 1. In general, H_n can be positive or negative (negative means borrowing or selling short), but sometimes there are constraints specified for the trading strategies to be admissible (for example, $H_n \geqslant 0$ for $n \geqslant 1$; that is, no short selling of the risky securities).

The *value process* $V = \{V_t : t = 0, 1\}$ describes the total value of the portfolio at each point in time. By simple bookkeeping this is

$$V_t \equiv H_o B_t + \sum_{n=1}^{N} H_n S_n(t), \qquad t = 0, 1$$

Note that the value process depends on the choice of the trading strategy H and that V_1 is a random variable.

The *gains process* G is a random variable that describes the total profit or loss generated by the portfolio between times 0 and 1. Since $H_n(S_n(1) - S_n(0))$ is the net profit due to investment in the nth security (similarly for the bank account), the gains process is

$$G \equiv H_0 r + \sum_{n=1}^{N} H_n \Delta S_n$$

where, by standard notation, $\Delta S_n \equiv S_n(1) - S_n(0)$.

A simple calculation verifies that

(1.1) $$V_1 = V_0 + G$$

Hence equation (1.1) says that any change in the value of the portfolio must be due to a profit or loss in the investment and not, for example, due to the addition of funds from an outside source.

The movement of the security prices relative to each other will be important to study, so it is convenient to normalize the prices in such a way that the bank account becomes constant. In other words, we are going to make the bank account the *numeraire*. We do this by defining the *discounted price process* $S^* = \{S_t^* : t = 0, 1\}$ by setting $S_t^* \equiv (S_1^*(t), \ldots, S_N^*(t))$ and

$$S_n^*(t) \equiv S_n(t)/B_t, \qquad n = 1, \ldots, N; \quad t = 0, 1$$

the *discounted value process* $V^* = \{V_t^* : t = 0, 1\}$ by

$$V_t^* \equiv H_0 + \sum_{n=1}^{N} H_n S_n^*(t), \qquad t = 0, 1$$

and the *discounted gains process* G^* by the random variable

$$G^* \equiv \sum_{n=1}^{N} H_n \Delta S_n^*$$

where, as one should guess, $\Delta S_n^* \equiv S_n^*(1) - S_n^*(0)$. With some more elementary bookkeeping, one eventually obtains

(1.2) $$V_t^{**} = V_t / B_t, \qquad t = 0, 1$$

as well as the discounted counterpart of equation (1.1), namely,

(1.3) $$V_1^* = V_0^* + G^*$$

Example 1.1 Suppose $K = 2$, $N = 1$, $r = 1/9$, $S_0 = 5$, $S_1(\omega_1) = 20/3$ and $S_1(\omega_2) = 40/9$. Then $B_1 = 1 + r = 10/9$, $S_1^*(\omega_1) = 6$, and $S_1^*(\omega_2) = 4$. For an arbitrary trading strategy H we have $V_0 = V_0^* = H_0 + 5H_1$ as well as

$$V_1 = (10/9)H_0 + H_1 S_1 \qquad V_1^* = H_0 + H_1 S_1^*$$
$$G = (1/9)H_0 + H_1(S_1 - 5) \qquad G^* = H_1(S_1^* - 5)$$

Hence in state ω_1

$$V_1 = (10/9)H_0 + (20/3)H_1 \qquad V_1^* = H_0 + 6H_1$$
$$G = (1/9)H_0 + (5/3)H_1 \qquad G^* = H_1$$

whereas in state ω_2

$$V_1 = (10/9)H_0 + (40/9)H_1 \qquad V_1^* = H_0 + 4H_1$$
$$G = (1/9)H_0 - (5/9)H_1 \qquad G^* = -H_1$$

It is easy to verify that equations (1.1) to (1.3) hold for both $\omega \in \Omega$.

Example 1.2 With everything else the same as in example 1.1, take $K = 3$ and set $S_1(\omega_3) = 30/9$, so that $S_1^*(\omega_3) = 3$. The other quantities of interest are left to the reader. Although this was a simple modification, it will be shown later that we have substantially changed the character of this model.

Example 1.3 For a simple model featuring two risky securities, suppose $K = 3$, $r = 1/9$ and the price process is as follows:

n	$S_n(0)$	$S_n(1)$		
		ω_1	ω_2	ω_3
1	5	60/9	60/9	40/9
2	10	40/3	80/9	80/9

It follows that the discounted price process is given by

n	$S_n^*(0)$	$S_n^*(1)$		
		ω_1	ω_2	ω_3
1	5	6	6	4
2	10	12	8	8

The other quantities of interest are left to the reader.

Example 1.4   Again, and as will be shown later, a small modification will create a model having substantially different character. With everything else the same as in example 1.3, we take $K = 4$ and set the prices in state ω_4 to be $S_1(1) = 20/9$ and $S_2(1) = 20/9$. Now the discounted price process is:

n	$S_n^*(0)$	$S_n^*(1)$			
		ω_1	ω_2	ω_3	ω_4
1	5	6	6	4	2
2	10	12	8	8	2

Exercise 1.1   Verify (1.2).

Exercise 1.2   Verify (1.3).

Exercise 1.3   Specify V, V^*, G and G^* for

(a)   Example 1.2
(b)   Example 1.3
(c)   Example 1.4

1.2   Arbitrage and other Economic Considerations

In order for the single period model to be reasonable from the economic standpoint, it must satisfy various criteria. For example, the model would be unreasonable if the investors were certain to be able to make a profit on a transaction, without any risk of losing money or even of failing to make a gain. Such would be the case if there existed a dominant trading strategy.

A trading strategy $\hat{H}$ is said to be *dominant* if there exists another trading strategy, say $\tilde{H}$, such that $\hat{V}_0 = \tilde{V}_0$ and $\hat{V}_1(\omega) > \tilde{V}_1(\omega)$ for all $\omega \in \Omega$. In other words, both trading strategies start with the same amount of money, but the dominant one is certain to end up with more.

If H is a trading strategy satisfying $V_0 = 0$ and $V_1(\omega) > 0$ for all $\omega \in \Omega$, then H is dominant because it dominates the strategy which starts with zero money and does no investment at all. Conversely, if the trading strategy $\hat{H}$ dominates the trading strategy $\tilde{H}$, then by defining a new trading strategy $H = \hat{H} - \tilde{H}$ it follows by the linearity in the definition of V that $V_0 = \hat{V}_0 - \tilde{V}_0 = 0$ and $V_1(\omega) = \hat{V}_1(\omega) - \tilde{V}_1(\omega) > 0$ for all $\omega \in \Omega$. In other words, the following is true:

(1.4) There exists a dominant trading strategy if and only if there exists a trading strategy satisfying $V_0 = 0$ and $V_1(\omega) > 0$ for all $\omega \subset \Omega$.

Note that the condition in (1.4) is unreasonable from the economic standpoint; an investor starting with zero money should not have a guaranteed way of ending up with a positive amount of money. Hence a securities market model having a dominant trading strategy cannot be a realistic one.

Not surprisingly, if there exists a dominant trading strategy, then there exists a trading strategy which can transform a strictly negative initial wealth into a non-negative wealth. To see this, suppose H satisfies the condition in (1.4). Then by (1.2) and the fact that $B_t > 0$, one has $V_0^* = 0$ and $V_1^*(\omega) > 0$ for all $\omega \in \Omega$. So by (1.3), $(H_1, \dots, H_N)$ must be such that $G^*(\omega) \succeq 0$ for all $\omega \in \Omega$. Now define a new strategy $\tilde{H}$ by setting $\tilde{H}_n = H_n$ for $n = 1, \dots, N$ and

$$\tilde{H}_0 = -\sum_{n=1}^{N} H_n S_n^*(0) - \delta$$

where

$$\delta \equiv \min_{\omega} G^*(\omega) > 0$$

It follows from the definition of $\cdot\tilde{V}_t^*$ that $\tilde{V}_0^* = -\delta < 0$ and $\tilde{V}_1^*(\omega) = \tilde{V}_0^* + \tilde{G}^*(\omega) = -\delta + \tilde{G}^*(\omega) \geq 0$ for all $\omega \in \Omega$. Hence by (1.2), again, $\tilde{H}$ is as desired.

Conversely, suppose there is a trading strategy such as $\tilde{H}$. Then by reversing the preceding argument one sees that $(\tilde{H}_1, \dots, \tilde{H}_N)$ is such that $\tilde{G}^*(\omega) > 0$ for all $\omega \in \Omega$. Hence upon setting $H_n = \tilde{H}_n$ for $n = 1, \dots, N$ and

$$H_0 = -\sum_{n=1}^{N} \tilde{H}_n S_n^*(0)$$

it follows that the new trading strategy H satisfies $V_0 = 0$ and $V_1(\omega) > 0$ for all $\omega \in \Omega$. In view of (1.4), this means there is another equivalent condition:

(1.5) There exists a dominant trading strategy if and only if there exists a trading strategy satisfying $V_0 < 0$ and $V_1(\omega) \geq 0$ for all $\omega \in \Omega$.

The existence of a dominant trading strategy is unsatisfactory from another standpoint: it leads to illogical pricing. For reasons which will soon become clear, it is often useful to interpret $V_1(\omega)$ as the time $t = 1$ payoff of a contract or claim when state ω pertains, in which case V_0 can be interpreted as the time $t = 0$ price of this claim. But if the trading strategy $\hat{H}$ dominates $\tilde{H}$, then the contingent claims $\hat{V}$ and $\tilde{V}$ have the same prices even though the former claim has a strictly greater payoff in every state ω. This is not consistent with reality.

The pricing of claims will be logically consistent if there is a *linear pricing measure*, that is, a non-negative vector $\pi = (\pi(\omega_1), \ldots, \pi(\omega_K))$ such that for every trading strategy H you have

$$V_0^* = \sum_\omega \pi(\omega) V_1^*(\omega) = \sum_\omega \pi(\omega) V_1(\omega)/B_1(\omega)$$

Now the illogical pricing associated with dominant trading strategies no longer exists; each claim has a unique price, and a claim that pays more than another in every state will have a higher time $t = 0$ price.

If there is a linear pricing measure π, then by its definition and that of V_t^* one has

(1.6) $$H_0 + \sum_{n=1}^{N} H_n S_n^*(0) = \sum_\omega \pi(\omega) \left[H_0 + \sum_{n=1}^{N} H_n S_n^*(1)(\omega) \right]$$

Taking $H_1 = \ldots = H_N = 0$, it can be seen that the linear pricing measure must satisfy $\pi(\omega_1) + \ldots + \pi(\omega_K) = 1$; thus one can interpret π as a probability measure on the sample space Ω. Taking for arbitrary $i \in \{1, \ldots, N\}$ a trading strategy with $H_n = 0$ for all $n \neq i$, one sees that this equation implies

(1.7) $$S_n^*(0) = \sum_\omega \pi(\omega) S_n^*(1)(\omega), \quad n = 1, \ldots, N$$

Conversely, suppose π is a probability measure on Ω satisfying (1.7). Then (1.6) is satisfied, and it follows that:

(1.8)   The vector π is a linear pricing measure if and only if it is a probability measure on Ω satisfying (1.7).

Since a linear pricing measure π can be taken to be a probability measure, (1.7) says that the initial price of each security is equal to the *expectation*[2] under π of the final discounted price. Similarly, by the original definition of π, the initial value V_0 of any portfolio is equal to the expectation under π of the final discounted value of the portfolio.

It turns out there exists a close relationship between the concepts of dominant trading strategies and linear pricing measures:

(1.9)   There exists a linear pricing measure if and only if there are no dominant trading strategies.

This important principle can be verified with linear programming duality theory.[3] In particular, let $\pi \in \mathbb{R}^K$ be a column vector, let $Z \in \mathbb{R}^{N+1}$ denote the column vector

$$Z = \begin{pmatrix} S_1^*(0) \\ \vdots \\ S_N^*(0) \\ 1 \end{pmatrix}$$

and let $\mathbb{Z}$ denote the $(N+1) \times K$ matrix

$$\mathbb{Z} \equiv \begin{pmatrix} S_1^*(1, \omega_1) \dots S_1^*(1, \omega_K) \\ \vdots \qquad \vdots \\ S_N^*(1, \omega_1) \dots S_N^*(1, \omega_K) \\ 1 \qquad \dots \qquad 1 \end{pmatrix}$$

Then by (1.8) the existence of a linear pricing measure implies the existence of a solution to the linear program

(**1.10**) $\qquad\qquad$ maximize $\quad (0, \dots, 0)\pi$

$\qquad\qquad\qquad$ subject to $\quad \mathbb{Z}\pi = Z$

$$\pi \geqslant 0.$$

By duality theory there must exist a solution $h = (h_1, \dots, h_{N+1})$ to the *dual linear* program

(**1.11**) $\qquad\qquad$ minimize $\quad hZ$

$\qquad\qquad\qquad$ subject to $\quad h\mathbb{Z} \geqslant 0$

and the two optimal objective values must coincide (in which case they obviously equal zero). Now interpret the solution h of (1.11) as a trading strategy, with the last component of h corresponding to H_0. The objective function in (1.11) says that $V_0^* = 0$, whereas the constraint says that $V_1^*(\omega) \geqslant 0$ for all $\omega \in \Omega$. Since the minimizing strategy h has an objective value equal to zero, there cannot be any trading strategies with $V_0 < 0$ and $V_1(\omega) \geqslant 0$ for all $\omega \in \Omega$. Hence by (1.5) the existence of a linear pricing measure implies there cannot be any dominant trading strategies.

Conversely, if there are no dominant trading strategies, then (1.11) has a solution, namely, $h = 0$. It follows by duality theory that (1.10) has a solution π which, as explained above, can be taken as the linear pricing measure.

To summarize matters up to this point, securities market models that permit dominant trading strategies are unreasonable from the economic point of view. Moreover, models without dominant strategies are reasonable, it would seem, because they are accompanied by linear pricing measures. Hence it makes sense to concentrate attention on the latter kind of model. But before agreeing to drop from consideration all models with dominant trading strategies, it is worth mentioning that one can have an even less reasonable securities market model.

It is said that the *law of one price* holds for a securities market model if there do not exist two trading strategies, say $\hat{H}$ and $\tilde{H}$, such that

$\hat{V}_1(\omega) = \tilde{V}_1(\omega)$ for all $\omega \in \Omega$ but $\hat{V}_0 > \tilde{V}_o$. In other words, if the law of one price holds, then there is no ambiguity about the time $t = 0$ price of any claim. On the other hand, the law of one price does not hold if there are two different trading strategies that yield the same time $t = 1$ payoff but the initial values of the two corresponding portfolios are different. This notion was mentioned above, just following principle (1.5).

Notice that if there do not exist two distinct trading strategies yielding the same payoff at time 1, then automatically the law of one price holds. On the other hand, if $\hat{H}$ and $\tilde{H}$ are as in the preceding paragraph, then $\hat{V}_1^* = \tilde{V}_1^*$ and $\hat{V}_0^* > \tilde{V}_0^*$ which, in turn, imply $\hat{G}^*(\omega) < \tilde{G}^*(\omega)$ for all $\omega \in \Omega$. Defining a new trading strategy H by taking $H_n = \tilde{H}_n - \hat{H}_n$ for $n = 1, \ldots, N$ yields $G^*(\omega) > 0$ for all $\omega \in \Omega$. Finally, taking $H_0 = -\sum H_n S_n^*(0)$ leads to $V_0 = 0$ and $V_1(\omega) > 0$ for all $\omega \in \Omega$. Hence by (1.4) the following is true:

(1.12)   If there are no dominant trading strategies, then the law of one price holds. The converse, however, is not necessarily true.

In other words, if the law of one price fails to hold, then there will exist a dominant trading strategy. The converse is not necessarily true, because, as will be illustrated in example 1.5 that follows, you can have a dominant trading strategy for a model that satisfies the law of one price. Thus failure of the law of one price is, in a sense, worse than having dominant trading strategies.

Example 1.5   For a trivial example where the law of one price fails to hold, suppose $K = 2$, $N = 1$, $r = 1$, $S_0 = 10$, and $S_1(\omega_1) = S_1(\omega_2) = 12$. Hence V_1 is constant on Ω, and for any scalar λ there is an infinite number of trading strategies with $V_1 = \lambda$, each of which has a different value of V_0.

Now suppose $S_1(\omega_2)$ is changed to the value 8. For any $X \in \mathbb{R}^2$ there is a unique H (and thus a unique time $t = 0$ price) such that $V_1 = X$, so the law of one price must hold. However, the trading strategy $H = (10, -1)$ satisfies $V_0 = 0$ and $V_1 = (8, 12)$, so it must be a dominant trading strategy.

Returning to the category of models that are without dominant trading strategies, it is clear that such models cannot have trading strategies that start with zero wealth and are certain to have a strictly positive amount of wealth at time $t = 1$. But what about trading strategies that start with zero wealth, cannot lose any money, and end up with a strictly positive amount of wealth at time $t = 1$ in at least one of the states ω, but not all? In other words, investors would have the possibility of being able to make a profit on a transaction without being exposed to the risk of incurring a loss. Such an investment opportunity is called an arbitrage opportunity, and it is unreasonable from the economic standpoint.

Formally, an *arbitrage opportunity* is some trading strategy H such that

(a) $V_0 = 0$.
(b) $V_1 \geqslant 0$, and
(c) $EV_1 > 0$.

Note that an arbitrage opportunity is a riskless way of making money: you start with nothing and, without any chance of going into debt, there is a chance of ending up with a positive amount of money. If such a situation were to exist, then everybody would 'jump in' with this trading strategy, affecting the prices of the securities. This economic model would not be in equilibrium. Hence for our single period model to be sensible from the economic standpoint, there cannot exist any arbitrage opportunities.

The following principle is true by (1.4) and example 1.6, which follows.

(1.13) If there exists a dominant trading strategy, then there exists an arbitrage opportunity, but the converse is not necessarily true.

Example 1.6 Suppose $K = 2$, $N = 1$, $r = 0$, $S_0 = 10$, $S_1(\omega_1) = 12$, and $S_1(\omega_2) = 10$ (with one stock, the subscript denotes time). The trading strategy $H = (-10, 1)$ is an arbitrage opportunity, because $V_0 = 0$ and $V_1 = (2, 0)$. However, there are no dominant trading strategies, because $\pi = (0, 1)$ is a linear pricing measure.

From (1.2) and the fact that $B_t > 0$ for all t and ω, it follows easily that H is an arbitrage opportunity if and only if

(a) $V_0^* = 0$,
(b) $V_1^* \geqslant 0$, and
(c) $EV_1^* > 0$.

In fact, there is still another equivalent condition:

(1.14) H is an arbitrage opportunity if and only if
     (a) $G^* \geqslant 0$, and
     (b) $EG^* > 0$.

To see this, suppose H is an arbitrage opportunity. By (1.3), $G^* = V_1^* - V_0^*$, so by the preceding remark $G^* \geqslant 0$ and $EG^* = EV_1^* - EV_0^* = EV_1^* > 0$. Conversely, suppose (a) and (b) in (1.14) are satisfied by some trading strategy $\hat{H}$. Then consider the strategy $H = (H_0, \hat{H}_1, \ldots \hat{H}_N)$, where

$$H_0 = -\sum_{n=1}^{N} \hat{H}_n S_n^*(0)$$

Under H one has $V_0^* = 0$. Moreover, by (1.3) one has $V_1^* = V_0^* + G^* = G^*$. Hence (a) and (b) in (1.14) imply $V_1^* \geqslant 0$ and $EV_1^* > 0$, in which case H is an arbitrage opportunity by the preceding remark.

In summary, and as illustrated in figure 1.1, all single period securities market models can be classified into four categories: (1) there are no arbitrage opportunities, (2) there are arbitrage opportunities but no dominant

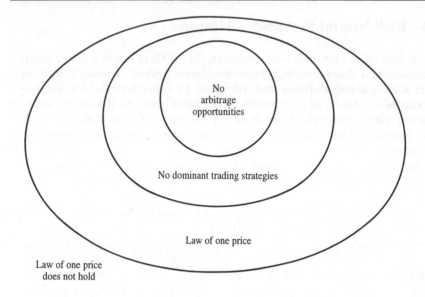

Figure 1.1   Classification of securities market models

trading strategies, (3) there are dominant trading strategies but the law of one price holds, and (4) the law of one price does not hold. And only the first category is reasonable from the economic point of view.

Unfortunately, it is not so easy to check directly whether a model has any arbitrage opportunities, at least when there are two or more risky securities. But there is an important necessary and sufficient condition for the model to be free of arbitrage opportunities. This condition involves the discounted price process and something called a risk neutral probability measure, which is a special kind of linear pricing measure. It will be the subject of the next section.

Exercise 1.4   Consider the model with $K = 3$, $N = 2$, $r = 0$, and the following security prices:

n	$S_n(0)$	$S_n(1)(\omega_1)$	$S_n(1)(\omega_2)$	$S_n(1)(\omega_3)$
1	4	8	6	3
2	7	10	8	4

Show that there exist dominant trading strategies and that the law of one price holds.

Exercise 1.5   Show for example 1.3 that there are no dominant trading strategies but there exists an arbitrage opportunity.

1.3   Risk Neutral Probability Measures

In the preceding section it was explained that if there exists a linear pricing measure, then there cannot be any dominant trading strategies, although there can still be arbitrage opportunities. In order to rule out arbitrage opportunities, we need a little bit more: there must exist a linear pricing measure which gives strictly positive mass to every state $\omega \in \Omega$.

A probability measure Q on Ω is said to be a *risk neutral* probability measure if

(a) $Q(\omega) > 0$, all $\omega \in \Omega$, and
(b) $E_Q[\Delta S_n^*] = 0$, $n = 1, 2, \ldots, N$.

Here the notation $E_Q[X]$ means the expected value of the random variable X under the probability measure Q. Note that

$$E_Q[\Delta S_n^*] = E_Q[S_n^*(1) - S_n^*(0)] = E_Q[S_n^*(1)] - S_n^*(0),$$

so $E_Q[\Delta S_n^*] = 0$ is equivalent to

(1.15) $$E_Q[S_n^*(1)] = S_n^*(0), \qquad n = 1, 2, \ldots, N$$

This is essentially the same as (1.7) and says that under the indicated probability measure the expected time $t = 1$ discounted price of each risky security is equal to its initial price. Hence a risk neutral probability measure is just a linear pricing measure giving strictly positive mass to every $\omega \in \Omega$.

We now come to a very important result.

(1.16)   There are no arbitrage opportunities if and only if there exists a risk neutral probability measure Q.

Before proving this result, it is worthwhile to look at some examples and provide some intuition.

Example 1.1 (continued)   We want to find strictly positive numbers $Q(\omega_1)$ and $Q(\omega_2)$ so that (1.15) is satisfied, that is,

$$5 = 6Q(\omega_1) + 4Q(\omega_2)$$

Also Q must be a probability measure, so it must satisfy

$$1 = Q(\omega_1) + Q(\omega_2)$$

It is easy to see that $Q(\omega_1) = Q(\omega_2) = 1/2$ satisfies both equations, so this is a risk neutral probability measure, and by (1.16) there cannot be any arbitrage opportunities.

Of course, with this simple example it is easy to see from the discounted price process that there cannot be any arbitrage opportunities. Indeed, principle (1.16) is easy to understand in the case where there is a single risky security (i.e., $N = 1$). From the definition, there is an arbitrage opportunity if and only if one can take a position H_1 in the discounted price process S^* that will possibly gain but cannot lose. This means that either

$\Delta S^* \geqslant 0$ with $\Delta S^*(\omega) > 0$ for at least one $\omega \in \Omega$ or $\Delta S^* \leqslant 0$ with $\Delta S^*(\omega) < 0$ for at least one $\omega \in \Omega$. Clearly, in both cases it is impossible to find a strictly positive probability measure satisfying (1.15). On the other hand, if neither of these two cases applies, then one can find a risk neutral probability measure and there are no arbitrage opportunities.

Example 1.2 (continued) The system of equations to be solved, namely,

$$5 = 6Q(\omega_1) + 4Q(\omega_2) + 3Q(\omega_3)$$
$$1 = Q(\omega_1) + Q(\omega_2) + Q(\omega_3)$$

involves three unknowns but only two equations, so we will solve for two of the unknowns in terms of the third, say $Q(\omega_1)$. Thus this system will be satisfied for an arbitrary real number $Q(\omega_1)$ if

$$Q(\omega_2) = 2 - 3Q(\omega_1) \quad \text{and} \quad Q(\omega_3) = -1 + 2Q(\omega_1)$$

Now for Q to be a strictly positive probability measure we must have $Q(\omega_i) > 0$ for all i. Using the preceding two equations, this leads to three inequalities for $Q(\omega_1)$, including $Q(\omega_1) > 0$. In view of its equation, $Q(\omega_2) > 0$ if and only if $Q(\omega_1) < 2/3$. Similarly, $Q(\omega_3) > 0$ if and only if $Q(\omega_1) > 1/2$. Hence our solution will be a strictly positive probability measure if and only if $1/2 < Q(\omega_1) < 2/3$. In other words, $Q = (\lambda, 2 - 3\lambda, -1 + 2\lambda)$ is a risk neutral probability measure for each value of the scalar λ satisfying $1/2 < \lambda < 2/3$, and there are no arbitrage opportunities.

Example 1.3 (continued)   We seek a solution of

$$5 = 6Q(\omega_1) + 6Q(\omega_2) + 4Q(\omega_3)$$
$$10 = 12Q(\omega_1) + 8Q(\omega_2) + 8Q(\omega_3)$$
$$1 = Q(\omega_1) + Q(\omega_2) + Q(\omega_3)$$

There exists a unique solution to these equations, namely, $Q(\omega_1) = Q(\omega_3) = 1/2$, $Q(\omega_2) = 0$. This is a linear pricing measure, but this solution is not strictly positive, so there does not exist a risk neutral probability measure. By (1.16), therefore, there must exist an arbitrage opportunity. It takes a bit of work to find one; we will come back to this example later.

Example 1.3 illustrates why the intuition which worked for the case of a single risky security does not work when there are two or more risky securities. Looking at the discounted price process for the first security, it is clear that we can find a strictly positive probability measure Q satisfying $E_Q[S_1^*(1)] = 5$. Similarly for the second risky security. The problem, however, is that we cannot find a single strictly positive probability measure that will simultaneously work for both securities. The interactions between these two securities permit arbitrage opportunities even though, taken individually, the securities seem acceptable. And it is these kinds of interactions which make the intuitive understanding of principle (1.16) much more difficult when there are two or more risky securities.

These three examples illustrate the three kinds of situations that can arise: either (1) there is a unique risk neutral probability measure, (2) there are infinitely many risk neutral probability measures, or (3) there are no risk neutral probability measures.

We now return to the explanation of (1.16) for the case where $N \geqslant 2$. For a general, single period model, consider the set

$$\mathbb{W} = \{X \in \mathbb{R}^K : X = G^* \text{for some trading strategy } H\}$$

One should think of $\mathbb{W}$ as a set of random variables, and because of (1.3) one should think of each $X \in \mathbb{W}$ as a possible time $t = 1$ discounted wealth when the initial value of the investment is zero. Note that $\mathbb{W}$ is actually a linear subspace of $\mathbb{R}^K$, that is, for any X, $\hat{X} \in \mathbb{W}$ and any scalars a and b one also has $aX + b\hat{X} \in \mathbb{W}$.

Next, consider the set

$$\mathbb{A} \equiv \{X \in \mathbb{R}^K : X \geqslant 0, X \neq 0\}$$

This is just the non-negative orthant of $\mathbb{R}^K$. In view of (1.14) it is apparent that there exists an arbitrage opportunity if and only if $\mathbb{W} \cap \mathbb{A} \neq \emptyset$, that is, if and only if the subspace $\mathbb{W}$ intersects with the non-negative orthant of $\mathbb{R}^K$. Hence to find an arbitrage opportunity in a model for which there is no risk neutral probability measure, one can use linear algebra to characterize $\mathbb{W}$ quantitatively and then compute a vector in its intersection with $\mathbb{A}$.

Now corresponding to the subspace $\mathbb{W}$ is the *orthogonal subspace*

$$\mathbb{W}^\perp \equiv \{Y \in \mathbb{R}^K : X \cdot Y = 0 \quad \text{for all} \quad X \in \mathbb{W}\}$$

where $X \cdot Y = X(\omega_1)Y(\omega_1) + \ldots + X(\omega_K)Y(\omega_K)$ denotes the *inner product* of X and Y. If you consider the geometric picture for the case $K = 2$ (see figure 1.2) or even the case $K = 3$, it should be easy to believe that $\mathbb{W} \cap \mathbb{A} = \emptyset$ implies the existence of a ray in $\mathbb{W}^\perp$ along which every component of every point not at the origin is strictly positive.[4] In particular, along this ray there will exist one point whose components sum to one, in which case this point can be interpreted as a probability measure. In other words, denoting

$$\mathbb{P}^+ \equiv \{X \in \mathbb{R}^K : X_1 + \ldots + X_K = 1, X_1 > 0, \ldots, X_K > 0\}$$

the geometry suggests that $\mathbb{W} \cap \mathbb{A} = \emptyset$ if and only if $\mathbb{W}^\perp \cap \mathbb{P}^+ \neq \emptyset$.

Since $\Delta S_n^* \in \mathbb{W}$ for all n, it follows that any element of the set $\mathbb{W}^\perp \cap \mathbb{P}^+$ is actually a risk neutral probability measure. Conversely, if Q is any risk neutral probability measure, then for any $G^* \in \mathbb{W}$ (with corresponding trading strategy H) we have

(1.17) $$E_Q G^* = E_Q \left[\sum_{n=1}^N H_n \Delta S_n^* \right] = \sum_{n=1}^N H_n E_Q [\Delta S_n^*] = 0$$

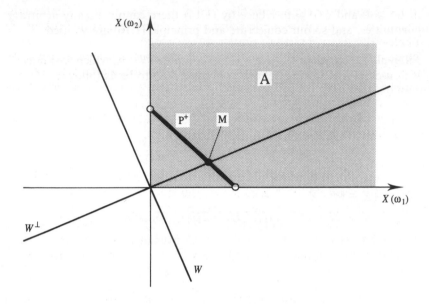

Figure 1.2 Geometric interpretation of the risk neutral probability measures

so $Q \in \mathbb{W}^{\perp} \cap \mathbb{P}^{+}$. Thus if we let $\mathbb{M}$ denote the set of all risk neutral probability measures, we have that

$$\mathbb{M} = \mathbb{W}^{\perp} \cap \mathbb{P}^{+}$$

Moreover, by the geometric intuition used above we conjecture that $\mathbb{W} \cap \mathbb{A} = \emptyset$ if and only if $\mathbb{M} \neq \emptyset$. This conjecture, of course, is the same as principle (1.16).

In order to make this argument more rigorous and apply it to the case of general K, it is convenient to use a version of the Hahn–Banach theorem called the *separating hyperplane theorem*. Consider the set

$$\mathbb{A}^{+} = \{ X \in \mathbb{A} : EX \geqslant 1 \}$$

This is a closed and convex[5] subset of $\mathbb{R}^{K}$, and the absence of arbitrage opportunities implies $\mathbb{W}$ and $\mathbb{A}^{+}$ are disjoint. Hence by the separating hyperplane theorem there exists some $Y \in \mathbb{W}^{\perp}$ such that $X \cdot Y > 0$ for all $X \in \mathbb{A}^{+}$. For each $k = 1, \ldots, K$ we can find a vector X in $\mathbb{A}^{+}$ whose kth component is positive and other components are zeros, so every component of Y must be strictly positive. By setting $Q(\omega_K) = Y(\omega_k)/[Y(\omega_1) + \ldots + Y(\omega_K)]$, it is clear that Q is a probability measure with $Q \in \mathbb{W}^{\perp}$. Since $\Delta S_n^{*} \in \mathbb{W}$ for all n, we conclude that Q is a risk neutral probability measure.

What about the converse of (1.16)? This is easy. If Q is a risk neutral probability measure, then, as explained above, for an arbitrary trading strategy H we have equation (1.17), which shows that G^{*} cannot satisfy both $G^* \geqslant 0$ and $EG^* > 0$. Hence by (1.14) there cannot be any arbitrage opportunities, and so our conjecture and principle (1.16) are verified.

Example 1.3 (continued)   We want to compute $\mathbb{W} \cap \mathbb{A}$, which we know is non-empty. Knowing S_n^*, one computes ΔS_n^* to be as follows:

n	$\Delta S_n^*(\omega_1)$	$\Delta S_n^*(\omega_2)$	$\Delta S_n^*(\omega_3)$
1	1	1	-1
2	2	-2	-2

It follows that

$$\mathbb{W} = \{X \in \mathbb{R}^3 : X$$
$$= (H_1 + 2H_2, H_1 - 2H_2, -H_1 - 2H_2) \quad \text{for some} \quad H_1, H_2 \in \mathbb{R}\}$$

Notice that $X_1 + X_3 = 0$ for all $X \in \mathbb{W}$. Conversely, given any vector X with $X_1 + X_3 = 0$, one can readily find a unique trading strategy H with $G^* = X$. Hence

$$\mathbb{W} = \{X \in \mathbb{R}^3 : X_1 + X_3 = 0\}$$

that is,

$$\mathbb{W}^\perp = \{Y \in \mathbb{R}^3 : Y = (\lambda, 0, \lambda) \text{for some } \lambda \in \mathbb{R}\}$$

Now comparing $\mathbb{W}$ and $\mathbb{A}$ we see that

$$\mathbb{W} \cap \mathbb{A} = \{X \in \mathbb{R}^3 : X_1 = X_3 = 0, X_2 > 0\}$$

So starting with any positive number X_2, we compute the trading strategy H which gives rise to the time $t = 1$ portfolio value $(0, X_2, 0)$. This will be the solution of

$$H_1 + 2H_2 = 0$$
$$H_1 - 2H_2 = X_2$$

namely, $H_1 = X_2/2$ and $H_2 = -X_2/4$. Finally, upon setting

$$H_0 = -H_1 S_1^*(0) - H_2 S_2^*(0) = -(X_2/2)(5) - (-X_2/4)(10),$$

one obtains $H_0 = 0$. It is apparent that $H = (0, X_2/2, -X_2/4)$ is an arbitrage opportunity for every $X_2 > 0$.

Exercise 1.6   Show that $\mathbb{W}$ and $\mathbb{W}^\perp$ are linear subspaces.

Exercise 1.7   Specify $\mathbb{W}$ and $\mathbb{W}^\perp$ in the case of

(a)   Example 1.1.
(b)   Example 1.2.
(c)   Example 1.4.

Exercise 1.8   Determine either all the risk neutral probability measures or all the arbitrage opportunities in the case of example 1.4.

Exercise 1.9   Suppose $K = 2$, $N = 1$, and the interest rate is a scalar parameter $r \geqslant 0$. Also, suppose $S_0 = 1$, $S_1(\omega_1) = u$ ('up'), and $S_1(\omega_2) = d$ ('down'), where the parameters u and d satisfy $u > d > 0$. For what values of r, u, and d does there exist a risk neutral probability measure? Say what this measure is. For the complementary values of these parameters, say what all the arbitrage opportunities are.

Exercise 1.10   Let A denote the $(K + 1) \times (K + 2N)$ matrix

$$
\begin{bmatrix}
0 & 0 & 0 & \cdots & 0 & 1 & 1 & \cdots & 1 \\
\Delta S_1^*(\omega_1) & -\Delta S_1^*(\omega_1) & \Delta S_2^*(\omega_1) & \cdots & -\Delta S_N^*(\omega_1) & -1 & 0 & \cdots & 0 \\
\Delta S_1^*(\omega_2) & -\Delta S_1^*(\omega_2) & \Delta S_2^*(\omega_2) & \cdots & -\Delta S_N^*(\omega_2) & 0 & -1 & \cdots & 0 \\
\vdots & \vdots & \vdots & & \vdots & \vdots & \vdots & & \vdots \\
\Delta S_1^*(\omega_K) & -\Delta S_1^*(\omega_K) & \Delta S_2^*(\omega_K) & \cdots & -\Delta S_N^*(\omega_K) & 0 & 0 & \cdots & -1
\end{bmatrix}
$$

and let b denote the $(K + 1)$-component column vector $(1, 0, \ldots, 0)'$. Show that

$$
Ax = b, \quad x \geqslant 0, \quad x \in \mathbb{R}^{K+2N}
$$

has a solution if and only if there exists an arbitrage opportunity.

Exercise 1.11   Farkas's Lemma, a variation of the separating hyperplane theorem, says that given an $m \times n$ matrix A and an m-dimensional column vector b, either

$$
Ax = b, \quad x \geqslant 0, \quad x \in \mathbb{R}^n
$$

has a solution or

$$
yA \leqslant 0, \quad yb > 0, \quad y \in \mathbb{R}^m
$$

has a solution, but not both. Use this and the results of exercise 1.10 to show that if there are no arbitrage opportunities, then there exists a risk neutral probability measure.

1.4   Valuation of Contingent Claims

A *contingent claim* is a random variable X representing a payoff at time $t = 1$. You can think of a contingent claim as part of a contract that a buyer and a seller make at time $t = 0$. The seller promises to pay the buyer the amount $X(\omega)$ at time $t = 1$ if $\omega \in \Omega$ turns out to be the true state of the world. Hence, when viewed at time $t = 0$, the payoff X is a random variable, and so the problem of interest is to determine the time $t - 0$ value of this payoff. In other words, what is the fair price that the buyer should pay the seller at time $t = 0$ in order for the two parties to be happy with their contract?

Now one might suppose that the value of a contingent claim would depend on the risk preferences and utility functions of the buyer and seller, but in a great many cases this is not so. It turns out that by the arguments of *arbitrage pricing theory* there is often a unique, correct, time $t = 0$ value for the contingent claim, a value that does not depend on the risk preferences of the parties who buy and sell this claim.

Here is the argument. A contingent claim X is said to be *attainable* or *marketable* if there exists some trading strategy H, called the *replicating portfolio*, such that $V_1 = X$. In this case one says that H generates X. Now suppose the time $t = 0$ price p of X is such that $p > V_0$. Then an astute individual would sell the contingent claim for p at time $t = 0$, follow the trading strategy H at a time $t = 0$ cost of V_0, and pocket the difference $p - V_0$. This individual has made a riskless profit, because at time $t = 1$ the value V_1 of the portfolio corresponding to H is exactly equal to the obligation X of the contingent claim in every state of the world. In other words, if $p > V_0$, then this astute individual could lock in a profit of $p - V_0$ by investing in a portfolio that provides exactly the right value to settle the obligation on the contingent claim.

Similarly, if $p < V_0$, then an astute individual would follow the trading strategy $-H$, thereby collecting the amount V_0 at time $t = 0$, and purchasing the contingent claim for the amount p, thereby locking in a risk free profit of $V_0 - p$. At time $t = 1$ the amount collected X is exactly what is needed to settle the obligation V_1 associated with the trading strategy $-H$. Again, if $p < V_0$, then this astute individual could lock in a riskless profit of $V_0 - p$.

If $p = V_0$, then apparently we cannot use H to create a riskless profit. So does this mean that V_0 is the correct value of X? Not necessarily, for suppose there is a second trading strategy, say $\hat{H}$, such that $\hat{V}_1 = X$ but $\hat{V}_0 \neq V_0$. Then even if $p = V_0$, one could use $\hat{H}$ and the argument above to lock in a riskless profit, thereby implying the different price $\hat{V}_0$. The problem here, of course, is that the law of one price does not hold. So for V_0 to be the unique, logical, time $t = 0$ price of X, it is necessary to assume that the law of one price does indeed hold. In this case we say that V_0 is the price of X as implied by arbitrage pricing theory.

As explained in section 1.2, if there are no arbitrage opportunities, then there are no dominant trading strategies, and if there are no dominant trading strategies, then the law of one price holds. Thus by (1.16) the existence of a risk neutral probability measure implies the law of one price. Alternatively, we can see this directly from the following, very important calculation:

(1.18)   If Q is any risk neutral probability measure, then for every trading strategy H one has

$$V_0 = V_0^* = E_Q V_0^* = E_Q[V_1^* - G^*] = E_Q V_1^* - E_Q\left[\sum_{n=1}^{N} H_n \Delta S_n^*\right]$$

$$= E_Q V_1^* - \sum_{n=1}^{N} H_n E_Q[\Delta S_n^*] = E_Q V_1^* - 0 = E_Q V_1^* = E_Q[V_1/B_1]$$

In other words, under Q the expected, discounted, time $t = 1$ value of any portfolio is equal to its initial value. So if there is a positive probability that the portfolio will go up in value, then there also must be a positive probability of going down in value, and vice versa. Moreover, there is no way you can have two trading strategies H and $\hat{H}$ with both $V_1 = \hat{V}_1$ and $V_0 \neq \hat{V}_0$, so the law of one price must hold.

Notice for future reference that the calculation in (1.18) does not depend on the choice of Q, because V_1^* is the time $t = 1$ discounted value of the portfolio under some trading strategy. In other words, for a model where there are two or more risk neutral probability measures, $E_Q V_1^*$ is constant with respect to such Q.

Returning to the contingent claim X, by the arguments near the beginning of this section we have the following important *valuation concept*:

(1.19)   If the law of one price holds, then the time $t = 0$ value of an attainable contingent claim X is $V_0 = H_0 B_0 + \sum_{n=1}^{N} H_n S_n(0)$, where H is the trading strategy that generates X.

If we have the stronger condition that the model is free of arbitrage opportunities, then we have the following, sensational result:

(1.20)   *Risk neutral valuation principle*: If the single period model is free of arbitrage opportunities, then the time $t = 0$ value of an attainable contingent claim X is $E_Q[X/B_1]$, where Q is any risk neutral probability measure.

This follows immediately from (1.2), (1.18), (1.19), and the fact that $B_0 = 1$. We now turn to several examples.

Example 1.1 (continued)   Suppose $r = 1/9$, $X(\omega_1) = 7$, and $X(\omega_2) = 2$. Then the time $t = 0$ value of X is

$$E_Q[X/B_1] = (1/2)(9/10)7 + (1/2)(9/10)2 = 4.05$$

providing X is attainable. How do we check this? One way is to try to compute the trading strategy H that generates X. This can be done by solving

$$X/B_1 = V_1^* = V_0^* + G^* = 4.05 + H_1 \Delta S_1^*$$

There is one unknown, H_1, and two equations, one for each ω, but both equations give the same solution, namely, $H_1 = 2.25$. To determine H_0 one can solve

$$4.05 = V_0 = H_0 + H_1 S_1 - H_0 + (2.25)(5)$$

to obtain $H_0 = -7.2$.

In summary, the contingent claim X is indeed attainable. To generate it you start with 4.05, you borrow 7.2 at the riskless interest rate $r = 1/9$, and you use the sum $4.05 + 7.2 = 11.25$ to purchase $11.25 \div 5 = 2.25$ shares of the risky asset. At time $t = 1$ you must pay $(7.2)(10/9) = 8$ to settle the loan. The amount of money remaining in the portfolio will depend on ω: in state ω_1 this will be $V_1 = (2.25)(20/3) - 8 = 7$, whereas in state ω_2 this will be $V_1 = (2.25)(40/9) - 8 = 2$. If the time $t = 0$ value of this contingent claim were different from 4.05, then you could use this trading strategy in the manner discussed at the beginning of this section to lock in a riskless profit.

Example 1.7 For a general securities model, taking

$$X(\omega) = \begin{cases} 1, & \omega = \hat{\omega} \\ 0, & \omega \neq \hat{\omega} \end{cases}$$

for some $\hat{\omega} \in \Omega$ leads to the time $t = 0$ price (if X is attainable)

$$E_Q[X/B_1] = \sum_{\omega} Q(\omega) X(\omega) / B_1(\omega) = Q(\hat{\omega})/B_1(\hat{\omega})$$

For this reason $Q(\hat{\omega})/B_1(\hat{\omega})$ is sometimes called the *state price* for state $\hat{\omega} \in \Omega$. Thus the time $t = 0$ price of an attainable contingent claim is simply the weighted sum across the states of the payoffs under X, with the weights being the state prices.

Example 1.8 – Call Options Suppose $N = 1$ and X has the form

$$X = (S_1 - e)^+ = \max\{0, S_1 - e\}$$

where e is a specified number called the *exercise price* or the *strike price*. Hence X is the contingent claim corresponding to the right to purchase the risky security at time $t = 1$ for the amount e. If it turns out that $S_1 \geq e$, then at time $t = 1$ this right will be worth the difference $S_1 - e$, and so the option should be exercised. On the other hand, if $S_1 \leq e$, then at time $t = 1$ this right will be worth nothing, and so the option should not be exercised. If X is attainable, then its time $t = 0$ price is

$$E_Q[X/B_1] = \sum_{\omega \in \Omega'} Q(\omega)[S_1(\omega) - e]/B_1(\omega)$$

where $\Omega' \equiv \{\omega \in \Omega : S_1(\omega) \geq e\}$.

Example 1.1 (continued) With $r = 1/9$ and $e = 5$, the time $t = 1$ value of the call option is

$$X(\omega) = \begin{cases} 5/3, & \omega = \omega_1 \\ 0, & \omega = \omega_2 \end{cases}$$

Hence if X is attainable, then its time $t = 0$ value is

$$E_Q[X/B_1] = (1/2)(9/10)(5/3) = 0.75$$

To check whether X is attainable, we shall try to compute a trading strategy that generates X. We solve the system of two equations (one for each state)

$$V_1 = H_0 B_1 + H_1 S_1 = X$$

for the two unknowns and obtain $H_1 = 0.75$ and $H_0 = -3$. So, indeed, $V_0 = H_0 + H_1 S_0 = -3 + (0.75)(5) = 0.75$ is the time $t = 0$ price of X.

Example 1.9 – Put options   Suppose $N = 1$ and X has the form

$$X = (e - S_1)^+ = \max\{0, e - S_1\}$$

Then X is the contingent claim that gives the owner the right to sell the risky security at time $t = 1$ for the amount e. This option should be exercised if and only if $S_1 < e$.

Example 1.2 (continued)   Consider an arbitrary contingent claim $X = (X_1, X_2, X_3)$. This claim is marketable if and only if $V_1 = H_0 B_1 + H_1 S_1 = X$ for some pair of numbers H_0 and H_1, that is, there exists a solution to the system of equations

$$\begin{aligned} \omega_1: & \quad (10/9)H_0 + (20/3)H_1 = X_1 \\ \omega_2: & \quad (10/9)H_0 + (40/9)H_1 = X_2 \\ \omega_3: & \quad (10/9)H_0 + (30/9)H_1 = X_3 \end{aligned}$$

Since there are three equations with only two unknowns, perhaps there is no solution. Let's see. Using the third equation to substitute for H_0 in the first two gives

$$H_1 = (3X_1 - 3X_3)/10 \quad \text{and} \quad H_1 = (9X_2 - 9X_3)/10$$

Hence the contingent claim is attainable if and only if these two values of H_1 are the same, that is, if and only if

(1.21) $$X_1 - 3X_2 + 2X_3 = 0$$

This example illustrates the general principle that not all the contingent claims are attainable whenever the underlying model has multiple risk neutral probability measures, a principle that will be developed in the next section.

Exercise 1.12   For example 1.1 with $r = 1/9$, what is the price of a put option with exercise price $e = 5$? What trading strategy generates this contingent claim?

Exercise 1.13 – Put-Call parity   Suppose the interest rate r is a scalar, and let c and p denote the prices of a call and put, respectively, both having the same exercise price e. Show that either both are marketable or neither is marketable. Use risk neutral valuation to show that in the former case one has

$$c - p = S_0 - e/(1 + r)$$

1.5   Complete and Incomplete Markets

Just because, as will be assumed throughout this section, there exists a risk neutral probability measure, it does not necessarily follow that one can use the risk neutral valuation principle to determine the time $t = 0$ price of a contingent claim. The problem, of course, is that the contingent claim might not be marketable, in which case it is not clear what its time $t = 0$ price should be. In particular, there is no reason to be sure that $E_Q[X/B_1]$ is the correct value. We therefore need a convenient method for checking whether a contingent claim is indeed marketable. One method, as illustrated with example 1.1 in the preceding section, is to try to compute a generating trading strategy by solving a system of linear equations. A solution to such a system will exist if and only if the contingent claim is marketable. But there exist alternative methods.

The model is said to be *complete* if every contingent claim X can be generated by some trading strategy. Otherwise, the model is said to be *incomplete*. It turns out there are simple ways to check whether a model is complete. One way is to understand when the system of linear equations mentioned just above will always have a solution.

(1.22)   Suppose there are no arbitrage opportunities. Then the model is complete if and only if the number of states in Ω equals the number of independent vectors in $\{B_1, S_1(1), \ldots, S_N(1)\}$.

To see this, define the $K \times (N + 1)$ matrix A by

$$A = \begin{bmatrix} B_1(\omega_1) & S_1(1)(\omega_1) & \cdots & S_N(1)(\omega_1) \\ B_1(\omega_2) & S_1(1)(\omega_2) & \cdots & S_N(1)(\omega_2) \\ \vdots & \vdots & & \vdots \\ B_1(\omega_K) & S_1(1)(\omega_K) & \cdots & S_N(1)(\omega_K) \end{bmatrix}$$

and consider column vectors $H = (H_0, H_1, \cdots, H_N)'$ and $X = (X_1, \ldots, X_K)$. Then the model is complete if and only if the system $AH = X$ has a solution

H for every X. By linear algebra, this last fact will be true if and only if the matrix A has rank K, that is, this matrix has K independent columns.

Example 1.1 (continued)   The matrix

$$A = \begin{bmatrix} 10/9 & 20/3 \\ 10/9 & 40/9 \end{bmatrix}$$

has two independent rows, so this model is complete

Example 1.10   Suppose we take example 1.1 and add a second risky security with $S_2(0) = 54$, $S_2(1)(\omega_1) = 70$, and $S_2(1)(\omega_2) = 50$. Note that $Q = (1/2, 1/2)$ is still a risk neutral probability measure because $54 = (1/2)(9/10)70 + (1/2)(9/10)50$. Now

$$A = \begin{bmatrix} 10/9 & 20/3 & 70 \\ 10/9 & 40/9 & 50 \end{bmatrix}$$

but this still has rank two. Hence this augmented model is still complete, although the risky securities are redundant.

Example 1.2 (continued)   The matrix

$$A = \begin{bmatrix} 10/9 & 20/3 \\ 10/9 & 40/9 \\ 10/9 & 10/3 \end{bmatrix}$$

has rank two, whereas $K = 3$, so this model is incomplete. Now we saw earlier that the risk neutral probability measures are of the form $Q = (\lambda, 2 - 3\lambda, -1 + 2\lambda)$, where λ is any scalar satisfying $1/2 < \lambda < 2/3$. Suppose we take any such Q and then use the formula from the risk neutral valuation principle (1.20):

$$E_Q[X/B_1] = \lambda(9/10)X_1 + (2 - 3\lambda)(9/10)X_2 + (-1 + 2\lambda)(9/10)X_3$$

If X is marketable, then this value will be the same for all λ because it must coincide with V_0 under the generating trading strategy. Note that this value is the same if and only if equation (1.21) holds. Moreover, recall from the discussion of (1.21) that a contingent claim is marketable if and only if (1.21) holds. Putting this together, we see that a contingent claim in this model is marketable if and only if $E_Q[X/B_1]$ is the same value under every risk neutral probability measure. It turns out that this necessary and sufficient condition holds in general.

As stated earlier, throughout this section it will be assumed that $\mathbb{M} \neq \emptyset$, where $\mathbb{M}$ is the set of all risk neutral probability measures. Now if the contingent claim X is attainable, then $E_Q[X/B_1]$ is constant with respect to all $Q \in \mathbb{M}$. This is because, as already discussed in connection with (1.18), one has $V_0 = E_Q[X/B_1]$ for all $Q \in \mathbb{M}$, where V_0 is the initial value of the replicating portfolio.

To show the converse, it suffices to suppose that the contingent claim X is *not* attainable and then demonstrate that $E_Q[X/B_1]$ does *not* take the same value for all $Q \in \mathbb{M}$. Consider the $K \times (N+1)$ matrix A, the $(N+1)$-dimensional column vector H, and the K-dimensional column vector X as described above in connection with (1.22). If X is not attainable, then there is no solution H to the system $AH = X$. By a slightly modified version of Farkas's Lemma (see exercise 1.11), it follows that there must exist a row vector $\pi = (\pi_1, \ldots, \pi_K)$ satisfying

$$\pi A = 0, \quad \pi X > 0.$$

Let $\hat{Q} \in \mathbb{M}$ be arbitrary, and let the scalar $\lambda > 0$ be small enough so that

$$Q(\omega_k) \equiv \hat{Q}(\omega_k) + \lambda \pi_k B_1(\omega_k) > 0, \quad \text{all} \quad k = 1, \ldots, K.$$

Since π times the 'zeroth' column of A is zero, it follows that the quantity Q which was just defined is actually a probability measure giving positive probability to each state $\omega \in \Omega$. Moreover, for any discounted price process S_n^* we have

$$\begin{aligned} E_Q S_n^*(1) &= \sum Q(\omega_k)[S_n(1, \omega_k)]/[B_1(\omega_k)] \\ &= \sum \hat{Q}(\omega_k)[S_n(1, \omega_k)]/[B_1(\omega_k)] + \lambda \sum \pi_k S_n(1, \omega_k) \\ &= \sum \hat{Q}(\omega_k) S_n^*(1, \omega_k) \end{aligned}$$

where we used the fact that π times the 'nth' column of A is zero. But $\hat{Q} \in \mathbb{M}$, so $\sum \hat{Q}(\omega_k) S_n^*(1)(\omega_k) = S_n^*(0)$, in which case we realize that $Q \in \mathbb{M}$.

It remains to show that the expected value of X/B_1 under Q is different from the expected value under $\hat{Q}$. Denote $\delta \equiv \pi X$ and note that $\delta > 0$. Then

$$\begin{aligned} E_Q[X/B_1] &= \sum Q(\omega_k) X(\omega_k)/[B_1(\omega_k)] \\ &= \sum \hat{Q}(\omega_k) X(\omega_k)/[B_1(\omega_k)] + \lambda \sum \pi_k X(\omega_k) \\ &= E_{\hat{Q}}[X/B_1] + \lambda \delta \end{aligned}$$

In other words, $E_Q[X/B_1] \neq E_{\hat{Q}}[X/B_1]$ since X is not attainable. In summary, therefore, we have the following important result.

(1.23)   The contingent claim X is attainable if and only if $E_Q[X/B_1]$ takes the same value for every $Q \in \mathbb{M}$.

Notice that if $\mathbb{M}$ is a singleton and X is an arbitrary contingent claim, then trivially $E_Q[X/B_1]$ takes the same value for all $Q \in \mathbb{M}$, in which case X must be attainable and the model must be complete. On the other hand, suppose every contingent claim X is attainable but $\mathbb{M}$ contains two distinct risk neutral probability measures, say Q and $\hat{Q}$. In this case there must exist some state ω_k with $Q(\omega_k) \neq \hat{Q}(\omega_k)$, so take the contingent claim X defined by

$$X(\omega) = \begin{cases} B_1(\omega_k), & \omega = \omega_k \\ 0, & \text{otherwise} \end{cases}$$

Then

$$E_Q[X/B_1] = Q(\omega_k) \neq \hat{Q}(\omega_k) = E_{\hat{Q}}[X/B_1]$$

But this contradicts (1.23), which says that if X is attainable, then $E_Q[X/B_1]$ takes the same value for all $Q \in \mathbb{M}$. Hence if the model is complete, then $\mathbb{M}$ cannot have more than one element. We can combine these observations as follows.

> **(1.24)**   The model is complete if and only if $\mathbb{M}$ consists of exactly one risk neutral probability measure.

To summarize matters, if the model is complete then we know how to price all the contingent claims. Moreover, if the model is not complete then we know how to price some of the contingent claims, namely, all the attainable ones. But what about the claims that are not attainable in an incomplete model? For such a claim we cannot pinpoint its time $t = 0$ price, but it turns out that at least we can identify an interval within which a fair, reasonable value for the time $t = 0$ price must fall.

For the rest of this section we shall be considering an incomplete model and we shall focus on an arbitrary contingent claim X that is not attainable. Consider the quantity

$$V_+(X) \equiv \inf\{E_Q[Y/B_1] : Y \geq X, Y \text{ is attainable}\}$$

and refer to figure 1.3 throughout this discussion. The choice of $Q \in \mathbb{M}$ here does not really matter since it is only being used to compute the price of attainable contingent claims. Note that λB_1 is an attainable contingent claim for all values of the scalar λ and that $\lambda B_1 \geq X$ for all large enough values of λ; hence $V_+(X)$ is well defined and finite. Notice also that $V_+(X)$ is bounded below by $\sup\{E_Q[X/B_1] : Q \in \mathbb{M}\}$.

The quantity $V_+(X)$ is important because it is a good upper bound on the fair price of X. This follows from an arbitrage argument that is similar to the one discussed in the preceding section. If X could be sold for a greater amount, say $p > V_+(X)$, then one should make use of the trading strategy that replicates Y, which is any attainable contingent claim satisfying $Y \geq X$ and $p > E_Q[Y/B_1] \geq V_+(X)$. In particular, one should sell X at time $t = 0$, use part of the proceeds to purchase for the amount $E_Q[Y/B_1]$ the portfolio which replicates Y, and pocket the difference $p - E_Q[Y/B_1]$ as a riskless profit. At time $t = 1$ the value of the portfolio Y will always be enough to cover the obligation X of the contingent claim. Hence $V_+(X)$ is the price of the cheapest portfolio that can be used to hedge a short position in the contingent claim X.

The unattainable contingent claim X cannot trade at a price higher than $V_+(X)$, or else there will exist an arbitrage opportunity. Similarly, this contingent claim cannot trade at a price lower than $V_-(X)$, where

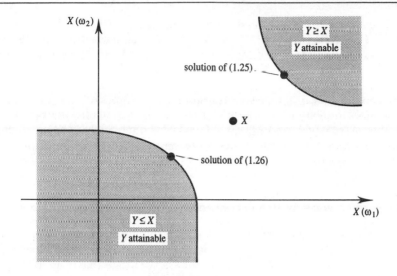

Figure 1.3   Determining fair prices for unattainable contingent claim X

$$V_-(X) = \sup\{E_Q[Y/B_1] : Y \leqslant X, Y \text{ is attainable}\}$$

As with $V_+(X)$, the quantity $V_-(X)$ is well defined and finite with $V_-(X) \leqslant \inf\{E_Q[X/B_1] : Q \in \mathbb{M}\}$. The fair price (or prices) of X must be in the interval $[V_-(X), V_+(X)]$. We therefore are interested in computing $V_+(X)$ as well as any attainable contingent claim $Y \geqslant X$ satisfying $V_+(X) - E_Q[Y/B_1]$, and similarly for $V_-(X)$.

Consider the linear program

(1.25)   minimize to λ

subject to $Y \geqslant X$
$$U - Y/B_1 = 0$$
$$\lambda - U \cdot Q_1 = 0$$
$$\vdots \qquad \vdots$$
$$\lambda - U \cdot Q_J = 0$$
$$\lambda \in \mathbb{R}, \quad Y \in \mathbb{R}^K, \quad U \in \mathbb{R}^K$$

Here $Q_j \in \mathbb{M} = \mathbb{W}^\perp \cap \mathbb{P}^+, j = 1 \ldots, J$, are chosen to be independent vectors, thereby forming a basis of $\mathbb{W}^\perp$, which is assumed to have dimension J. This means that the subspace $\mathbb{W}$ of discounted gains has dimension $K - J$ and can be expressed as

$$\mathbb{W} = \{X \in \mathbb{R}^K : X \cdot Q_j = 0 \quad \text{for} \quad j = 1, \cdots, J\}$$

Now suppose Y is an attainable contingent claim with time $t = 0$ price λ, and set $U = Y/B_1$. Because $V_1^* = V_0^* + G^*$, this statement is equivalent to the statement that $U - \lambda e \in \mathbb{W}$ and $U = Y/B_1$, where e here is a column vector of 1's. But $e \cdot Q_j = 1$ for all j, so this statement, in turn, is equivalent to the statement that $U = Y/B_1$ and $U \cdot Q_j - \lambda = 0$ for $j = 1, \cdots J$. Hence the feasible region in the linear program (1.25) can be interpreted as being the set of all attainable contingent claims Y with $Y \geqslant X$. It follows that if λ and Y are part of an optimal solution of this linear program, then $V_+(X) = \lambda$ and Y is an attainable contingent claim with $Y \geqslant X$ and time $t = 0$ price equal to $V_+(X)$. Note that an optimal solution always exists to this linear program because the feasible region is nonempty and the objective function is bounded below.

Similarly, if you solve the linear program

(**1.26**)   maximize λ

subject to $Y \leqslant X$

$$U - Y/B_1 = 0$$
$$\lambda - U \cdot Q_1 = 0$$
$$\vdots \qquad \vdots$$
$$\lambda - U \cdot Q_J = 0$$
$$\lambda \in \mathbb{R}, \quad Y \in \mathbb{R}^K, \quad U \in \mathbb{R}^K$$

and obtain an optimal solution (λ, Y, U), then $V_-(X)$ and Y is an attainable contingent claim with $Y \leqslant X$ and time $t = 0$ price equal to $V_-(X)$.

It turns out that not only does linear programming enable us to completely solve for the quantities of interest, but it gives us something extra as a bonus. Consider another linear program:

(**1.27**)   maximize $\displaystyle\sum_{k=1}^{K}[X(\omega_k)/B_1(\omega_k)]\psi_k$

subject to $\theta_1 + \cdots + \theta_J = 1$

$$\psi_1 - Q_1(\omega_1)\theta_1 - \cdots - Q_J(\omega_1)\theta_J = 0$$
$$\vdots \qquad \vdots \qquad\qquad \vdots \qquad \vdots$$
$$\psi_K - Q_1(\omega_K)\theta_1 - \cdots - Q_J(\omega_K)\theta_J = 0$$
$$\psi \in \mathbb{R}^K \qquad \theta \in \mathbb{R}^J \qquad \psi \geqslant 0$$

If (ψ, θ) is an arbitrary feasible solution, then

$$\psi = \theta_1 Q_1 + \theta_2 Q_2 + \cdots + \theta_J Q_J,$$

which is non-negative. Moreover, with e a row vector of 1's we have

$$e \cdot \psi = \theta_1 e \cdot Q_1 + \cdots + \theta_J e \cdot Q_J = \theta_1 + \cdots + \theta_J = 1$$

since each Q_j is a probability measure, so ψ can be interpreted as a probability measure too. For any discounted price process S_n^* we have

$$E_\psi[\Delta S_n^*] = \theta_1 Q_1 \cdot \Delta S_n^* + \cdots + \theta_J Q_J \cdot \Delta S_n^* = 0$$

since each $Q_j \in M$. Hence ψ can be interpreted as a linear pricing measure (but not, necessarily, as a risk neutral probability measure). In other words the feasible region can be interpreted as the closure of M. It follows that the optimal value of the objective function in linear program (1.27) is precisely equal to $\sup\{E_Q[X/B_1] : Q \in M\}$.

Now here comes a startling result of fundamental importance. By linear programming theory the linear programs (1.25) and (1.27) are duals of each other. Both programs are feasible, so by linear programming duality theory, their optimal objective values are equal to each other. Analogous results hold for linear program (1.26), of course, so all these results can be summarized as follows:

(1.28) If $M \neq \emptyset$, then for any contingent claim X one has

$$V_+(X) = \sup\{E_Q[X/B_1] : Q \in M\} \quad \text{and}$$
$$V_-(X) = \inf\{E_Q[X/B_1] : Q \in M\}.$$

Of course, if X is attainable, then $V_+(X) = V_-(X)$ is its usual time $t = 0$ price.

Example 1.2 (continued) Consider the contingent claim $X = (30, 20, 10)$. This is not attainable, because it does not satisfy equation (1.21). Recalling that M consists of all probability measures of the form $Q = (q, 2 - 3q, -1 + 2q)$ where $1/2 < q < 2/3$, it is straightforward to compute (making a slight and obvious change of notation for this particular example) $E_q[X/B_1] = 27 - 9q$. Hence

$$V_+(X) = \sup_q E_q[X/B_1] = \sup_q \{27 - 9q\} = 27 - 9(1/2) = 22 \ 1/2$$

and

$$V_-(X) = \inf_q E_q[X/B_1] = \inf_q \{27 - 9q\} = 27 - 9(2/3) = 21$$

Upon solving the linear program (1.25) one obtains the attainable contingent claim corresponding to $V_+(X)$; this is $Y = (30, 20, 15)$, as can be verified by checking equation (1.21) and checking that the time $t = 0$ price of Y is indeed 22 1/2. Similarly, the attainable contingent claim corresponding to $V_-(X)$ is verified to be $Y = (30, 50/3, 10)$.

Exercise 1.14 Explain why the model in example 1.4 is not complete. Characterize the set of all the attainable contingent claims. Compute $V_+(X)$ and $V_-(X)$ for $X = (40, 30, 20, 10)$.

Exercise 1.15 Use (1.23) to verify whether there are any values of the exercise price e such that the call option is attainable for the model in example 1.2. Similarly, specify which put options are attainable. Assume $r = 1/9$.

Exercise 1.16 Just after linear program (1.25) it was asserted that one can choose $Q_j \in \mathsf{M} = \mathsf{W}^\perp \cap \mathsf{P}^+$, $j = 1, \cdots, J$, to be independent vectors, thereby forming a basis of $\mathsf{W}^\perp$, which is assumed to have dimension J. Use linear algebra to carefully verify this assertion. Compute Q_j vectors for example 1.4.

1.6   Risk and Return

With Q a risk neutral probability measure and $\omega \in \Omega$, recall that $Q(\omega)/B_1(\omega)$ is sometimes called the state price of ω. For this reason, the random variable

$$L(\omega) \equiv \frac{Q(\omega)}{P(\omega)}$$

is called the *state price vector* or the *state price density*. The main result to be shown in this section is that the risk premium of an arbitrary portfolio is proportional to the covariance[6] between a return corresponding to the state price density and the return for the portfolio, a result that resembles a principal finding of the capital asset pricing model.

Assuming the time $t = 0$ price $S_n(0)$ is strictly positive, the *return* R_n for risky security n is defined to be the random variable

$$R_n \equiv \frac{S_n(1) - S_n(0)}{S_n(0)}, \qquad n = 1, \cdots, N$$

Similarly, the return corresponding to the bank account is defined by

$$R_0 \equiv \frac{B_1 - B_0}{B_0} = r$$

The returns are useful quantities for a variety of purposes, one of which is that if you know the time $t = 0$ prices and the returns, then you can compute time $t = 1$ prices. Since prices are non-negative one has $R_n \geqslant -1$, with equality if and only if $S_n(1) = 0$. It is left as an exercise to verify that the gain for a portfolio can be written as

$$(1.29) \qquad G = H_0 B_0 R_0 + \sum_{n=1}^{N} H_n S_n(0) R_n$$

Hence the gain for a portfolio is a weighted combination of the underlying returns, each weight being the amount of money invested at time $t = 0$ in the corresponding security.

The returns can also be used to compute risk neutral probability measures. Since

$$S_n^*(1) \quad S_n^*(0) = \frac{S_n^*(1) - B_1 S_n(0)}{B_1}$$

$$= \frac{[1 + R_n]S_n(0) - [1 + R_0]S_n(0)}{1 + R_0}$$

$$= S_n(0)\left(\frac{R_n - R_0}{1 + R_0}\right)$$

it follows from (1.15) that

(1.30)   If Q is a probability measure with $Q(\omega) > 0$ for all $\omega \in \Omega$, then Q is a risk neutral probability measure if and only if

$$E_Q\left(\frac{R_n - R_0}{1 + R_0}\right) = 0, \qquad n = 1, \ldots, N$$

Notice that when the interest rate $R_0 = r$ is deterministic, the equation in (1.30) becomes simply

$$E_Q[R_n] = r, \qquad n = 1, \ldots, N$$

This is one example of many situations where, under the assumption of a deterministic interest rate, one has a nice, and often important, relationship involving returns. Therefore, this assumption will be in force for the balance of this section, as will be the assumption that there exists a risk neutral probability measure Q.

The mean return for security n, denoted $\bar{R}_n = E[R_n]$, often plays an important role. For example, it is easy to see that $\operatorname{cov}(R_n, L) = E[R_n L] - E[R_n]E[L] = E_Q[R_n] - E[R_n] = r - \bar{R}_n$. In other words,

(1.31) $\bar{R}_n - r = -\operatorname{cov}(R_n, L), \qquad n = 1, \cdots, N$

The difference $\bar{R}_n - r$ here is called the *risk premium* for the security; normally this is positive because investors usually insist that the expected returns of risky securities be higher than the riskless return r. Thus (1.31) says that the risk premium of a security is related to the correlation[7] between the security's return and the state price density.

Consider the return R of a portfolio corresponding to an arbitrary trading strategy $H = (H_0, H_1, \ldots, H_N)$. Assuming $V_0 > 0$, this is

$$R = \frac{V_1 - V_0}{V_0}$$

Using $S_n(1) = S_n(0)[1 + R_n]$ and the definition of V_t one obtains

(1.32) $$R = \frac{H_0}{V_0}r + \sum_{n=1}^{N}\left[\frac{H_n S_n(0)}{V_0}\right]R_n$$

If you interpret H_o/V_o as the fraction of money invested in the savings account (recall $B_0 = 1$) and $H_n S_n(0)/V_0$ as the fraction of money invested in the nth security, then (1.32) says that the return on the portfolio is a convex combination of the returns of the individual securities. Using (1.31), (1.32), and some basic properties of the covariance, it is straightforward to verify that

$$(1.33) \qquad\qquad \bar{R} - r = -\text{cov}(R, L)$$

where, of course, $\bar{R} = E[R]$.

Now fix two scalars a and b with $b \neq 0$, and assume the contingent claim $a + bL$ is attainable, that is, suppose there exists some trading strategy H' such that $V_1' = a + bL$. Since $V_0'(1 + R') = a + bL$ (here V' and R' denote the value and return processes, respectively, corresponding to H'), one can substitute for L and use the properties of the covariance relationship to verify that

$$\text{cov}(R, L) = \frac{V_0'}{b} \text{cov}(R, R')$$

(R still corresponds to an arbitrary trading strategy). Hence (1.33) can be rewritten as

$$(1.34) \qquad\qquad \bar{R} - r = -\frac{V_0'}{b} \text{cov}(R, R')$$

In particular, in the special case where you choose $H = H'$, (1.34) says that

$$\bar{R}' - r = -\frac{V_0'}{b} \text{cov}(R', R') = -\frac{V_0'}{b} \text{var}(R')$$

Using this to substitute for V_0'/b in (1.34), where now we are back to an arbitrary trading strategy H, we obtain the following:

(1.35)   Suppose for scalars a and b the contingent claim $a + bL$ is generated by some portfolio having return R' and suppose the interest rate r is deterministic. Let R be the return of an arbitrary portfolio. Then

$$\bar{R} - r = \frac{\text{cov}(R, R')}{\text{var}(R')}(\bar{R}' - r)$$

The ratio $\text{cov}(R, R')/\text{var}(R')$ is called the *beta* of the trading strategy H with respect to the trading strategy H'. This result says that the risk premium of H is proportional to the risk premium of H', with the proportionality constant being this beta. Or from a slightly different perspective, (1.35) says that the risk premium is proportional to its beta with respect to a linear transformation of the state price density. This result resembles the traditional capital asset pricing model, only here H' corresponds to a linear transformation of the state price density instead of the market portfolio.

Notice that with a deterministic interest rate r and with arbitrary scalars a and b $(b \neq 0)$, the contingent claim $a + bL$ is attainable if and only if the state price density L is. This is because $\Pi_0(1+r) + \sum H_n S_n(1) = a + bL$ if and only if

$$\frac{1}{b}\left[H_0 - \frac{a}{1+r}\right](1+r) + \sum_{n=1}^{N}\frac{1}{b}H_n S_n(1) = L$$

Exercise 1.17   Verify equation (1.29), both in general and by applying it to example 1.1.

Exercise 1.18   Assuming the time $t = 0$ price is strictly positive, the *discounted return* R_n^* is defined by $R_n^* \equiv [S_n^*(1) - S_n^*(0)]/S_n^*(0)$ for $n = 1, \ldots, N$. Show that

(a) $G^* = \displaystyle\sum_{n=1}^{N} H_n S_n^*(0) R_n^*$

(b) $R_n^* = \dfrac{R_n - R_0}{1 + R_0} \qquad n = 1, \ldots, N$

(c)   The strictly positive probability measure Q is a risk neutral probability measure if and only if $E_Q[R_n^*] = 0$ for $n = 1, \ldots, N$.

Exercise 1.19   Analyze the risk and return properties of example 1.1 assuming $P(\omega_1) = p$ for a general parameter $0 < p < 1$.

(a)   What are R_1 and $\bar{R}_1$?
(b)   What is L?
(c)   Verify (1.31) for $n = 0$ and 1.

From now on suppose $H = (H_0, H_1) = (1, 3)$.

(d)   What are R and $\bar{R}$?
(e)   Verify (1.32).
(f)   Verify (1.33).
(g)   What are Π', V_0', and R'?
(h)   Verify (1.34).
(i)   Verify (1.35).

NOTES

1   If X is a *random variable*, this means X is a real-valued function on the sample space Ω. In other words, we know the value $X(\omega)$ for each state of the world $\omega \in \Omega$.
2   The *expected value* (also called the *mean* or *average*) of the random variable X is denoted EX or $E[X]$ and defined to be

$$EX \equiv \sum_{k=1}^{K} X(\omega_k) P(\omega_k)$$

More generally, if f is a real-valued function on the real line,

$$Ef(X) \equiv \sum_{k=1}^{K} f\Big(X(\omega_k)\Big) P(\omega_k)$$

In particular, for scalars a and b, $E[aX + b] = aEX + b$.

3 See the appendix on linear programming.

4 In other words, for some $\hat{Y} \in \mathbb{W}^{\perp}$ whose components are all strictly positive, the ray is of the form $\{Y \in \mathbb{R}^N : Y = \lambda \hat{Y}, \lambda > 0, \lambda \in \mathbb{R}\}$.

5 *Closed* means that if $\{X_1\}$ is a sequence of points in $\mathbb{A}^+$ that converges to some $X \in \mathbb{R}^K$, then $X \in \mathbb{A}^+$; *convex* means that for any $X, \hat{X} \in \mathbb{A}^+$ and any scalar λ with $0 < \lambda < 1$, then $\lambda X + (1 - \lambda)\hat{X} \in \mathbb{A}^+$.

6 For two random variables X and Y, the *covariance* $\text{cov}(X, Y)$ is defined to be $E[XY] - E[X]E[Y]$. Note that $\text{cov}(X - E[X], Y) = \text{cov}(X, Y)$. Moreover, given three random variables X, Y, and Z and two scalars a and b, one has $\text{cov}(aX + bZ, Y) = a\,\text{cov}(X, Y) + b\,\text{cov}(Z, Y)$.

7 The *variance*, denoted $\text{var}(X)$, of a random variable X is defined by $\text{var}(X) \equiv E[X^2] - (E[X])^2 = E[(X - E[X])^2]$. The *standard deviation* of X is $\sigma_X \equiv \sqrt{\text{var}(X)}$. The *correlation* between the random variables X and Y (assuming $\sigma_X > 0$ and $\sigma_Y > 0$) is defined by $\rho(X, Y) \equiv \text{cov}(X, Y)/(\sigma_X \sigma_Y)$. Hence the risk premium for security n equals $-\rho(R_n, L)\rho_{R_n}\sigma_L$.

2 Single Period Consumption and Investment

2.1 Optimal Portfolios and Viability

This chapter is concerned with the problem of choosing the best trading strategy for the purpose of transforming wealth invested at time $t = 0$ into time $t = 1$ wealth. With some variations of this problem that will be considered in later sections, a portion of the wealth is consumed at time $t = 0$. The problem is to compute an optimal trading strategy, and for this a measure of performance is needed.

The measure of performance that will be used here is that of expected utility. In particular, suppose $u : \mathbb{R} \times \Omega \to \mathbb{R}$ is a function such that $w \to u(w, \Omega)$ is differentiable, concave, and strictly increasing for each $\omega \in \Omega$. If w is the value of the portfolio at time $t = 1$ and ω is the state, then $u(w, \omega)$ will represent the *utility* of the amount w. Hence our measure of performance will be the expected utility of terminal wealth, that is,

$$Eu(V_1) = \sum_{\omega \in \Omega} P(\omega)u(V_1(\omega), \omega)$$

Note that the utility function u can depend explicitly on both the terminal wealth w and the state ω. However, for many applications it suffices for u to depend only on the wealth, in which case u is simply a concave, strictly increasing function with a single argument.

Let $\mathbb{H}$ denote the set of all trading strategies, that is, $\mathbb{H} = \mathbb{R}^{N+1}$, the linear space of all vectors of the form $(H_0, H_1, \ldots, H_N)$. Let $v \in \mathbb{R}$ be a specified scalar representing the initial, time $t = 0$ wealth. We are interested in the following optimal portfolio problem:

(2.1)
$$\text{maximize} \quad Eu(V_1)$$
$$H \in \mathbb{H}$$

$$\text{subject to} \quad V_0 = v$$

Since $V_1 = B_1 V_1^*$ and $V_1^* = V_0^* + G^*$, this is the same as

(2.2)
$$\text{maximize} \quad E[u(B_1\{v + H_1 \Delta S_1^* + \ldots + H_N \Delta S_N^*\})]$$

Notice that if there exists an arbitrage opportunity, then there cannot exist a solution to (2.1). In other words, if $\hat{H}$ is a solution and H is an arbitrage opportunity, then setting $\tilde{H} = \hat{H} + H$ gives

$$v + \sum_{n=1}^{N} \tilde{H}_n \Delta S_n^* = v + \sum_{n=1}^{N} \hat{H}_n \Delta S_n^* + \sum_{n=1}^{N} H_n \Delta S_n^* \geqslant v + \sum_{n=1}^{N} \hat{H}_n \Delta S_n^*$$

where the inequality follows because H is an arbitrage opportunity. In fact, this inequality is actually strict for at least one $\omega \in \Omega$. Since u is strictly increasing in wealth and since $P(\omega) > 0$ for all $\omega \in \Omega$, this means the objective value in (2.2) is strictly greater under $\tilde{H}$ than under $\hat{H}$. This contradicts the assertion that $\hat{H}$ is an optimal solution of (2.2), in which case the following must be true:

> **(2.3)**   If there exists an optimal solution of the portfolio problem (2.1) or (2.2), then there are no arbitrage opportunities.

In other words, (2.3) says that if there exists an optimal solution to (2.1) or (2.2), then there exists a risk neutral probability measure. By a result that is somewhat surprising, there exists an explicit relationship between any such solution and the risk neutral probability measures. This relationship can be derived from the first order conditions necessary for optimality. To see this, rewrite the objective function in (2.2) as

$$\sum_{\omega \in \Omega} P(\omega) u(B_1(\omega)\{v + H_1 \Delta S_1^*(\omega) + \ldots + H_N \Delta S_N^*(\omega)\}, \omega)$$

so that the first order necessary condition can be expressed as

(2.4)
$$0 = \frac{\partial E[u(B_1\{v + H_1 \Delta S_1^* + \ldots + H_N \Delta S_N^*\})]}{\partial H_n}$$

$$= \sum_{\omega \in \Omega} P(\omega) u'(B_1(\omega)\{v + H_1 \Delta S_1^*(\omega) + \ldots + H_N \Delta S_N^*(\omega)\}, \omega) B_1(\omega) \Delta S_n^*(\omega)$$

$$= E[B_1 u'(V_1) \Delta S_n^*], \quad n = 1, \ldots, N$$

where u' denotes the partial derivative of u with respect to the first argument. Hence if (H, V) is a solution of (2.2), then it must satisfy this system of N equations. But recall the condition which a risk neutral probability measure must satisfy:

(2.5)
$$0 = E_Q[\Delta S_n^*] = \sum_{\omega \in \Omega} Q(\omega) \Delta S_n^*(\omega), \quad n = 1, \ldots, N$$

Comparing (2.4) and (2.5) it is apparent that upon setting $Q(\omega) = P(\omega)B_1(\omega)u'(V_1(\omega),\omega)$ one has obtained a measure satisfying (2.5). Note that $Q(\omega) > 0$ for all ω since u is strictly increasing. However, $Q(\omega_1) + \ldots + Q(\omega_K)$ is not necessarily equal to one, so Q is only a probability measure up to a constant. It is easy to see what this constant should be, and so we have the following:

(2.6) If (H, V) is a solution of the optimal portfolio problem (2.1) or (2.2), then

$$Q(\omega) \equiv \frac{P(\omega)B_1(\omega)u'(V_1(\omega),\omega)}{E[B_1u'(V_1)]}, \qquad \omega \in \Omega$$

defines a risk neutral probability measure.

Rewriting (2.6) slightly in the case where $B_1 = 1 + r$ is constant, we obtain $L(\omega) = Q(\omega)/P(\omega) = u'(V_1(\omega),\omega)/E[u'(V_1)]$. In other words, when the interest rate is deterministic, the *state price density* is proportional to the *marginal utility of terminal wealth*.

What about the converse? If there exists a risk neutral probability measure Q, then does the optimal portfolio problem (2.1) have a solution? Not necessarily, for some u and v may be such that no solution H exists. However, one can always find some u and v such that a solution H does exist. Formalizing this idea, we will say that the model is *viable* if there exists a function $u : \mathbb{R} \times \Omega \to \mathbb{R}$ and an initial wealth v such that $w \to u(w,\omega)$ is concave and strictly increasing for each $\omega \in \Omega$ and such that the corresponding optimal portfolio problem (2.1) has an optimal solution H.

(2.7) The securities market model is viable if and only if there exists a risk neutral probability measure Q.

In view of (2.6), to verify this principle it suffices to assume the existence of a risk neutral probability measure, cleverly select u and v, and then demonstrate the existence of a solution of (2.2). The choice of u will be

$$u(w, \omega) = w\frac{Q(\omega)}{P(\omega)B_1(\omega)}$$

while v will be arbitrary. Now for an arbitrary $(H_1, \ldots, H_N)$ we have

$$E[u(B_1\{v + H_1\Delta S_1^* + \ldots + H_N\Delta S_N^*\}, \omega)]$$
$$= \sum P(\omega)B_1(\omega)\{v + H_1\Delta S_1^* + \ldots + H_N\Delta S_N^*\}Q(\omega)/[P(\omega)B_1(\omega)]$$
$$= \sum Q(\omega)\{v + H_1\Delta S_1^* + \ldots + H_N\Delta S_N^*\}$$
$$= v + H_1E_Q[\Delta S_1^*] + \ldots + H_NE_Q[\Delta S_N^*] = v$$

so every vector $(H_1, \ldots, H_N)$ gives rise to the same objective value in (2.2). Equivalently, every trading strategy with initial wealth v gives rise to the same objective value in (2.1), which means that all such trading strategies are optimal. Hence (2.7) is true by this clever choice of utility function.

The optimal portfolio problem (2.1) or (2.2) is a standard convex optimization problem, so one can use standard techniques to compute a solution. One such approach is to work with the necessary equations (2.4), a system of N equations and N unknowns. Unfortunately, as seen in the following example, these equations can be nonlinear in H and thus difficult to solve.

Example 2.1   Suppose $N = 2$, $K = 3$, $r = 1/9$, and the discounted price process is as follows:

n	S_n^*	$S_n^*(1)$		
		ω_1	ω_2	ω_3
1	6	6	8	4
2	10	13	9	8

Note that there exists a unique risk neutral probability measure, because $Q = (1/3, 1/3, 1/3)$ is the unique solution of the following system of equations:

$$6 = 6Q(\omega_1) + 8Q(\omega_2) + 4Q(\omega_3)$$
$$10 = 13Q(\omega_1) + 9Q(\omega_2) + 8Q(\omega_3)$$
$$1 = Q(\omega_1) + Q(\omega_2) + Q(\omega_3)$$

With the exponential utility function $u(w) = -\exp\{-w\}$, the marginal utility function is $u'(w) = \exp\{-w\}$. Hence the necessary conditions (2.4) are:

$$0 = P(\omega_1)\,\exp\{-(10/9)(v + 0H_1 + 3H_2)\}(10/9)(0)$$
$$+ P(\omega_2)\,\exp\{-(10/9)(v + 2H_1 - H_2)\}(10/9)(2)$$
$$+ P(\omega_3)\,\exp\{-(10/9)(v - 2H_1 - 2H_2)\}(10/9)(-2)$$

$$0 = P(\omega_1)\,\exp\{-(10/9)(v + 0H_1 + 3H_2)\}(10/9)(3)$$
$$+ P(\omega_2)\,\exp\{-(10/9)(v + 2H_1 - H_2)\}(10/9)(-1)$$
$$+ P(\omega_3)\,\exp\{-(10/9)(v - 2H_1 - 2H_2)\}(10/9)(-2)$$

Needless to say, these are not so easy to solve for H_1 and H_2.

Exercise 2.1   Suppose $N = 1$, $K = 2$, $S_0 = 5$, $S_1(\omega_1) = 20/3$, and $S_1(\omega_2) = 40/9$. Solve (2.1) in the case of $r = 1/9$ and general scalar parameters for the initial wealth $v \geqslant 0$ and the probability $P(\omega_1) = p$ under the utility functions

(a) $u(w) = \ln w$
(b) $u(w) = -\exp(-w)$
(c) $u(w) = \gamma^{-1}w^\gamma$, where $-\infty < \gamma < 1$, $\gamma \neq 0$.

2.2 Risk Neutral Computational Approach

As seen in example 2.1, solving the optimal portfolio problem (2.1) can be computationally difficult. Fortunately, there is an alternative technique which involves the risk neutral probability measure and is much more efficient. The idea is based on the observation that the objective function $H \to Eu(V_1)$ in (2.1) can be viewed as the composition of two functions, as illustrated in figure 2.1. The first function $H \to V_1$ maps trading strategies into random variables which represent the time $t = 1$ value of the portfolio. The second function $V_1 \to Eu(V_1)$ maps random variables into numbers on the real line. Corresponding to this composition, the risk neutral computation technique involves a two-step process. First you identify the optimal random variable V_1, that is, the value of V_1 maximizing $Eu(V_1)$ over the subset of feasible random variables. Then you compute the trading strategy H that generates this V_1, that is, you solve for the trading strategy that replicates the contingent claim V_1.

Step 2 is easy. This is exactly the same as was discussed in section 1.4 for computing the trading strategy which replicates an attainable contingent claim. If the subset of feasible random variables were chosen correctly for step 1, then the computed trading strategy which replicates V_1 will correspond to a portfolio having time $t = 0$ value equal to v. In other words, the attainable contingent claim V_1 will have time $t = 0$ price equal to v, the specified initial value of the portfolio.

Step 1 is a bit more challenging, but it just involves straightforward optimization theory. The key to success is to specify the subset of feasible random variables correctly and conveniently. If the model is complete, this subset is simply

$$(2.8) \qquad \mathbb{W}_v \equiv \{ W \in \mathbb{R}^K : E_Q[W/B_1] = v \}$$

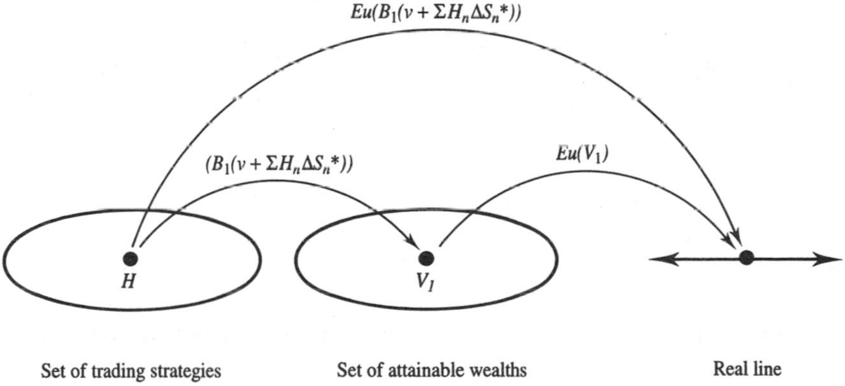

Figure 2.1 The risk neutral computational approach

(the specification of W_v for incomplete models is more complex and will be discussed below). To see this, note that under any trading strategy H with $V_0 = v$ one has $E_Q[V_1/B_1] = v$ by the risk neutral valuation principle. Conversely, for any contingent claim $W \in W_v$ there exists, again by the risk neutral valuation principle, a trading strategy H such that $V_0 = v$ and $V_1 = W$. In the context of optimal portfolio problems, the subset W_v (actually, an affine subspace) is called the *set of attainable wealths*.

The first step in the risk neutral computation technique is to solve the subproblem:

$$(2.9) \qquad \text{maximize} \quad Eu(W)$$
$$\text{subject to} \quad W \in W_v$$

When the model is complete, this problem can be conveniently solved with a Lagrange multiplier. In view of (2.8), problem (2.9) is equivalent to

$$(2.10) \qquad \text{maximize} \quad Eu(W) - \lambda E_Q[W/B_1]$$

where the Lagrange multiplier λ is chosen so that the solution in (2.10) satisfies

$$(2.11) \qquad E_Q[W/B_1] = v$$

Introducing the state price density $L = Q/P$, the objective function in (2.10) can be rewritten as

$$Eu(W) - \lambda E[LW/B_1] = E[u(W) - \lambda LW/B_1]$$
$$= \sum_{\omega} P(\omega)[u(W(\omega)) - \lambda L(\omega)W(\omega)/B_1(\omega)]$$

If W maximizes this expression, then the necessary conditions must be satisfied, giving rise to one equation for each $\omega \in \Omega$:

$$u'(W(\omega)) = \lambda L(\omega)/B_1(\omega), \qquad \text{all } \omega \in \Omega$$

Note that this equation is exactly the same as the one in (2.6); in fact, since $W = V_1$ one can deduce that λ is equal to $E[B_1 u'(W)]$, where W is the optimal solution. To compute W we solve the preceding displayed equation for $W(\omega)$ giving

$$(2.12) \qquad W(\omega) = I[\lambda L(\omega)/B_1(\omega)]$$

where I denotes the *inverse function* corresponding to u'.

Hence (2.12) gives the optimal solution of (2.9) when λ takes the correct value. But what is the correct value? It is simply the value such that (2.11) is satisfied when (2.12) is substituted for W, that is,

$$(2.13) \qquad E_Q[I(\lambda L/B_1)/B_1] = v$$

The inverse function I is decreasing, and its range will normally include $(0, \infty)$, so normally a solution λ to (2.11) will exist for $v > 0$.

Example 2.2 Suppose $u(w) = -\exp(-w)$, so that $u'(w) = \exp(-w)$. Then $u'(w) = i$ if and only if $w = -\ln(i)$, so $I(i) = -\ln(i)$. Hence the optimal solution of (2.9) is of the form

$$W = -\ln(\lambda L/B_1) = -\ln(\lambda) - \ln(L/B_1)$$

and (2.13) becomes

$$v = -E_Q[B_1^{-1}\ln(\lambda L/B_1)] = -\ln(\lambda)E_Q B_1^{-1} - E_Q[\ln(L/B_1)/B_1]$$

Hence the correct value of λ is given by

$$\lambda = \exp\left\{\frac{-v - E_Q[B_1^{-1}\ln(L/B_1)]}{E_Q B_1^{-1}}\right\}$$

so

$$W = \frac{v + E_Q[B_1^{-1}\ln(L/B_1)]}{E_Q B_1^{-1}} - \ln(L/B_1)$$

Substituting this into $-\exp(-W)$ gives

$$u(W) = -\exp\left\{\frac{-v + \ln(L/B_1)E_Q B_1^{-1} - E_Q[B_1^{-1}\ln(L/B_1)]}{E_Q B_1^{-1}}\right\}$$
$$= -\lambda L/B_1$$

so the optimal value of the objective function in (2.9) is

$$Eu(W) = -\lambda E[L/B_1] = -\lambda E_Q B_1^{-1}$$

This example illustrates a general pattern: general formulas for the optimal wealth W and so forth are obtained which depend on the underlying securities market model only via the probability measures P and Q. In other words, P and Q comprise what can be thought of as a sufficient statistic for the optimal portfolio subproblem (2.9). After deriving the formulas like those in example 2.2 for a particular utility function, one can quickly analyse any complete securities market model having the same utility function.

Examples 2.1 and 2.2 (continued)   Suppose $P(\omega_1) = 1/2$ and $P(\omega_2) = P(\omega_3) = 1/4$ so the state price density L is given by $L(\omega_1) = 2/3$ and $L(\omega_2) = L(\omega_3) - 4/3$. With $r = 1/9$ and $B_1 = 10/9$ we compute

$$E_Q[\ln(L/B_1)] = (1/3)\left[\ln\left(\frac{2}{3}\cdot\frac{9}{10}\right) + 2\ln\left(\frac{4}{3}\cdot\frac{9}{10}\right)\right] = -0.04873$$

so the optimal attainable wealth is

$$W = v(1+r) + E_Q[\ln(L/B_1)] - \ln(L/B_1)$$
$$= \begin{cases} v(10/9) + 0.46209, & \omega = \omega_1 \\ v(10/9) - 0.23105, & \omega = \omega_2, \omega_3 \end{cases}$$

Note that $E_Q[W/B_1] = v$, as desired. Now $\lambda = \exp\{-(10/9)v + 0.04873\}$, so the optimal value of the objective function is

$$Eu(W) = -\lambda E_Q B_1^{-1} = -\frac{9}{10}\lambda$$

Notice that, consistent with (2.6), $\lambda = E[B_1 u'(V_1)]$. Also, having computed the optimal attainable wealth W, we can now easily compute the optimal trading strategy H by solving $W/B_1 = v + G^*$. In state ω_1 the discounted terminal wealth $W(\omega_1)/B_1$ equals $v + (9/10)(0.46209) = v + 0.41490$, whereas the initial wealth plus the discounted gain $v + G^*(\omega_1)$ equals $v + H_1(6-6) + H_2(13-10) = v + 3H_2$. Similarly, equations are obtained corresponding to states ω_2 and ω_3, yielding the following system of three equations:

$$\omega_1 : \quad 0.41590 = \quad 0H_1 + 3H_2$$
$$\omega_2 : -0.20795 = \quad 2H_1 - H_2$$
$$\omega_3 : -0.20795 = -2H_1 - 2H_2$$

These equations are redundant and there exists a unique solution, which is $H_1 = -0.03466$ and $H_2 = 0.13863$. Using $v = V_0 = H_0 + 6H_1 + 10H_2$ to solve for H_0 yields $H_0 = v - 1.17834$. Finally, notice that, as desired, this trading strategy satisfies the necessary conditions (2.4) (see example 2.1 above).

Exercise 2.2 (log utility) Suppose $u(w) = \ln(w)$. Show that the inverse function $I(i) = i^{-1}$, the Lagrange multiplier $\lambda = v^{-1}$, the optimal attainable wealth is $W = vL^{-1}B_1$, and the optimal objective value is $\ln(v) - E[\ln(L/B_1)]$. Compute these expressions and solve for the optimal trading strategy in the case where $N = 1$, $K = 2$, $r = 1/9$, $S_0 = 5$, $S_1(\omega_1) = 20/3$, $S_1(\omega_2) = 40/9$, and $P(\omega_1) = 3/5$.

Exercise 2.3 (isoelastic utility) Suppose $u(w) = \gamma^{-1} w^\gamma$, where $-\infty < \gamma < 1$ and $\gamma \neq 0$. Show that the inverse function $I(i) = i^{-1/(1-\gamma)}$, the Lagrange multiplier

$$\lambda = v^{-(1-\gamma)}\{E[(L/B_1)^{-\gamma/(1-\gamma)}]\}^{(1-\gamma)}$$

the optimal attainable wealth

$$W = \frac{v(L/B_1)^{-1/(1-\gamma)}}{E[(L/B_1)^{-\gamma/(1-\gamma)}]}$$

and the optimal objective value $E[u(W)] = \lambda v/\gamma$. Compute these expressions and solve for the optimal trading strategy in the case where the underlying model is as in exercise 2.2.

2.3   Consumption Investment Problems

A *consumption process* $C = (C_0, C_1)$ consists of a non-negative scalar C_0 and a non-negative random variable C_1. A *consumption-investment plan* consists of a pair (C, H), where C is a consumption process and H is a trading strategy. A consumption investment plan is said to be *admissible* if (1) $C_0 + V_0 - v$, the money available at time $t = 0$, and (2) $C_1 - V_1$. We always assume $v \geqslant 0$.

The quantity C_t should be interpreted as the amount consumed by the investor at time t. Since C_0 equals time zero consumption and since $V_0 = H_0 + \sum H_n S_n(0)$ is the amount invested at time $t = 0$, the amount of money v available at time zero must be at least $C_0 + V_0$. Since $V_1 = H_0 B_1 + \sum H_n S_n(1)$ is the amount of money available at time $t = 1$, it must be that $C_1 \leqslant V_1$. Now a sensible investor who can consume only at times $t = 0$ and $t = 1$ would not leave money 'lying on the table' at either time, so this investor would probably not want to adopt a consumption-investment plan unless it is admissible.

A question that naturally arises is, given a consumption-investment plan (C, H) and an initial amount of funds v, how do you check whether (C, H) is admissible? Of course one way is to compute V_t and then check whether both $C_0 + V_0 = v$ and $C_1 = V_1$. Notice that if (C, H) is indeed admissible, then C_1 is an attainable contingent claim with

$$E_Q[C_1/B_1] = E_Q[V_1/B_1] = V_0$$

for every risk neutral probability measure Q, in which case

$$(2.4) \qquad\qquad E_Q[C_0 + C_1/B_1] = v$$

Now here is a harder question: given some $v \geqslant 0$ and some consumption process C, how do you know whether there exists some trading strategy H such that (C, H) is admissible? Well, if C_1 is an attainable contingent claim, then there exists some trading strategy H such that $C_1 = V_1 - H_0 B_1 + \sum H_n S_n$. If, moreover, (2.14) is satisfied for some Q, then $C_0 + V_0 = v$, in which case (C, H) is admissible. Notice that $E_Q[C_0 + C_1/B_1]$ is constant with respect to all risk neutral probability measures if and only if C_1 is attainable. Hence we can summarize all these findings as follows:

(2.15)   Let the initial amount of money $v \geqslant 0$ and the consumption process C be fixed. There exists a trading strategy H such that the consumption-investment plan (C, H) is admissible if and only if

$$C_0 + E_Q[C_1/B_1] = v$$

for every risk neutral probability measure Q.

Example 2.1 (continued)   This model is complete with $Q = (1/3, 1/3, 1/3)$. In order for the consumption process (C_0, C_1) to be part of an admissible consumption-investment plan we must have, of course, $0 \leqslant C_0 \leqslant v$ and $C_1 \geqslant 0$. In addition, we must have by (2.15)

$$v - C_0 = \frac{9}{10} E_Q C_1 = \frac{3}{10} [C_1(\omega_1) + C_1(\omega_2) + C_1(\omega_3)]$$

Suppose an investor starts with initial wealth v and wants to choose an admissible consumption-investment plan so as to maximize the expected value of the utility of consumption at both times 0 and 1. Here the utility function $u : \mathbb{R}_+ \to \mathbb{R}$ is assumed to be concave, differentiable, and strictly increasing. Mathematically this problem is:

$$\text{maximize} \quad u(C_0) + E[u(C_1)]$$

$$\text{subject to} \quad C_0 + H_0 B_0 + \sum_{n=1}^{N} H_n S_n(0) = v$$

(2.16)

$$C_1 - H_0 B_0 - \sum_{n=1}^{N} H_n S_n(1) = 0$$

$$C_0 \geqslant 0 \quad C_1 \geqslant 0 \quad H \in \mathbb{R}^{N+1}$$

As with the optimal portfolio problem, this consumption-investment problem can be solved either with standard optimization theory or with a risk neutral computational approach. To illustrate the former, consider the following:

Example 2.1 (continued)   Suppose $u(c) = \ln(c)$. Since $\ln(c) \to -\infty$ as $c \searrow 0$, we can drop the explicit non-negativity constraints in (2.16). With $P(\omega_1) = 1/2$ and $P(\omega_2) = P(\omega_3) = 1/4$ and $r = 1/9$, the optimization problem becomes

$$\text{maximize} \quad \ln(C_0) + \tfrac{1}{2}\ln(C_1(\omega_1)) + \tfrac{1}{4}\ln(C_1(\omega_2)) + \tfrac{1}{4}\ln(C_1(\omega_3))$$

$$\text{subject to} \quad C_0 = v - H_0 - 6H_1 - 10H_2$$

$$C_1(\omega_1) = \frac{10}{9} H_0 + \frac{60}{9} H_1 + \frac{130}{9} H_2$$

(2.17)

$$C_1(\omega_2) = \frac{10}{9} H_0 + \frac{80}{9} H_1 + \frac{90}{9} H_2$$

$$C_1(\omega_3) = \frac{10}{9} H_0 + \frac{40}{9} H_1 + \frac{80}{9} H_2$$

This simplifies to become

$$\text{maximize} \quad \ln(v - H_0 - 6H_1 - 10H_2)$$

$$+ \frac{1}{2}\ln\left(\frac{10}{9} H_0 + \frac{60}{9} H_1 + \frac{130}{9} H_2\right)$$

$$+ \frac{1}{4}\ln\left(\frac{10}{9} H_0 + \frac{80}{9} H_1 + \frac{90}{9} H_2\right)$$

$$+ \frac{1}{4}\ln\left(\frac{10}{9} H_0 + \frac{40}{9} H_1 + \frac{80}{9} H_2\right)$$

Computing the partial derivatives with respect to the H_n and then setting them equal to zero, we obtain the necessary conditions.

$$(2.18) \quad \frac{-1}{C_0} + \frac{1}{2} \cdot \frac{10}{9} \cdot \frac{1}{C_1(\omega_1)} + \frac{1}{4} \cdot \frac{10}{9} \cdot \frac{1}{C_1(\omega_2)} + \frac{1}{4} \cdot \frac{10}{9} \cdot \frac{1}{C_1(\omega_3)} = 0$$

$$\frac{-6}{C_0} + \frac{1}{2} \cdot \frac{60}{9} \cdot \frac{1}{C_1(\omega_1)} + \frac{1}{4} \cdot \frac{80}{9} \cdot \frac{1}{C_1(\omega_2)} + \frac{1}{4} \cdot \frac{40}{9} \cdot \frac{1}{C_1(\omega_3)} = 0$$

$$\frac{10}{C_0} + \frac{1}{2} \cdot \frac{130}{9} \cdot \frac{1}{C_1(\omega_1)} + \frac{1}{4} \cdot \frac{90}{9} \cdot \frac{1}{C_1(\omega_2)} + \frac{1}{4} \cdot \frac{80}{9} \cdot \frac{1}{C_1(\omega_3)} = 0$$

Here the four equations in (2.17) were used in order to be concise, so actually the three equations in (2.18) involve just the three unknowns H_0, H_1, and H_2. Hence, although it is not particularly easy to do so, these three equations can be solved for the optimal trading strategy H, and then finally the four equations in (2.17) can be used to obtain the optimal consumption process C.

A general consumption investment problem (2.16) can be solved in a manner similar to that just used for example 2.1. The $N+1$ first order necessary conditions are, in general:

$$(2.19) \qquad\qquad u'(C_0) = E[B_1 u'(C_1)]$$

$$(2.20) \qquad u'(C_0)S_n(0) = E[u'(C_1)S_n(1)], \qquad n = 1, \ldots, N$$

Using the constraints in (2.16) to substitute for C_0 and C_1 gives rise to $N+1$ equations which, in principle, can be solved for the $N+1$ unknowns $H_0, H_1, \ldots, H_N$. Substituting these values into the constraints of (2.16) gives the values of C_0 and C_1. This procedure yields a solution of (2.16) provided C_0 and C_1 are both non-negative (suitable assumptions about the utility function, such as $u'(c) \to \infty$ as $c \searrow 0$, will guarantee the success of this procedure).

For some utility functions it is possible that one or more of the non-negativity constraints will be binding, in which case the procedure just described would be unsuccessful. Standard methods can be used to cope with such complications, but they will not be described here.

Notice that equation (2.20) is similar to the condition that must be satisfied by a risk neutral probability measure. Not surprisingly, therefore, we have the following counterpart to (2.6):

(2.21) If C is part of a solution to the optimal consumption investment problem (2.16) with $C_0 > 0$ and $C_1(\omega) > 0$ for all ω, then

$$Q(\omega) = P(\omega)B_1(\omega)\frac{u'(C_1(\omega))}{u'(C_0)}$$

defines a risk neutral probability measure.

To see this, simply note that

$$E_Q[S_n(1)/B_1] = \sum Q(\omega)S_n(1,\omega)/B_1(\omega)$$

$$= \sum P(\omega)B_1(\omega)\left(\frac{u'(C_1(\omega))}{u'(C_0)}\right)\left(\frac{S_n(1,\omega)}{B_1(\omega)}\right)$$

$$= \frac{1}{u'(C_0)}E[u'(C_1)S_n(1)]$$

Meanwhile, if $C_0 > 0$ and $C_1(\omega) > 0$ for all $\omega \in \Omega$, then the first order necessary condition (2.20) must hold. In this case it follows that $E[u'(C_1)S_n(1)]/u'(C_0)$ and thus $E_Q[S_n(1)/B_1]$ equal $S_n(0)$. Finally, using (2.19) it is easy to show that $\sum Q(\omega) = 1$, and so, indeed, Q as defined in (2.21) is a risk neutral probability measure.

We now turn to the risk neutral computational approach for solving the consumption-investment problem (2.16) in the case of a complete model. The idea is to first use principle (2.15) to rewrite (2.16) as follows:

(**2.22**)   maximize $u(C_0) + E[u(C_1)]$
           subject to $C_0 + E_Q[C_1/B_1] = v$
                   $C_0 \geqslant 0$ $C_1 \geqslant 0$

The optimization problems (2.16) and (2.22) are essentially the same, because if the pair (C, H) is feasible for (2.16), then C is feasible for (2.22); conversely, if C is feasible for (2.22), then there exists some H such that (C, H) is feasible for (2.16).

Notice the trading strategy H does not appear at all in (2.22), so the first step with the risk neutral computational approach, solving (2.22), is much easier than solving (2.16). This leaves for the second and final step the computation of the trading strategy H that generates the contingent claim C_1, where C_1 is time $t = 1$ consumption under the solution of subproblem (2.22). Analogous to the optimal portfolio problem, these two steps can be readily solved with standard methods.

To solve (2.22) with a Lagrange multiplier, one first analyses the unconstrained problem

(**2.23**)   maximize $u(C_0) + E[u(C_1)] - \lambda\{C_0 + E[C_1 L/B_1]\}$

(recall $E[C_1 L/B_1] = E_Q[C_1/B_1]$). With suitable assumptions about the utility function u to ensure the optimal solution of (2.22) will feature strictly positive consumption values, the following first order necessary conditions must be satisfied:

$$u'(C_0) = \lambda \quad \text{and} \quad u'(C_1(\omega)) = \lambda L/B_1$$

Hence

(**2.24**) $C_0 = I(\lambda) \quad \text{and} \quad C_1(\omega) = I(\lambda L/B_1)$

where $I(\cdot)$ is the inverse of the marginal utility function $u'(\cdot)$. Of course, the Lagrange multiplier λ must take the correct value, namely, the value such that the constraint in (2.22) is satisfied. This is

(2.25) $$I(\lambda) + E_Q[I(\lambda L/B_1)/B_1] = v$$

As is the case with (2.13), the inverse function I is decreasing so this equation will normally have a solution λ. If the corresponding values of C_0 and C_1, as given by (2.24), are non-negative, then they must be an optimal solution of (2.22).

If this procedure yields a consumption value that is not non-negative, then a more complicated algorithm must be used to derive the solution of (2.22). Such algorithms are standard, although they will not be discussed here. Suffice it to say that in this case it is still much easier to solve (2.22) than (2.16).

Example 2.3 Suppose $u(C) = \ln(c)$, so that $u'(c) = 1/c$ and the inverse function $I(i) = 1/i$. Equations (2.24) and (2.25) become

$$C_0 = 1/\lambda \quad \text{and} \quad C_1(\omega) = 1/(\lambda L/B_1)$$

and

$$\frac{1}{\lambda} + \frac{1}{\lambda} E_Q[L^{-1}] = \frac{1}{\lambda} + \frac{1}{\lambda} E[1] = \frac{2}{\lambda} = v$$

so $\lambda = 2/v$, $C_0 = v/2$, and $C_1(\omega) = vB_1(\omega)P(\omega)/[2Q(\omega)]$. Notice that these are non-negative as long as $v \geqslant 0$. Substituting these values gives the maximum value of the objective function in (2.22) to be $2\ln(v/2) + E[\ln(vB_1/L)]$.

Example 2.1 and 2.3 (continued) With $L(\omega_1) = 2/3$, $L(\omega_2) = L(\omega_3) = 4/3$, and $r = 1/9$ as before, we have

$$C_1(\omega) = v\frac{5}{9}L^{-1} = \begin{cases} \dfrac{5}{6}v, & \omega = \omega_1 \\[2mm] \dfrac{5}{12}v, & \omega = \omega_2, \omega_3 \end{cases}$$

Note that the equation in (2.15) as well as the necessary conditions (2.18) are satisfied, as desired. We compute the optimal H_1 and H_2 by solving the system $C_1/B_1 = v/2 + G^*$, that is,

$$\frac{3}{4}v = \frac{1}{2}v + 0H_1 + 3H_2$$

$$\frac{3}{8}v = \frac{1}{2}v + 2H_1 - 1H_2$$

$$\frac{3}{8}v = \frac{1}{2}v - 2H_1 - 2H_2$$

Although there are three equations and two unknowns, the solution is unique: $H_1 = -v/48$ and $H_2 = v/12$. Since $v/2 = H_0 + 6H_1 + 10H_2$, it follows that $H_0 = -(5/24)v$.

In summary, principle (2.15) greatly simplifies the solution of the optimal consumption investment problem because it allows one to decompose the original problem into two simpler subproblems: in the first you solve for the optimal consumption process without worrying about the trading strategy, and in the second you derive the trading strategy that corresponds to the solution of the first subproblem.

The basic consumption investment problem (2.16) can be generalized in several directions. For example, the objective function can be written as

(2.26) $u(C_0) + \beta E[u(C_1)]$

where the scalar β satisfies $0 < \beta \leqslant 1$. The idea here is to model the time-value of when consumption occurs by regarding the specified parameter β as a discount factor.

A second generalization of (2.16) is to allow the consumer to have income or endowment $\tilde{E}$ at time $t = 1$, where $\tilde{E}$ is a specified random variable. The optimization problem thus is:

(2.27)   maximize $u(C_0) + E[u(C_1)]$

$$\text{subject to} \quad C_0 + H_0 B_0 + \sum_{n=1}^{N} H_n S_n(0) = v$$

$$C_1 - H_0 B_1 - \sum_{n=1}^{N} H_n S_n(1) = \tilde{E}$$

$$C_0 \geqslant 0 \qquad C_1 \geqslant 0 \qquad H \in \mathbb{R}^{N+1}$$

The pair $(v, \tilde{E})$ is sometimes called the *endowment process* for the consumer.

Exercise 2.4   Derive formulas for λ, C_0, and C_1 for the consumption investment problem in the case where the utility function is:

(a) $u(c) = -\exp\{-c\}$.
(b) $u(c) = \gamma^{-1} c^\gamma$, where $-\infty < \gamma < 1$ and $\gamma \neq 0$.

Exercise 2.5   Show that if the objective function for the consumption investment problem is as in (2.26), then the equation in (2.21) should be generalized to:

$$Q(\omega) = \beta P(\omega) B_1(\omega) \frac{u'(C_1(\omega))}{u'(C_0)}$$

Exercise 2.6   For the consumption investment problem (2.27) with an endowment, show that the equation in (2.15) generalizes to

$$C_0 + E_Q[(C_1 - \tilde{E})/B_1] = v$$

Exercise 2.7   For example 1.4, suppose the initial wealth $v = 100$. Characterize the set of all consumption processes C such that there is a trading strategy H making the consumption-investment plan (C, H) admissible.

2.4   Mean-Variance Portfolio Analysis

Throughout this section it will be assumed that the interest rate r is deterministic, there are no arbitrage opportunities, and there exists some portfolio with $E[R] \neq r$. A classical problem in this case is to solve the mean-variance portfolio problem:

(2.28)
$$\text{minimize} \quad \text{var}(R)$$
$$\text{subject to} \quad E[R] = \rho$$
$$R \text{ is a portfolio return}$$

where ρ is a specified scalar. Notice that for each value of $\rho \geqslant r$, the feasible region in (2.28) is non-empty (to see this, just take a suitable linear combination of the riskless portfolio and a specific one with $E[R] \neq r$), and so the solution of (2.28) is well defined. In particular, the optimal value of the objective function equals zero if and only if $\rho = r$; otherwise, it will be a finite, positive number.

Recalling that the return for a portfolio can be expressed as

$$R = \frac{H_0}{V_0} r + \sum_{n=1}^{N} \left[\frac{H_n S_n(0)}{V_0} \right] R_n$$

it follows that R is the return for a portfolio if and only if it can be written in the form $R = (1 - F_1 - \ldots - F_N)r + \sum F_n R_n$, where F_n can be interpreted as the fraction of time $t = 0$ wealth that is invested in security n. Hence (2.28) can be rewritten as

(2.29)
$$\text{minimize} \quad F \mathbb{C} F'$$
$$\text{subject to} \quad (1 - F_1 - \ldots - F_N)r + \sum F_n \bar{R}_n = \rho$$

where $\mathbb{C}$ is the $N \times N$ matrix of the covariances for the returns (its ijth element is $\text{cov}(R_i, R_j)$, $\bar{R}_n = ER_n$, and $F \equiv (F_1, \ldots, F_N)$. This is a quadratic programming problem, a well-known kind of problem in the area of optimization theory, and it has been the subject of extensive study by financial researchers and mathematical programmers.

In this section, problem (2.28) will be solved with a different approach, one that relies on the modern theory developed in section 2.2. Consider the following problem:

(2.30)
$$\text{minimize} \quad \text{var}(V_1)$$
$$\text{subject to} \quad E[V_1] = v(1 + \rho)$$
$$V_0 = v$$

Here the constraints identify the set of all time $t = 1$ portfolio values that can be achieved starting with initial wealth v and which have mean $v(1 + \rho)$, where $\rho \geqslant r$ is as in (2.28) and $v > 0$ is a specified scalar. Notice that if $\hat{V}_1$ is a solution of (2.30), then $\hat{R} \equiv (\hat{V}_1 - v)/v$ satisfies the constraints in (2.28). Moreover, if R is any other return that is feasible for (2.28), then $V_1 \equiv v(1 + R)$ satisfies $E(V_1) = v(1 + \rho)$, which means V_1 is feasible for (2.30). Hence

$$\text{var}(\hat{R}) = \frac{1}{v^2}\text{var}(\hat{V}_1) \leqslant \frac{1}{v^2}\text{var}(V_1) = \text{var}(R)$$

which means $\hat{R}$ is a solution of (2.28). Conversely, a solution of (2.28) gives just as easily a solution of (2.30), so really (2.28) and (2.30) are equivalent problems. In other words,

>   **(2.31)**   The relationship $V_1 = v(1 + R)$ establishes a one-to-one correspondence between feasible solution of (2.28) and (2.30).

You can see where we are headed: we want to reformulate (2.28) so we can apply the results of section 2.2, and (2.30) is a step in this direction. For the next step, consider how to solve (2.30) with a Lagrange multiplier. Introducing the scalar β, one is interested in minimizing the objective function $\text{var}(V_1) - \beta E[V_1]$, subject to the constraint $V_0 = v$. But $\text{var}(V_1) = E[V_1^2] - (EV_1)^2$, so, as will be verified later, this objective function can be written as $E[\frac{1}{2}V_1^2 - \beta V_1]$. In other words, with the Lagrange multiplier approach we are interested in solving

(2.32) $$\text{maximize} \quad E[-\frac{1}{2}V_1^2 + \beta V_1]$$

$$\text{subject to} \quad V_0 = v.$$

Problem (2.32) is in the form studied in section 2.2, so applying the results there one concludes the optimal solution, denoted $\hat{V}$, is given by (this is left as an exercise)

(2.33) $$\hat{V} = \frac{\beta}{E_Q L}(E_Q L - L) + v(1 + r)\frac{L}{E_Q L}$$

in which case $E[\hat{V}] = \beta(E_Q L - 1)/E_Q L + v(1 + r)/E_Q L$ (recall $L = Q/P$ is the state price density). Now assuming Q and P are not identical, one has $E_Q L > 1$ (this is also left as an exercise). Hence $E[\hat{V}] = v(1 + \rho)$ if and only if

(2.34) $$\beta = \frac{v[(1 + \rho)E_Q L - (1 + r)]}{E_Q L - 1}$$

Substituting this into (2.33) means that $\hat{V}$ is feasible for (2.30). If V is any other random variable that is feasible for (2.30), then the facts that $E[\hat{V}] = E[V]$ and that $E[-\frac{1}{2}\hat{V}^2 + \beta\hat{V}] \geqslant E[-\frac{1}{2}V^2 + \beta V]$ imply $\text{var}(\hat{V}) \leqslant \text{var}(V)$. Hence $\hat{V}$ is an optimal solution of (2.30).

Conversely, suppose $\hat{V}$ is a solution of (2.30) with β as in (2.34). If V is any other random variable that is feasible for (2.30), then $E[-\frac{1}{2}\hat{V}^2 + \beta\hat{V}] \geqslant E[-\frac{1}{2}V^2 + \beta V]$. We saw above that any solution of (2.32) must be feasible for (2.30), so we conclude that $\hat{V}$ must be an optimal solution of (2.32). The relationship between (2.30) and (2.32) is summarized as follows:

(2.35) Portfolio problems (2.30) and (2.32) are equivalent provided ρ and β are related according to (2.34).

Notice according to (2.34) that β is a strictly increasing function of ρ which equals $v(1+r)$ when $\rho = r$. Moreover, when $\rho = r$, the optimal solution (2.33) is $\hat{V} = v(1+r)$. This is a constant, as anticipated.

Problem (2.32) has the standard form of sections 2.1 and 2.2 if the investor's utility function is taken to be the quadratic function $u(w) = -w^2/2 + \beta w$. Although quadratic utility functions are dubious because they are not non-decreasing with respect to wealth (this function is concave but attains its maximum value at $w = \beta < \infty$), they are accepted for various applications. In particular, principle (2.31) implies there is a one-to-one correspondence between solutions of the quadratic utility portfolio problem (2.32) and solutions of the mean-variance portfolio problem (2.28).

This correspondence has a fundamental consequence. Looking at (2.33) we see that the solution of (2.28) must be an affine[1] function of the state price density. Indeed, substituting (2.34) in (2.33) we compute that the return $\hat{R}$ corresponding to $\hat{V}$ is

(2.36)
$$\hat{R} = \frac{\rho E_Q L - r}{E_Q L - 1} - \frac{\rho - r}{E_Q L - 1} L$$

Hence we conclude (this also could have been worked out using (2.12) for the case of a quadratic utility function):

(2.37) The optimal solution R of the mean-variance portfolio problem (2.28) is an affine function of the state price density L.

A further consequence is realized if you tie this together with result (1.35) concerning the relationship between the risk premium of an arbitrary portfolio and its beta with respect to a portfolio whose return is an affine function of the state price density. It is apparent that we have established the famous security market line result of the capital asset pricing model (CAPM) theory:

(2.38) CAPM: If R' is a solution of the mean-variance portfolio problem (2.28) for $\rho \geqslant r$ and if R is the return of an arbitrary portfolio, then

$$E[R] - r = \frac{\text{cov}(R, R')}{\text{var}(R')} (E[R'] - r)$$

This relationship is quite important, because in a world of mean-variance investors there is often a portfolio (for example, a stock index) which can be assumed to be a solution of (2.28) and whose mean return can be estimated, thereby giving via (2.38) estimates of the mean return of arbitrary portfolios.

Principle (2.37) has another important consequence. Fix some arbitrary $\hat{\rho} > r$ and consider the corresponding return $\hat{R}$ as given by (2.36). Think of $\hat{R}$

as corresponding to some portfolio or mutual fund that is available for investment. Suppose an investor puts the fraction λ of his money in the riskless security and the balance $1 - \lambda$ in this mutual fund, where $\lambda = (\hat{\rho} - \rho)/(\hat{\rho} - r)$ and $\rho \geqslant r$ ($\lambda < 0$ corresponds to borrowing at the riskless rate). Since this portfolio's return $R = \lambda r + (1 - \lambda)\hat{R}$, one can do some tedious algebra to verify that, in fact, R is given precisely by (2.36), only with ρ instead of $\hat{\rho}$ on the right hand side. Hence to achieve any solution of the mean-variance portfolio problem (2.28) it is not necessary to trade the individual securities, provided there is a mutual fund available which corresponds to one solution. It is just a question of dividing up the invested funds between the riskless security and the mutual fund. Since all the risky securities are in the mutual fund, it must mean that the relative proportions invested in the risky securities (that is, the money invested in security n divided by the money invested in the mutual fund) are constants with respect to ρ. This all can be summarized as follows:

(**2.39**)   *Mutual fund principle*: Suppose you fix a portfolio whose return is a solution of the mean-variance portfolio problem (2.28) corresponding to some mean return $\hat{\rho} > r$. Then the solution of (2.28) can be achieved for any other mean return by a portfolio consisting of investments in just the riskless security and the fixed portfolio.

Hence a world of mean-variance investors is quite nice; it enjoys many nice properties. However, it should be stressed that many of these nice properties may disappear in the presence of investors whose decisions are not consistent with quadratic utility functions. For example, as seen in section 2.2, log utility investors will want to choose portfolios whose time $t = 1$ values are proportional to the *inverse* of the state price density. In this case the time $t = 1$ wealth cannot, in general, be expressed as an affine function of the state price density, and the security market line result will not hold with respect to any portfolio in which the log utility investor would desire to invest his or her money.

Indeed, it is almost a lucky accident that the CAPM security market line result holds for a reasonable class of utility functions. With most utility functions the return of the optimal portfolio will not be an affine function of the state price density and thus cannot play the role of R' in (1.35). Result (1.35) is more fundamental in the sense that it applies to any single period securities market provided its general hypotheses are satisfied, whereas the CAPM result (2.38) is a special case or corollary. But the general version is not particularly useful unless you can identify R' with an economically meaningful portfolio. In the mean-variance world you can do this, and that is why the CAPM result (2.38) is so important.

Example 2.4   Suppose $N = 2$, $K = 3$, and the return processes R_n and the probability measure P are as indicated in table 2.1.

Table 2.1   Data for example 2.4

	ω_1	ω_2	ω_3
$R_1(\omega)$	0.2	-0.2	0.05
$R_2(\omega)$	0.15	0	-0.1
$P(\omega)$	1/3	1/3	1/3
$R_1^*(\omega)$	$\frac{0.2-r}{1+r}$	$\frac{-0.2-r}{1+r}$	$\frac{0.05-r}{1+r}$
$R_2^*(\omega)$	$\frac{0.15-r}{1+r}$	$\frac{-r}{1+r}$	$\frac{-0.1-r}{1+r}$
$Q(\omega)$	$0.258 + 4.52r$	$0.355 - 1.3r$	$0.387 - 3.22r$
$L(\omega)$	$0.774 + 13.56r$	$1.065 - 3.9r$	$1.161 - 9.66r$

Solving $E_Q R_n^* = 0$ for the risk neutral probability measure Q, it is apparent that this exists, provided $r < 0.387/3.22 = 0.12$. These quantities along with the resulting state price density L are displayed in table 2.1.

To solve the classical mean-variance problem (2.29), we first compute $ER_1 = ER_2 = 1/60$, $\text{var}(R_1) = 0.02722$, $\text{var}(R_2) = 0.01056$, and $\text{cov}(R_1, R_2) = 0.00805$. Assuming (for simplicity) from now on that $r = 0$, this leads to the solution $F_1 = 6.95\rho$ and $F_2 = 53.05\rho$. Hence, for example, if $\rho = 1$ percent, then 6.95 percent of the funds should be invested in the first risky security, 53.05 percent in the second risky security, and 40 percent in the riskless security. Moreover, the return of the resulting portfolio is

$$R = F_1 R_1 + F_2 R_2 - \begin{cases} 0.0936, & \omega = \omega_1 \\ -0.0140, & \omega = \omega_2 \\ -0.0496, & \omega = \omega_3 \end{cases}$$

Alternatively, using formulas (2.33) and (2.34) one computes $E_Q L = 1.027$, $\beta = v[1 + 38.04\rho]$, $\hat{V} = v[1 + 38.04\rho - 37.04\rho L]$, and $\hat{R} = 38.04\rho - 37.04\rho L$. To get F_1 and F_2, you solve $\hat{R} = F_1 R_1 + F_2 R_2$. Hence, for example, if $\rho = 1$ percent, then you get the values already presented above.

Exercise 2.8   With Q a risk neutral probability measure, P the original probability measure, and L the corresponding state price density, show that $E_Q L \geqslant 1$, with equality if and only if $Q = P$ (hint: minimize $\sum Q^2(\omega_k)/P(\omega_k)$ subject to suitable constraints).

Exercise 2.9   Verify equation (2.33).

Exercise 2.10   Verify the assertion made in connection with the mutual fund principle (2.39): $R = \lambda r + (1 - \lambda)\hat{R}$ satisfies (2.36), where $\lambda = (\hat{\rho} - \rho)/(\hat{\rho} - r)$.

2.5   Portfolio Management with Short Sales Restrictions and Similar Constraints

The basic optimal portfolio problem studied in earlier sections may be inappropriate for many practical situations because important constraints are ignored. For example, the investor might be prohibited by stock exchange rules from selling stocks short or from financing the purchase of stocks by borrowing money. Consequently, it is important to be able to solve versions of problem (2.1) where constraints are imposed on the admissible trading strategies.

In actual situations it is usually more natural to express the constraints in terms of the fractions $F_n \equiv H_n S_n(0)/V_0$ of money invested in security $n, n = 1, \ldots, N$, rather than in terms of the number H_n of shares invested in security n. For example, no short selling of security n is $F_n \geq 0$, no borrowing from the bank account is $F_1 + \ldots + F_N \leq 1$, and a stipulation that no more than 4 percent of the wealth can be invested in security n is $F_n \leq 0.04$. In general, therefore, the constraints of interest will be expressed by stipulating that $F \equiv (F_1, \ldots, F_N) \in \mathbb{K}$, where $\mathbb{K} \subset \mathbb{R}^N$ is a specified subset that is assumed to be closed and convex. In order to simplify the presentation later in this section, it will also be assumed that the strategy $0 \in \mathbb{K}$, that is, it is always feasible to invest all the funds in the bank account. For example, $\mathbb{K}$ is equal to $\{F \in \mathbb{R}^N : F_n \geq 0\}$, $\{F \in \mathbb{R}^N : F_1 + \ldots + F_N \leq 1\}$, and $\{F \in \mathbb{R}^N : F_n \leq 0.04\}$, respectively, in the three cases mentioned just above.

With the trading strategy expressed in the form F, it is convenient to express the time $t = 1$ wealth $V_1 = V_0(1 + R)$ in terms of R, the return process for the portfolio. In view of (1.32) this is

$$R = \left(1 - \sum_{n=1}^{N} F_n\right)r + \sum_{n=1}^{N} F_n R_n = r + \sum_{n=1}^{N} F_n(R_n - r)$$

where R_n is the return process for security n. Hence the optimal portfolio problem can be written as

(2.40) $$\begin{array}{c} \text{maximize} \\ F \in \mathbb{K} \end{array} \quad Eu\left(v\left(1 + r + \sum_{n=1}^{N} F_n(R_n - r)\right)\right)$$

where $v = V_0$ is the initial value of the portfolio.

It is straightforward to solve this kind of problem with traditional methods, similar to those used in section 2.1 for the unconstrained problem. This is best explained by considering a simple example.

Example 2.5   The security processes are the same as in example 2.4, but now $r = 0$, $P(\omega_1) = 0.26$, $P(\omega_2) = P(\omega_3) = 0.37$, and the utility function is the log function. Thus the objective function is

$$0.26 \ln[1 + 0.2F_1 + 0.15F_2] + 0.37 \ln[1 - 0.2F_1]$$
$$+ 0.37 \ln[1 + 0.05F_1 - 0.1F_2]$$

and the corresponding partial derivatives are

$$\frac{\partial}{\partial F_1} = \frac{0.052}{1 + 0.2F_1 + 0.15F_2} - \frac{0.074}{1 - 0.2F_1} + \frac{0.0185}{1 + 0.05F_1 - 0.1F_2}$$

and

$$\frac{\partial}{\partial F_2} = \frac{0.039}{1 + 0.02F_1 + 0.15F_2} - \frac{0.037}{1 + 0.05F_1 - 0.1F_2}$$

Hence the optimal solution for the unconstrained problem, obtained by setting these partials equal to zero, is $F_1 - -0.21333$ and $F_2 = 0.33467$.

Now suppose that short sales of the risky securities are prohibited, that is, $\mathbb{K} = \{F \in \mathbb{R}^2 : F_1 \geqslant 0 \text{ and } F_2 \geqslant 0\}$. In this case the unconstrained optimal solution is not feasible, and so we must do some more work. It is apparent that the new optimal solution must be on the boundary of $\mathbb{K}$ at a point where the directional derivative is normal to $\mathbb{K}$. In view of the unconstrained optimal solution, we conjecture the new optimal solution satisfies $F_1 = 0$ and $F_2 > 0$. We therefore look for a point satisfying $F_1 = 0$, $F_2 > 0$, $\delta/\delta F_2 = 0$, and $\delta/\delta F_1 < 0$. Using the above expressions for the partials, we readily compute the optimal solution for the constrained problem to be $F_1 = 0$ and $F_2 = 0.21164$. Note that the optimal attainable wealth is

$$W = v[1 + F_1 R_1 + F_2 R_2] = \begin{cases} 1.03175v & \omega = \omega_1 \\ v, & \omega = \omega_2 \\ 0.97884v, & \omega = \omega_3 \end{cases}$$

and the optimal objective value is

$$E \ln W = \ln v + 0.26 \ln(1.03175) + 0.37 \ln(0.97884) = \ln v + 0.002$$

To summarize the traditional method for solving problem (2.40), first obtain the unconstrained optimal solution and check to see if it is feasible; if not, then look for a point on the boundary of $\mathbb{K}$ where the directional derivative is normal to $\mathbb{K}$, using the partial derivatives throughout. While this method was easy to apply in the case of example 2.5, the computations could become formidable in a case where there are many securities and/or there is a different kind of utility function. Furthermore, these computational difficulties are compounded when dealing with multiperiod models. We therefore are interested in an alternative method, a risk neutral computational approach.

The risk neutral computational approach for constrained portfolio problems is roughly as follows. For each value of a parameter κ contained in a certain subset $\mathbb{K} \subset \mathbb{R}^N$ define a modified securities market denoted $\mathcal{M}_\kappa$ ($\kappa = 0$ corresponds to the original market). Then consider the unconstrained problem for the market $\mathcal{M}_\kappa$. In particular, using the formulas developed in section 2.2 focus on the optimal objective value, denoted $J_\kappa(v)$, for each $\kappa \in \tilde{\mathbb{K}}$. Then solve the *dual problem*:

(2.41) $$\underset{\kappa \in \tilde{\mathbb{K}}}{\text{minimize}} \quad J_\kappa(v)$$

If $\hat{\kappa}$ denotes the optimal solution of (2.41), then the optimal solution for the unconstrained problem in the market $\mathcal{M}_{\hat{\kappa}}$ will turn out to be the optimal solution for the constrained problem in the original market $\mathcal{M}_0$. Moreover, the corresponding optimal objective values will coincide.

Although the risk neutral computational approach still requires one to solve a constrained optimization problem with traditional methods, it turns out that solving (2.41) is often easier than solving (2.40).

Turning to some details, the set $\tilde{\mathbb{K}}$ is simply

$$\tilde{\mathbb{K}} \equiv \{\kappa \in \mathbb{R}^N : \delta(\kappa) < \infty\}$$

where the function $\delta : \mathbb{R}^N \to \mathbb{R} \cup \{+\infty\}$ is defined by

$$\delta(\kappa) \equiv \sup_{F \in \mathbb{K}} (-F\kappa')$$

and κ' denotes the transpose of the row vector κ. The function δ is convex and is called the *support function* of $-\mathbb{K}$. Notice that δ is non-negative, because $0 \in \mathbb{K}$. It will be assumed that $\mathbb{K}$ is such that δ is continuous on $\tilde{\mathbb{K}}$. The set $\tilde{\mathbb{K}}$, called the *effective domain* of δ, is a convex cone that contains the point $\kappa = 0$. For example, if $\mathbb{K} = \{F \in \mathbb{R}^N : F_n \geqslant 0, n = 1, \ldots, N\}$, then

(2.42) $$\delta(\kappa) = \begin{cases} 0, & \kappa \in \mathbb{K} \\ \infty, & \kappa \notin \mathbb{K} \end{cases}$$

and $\tilde{\mathbb{K}} = \mathbb{K}$. For another example, if $\mathbb{K} = \{F \in \mathbb{R}^N : F_1 + \ldots + F_N \leqslant 1\}$, then

(2.43) $$\delta(\kappa) = \begin{cases} -\lambda, & \kappa_1 = \ldots = \kappa_N = \lambda \leqslant 0 \\ \infty, & \text{otherwise} \end{cases}$$

and $\tilde{\mathbb{K}} = \{\kappa \in \mathbb{R}^N : \kappa_1 = \ldots = \kappa_n \leqslant 0\}$.

To define the auxiliary market $\mathcal{M}_\kappa$ for each $\kappa \in \tilde{\mathbb{K}}$, we simply modify the return processes for the bank account and the risky securities according to

$$r \to r + \delta(\kappa)$$
$$R_n \to R_n + \delta(\kappa) + \kappa_n, \qquad n = 1, \ldots, N$$

In other words, in the market $\mathcal{M}_\kappa$ the bank's interest rate is replaced by the original rate plus the non-negative quantity $\delta(\kappa)$, and so forth. Notice that the case $\kappa = 0$ does indeed coincide with the original market.

In order to solve the unconstrained problem in the market $\mathcal{M}_\kappa$, we will need to use the corresponding risk neutral probability measure, which is denoted Q_κ. Throughout this section it will be assumed that the risk neutral probability measure $Q = Q_0$ for the original market exists and is unique. Since Q_0 is the unique probability measure satisfying

$$E_Q\left(\frac{R_n - r}{q + r}\right) = 0, \qquad n = 1, \ldots, N$$

it follows for other $\kappa \in \tilde{\mathbb{K}}$ that Q_κ must be a probability measure satisfying for $Q - Q_\kappa$

(2.44) $$E_Q\left(\frac{R_n + \kappa_n - r - \delta(\kappa)}{1 + r + \delta(\kappa)}\right) = 0, \qquad n - 1, \ldots, N$$

It is not clear whether Q_κ will exist for all $\kappa \in \tilde{\mathbb{K}}$, but a unique Q_κ will exist and the function $\kappa \to Q_\kappa$ will be continuous at least for all $\kappa \in \tilde{\mathbb{K}}$ in some open neighborhood of $\kappa = 0$, by the assumed continuity of $\delta(\cdot)$.

In the market $\mathcal{M}_\kappa$ the state price density and the bank account process are denoted respectively by

$$L_\kappa \equiv \frac{Q_\kappa}{P} \qquad \text{and} \qquad B_1^\kappa = (1 + r + \delta(\kappa)$$

Moreover, given any trading strategy F, the time $t = 1$ value of the portfolio in the market $\mathcal{M}_\kappa$ is given by

(2.45) $$V_1^\kappa = v(1 + R^\kappa) = v\left[1 + r + \delta(\kappa) + \sum_{n=1}^N F_n(R_n + \kappa_n - r)\right]$$

$$= v\left[1 + r + \sum_{n=1}^N F_n(R_n - r) + \delta(\kappa) + \sum_{n=1}^N F_n\kappa_n\right]$$

$$= V_1^0 + v[\delta(\kappa) + F\kappa']$$

It is important to note that if $F \in \mathbb{K}$, then by the definition of $\delta(\cdot)$ one has $\delta(\kappa) + F\kappa' \geqslant 0$, in which case $V_1^\kappa \geqslant V_1^0$. On the other hand, if $F \notin \mathbb{K}$, then possibly $\delta(\kappa) + F\kappa' < 0$, in which case $V_1^\kappa < V_1^0$ and $Eu(V_1^\kappa) < Eu(V_1^0)$. This is the reason why it is possible to have the optimal objective values satisfy $J_\kappa(v) \prec J_0(v)$.

We are now in a position to illustrate how the risk neutral computational approach works.

Example 2.5 (continued) With $\mathbb{K} = \{F \in \mathbb{R}^2 : F_1 \geqslant 0, F_2 \geqslant 0\}$, we have $\tilde{\mathbb{K}} = \mathbb{K}$ and $\delta(\cdot)$ as in (2.42) above. With $r = \delta(\kappa) = 0$ for $\kappa \in \tilde{\mathbb{K}}$, (3.44) reduces to

$$0.2Q_\kappa(\omega_1) - 0.2Q_\kappa(\omega_2) + 0.05Q_\kappa(\omega_3) = -\kappa_1$$
$$0.15Q_\kappa(\omega_1) \qquad\qquad - 0.1Q_\kappa(\omega_3) = -\kappa_2$$

Solving this system along with $E_{Q_\kappa}[1] = 1$ leads to

$$Q_\kappa(\omega) = \begin{cases} [8 - 40\kappa_1 - 100\kappa_2]/31, & \omega = \omega_1 \\ [11 + 100\kappa_1 - 60\kappa_2]/31, & \omega = \omega_2 \\ [12 - 60\kappa_1 + 160\kappa_2]/31, & \omega = \omega_3 \end{cases}$$

These probabilities are strictly positive, and thus Q_κ is a valid risk neutral probability measure for the market $\mathcal{M}_\kappa$, as long as $\kappa \in \tilde{\mathbb{K}}$ and $40\kappa_1 + 100\kappa_2 < 8$.

The next step is to solve the unconstrained optimization problem for the market $\mathcal{M}_\kappa$. Letting W_κ denote the corresponding optimal attainable wealth, we have by exercise 2.2 in section 2.2

(**2.46**) $$W_\kappa = \kappa B_1^\kappa / L = \kappa P / Q_\kappa$$

Moreover, the optimal value of the objective function is

(**2.47**) $\quad J_\kappa(v) = \ln(v) - E\ln(L_\kappa / B_1^\kappa) = \ln(v) + E\ln P - E\ln Q_\kappa$
$$= \ln(v) + [0.26\ln(0.26) + 2(0.37)\ln(0.37)]$$
$$- [0.26\ln(8 - 40\kappa_1 - 100\kappa_2) + 0.37\ln(11 - 100\kappa_1 - 60\kappa_2)$$
$$+ 0.37\ln(12 - 60\kappa_1 + 160\kappa_2) - \ln(31)]$$

The next step is to minimize $J_\kappa(v)$ with respect to $\kappa \in \tilde{\mathbb{K}}$. In view of the preceding expression, this is the same as solving

maximize $\quad 0.26\ln(8 - 40\kappa_1 - 100\kappa_2) + 0.37\ln(11 - 100\kappa_1 - 60\kappa_2)$
$$+ 0.37\ln(12 - 60\kappa_1 + 160\kappa_2)$$

subject to $\quad \kappa_1 \geqslant 0, \quad \kappa_2 \geqslant 0$

Using partial derivatives in the standard way, the optimal solution is computed to be $\hat{\kappa}_1 = 0.0047$ and $\hat{\kappa}_2 = 0$. Substituting these values in (2.46) and (2.47) yields the same values for the optimal attainable wealth and the optimal objective value as were obtained earlier with the traditional approach.

Why does this risk neutral approach work? The key is expression (2.45) for the attainable wealths in the market $\mathcal{M}_\kappa$ as well as the observations made immediately thereafter. By the same considerations, the optimal objective value for the constrained problem in the original market $\mathcal{M}_0$, which we denote by $J(\kappa)$, must be less than or equal to the optimal objective value for the constrained problem in the market $\mathcal{M}_\kappa$ for any $\kappa \in \tilde{\mathbb{K}}$. And the latter, of course, must be less than or equal to the optimal objective value for the unconstrained problem in the market $\mathcal{M}_\kappa$. Hence we must have

(**2.48**) $$J(\kappa) \leqslant J_\kappa(v), \quad \text{all} \quad \kappa \in \tilde{\mathbb{K}}$$

Apparently this inequality can be an equality for the κ that minimizes the right hand side of (2.48), as explained in the following.

(**2.49**) Suppose for some $\hat{\kappa} \in \tilde{\mathbb{K}}$ that F, the optimal trading strategy for the unconstrained portfolio problem in the market $\mathcal{M}_{\hat{\kappa}}$, satisfies

(a) $F \in \mathbb{K}$
(b) $\delta(\hat{\kappa}) + F\hat{\kappa}' = 0.$

Then F is optimal for the constrained problem in the original market $\mathcal{M}_0$, and $J(\kappa) = J_{\hat{\kappa}}(v) \leqslant J_\kappa(v)$ for all $\kappa \in \tilde{\mathbb{K}}$.

To see this, note by (2.45) that (b) implies W, the attainable wealth under F in the market $\mathcal{M}_\kappa$, satisfies

$$W = v\left[1 + r + \sum_{n=1}^{N} F_n(R_n - r)\right]$$

which means that W is also the attainable wealth under F in the original market $\mathcal{M}_0$. Since F is feasible for the constrained problem, it follows that $Eu(W) \leqslant J(v)$. But $Eu(W) = J_{\hat{\kappa}}(v)$, so by (2.48) we must have $Eu(W) = J(v) = J_{\hat{\kappa}}(v) \leqslant J_\kappa(v)$ for all $\kappa \in \mathbb{K}$.

In summary, the obvious candidate for the $\hat{\kappa}$ in (2.49) is the solution of the dual problem (2.41). Having computed this $\hat{\kappa}$, you then verify whether F, the optimal trading strategy for the unconstrained optimal portfolio problem in the market $\mathcal{M}_{\hat{\kappa}}$, satisfies $F \in \mathbb{K}$ and $\delta(\hat{\kappa}) + F\hat{\kappa}' = 0$ (there is no guarantee that both these conditions will be satisfied, but in a wide variety of cases they will both automatically hold). If so, then F will be optimal for the constrained problem in the original market $\mathcal{M}_0$.

This section concludes with another example.

Example 2.6   The security processes are the same as in examples 2.4 and 2.5, but now $r = 0$, $P(\omega_1) = P(\omega_2) = P(\omega_3) = 1/3$, the utility function is the log function, and borrowing funds from the bank is prohibited. Thus $\mathbb{K} = \{F \in \mathbb{R}^2 : F_1 + F_2 \leqslant 1\}$, $\tilde{\mathbb{K}} = \{\kappa \in \mathbb{R}^2 : \kappa_1 = \kappa_2 \leqslant 0\}$, and

$$\delta(\kappa) = \begin{cases} -\lambda, & \kappa_1 = \kappa_2 = \lambda \leqslant 0 \\ \infty, & \text{otherwise}, \end{cases}$$

and so for case of exposition we will identify the vector $\kappa \in \tilde{\mathbb{K}}$ with the scalar $\lambda \leqslant 0$.

The interest rate for the bank account in the market $\mathcal{M}_\kappa$ will be $-\lambda$, but the return processes for the risky securities in the market $\mathcal{M}_\kappa$ will be the same as in the original market $\mathcal{M}_0$. Hence by (2.44) the risk neutral probability measure Q_κ can be obtained by solving the system

$$0.2Q_\kappa(\omega_1) - 0.2Q_\kappa(\omega_2) + 0.05Q_\kappa(\omega_3) = -\lambda$$
$$0.15Q_\kappa(\omega_1) \qquad\qquad - 0.1Q_\kappa(\omega_3) = -\lambda$$
$$Q_\kappa(\omega_1) + Q_\kappa(\omega_2) \quad + Q_\kappa(\omega_3) = 1$$

This leads to

$$Q_\kappa(\omega) = \begin{cases} [8 - 140\lambda]/31, & \omega = \omega_1 \\ [11 + 40\lambda]/31, & \omega = \omega_2 \\ [12 + 100\lambda]/31, & \omega = \omega_3 \end{cases}$$

These probabilities are all strictly positive and thus Q_κ is a legitimate risk neutral probability measure if $-0.12 < \lambda \leqslant 0$.

With $B_1^\kappa = (1 - \lambda)$, the optimal objective value for the unconstrained problem in the market $\mathscr{M}_\kappa$ is given by

$$J_\kappa(v) = \ln(v) - E\ln(L_\kappa/B_1^\kappa) = \ln(v) - E\ln Q_\kappa + E\ln P + \ln(1 - \lambda)$$

Hence dual problem (2.41) amounts to the same thing as

$$\underset{-0.12 < \lambda \leq 0}{\text{maximize}} \quad \frac{1}{3}\ln(8 - 140\lambda) + \frac{1}{3}\ln(11 + 40\lambda)$$

$$+ \frac{1}{3}\ln(12 + 100\lambda) - \ln(1 - \lambda)$$

Although this objective function is not concave on the real line, the solution of this constrained problem is easily found to be approximately $\lambda = -0.00711$, that is, $\hat{\kappa} = (-0.00711, -0.00711)$.

The next step is to compute the optimal trading strategy F for the unconstrained problem in the market $\mathscr{M}_{\hat{\kappa}}$. The corresponding optimal attainable wealth is

$$W_{\hat{\kappa}} = vB_1^{\hat{\kappa}}/L_{\hat{\kappa}} = \frac{1.0071vP}{Q_{\hat{\kappa}}} = \begin{cases} 1.157v, & \omega = \omega_1 \\ 0.972v, & \omega = \omega_2 \\ 0.921v, & \omega = \omega_3 \end{cases}$$

so F can be computed by solving (2.45), that is,

$$W_{\hat{\kappa}}(\omega) = v[1.00711 + F_1(R_1(\omega) - 0.00711) + F_2(R_2(\omega) - 0.00711)]$$

This yields $F = (0.14, 0.86)$. Clearly $F \in \mathbb{K}$ and $\delta(\hat{\kappa}) + F\hat{\kappa}' = 0$, so by (2.49) F must be the optimal solution for the constrained problem. Substituting $\hat{\kappa} = -0.00711$ in the above expression for $J_\kappa(v)$ gives the optimal objective value equal to $\ln v + 0.01171$.

Exercise 2.11   Solve example 2.6 assuming $P(\omega_1) = 0.5$, $P(\omega_2) = 0.3$, and $P(\omega_3) = 0.2$.

2.6   Optimal Portfolios in Incomplete Markets

Throughout this chapter up to this point it has been assumed that the model is complete, a crucial assumption for the risk neutral computational approach. Under this assumption the set of attainable wealths is easy to identify and characterize, and so after using convex optimization theory to identify the optimal attainable wealth, one is assured of finding the trading strategy which generates this wealth. In the case of incomplete markets the principles are the same, but more work must be done to properly identify the set of attainable wealths. Having done so, one computes the optimal attainable wealth and finally the trading strategy which generates this wealth, the same as before.

Of course, one could always revert to the standard approach, working with the first order necessary conditions and so forth, exactly the same as described in section 2.1. The standard approach is no more difficult with incomplete than with complete models, so the relative advantages of the risk neutral computational approach are diminished in the case of incomplete models. However, the risk neutral approach is still preferred when dealing with certain utility functions and, as will be seen later, when analyzing multiperiod models.

It turns out there is even a third approach for solving optimal portfolio problems in incomplete markets. This approach relies on the constrained optimization methods presented in the preceding section, and so it lends itself well to the introduction of short sales restrictions and/or similar constraints. The idea is to introduce fictitious securities to the market in such a way as to make the model complete, and then use constraints to prohibit any positions in these fictitious securities. This *fictitious security* approach will be described later in this section, after examining the risk neutral computational approach.

A key to the identification of the set of attainable wealths is principle (1.23), which says that a contingent claim (i.e., wealth) W is attainable if and only if $E_Q[W/B_1]$ takes the same value for every risk neutral probability measure $Q \in \mathsf{M}$. Thus W_v, the set of wealths that can be generated starting with initial capital v, is given by $\mathsf{W}_v = \{W \in \mathbb{R}^K : E_Q[W/B_1] = v,$ all $Q \in \mathsf{M}\}$. But this characterization of W_v is not practical, because with incomplete models the set M of risk neutral probability measures contains an infinite number of elements. This difficulty is resolved with the help of relationship (1.17), which says that M is the intersection of a linear subspace and the set of strictly positive probability measures. In particular, there exists a finite number of independent vectors in $\bar{\mathsf{M}}$ (the closure of M), say $Q(1), Q(2), \ldots, Q(J)$, such that each element of M can be expressed as a linear combination of these J vectors (see the linear program (1.25)), where the weights, some of which can be zero or negative, add up to one. Hence $E_Q[W/B_1] = v$ for all $Q \in \mathsf{M}$ if and only if $E_{Q(j)}[W/B_1] = v$ for $j = 1, \ldots, J$, and so

$$\mathsf{W}_v = \{W \in \mathbb{R}^K : E_{Q(j)}[W/B_1] = v \quad \text{for} \quad j = 1, \ldots, J\}$$

It follows that the optimal portfolio problem (2.1) (or (2.9)) can be written as

(2.50)

$$\begin{aligned} &\text{maximize} \quad Eu(W) \\ &\text{subject to} \quad E_{Q(j)}[W/B_1] = v, \quad j = 1, \ldots, J \end{aligned}$$

As in section 2.2, problem (2.50) can be solved by introducing J Lagrange multipliers as well as J corresponding state price densities $L_j \equiv Q(j)/P$:

(2.51)

$$\text{maximize} \quad Eu(W) - \sum_{j=1}^{J} \lambda_j E[L_j W/B_1]$$

The first order necessary conditions, one for each $\omega \in \Omega$, are:

$$u'(W(\omega)) = \sum_{j=1}^{J} \lambda_j L_j(\omega)/B_1(\omega), \qquad \text{all} \quad \omega \in \Omega$$

or

(2.52) $$W(\omega) = I\left[\sum_{j=1}^{J} \lambda_j L_j(\omega)/B_1(\omega)\right], \qquad \text{all} \quad \omega \in \Omega$$

where $I(\cdot)$ is the inverse function of u'. This gives the solution of (2.51) as a function of the J Lagrange multipliers. Substituting this expression into the J constraints of (2.50) enables one to solve for the values of the Lagrange multipliers which provide the solution of (2.50). In other words, substituting the values of the Lagrange multipliers satisfying

(2.53) $$E[L_j I(\lambda_1 L_1/B_1 + \ldots + \lambda_J L_J/B_1)/B_1] = v, \quad j = 1, \ldots, J$$

into (2.52) provides the optimal solution of (2.50). From this solution, the optimal attainable wealth, one finally computes the optimal trading strategy in the usual way.

The system (2.53) will normally have a unique, non-negative solution, depending upon the properties of the utility function. If the utility function is strictly concave, then the solution of (2.50) will be unique. This computational procedure will now be illustrated with an example.

Example 2.7   The securities model is the same as in example 1.2, namely, $K = 3$, $N = 1$, $r = 1/9$, $S_0 = 5$, and

ω	$S_1(\omega)$	$S_1^*(\omega)$	$P(\omega)$
ω_1	20/3	6	1/3
ω_2	40/9	4	1/3
ω_3	30/9	3	1/3

In chapter 1 it was established that this model is incomplete with M consisting of all probability measures of the form

$$Q = (\theta, 2 - 3\theta, -1 + 2\theta), \qquad \text{where} \quad \frac{1}{2} < \theta < \frac{2}{3}$$

and with a contingent claim $X = (X_1, X_2, X_3)$ being attainable if and only if

(2.54) $$X_1 - 3X_2 + 2X_3 = 0$$

In this case a 'basis' for M can be obtained by taking any two distinct elements of M. In fact, one can take the two endpoints, corresponding to $\theta = 1/2$ and $\theta = 2/3$, and this is what we will do:

$$Q(1) = (1/2, 1/2, 0) \quad Q(2) = (2/3, 0, 1/3)$$
$$L_1 = (3/2, 3/2, 0) \qquad L_2 = (2, 0, 1)$$

Taking $u(w) = \ln(w)$ one has $u'(w) = 1/w$ and $I(i) = 1/i$, so system (2.53) becomes, after a little algebra,

$$\frac{1}{3\lambda_1 + 4\lambda_2} + \frac{1}{3\lambda_1} = v$$

$$\frac{1}{9\lambda_1 + 12\lambda_2} + \frac{1}{3\lambda_2} = v$$

The unique, non-negative solution is found to be

$$\lambda_1 = 0.46482\, v^{-1} \qquad \lambda_2 = 0.53519\, v^{-1}$$

Substituting these values into (2.52) yields

$$W(\omega) = \frac{v}{0.46482(9/10)L_1(\omega) + 0.53519(9/10)L_2(\omega)}$$

$$= \begin{cases} 0.62860\, v, & \omega = \omega_1 \\ 1.59360\, v, & \omega = \omega_2 \\ 2.076611\, v, & \omega = \omega_3 \end{cases}$$

for the optimal attainable wealth. Notice, as verification, that W satisfies equation (2.54). Solving $H_0 + 6H_1 = (9/10)(0.6286)v$ and $H_0 + 4H_1 = (9/10)(1.5936)v$ for the optimal trading strategy yields

$$H_0 = 3.17124\, v \quad \text{and} \quad H_1 = -0.43425\, v$$

The optimal objective value is $0.24409 + \ln v$.

In summary, the risk neutral computational approach for incomplete models is essentially the same as for complete models, but the computational difficulties are increased due to the need to first specify and then cope with the additional constraints in (2.50).

We now turn to an alternative computational approach that features fictitious securities. The idea is to add one or more securities to the model in such a way as to make it complete (without, of course, creating any arbitrage opportunities). Then one solves, using the methods of the preceding section, the optimal portfolio problem with the constraint that no position can be taken in any of the added, fictitious securities. Since this optimization problem is done for a complete market, the computations may be simpler than with the two alternative approaches, even with the constraints.

While this concept is simple, a key step is to properly specify the added, fictitious securities. A good way to do this is to work with the $K \times N$ matrix A of chapter 1:

$$A = \begin{bmatrix} B_1(\omega_1) & S_1(1)(\omega_1) & \cdots & S_N(1)(\omega_1) \\ B_1(\omega_2) & S_1(1)(\omega_2) & \cdots & S_N(1)(\omega_2) \\ \vdots & \vdots & & \vdots \\ B_1(\omega_K) & S_1(1)(\omega_K) & \cdots & S_N(1)(\omega_K) \end{bmatrix}$$

This matrix has rank less than K, since the market is incomplete. We need to add some fictitious securities, that is, column vectors of non-negative numbers to A, so that the rank of A becomes equal to K. When selecting column vectors one must be careful to avoid adding arbitrage opportunities. A little linear algebra will ensure a successful result, as illustrated in the following example.

Example 2.7 (continued)   It suffices to add one fictitious security, so that the matrix A has the form

$$A = \begin{bmatrix} 10/9 & 60/9 & S_2(1)(\omega_1) \\ 10/9 & 40/9 & S_2(1)(\omega_2) \\ 10/9 & 30/9 & S_2(1)(\omega_3) \end{bmatrix}$$

Taking, for instance, $S_2(1) = (50/9, 20/9, 70/9)$, it is easy to verify that the matrix A will have full rank 3. Since all the risk neutral probabilities in the original market satisfy $Q = (\theta, 2 - 3\theta, -1 + 2\theta)$ for $1/2 < \theta < 2/3$, it follows that the unique risk neutral probability measure in the new market must be of this form as well. Taking, for instance, $\theta = 7/13$ gives $Q = (7/13, 5/13, 1/13)$ as well as $S_2(0) = E_Q[(9/10)S_2(1)] = 4$.

It remains to solve the optimal portfolio problem in the new market with the constraint that positions in security #2 are prohibited. Taking the approach described in the preceding section, this means that $\mathbb{K} = \{F \in \mathbb{R}^2 : F_2 = 0\}$,

$$\delta(\kappa) = \sup_{F \in \mathbb{K}} (-F\kappa') = \sup_{F_1 \in \mathbb{R}} (-F_1\kappa_1) = \begin{cases} 0, & \kappa_1 = 0 \\ \infty & \text{otherwise} \end{cases}$$

and $\tilde{\mathbb{K}} = \{\kappa \in \mathbb{R}^2 : \kappa_1 = 0\}$. The return processes in the market $\mathcal{M}_\kappa$ are

	ω_1	ω_2	ω_3
$R_1(\omega)$	$1/3$	$-1/9$	$-1/3$
$R_2(\omega)$	$7/18 + \kappa_2$	$-4/9 + \kappa_2$	$17/18 + \kappa_2$

and the corresponding risk neutral probability measure is computed to be

$$Q_\kappa(\omega) = \begin{cases} 7/13 - (18/65)\kappa_2, & \omega = \omega_1 \\ 5/13 + (54/65)\kappa_2, & \omega = \omega_2 \\ 1/13 - (36/65)\kappa_2, & \omega = \omega_3 \end{cases}$$

Notice that these probabilities are strictly positive as long as $-25/54 < \kappa_2 < 5/36$. Since $B_1^\kappa = 10/9$ and we are still using log utility, the optimal objective value for the unconstrained problem in the market $\mathcal{M}_\kappa$ is $J_\kappa(v) = \ln v - \ln(9/10) - E\ln Q_\kappa + E\ln P$. The dual problem is therefore the same as maximizing $E\ln Q_\kappa$ over $\tilde{\mathbb{K}}$, that is, with respect to κ_2 over the interval $(-25/54, 5/36)$. Some simple calculus provides the optimal solution: $\hat{\kappa} = (0, -0.18321)$.

The corresponding optimal attainable wealth is

$$W_{\hat{\kappa}} = vB_1^{\hat{\kappa}}/L_{\hat{\kappa}} = \frac{10v}{27Q_{\hat{\kappa}}} = \begin{cases} 0.62860\, v & \omega = \omega_1 \\ 1.59360\, v, & \omega = \omega_2 \\ 2.07611\, v, & \omega = \omega_3 \end{cases}$$

which is seen to be generated by the trading strategy $F = (-2.17125, 0)$. Since $F \in \mathbb{K}$ and $\delta(\hat{\kappa}) + F\hat{\kappa}' = 0$, it follows that this is also the optimal solution for the constrained problem as well as for the original unconstrained problem in the incomplete market.

A virtue of the fictitious securities approach is that it readily lends itself to problems which have short sales restrictions or similar constraints on the real securities. One proceeds in exactly the same way, only choosing the constraint set $\mathbb{K}$ so as to capture the explicit constraints on the real securities as well as the prohibition from taking a position in the fictitious securities. A return to the same example will illustrate this.

Example 2.7 (continued)   Suppose we prohibit short sales, so the solution obtained earlier is now infeasible. With the fictitious security the same as before, take $\mathbb{K} = \{F \in \mathbb{R}^2 : F_1 \geqslant 0, F_2 = 0\}$, so that

$$\delta(\kappa) = \sup_{F \in \mathbb{K}} (-F\kappa') = \sup_{F_1 \geqslant 0} (-F_1\kappa_1) = \begin{cases} 0, & \kappa_1 \geqslant 0 \\ \infty & \text{otherwise} \end{cases}$$

and $\tilde{\mathbb{K}} = \{\kappa \in \mathbb{R}^2 : \kappa_1 \geqslant 0\}$. The return processes in the market $\mathcal{M}_\kappa$ are

	ω_1	ω_2	ω_3
$R_1(\omega)$	$1/3 + \kappa_1$	$-1/9 + \kappa_1$	$-1/3 + \kappa_1$
$R_2(\omega)$	$7/18 + \kappa_2$	$-4/9 + \kappa_2$	$17/18 + \kappa_2$

and the corresponding risk neutral probability measure is

$$Q_\kappa(\omega) = \begin{cases} 7/13 - (45/26)\kappa_1 - (18/65)\kappa_2, & \omega = \omega_1 \\ 5/13 + (9/13)\kappa_1 + (54/65)\kappa_2, & \omega = \omega_2 \\ 1/13 + (27/26)\kappa_1 - (36/65)\kappa_2, & \omega = \omega_3 \end{cases}$$

Note these probabilities are strictly positive on the triangular subset of $\mathbb{R}^2$ where $\kappa_2 < -(25/4)\kappa_1 + 35/18$, $\kappa_2 > -(5/6)\kappa_1 - 25/54$, and

$\kappa_2 < (15/8)\kappa_1 + 5/36$. The optimal objective value for the unconstrained problem in the market $\mathcal{M}_\kappa$ has the same form as before, so the dual problem comes down to maximizing $E \ln Q_\kappa$ on the intersection of this triangular subset with the half-plane where $\kappa_1 \geqslant 0$. Using the first order conditions, it is easy to verify that $\hat{\kappa} = (4/27, -5/27)$ is the optimal solution. Corresponding to this are $Q_{\hat{\kappa}} = (1/3, 1/3, 1/3)$ and $W_{\hat{\kappa}} = 10v/(27Q_{\hat{\kappa}}) = (10v/9)(1,1,1)$, both constants on Ω. The trading strategy that generates $W_{\hat{\kappa}}$ is easily computed to be $F = (0,0)$, that is, invest all the money in the bank account. Clearly $F \in \mathbb{K}$ and $\delta(\hat{\kappa}) + F\hat{\kappa}' = 0$, so F is also the optimal trading strategy for the original constrained optimal portfolio problem, which is what we suspected from the start. The optimal objective value is $\ln v + \ln(10/9)$.

Exercise 2.12 Solve example 2.7 with $P(\omega_1) = 0.5$, $P(\omega_2) = 0.3$, and $P(\omega_3) = 0.2$, assuming

(a)   short sales are allowed,
(b)   short sales are prohibited.

2.7   Equilibrium Models

Until now, the specification of the security price processes $S_1, S_2, \ldots, S_N$, has been part of the data, external to the model. But it is important to understand prices, and so financial economists develop and study models where the price processes are internal, that is, endogenous.

An important category of models of this type is the class of *equilibrium* models. Sometimes the prices at both time $t = 0$ and time $t = 1$ are internal. Other times, and this is the kind of equilibrium model that will be looked at in this section, the prices at time $t = 1$ are specified and only the prices at time $t = 1$ are internal.

The data for the one-period equilibrium model will consist of the sample space Ω, the probability measure P, the bank account process B, and the N random variables $S_1(1), S_2(1), \ldots, S_N(1)$ representing the time $t = 1$ prices of the risky securities. In addition, there are I investors (or traders or consumers), numbered $i = 1, 2, \ldots, I$. Corresponding to each trader is a utility function u_i (differentiable, concave, strictly increasing) and an endowment process (v_i, E_i).

Internal to the model are three kinds of variables: the time $t = 0$ security prices $S_1(0), S_2(0), \ldots, S_N(0)$; a consumption process $C^i = (C_0^i, C_1^i)$ for each investor; and a trading strategy $H^i = (H_0^i, H_1^i, \ldots H_N^i)$ for each investor. The *equilibrium solution concept* involves finding values of all these variables such that a set of internally consistent conditions is satisfied. In particular,

The variables $S_n(0)$, $n = 1, \ldots, N$, and $\{C^i, H^i\}$, $i = 1, \ldots, I$, are said to be an *equilibrium solution* if for each i the consumption investment plan (C^i, H^i) is optimal for investor i, that is, (C^i, H^i) is a solution of

$$(2.55) \qquad \text{maximize} \quad u_i(C_0^i) + E[u_i(C_1^i)]$$

$$\text{subject to} \quad C_0^i + H_0^i B_0 + \sum_{n=1}^{N} H_n^i S_n(0) = v_i$$

$$C_1^i - H_0^i B_1 - \sum_{n=1}^{n} H_n^i S_n(1) = E_i$$

$$H^i \in \mathbb{R}^{N+1}$$

and the security market clears, that is, the aggregate demand for each security is zero, that is

$$(2.56) \qquad \sum_{i=1}^{I} H_n^i = 0 \qquad \text{for} \quad n = 0, 1, \ldots, N$$

Note that (2.55) does not include any explicit constraints requiring the consumption to be non-negative; if negative consumption is a problem, then one could specify utility functions that would force the consumption to be non-negative. It is possible to add explicit non-negativity constraints, but doing so would make the analysis of the equilibrium model more complicated. The requirement (2.56) that aggregate demand be zero does not make much sense for securities such as stocks and bonds, but it does hold perfectly well for things like futures contracts. Alternatively, one can imagine that some individuals act as firms, raising capital by selling stocks and bonds, and investing in the technologies that produce returns. These individuals are short the securities while everybody else is long. In the aggregate, the net positions in the securities are zero, and real aggregate wealth is equal to the total investment in the fundamental technologies.

Since the traders have strictly increasing utility functions, if there exists a solution to the equilibrium problem, then by (2.21) there must exist a risk neutral probability measure, say Q. It follows, therefore, that the time $t = 0$ prices must satisfy

$$S_n(0) = E_Q[S_n(1)/B_1]$$

Hence if we can derive the equilibrium consumption processes, then everything else will fall into place: (2.21) and the preceding equation will provide time zero prices, and investor i's trading strategy H^i will be the one which generates the contingent claim $C_1^i - E_i$ (assuming $C_1^i - E_i$ is attainable for all i, which will be the case if the model is complete).

Unfortunately, it is rather difficult to compute equilibrium consumption processes. In fact, an equilibrium solution does not necessarily exist, in general, so we shall not attempt to compute one. We shall need to be content with a study of the relationship between the equilibrium solution and something called Pareto efficiency.

But first notice that if you add up the time $t = 0$ budget constraint in (2.55) across i and rearrange terms you get

$$B_0 \sum_{i=1}^{I} H_0^i + \sum_{n=1}^{N} S_N(0) \sum_{i=1}^{I} H_n^i = \sum_{i=1}^{I} v_i - \sum_{i=1}^{I} C_0^i$$

In view of (2.56), if this is an equilibrium solution, then the left hand side equals zero, in which case the same can be said for the right hand side. One obtains a similar conclusion from the time $t = 1$ budget constraint in (2.55), and so

(2.57) If the consumption processes C^i, $i = 1, \ldots, I$, are part of an equilibrium solution, then

$$\sum_{i=1}^{I} C_0^i = \sum_{i=1}^{I} v_i \quad \text{and} \quad \sum_{i=1}^{I} C_1^i = \sum_{i=1}^{I} E_i$$

A collection of consumption processes satisfying these two equations is said to be *feasible*. In other words, the aggregate consumption equals the aggregate endowment, which is a kind of budget constraint.

The collection $\{\hat{C}^1, \hat{C}^2, \ldots, \hat{C}^I\}$ of consumption processes is said to be *Pareto efficient* if they are feasible (as in (2.57)) and there is no other collection $\{C^1, C^2, \ldots, C^I\}$ of feasible consumption processes such that

(2.58) $u_i(C_0^i) + Eu_i(C_1^i) \geqslant u_i(\hat{C}_0^i) + Eu_i(\hat{C}_1^i), \quad i = 1, \ldots, I$

with this inequality being strict for at least one i.

The condition for Pareto efficiency says that there is no feasible collection of consumption processes such that all of the investors are just as happy as they would be under the feasible collection $\{\hat{C}^1, \hat{C}^2, \ldots \hat{C}^I\}$, with at least one being strictly happier. Hence one might conjecture that a necessary and sufficient condition for $\{\hat{C}^1, \hat{C}^2, \ldots, \hat{C}^I\}$ to be part of an equilibrium solution is that it be Pareto efficient. While this is not exactly right, we do have the following:

(2.59) If the model is complete and $\{\hat{C}^1, \hat{C}^2, \ldots, \hat{C}^I\}$ is part of an equilibrium solution, then $\{\hat{C}^1, \hat{C}^2, \ldots, \hat{C}^I\}$ is Pareto efficient.

To see why this is true, suppose $\{\hat{C}^1, \hat{C}^2, \ldots, \hat{C}^I\}$ is part of an equilibrium solution, but there exists a feasible collection $\{C^1, C^2, \ldots, C^I\}$ of consumption processes as in (2.58), with at least one inequality being strict. I will show this leads to a contradiction. Since the model is complete, for each investor i there exists a trading strategy H^i satisfying

(2.60) $$H_0^i B_1 + \sum_{n=1}^{N} H_n^i S_n(1) = C_1^i - E_i$$

In view of (2.56), this means that

$$0 = \sum_{i=1}^{I} \left[H_0^i B_1 + \sum_{n=1}^{N} H_n^i S_n(1) \right] = \left(\sum_{i=1}^{I} H_0^i \right) B_1 + \sum_{n=1}^{N} \left(\sum_{i=1}^{I} H_n^i \right) S_n(1)$$

So defining a new trading strategy $\tilde{H}$ by

$$\tilde{H}_n = \sum_{i=1}^{n} H_n^i, \qquad n = 0, 1, \ldots, N$$

we see that the time $t = 1$ value of the portfolio corresponding to $\tilde{H}$ is identical to zero. Since there are no arbitrage opportunities (recall that there must exist a risk neutral probability measure), by the law of one price the time $t = 0$ value of this portfolio must be zero, that is,

$$(2.61) \qquad 0 = \tilde{H}_0 B_0 + \sum_{n=1}^{N} \tilde{H}_n S_n(0) = \left(\sum_{i=1}^{I} H_0^i \right) B_0 + \sum_{n=1}^{N} \left(\sum_{i=1}^{I} H_n^i \right) S_n(0)$$

This equation will be used in a moment. Meanwhile, define the scalars

$$(2.62) \qquad \psi_i \equiv C_0^i - v_i + H_0^i B_0 + \sum_{n=1}^{N} H_n^i S_n(0), \qquad i = 1, \ldots, I$$

Think of $C_0^i - \psi_i$ as time $t = 0$ consumption for investor i. The consumption process $\{C_0^i - \psi_i, C_1^i\}$ is attainable by (2.60) and (2.62). If $\psi_i < 0$, then investor i strictly prefers the consumption process $\{C_0^i - \psi_i, C_1^i\}$ to the consumption process $\{C_0^i, C_1^i\}$. Moreover, $\{C_0^i - \psi_i, C_1^i\}$ satisfies the budget constraints in investor i's optimization problem (2.55), and $\{C_0^i, C_1^i\}$ is preferred to $\{\hat{C}_0^i, \hat{C}_1^i\}$ by inequality (2.58). Hence $\psi_1 < 0$ would imply $\{C_0^i, C_1^i\}$ is strictly preferred to $\{\hat{C}_0^i, \hat{C}_1^i\}$, thereby contradicting the fact that the latter is an optimal solution of (2.55). It must be that $\psi_i \geqslant 0$ for all $i = 1, \ldots, I$.

By almost the same logic, if inequality (2.58) for investor i is strict, then $\psi_i = 0$ leads to a contradiction, and so this same ψ_i must be strictly positive. Since at least one inequality in (2.58) is supposed to be strict, if we sum equation (2.62) across i, we see that both sides of the resulting equation must be strictly positive. Using (2.61), we see that the right hand side is simply

$$\sum_{i=1}^{I} C_0^i - \sum_{i=1}^{I} v_i > 0$$

But this contradicts the supposition that $\{C^1, C^2, \ldots, C^I\}$ satisfy the feasibility requirement (2.57); we conclude the collection $\{\hat{C}^1, \hat{C}^2, \ldots, \hat{C}^I\}$ must be Pareto efficient.

In summary, if the market is complete, then a necessary condition for a collection of consumption processes to be part of an equilibrium solution is that the collection be Pareto efficient. Hence to compute an equilibrium solution, a reasonable approach might be first to identify all the Pareto efficient collections of consumption processes and then to search among these for one that is part of an equilibrium solution. Unfortunately, this approach is easier said than done, in general, and so this idea will not be pursued any further. Instead, we will study a variation of the equilibrium problem for which it is easier to compute equilibrium solutions.

Suppose we simplify the basic equilibrium problem by stipulating that $C_0^i = 0$ and $E_i = 0$ for every investor $i = 1, \ldots, I$ and ignoring the utility of time $t = 0$ consumption, so that (2.55) for each investor is simply a standard optimal portfolio problem. Furthermore, condition (2.56) for an equilibrium solution is replaced by

$$(2.63) \qquad \sum_{i=1}^{I} H_n^i = s_n, \qquad \text{for} \quad n = 1, \ldots, N$$

where $s_n > 0$ represents the total supply or number of units or shares of security n that are present in the market. The equilibrium problem can now be thought of as a market where all the investors share common beliefs about the time $t = 1$ prices in each of the states, and the question is, 'What are the appropriate time $t = 0$ prices?' Or perhaps N companies are making initial public offerings of their securities, they can assess the correct time $t = 1$ prices of their securities in each of the states, and they want to set the time $t = 0$ offering prices properly. In any event, the equilibrium solution will now consist of time $t = 0$ prices and a trading strategy for each investor such that the optimal portfolio problem (2.55) is satisfied for each investor and the market clearing condition (2.63) is satisfied.

To solve this kind of problem, a good approach is first to compute $H^i(S_0) = \{H_1^i(S_0), \ldots, H_N^i(S_0)\}$, the optimal solution of the portfolio problem (2.55) as a function of the specified time $t = 0$ prices $S_0 = \{S_1(0), \ldots, S_N(0)\}$. Thus $S_0 \to H_n^i(S_0)$ should be thought of as investor i's demand 'curve' or *demand function* for security n. Knowing these demand functions for all i and n, it remains to substitute them in (2.63) and solve for a time $t = 0$ price vector S_0 such that the market clearing condition (2.63) is satisfied.

We know something about the demand functions right away: they are finite at the point S_0 if and only if there exists a risk neutral probability measure at the point S_0. This is because if there is no risk neutral probability measure, then there is some arbitrage opportunity, in which case the investors would find it desirable to buy long or sell short an infinite quantity of one or more of the securities. It follows that the region where the demand functions are all finite, which will be denoted $\mathbb{S}$, is a subset of the n-dimensional interval

$$\underset{n=1}{\overset{N}{\mathrm{X}}} [\min\{S_n^*(1)(\omega) : \omega \in \Omega\}, \ \max\{S_n^*(1)(\omega) : \omega \in \Omega\}]$$

If $N = 1$, then this interval coincides with $\mathbb{S}$. With $N \geqslant 2$, $\mathbb{S}$ can either coincide with the n-dimensional interval or be a proper subset of its interior.

Consideration of this interval helps to organize the computation of the demand functions.

If the utility functions are suitably smooth with $u'(\cdot)$ taking all the non-negative values on the real line, then the demand functions $S_0 \to H^i(S_0)$ are continuous on $\mathbb{S}$. This is because the first order necessary conditions (2.4) are satisfied for each investor i, namely,

$$(2.64) \qquad 0 = E[B_1 u'(v_i + H_1^i\{S_1^*(1) - S_1(0)\} + \ldots + H_n^i\{S_n^*(1)$$
$$- S_n(0)\})\{S_n^*(1) - S_n(0)\}], \qquad n = 1,\ldots,N$$

(recall $S_n(0) = S_n^*(0)$). These equations are satisfied by some H^i for each S_0 in $\mathbb{S}$, and with modest assumptions the solution $H^i(S_0)$ will vary in a continuous fashion with respect to S_0 by what is called the implicit function theorem.[2] Moreover, the absolute value of one or more components of the demand functions will become arbitrarily large as S_0 approaches the boundary of $\mathbb{S}$. For example, in the case $N = 1$ the function $H_1^i(S_0)$ becomes arbitrarily large (small) as S_0 approaches the lower (respectively, upper) endpoint of the interval $\mathbb{S}$.

As stated above, to compute an equilibrium solution the recommended approach is first to compute the demand functions and then to substitute them in the market clearing condition (2.63) to solve for S_0. But one should be warned that this recipe will usually entail some nasty calculations; in fact, this approach is not guaranteed to be successful. It is instructive to now look at an example.

Example 2.8   Suppose $N = 2$, $K = 3$, $P = (1/3, 1/3, 1/3)$, $r = $ constant, and there are I identical investors with $u_i(w) = \ln(w)$ and $v_i = v$. The time $t = 1$ discounted prices are:

n	$S_n^*(1)$		
	ω_1	ω_2	ω_3
1	6	8	4
2	13	9	8

Recalling the matrix A that was studied in chapter 1, it is apparent that if there is a risk neutral probability measure, then this market must be complete. To compute the risk neutral probability measure as a function of the still unknown time $t = 0$ prices, one solves the usual system of equations and obtains

$$Q(\omega) = \begin{cases} \dfrac{-28 - S_1(0) + 4S_2(0)}{18}, & \omega = \omega_1 \\[2mm] \dfrac{-4 + 5S_1(0) - 2S_2(0)}{18}, & \omega = \omega_2 \\[2mm] \dfrac{50 - 4S_1(0) - 2S_2(0)}{18}, & \omega = \omega_3 \end{cases}$$

The region where these three fractions are all strictly positive coincides with the region $\mathbb{S}$ where the demand functions are finite; some simple algebra reveals this to be the interior of the triangle with vertices at $(4,8)$, $(6,13)$, and $(8,9)$. With log utility the optimal attainable wealth is of the form $W = vP(1+r)/Q$ (see exercise 2.2), so solving the system $H_0(1+r) + H_1S_1(\omega) + H_2S_2(\omega) = W(\omega)$, one obtains the demand functions

$$H_1^i(S_0) = \frac{-(1/3)v}{-28 - S_1(0) + 4S_2(0)} - \frac{(4/3)v}{50 - 4S_1(0) - 2S_2(0)}$$
$$+ \frac{(5/3)v}{-4 + 5S_1(0) - 2S_2(0)}$$

$$H_2^i(S_0) = \frac{(4/3)v}{-28 - S_1(0) + 4S_2(0)} - \frac{(2/3)v}{50 - 4S_1(0) - 2S_2(0)}$$
$$- \frac{(2/3)v}{-4 + 5S_1(0) - 2S_2(0)}$$

Hence knowing the values s_1, s_2, I, and v, one can substitute these two functions in the two market clearing equations (2.63) and solve for the two unknown time $t = 0$ prices. For example, if there are $I = 2$ investors each having $v = \$6000$ to invest, and if there are available $s_1 = 4000$ and $S_2 = 2000$ shares of securities 1 and 2, respectively, then system (2.63) yields $S_1(0) = 5$ and $S_2(0) = 9$. Substituting these values back into the demand functions gives $H_1^i = 2000$ and $H_2^i = 1000$, numbers which are as anticipated, since with I identical investors the equilibrium trading strategies will necessarily satisfy $H_n^i = s_n/I$. Note that $H_0 = v - H_1S_1(0) - H_2S_2(0) = -13,000$, so each investor will borrow $\$13,000$ in order to finance these transactions.

Exercise 2.13   Suppose $N = 1$, $K = 2$, $r = $ constant, $S_1(\omega_1) = 6$, $S_1(\omega_2) = 4$, and $P(\omega_1) = 2/3$. There are I identical investors, each with initial capital v and with log utility preferences.

(a) Show that the risk neutral probability measure must be of the form $Q(\omega_1) = [S_0(1+r) - 4]/2$ with $\mathbb{S} = (4/(1+r), 6/(1+r))$.
(b) Show that the demand function is

$$H(S_0) = \frac{v(1+r)\{3S_0(1+r) - 16\}}{3\{4 - S_0(1+r)\}\{6 - S_0(1+r)\}}$$

and is strictly decreasing on $\mathbb{S}$.

(c) Derive a formula for the equilibrium price S_0 in terms of general parameters I, v, s_1, and r. What is the equilibrium price when $I = 3$, $v = s_1 = 1000$, and $r = 0$?

NOTES

1 An *affine* function is equal to a constant plus a linear function.
2 For the situation here, suppose the N partial derivatives of the right hand side of (2.64) with respect to each H_n^i as well as to each $S_n(0)$ is a continuous function. Moreover, suppose the determinant of the $N \times N$ matrix of the partial derivatives of the right hand side of (2.64) with respect to each $H_n^i, n = 1, \ldots, N$ (this is called a *Jacobian*), is non-zero at some point $\hat{S}_0$ where (2.64) is satisfied. Then the implicit function theorem says there exist continuous functions $H_1^i(S_0), \ldots, H_N^i(S_0)$ such that, when substituted in (2.64), this equation is satisfied for all S_0 in some neighborhood of $\hat{S}_0$.

3 Multiperiod Securities Markets

3.1 Model Specifications, Filtrations, and Stochastic Processes

Multiperiod models of securities markets are much more realistic than single period models. In fact, they are extensively used for practical purposes in the financial industry.

The following elements of the basic, multiperiod model are specified as data:

- $T + 1$ trading dates: $t = 0, 1, \ldots, T$.
- A finite sample space Ω with $K < \infty$ elements:

$$\Omega = \{\omega_1, \omega_2, \ldots, \omega_K\}$$

- A probability measure P on Ω with $P(\omega) > 0$ for all $\omega \in \Omega$.
- A *filtration* $\mathbb{F} = \{\mathscr{F}_t; t = 0, 1, \ldots, T\}$, which is a submodel describing how the information about the security prices is revealed to the investors.
- A *bank account* process $B = \{B_t; t = 0, 1, \ldots, T\}$, where B is a stochastic process with $B_0 = 1$ and with $B_t(\omega) > 0$ for all t and ω. Here B_t should be thought of as the time t value of a savings account when \$1 is deposited at time 0. Usually B is a non-decreasing process, and the (possibly random) quantity $r_t \equiv (B_t - B_{t-1})/B_{t-1} \geqslant 0, t = 1, \ldots, T$, should be thought of as the *interest rate* pertaining to the time interval $(t - 1, t)$.

- *N risky security* processes $S_n = \{S_n(t); t = 0, 1, \ldots T\}$, where S_n is a non-negative stochastic process for each $n = 1, 2, \ldots N$. Here $S_n(t)$ should be thought of as the time t price of risky security n, for example, the price of one share of common stock of a particular corporation.

Note the multiperiod securities market model has two new features not shared with single period models: the information submodel and stochastic process submodels of prices. These will now be described.

3.1.1 Information Structures

It is important to have a clear idea about how information concerning the security prices is revealed to the investors. This is done in terms of subsets of the sample space Ω.

Consider that at time $t = 0$ every state $\omega \in \Omega$ is possible. Some states may be more likely than others, but none is ruled out. Meanwhile, at time $t = T$ (it will always be assumed) the investors learn the true state ω of the world (and thus the true value of every random variable). This is because as time evolves the investors will be able to deduce the true state by observing the information as it unfolds, since it will be assumed there exists a one-to-one correspondence between each possible sequence of information and each state.

What about the information at intermediate times, namely, when $0 < t < T$? How do we model the way the information evolves? Well, the new information observed over one time period enables the investors to rule out certain states as being impossible. Hence one can view the evolution of information as a random sequence $\{A_t\}$ of subsets of Ω, where $A_0 = \Omega$, $A_T = \{\omega\}$ for some $\omega \in \Omega$ and $A_0 \supseteq A_1 \supseteq \ldots \supseteq A_{T-1} \supseteq A_T$. The investors know at time t that for some subset A_t the true state is some $\omega \in A_t$, but they are not sure which one it is. Some states $\omega \in A_t$ may be more likely than others, but none is ruled out. On the other hand, every state $\omega \in A_t^c$ (the complement of A_t) is ruled out by the investors at time t. The investors know the true state of the world is not outside A_t. Logically, one period later the relevant subset A_{t+1} describing investor information must be, in turn, a subset of A_t. Thus the sequence $\{A_t\}$ of subsets that unfolds for the investors must satisfy $A_{t+1} \subseteq A_t$ for all t.

Notice there exist K possible information sequences $\{A_t\}$ of subsets. At time $t = 0$ the investors are aware of all these sequences, but they do not know which one is going to unfold. Arbitrarily select one such sequence $\{\hat{A}_t\}$ and some time $s < T$, and consider the collection of all the sequences $\{A_t\}$ which coincide with $\{\hat{A}_t\}$ up through time s along with $\{\hat{A}_t\}$ itself. In particular, consider all the time $s + 1$ subsets A_{s+1} from the sequences in this collection. If $\omega \in \hat{A}_s$, then there must exist at least one subset A_{s+1} containing ω (if none of the sequences coinciding with $\{\hat{A}_t\}$ through time s ends up in state ω, then ω should not have been in $\hat{A}_s$ to begin with). Hence the union of all the subsets A_{s+1} that can possibly follow $\hat{A}_s$ must be equal to $\hat{A}_s$. Moreover, this collection $\{A_{s+1}\}$ of subsets must be mutually exclusive (if ω, say, were contained in two distinct subsets, then there would exist two or more distinct sequences $\{A_t\}$ corresponding to state ω, a contradiction). Hence the collection $\{A_{s+1}\}$ of subsets that can possibly follow $\hat{A}_s$ forms a *partition* of $\hat{A}_s$, that is, a collection of disjoint subsets whose union equals $\hat{A}_s$.

In particular, taking $s = 0$, we see that the collection $\{A_1\}$ of all possible time $t = 1$ subsets forms a partition of Ω. This partition is denoted $\mathscr{P}_1$. Moreover, the collection $\{A_2\}$ of all possible time $t = 2$ subsets also forms a partition, denoted $\mathscr{P}_2$, of Ω; it has the property that each $A \in \mathscr{P}_1$ is equal to the union of one or more of the elements of $\mathscr{P}_2$. It follows, therefore, that the information structure is fully described by a sequence $\mathscr{P}_0, \mathscr{P}_1, \ldots \mathscr{P}_T$ of partitions of Ω, with $\mathscr{P}_0 \equiv \{\Omega\}$, $\mathscr{P}_T \equiv \{\{\omega_1\}, \ldots, \{\omega_K\}\}$, and satisfying the property that each $A \in \mathscr{P}_t$ is equal to the union of some elements in $\mathscr{P}_{t+1}$ for every $t < T$. This sequence $\{\mathscr{P}_t\}$ of partitions is uniquely constructed from the collection of possible information sequences $\{A_t\}$. Conversely, given a sequence $\{\mathscr{P}_t\}$ of partitions as above, there is a unique, corresponding collection of possible information sequences $\{A_t\}$.

There are several good ways to visualize the information structure. The sequence of partitions can, of course, be described with a sequence of pictures of the sample space, one picture for each point in time showing the corresponding partition. Alternatively, the sequence of partitions can be described with a network diagram known as a *tree*, where each node corresponds to one element A_t of the time t partition, and there is one arc going from this node to each node corresponding to some $A_{t+1} \subseteq A_t$. There will thus be one path from the time $t = 0$ node (i.e., $A_0 = \Omega$) to each $t = T$ node (i.e., $A_T = \omega$ for each state ω), and each such path will indicate a possible information sequence $\{A_t\}$.

Example 3.1   With $K = 8$ and $T = 3$, suppose the time $t = 1$ partition is

$$\mathscr{P}_1 = \{\{\omega_1, \omega_2, \omega_3, \omega_4\}, \quad \{\omega_5, \omega_6, \omega_7, \omega_8\}\}$$

Then for the time $t = 2$ partition we could take

$$\mathscr{P}_2 = \{\{\omega_1, \omega_2\}, \quad \{\omega_3, \omega_4\}, \quad \{\omega_5, \omega_6\}, \quad \{\omega_7, \omega_8\}\}$$

or

$$\mathscr{P}_2 = \{\{\omega_1\}, \quad \{\omega_2, \omega_3, \omega_4\}, \quad \{\omega_5, \omega_6, \omega_7, \omega_8\}\}$$

for example, but we could not take

$$\mathscr{P}_2 = \{\{\omega_1, \omega_2, \omega_3\}, \quad \{\omega_3, \omega_4\}, \quad \{\omega_5, \omega_6\}, \quad \{\omega_7, \omega_8\}\}$$

for example, because two of the subsets are not disjoint, nor could we take

$$\mathscr{P}_2 = \{\{\omega_1, \omega_2\}, \quad \{\omega_3, \omega_4, \omega_5\}, \quad \{\omega_6, \omega_7, \omega_8\}\}$$

because no union of any of these subsets equals $\{\omega_5, \omega_6, \omega_7, \omega_8\}$. Adopting the first suggestion for the time $t = 2$ partition, this example can be conveniently described by the sequence of pictures shown in figure 3.1 or by the tree diagram in figure 3.2.

In summary, the submodel of information structure can be organized as a sequence of partitions, with each successive partition becoming *finer*. Or it can be organized as a tree. There is still another way to specify the submodel.

A collection $\mathscr{F}$ of subsets of Ω is called an *algebra* on Ω if

(a) $\Omega \in \mathscr{F}$
(b) $F \in \mathscr{F} \Rightarrow F^c = \Omega \backslash F \in \mathscr{F}$
(c) F and $G \in \mathscr{F} \Rightarrow F \cup G \subset \mathscr{F}$.

Note that the empty set $\phi = \Omega^c$, so if $\mathscr{F}$ is an algebra, then it must contain the empty set. Note also that $F \cap G = (F^c \cup G^c)^c$, so if $\mathscr{F}$ is an algebra containing F and G, then $\mathscr{F}$ must contain the intersection $F \cap G$ of F and G. Hence an algebra on Ω is a family of subsets of Ω that is stable under finitely many set operations.

Given an algebra on Ω, denoted $\mathscr{F}_t$, you can always find a unique collection $\{F_n\}$ of subsets F_n such that

(a) each $F_n \in \mathscr{F}_t$,
(b) the subsets $\{F_n\}$ are disjoint, and
(c) the union of the subsets $\{F_n\}$ equals Ω.

In other words, corresponding to the algebra $\mathscr{F}_t$ is a partition of Ω, which is unique.

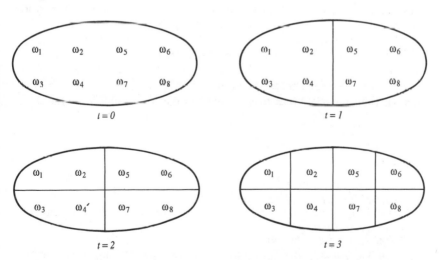

Figure 3.1 Partitions corresponding to information submodel for example 3.1

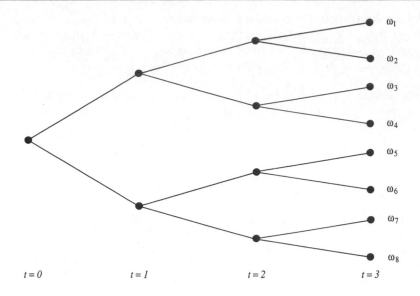

Figure 3.2   Information tree submodel for example 3.1

Conversely, given a partition you can perform a variety of elementary set operations (taking complements, intersections, unions, and so forth), generating as many new subsets as possible. You thereby end up with an algebra, which is unique.

Hence there is a one-to-one correspondence between partitions of Ω and algebras on Ω, and so the submodel of the information structure can be organized as a sequence $\{\mathscr{F}_t\}$ of algebras. We write $\mathbb{F} = \{\mathscr{F}_t; t = 0, 1, \ldots, T\}$ and call $\mathbb{F}$ a *filtration*. Note that $\mathscr{F}_0 = \{\phi, \Omega\}$ and $\mathscr{F}_T$ consists of all the subsets of Ω. Since each subset in the time t partition equals the union of some subsets in the time $(t + 1)$ partition, we must have $\mathscr{F}_t \subseteq \mathscr{F}_{t+1}$, that is, each subset of $\mathscr{F}_t$ must be an element of $\mathscr{F}_{t+1}$. One thus can say that our filtration is a nested sequence of algebras.

Example 3.1 (continued)   Corresponding to the time $t = 1$ partition is the algebra

$$\mathscr{F}_1 = \{\phi, \Omega, \{\omega_1, \omega_2, \omega_3, \omega_4\}, \{\omega_5, \omega_6, \omega_7, \omega_8\}\}$$

Corresponding to the time $t = 2$ partition we adopted is the algebra

$$\begin{aligned}
\mathscr{F}_2 = \{&\phi, \Omega, \{\omega_1, \omega_2\}, \{\omega_3, \omega_4\}, \{\omega_5, \omega_6\}, \{\omega_7, \omega_8\}, \{\omega_1, \omega_2, \omega_3, \omega_4\}, \\
&\{\omega_5, \omega_6, \omega_7, \omega_8\}, \{\omega_1, \omega_2, \omega_5, \omega_6\}, \{\omega_1, \omega_2, \omega_7, \omega_8\}, \{\omega_3, \omega_4, \omega_5, \omega_6\}, \\
&\{\omega_3, \omega_4, \omega_7, \omega_8\}, \{\omega_1, \omega_2, \omega_3, \omega_4, \omega_5, \omega_6\}, \{\omega_1, \omega_2, \omega_3, \omega_4, \omega_7, \omega_8\}, \\
&\{\omega_1, \omega_2, \omega_5, \omega_6, \omega_7, \omega_8\}, \{\omega_3, \omega_4, \omega_5, \omega_6, \omega_7, \omega_8\}\}.
\end{aligned}$$

3.1.2 Stochastic Process Models of Security Prices

A *stochastic process* S_n is a real-valued function $S_n(t, \omega)$ of both t and ω. Hence the domain is $\{0, 1, \ldots, T\}/ \times \Omega$. For each fixed $\omega \in \Omega$, the function $t \to S_n(t, \omega)$ is called the *sample path*. For each fixed t, the function $\omega \to S_n(t, \omega)$ is a random variable.

For modeling purposes, we want our stochastic process model of the security prices to be consistent with the information structure. In particular, we want the information available to the investors at any point in time to include knowledge of the present and past security prices. This is accomplished by introducing the concept of measurability of random variables.

The random variable X is said to be *measurable* with respect to the algebra $\mathscr{F}$ if the function $\omega \to W(\omega)$ is constant on any subset in the partition corresponding to $\mathscr{F}$. Equivalently, for every real number x, the subset $\{\omega \in \Omega : X(\omega) = x\}$ is an element of the algebra $\mathscr{F}$.

Example 3.2 With $\mathscr{F}_1 = \{\phi, \Omega, \{\omega_1, \omega_2, \omega_3, \omega_4\}, \{\omega_5, \omega_6, \omega_7, \omega_8\}\}$ as in Example 3.1, suppose

$$X(\omega) = \begin{cases} 6, & \omega = \omega_1, \omega_2, \omega_3, \text{ or } \omega_4 \\ 8, & \omega = \omega_5, \omega_6, \omega_7, \text{ or } \omega_8 \end{cases}$$

and

$$Y(\omega) = \begin{cases} 1, & \omega = \omega_1, \omega_3, \omega_5, \text{ or } \omega_7 \\ 0, & \omega = \omega_2, \omega_4, \omega_6, \text{ or } \omega_8 \end{cases}$$

Then X is measurable with respect to $\mathscr{F}_1$, but Y is not.

A stochastic process $S_n = \{S_n(t); t = 0, 1, \ldots, T\}$ is said to be *adapted* to the filtration $\mathbb{F} = \{\mathscr{F}_t; t = 0, 1, \ldots, T\}$ if the random variable $S_n(t)$ is measurable with respect to $\mathscr{F}_t$ for every $t = 0, \ldots, T$. It will be assumed in all that follows that the price of the nth risky security is an adapted stochastic process S_n for $n = 1, \ldots, N$, and the same for the bank account process B.

So how does the requirement that the stochastic processes be adapted ensure that each investor has full knowledge of the past and present prices? The investors know at time t that the true state ω is contained in a particular subset in the time t partition $\mathscr{P}_t$. The time t price $S_n(t)$ of each security must be constant on this subset, so the investors can work out what the time t values of the securities must actually be. Moreover, since the partitions form a nested sequence, the investors can infer the observed subsets in earlier partitions and thereby deduce the actual security prices at earlier times.

In summary, our securities market model will consist of security processes that are adapted to the filtration, so the investors will have full knowledge of the past and present prices. While the information and security submodels can be specified simultaneously, in practice the filtration is often specified only after first specifying the stochastic process submodel of the securities.

But starting with a specification of the stochastic processes, it is usually possible to specify two or more filtrations such that the security prices will be adapted. Some of these filtrations may be unacceptable, however, because they may be consistent with allowing the investors to look into the future. For example, if time $t + 1$ prices are $\mathscr{F}_t$ measurable, then the investors know at time t what the prices will be at time $t + 1$. Nevertheless, there is always one filtration that corresponds to learning about the prices as time goes on, but learning nothing more. The derivation of this kind of filtration is illustrated in the following example.

Example 3.3 Consider an investor who watches a security and knows that it is going to evolve as follows:

ω_k	$t = 0$	$t = 1$	$t = 2$
ω_1	$S_0 = 5$	$S_1 = 8$	$S_2 = 9$
ω_2	$S_0 = 5$	$S_1 = 8$	$S_2 = 6$
ω_3	$S_0 = 5$	$S_1 = 4$	$S_2 = 6$
ω_4	$S_0 = 5$	$S_1 = 4$	$S_2 = 3$

Here $N = 1$, and we are using the convention that when $N = 1$ the subscript can denote the time index instead of the identification of the risky security. Moreover, $T = 2$ and $K = 4$, so the stochastic process S has been specified for every (t, ω).

Now at time $t = 0$ all the investor observes is $S_0 = 5$; in other words, the investor does not have a clue about the true state, so $\mathscr{F}_0 = \{\phi, \Omega\}$. But at time $t = 1$ the investor observes either $S_1 = 8$ or $S_1 = 4$. In the former case the investor infers the true state must be either ω_1 or ω_2; in the latter case it must be either ω_3 or ω_4. Hence the relevant partition is $\{\omega_1, \omega_2\} \cup \{\omega_3, \omega_4\}$, and the corresponding algebra is

$$\mathscr{F}_1 = \{\phi, \Omega, \{\omega_1, \omega_2\}, \{\omega_3, \omega_4\}\}$$

At time $t = 2$ the investor observes S_2 and thereby deduces the true state ω (the investor distinguishes ω_2 from ω_3 by remembering S_1). Hence the relevant partition is $\omega_1 \cup \omega_2 \cup \omega_3 \cup \omega_4$ and $\mathscr{F}_2$ is the collection of all subsets of Ω. The resulting information structure can be described as the tree in figure 3.3. Note that, indeed, the stochastic process S is adapted to the filtration.

A filtration constructed in the manner illustrated in example 3.3 is said to be *generated* by the stochastic process. The resulting filtration is the coarsest one possible, that is, the various algebras have the fewest possible subsets such that the stochastic process under discussion is adapted.

But there is another useful way to construct the securities market model. You can start with a filtration submodel, based upon, perhaps, a variety of information reports. Then you add stochastic process models of security

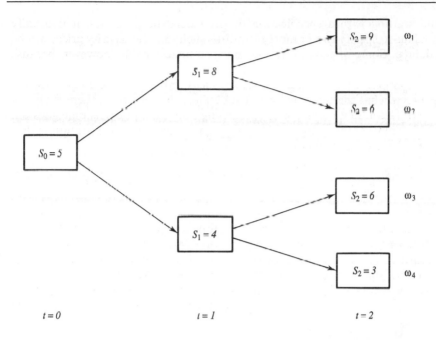

Figure 3.3   Information structure and risky security for example 3.3

prices, making sure the processes are adapted to ensure appropriate investor knowledge of past and present prices. This is illustrated in the following example.

Example 3.4   Suppose, with $K = 4$, $N = 1$, and $T = 2$, that at time $t = 1$ a marketing survey will be conducted that will be either favorable (corresponding to the subset $\{\omega_1, \omega_3\}$) or unfavorable $\{\omega_2, \omega_4\}$, respectively). Morever, in either case the risky security will possibly take one of two distinct values. Hence the relevant partition at time $t = 1$ is $\omega_1 \cup \omega_2 \cup \omega_3 \cup \omega_4$ and the corresponding algebra $\mathcal{F}_1$ is the collection of all subsets of Ω. Note that the risky process defined in example 3.3 is adapted to this filtration and thus consistent with the information submodel. But since the investors can distinguish ω_1 from ω_2 as well as ω_3 from ω_4 at time $t = 1$ by observing the marketing report, they learn more information than by only observing the price process. In fact, the investors can now look into the future, for they know at time $t = 1$ what the prices will be at time $t = 2$. The filtrations in examples 3.3 and 3.4 are different, although the price processes are the same. This modeling flexibility is one reason why we go to the trouble of having filtration submodels of the information structure.

3.1.3   Trading Strategies

A *trading strategy* $H = (H_0, H_1, \cdots, H_N)$ is a vector of stochastic processes $H_n = \{H_n(t); t = 1, 2, \cdots, T\}$, $n = 0, 1, \cdots, N$. Note that $H_n(0)$ is not specified; this is because, for $n \geqslant 1$, $H_n(t)$ should be interpreted as the number of units (e.g., shares of stock) that the investor owns (i.e., carries forward) from time $t - 1$ to time t, whereas $H_0(t)B_{t-1}$ equals the amount of money invested in the bank account at time $t - 1$. Note also that $H_n(t)$ can be negative; this corresponds to borrowing money from the bank (in the case $n = 0$) or selling short security n (in the cases $n \geqslant 1$).

It may seem odd to model an investor's trading strategy as a stochastic process, but upon recalling that a stochastic process is little more than a real-valued function of time and the state, this begins to make sense. A trading strategy should be a rule (i.e., a function) that specifies the investor's position in each security at each point in time and in each state of the world. Moreover, this rule should allow the investor to choose a position in the securities based on all the available information, but it should not allow, for example, the investor to 'look into the future.' Hence the trading strategies must be related to the filtration submodel of the information structure in just the right way so that the investor can base the trading position on the available information, but nothing more. This is done by introducing the concept of predictibility.

A stochastic process H_n is said to be *predictable* with respect to the filtration $\mathbb{F}$ if each random variable $H_n(t)$ is measurable with respect to $\mathscr{F}_{t-1}$ for all $t = 1, 2, \cdots, T$. Since $\mathscr{F}_{t-1} \subseteq \mathscr{F}_t$, this means that all predictable stochastic processes are *adapted*.

It will be assumed in all that follows that each component of a trading strategy H is a predictable stochastic process. Since the trading position $H_n(t)$ established by the investor at time $t - 1$ is constant on the subset that is observed in the time $t - 1$ partition $\mathscr{P}_{t-1}$, the investor can take into account all of the information available at that time, but nothing more.

Example 3.1 (continued)   Since $H_n(1) \in \mathscr{F}_0$, the position in security n carried forward from time $t = 0$ to time $t = 1$ must be the same for all $\omega \in \Omega$. At time $t = 1$ the trader can adjust this position based on the information which becomes available, that is, on the observation as to whether the true state $\omega \in \{\omega_1, \omega_2, \omega_3, \omega_4\}$. Consequently, the investor can choose one value for $H_n(2, \omega)$ if $\omega \in \{\omega_1, \omega_2, \omega_3, \omega_4\}$ and a second value for $H_n(2, \omega)$ if $\omega \notin \{\omega_1, \omega_2, \omega_3, \omega_4\}$. In other words, the investor's new position at time $t = 1$ can be according to any rule $H_n(2)$ with $H_n(2) \in \mathscr{F}_1$. Finally, and in a similar fashion, at time $t = 2$ the investor learns the information corresponding to $\mathscr{F}_2$; the investor ean take a new position according to any rule $H_n(3)$ with $H_n(3) \in \mathscr{F}_2$; and this rule will have the property that $H_n(1, \omega_1) = H_n(1, \omega_2), \cdots$, and $H_n(1, \omega_7) = H_n(1, \omega_8)$.

3.1.4 Value Processes and Gains Processes

The *value process* $V = \{V_t; t = 0, 1, \cdots, T\}$ is a stochastic process defined by

$$V_t = \begin{cases} H_0(1) B_0 + \sum_{n=1}^{N} H_n(1) S_n(0), & t = 0 \\ H_0(t) B_t + \sum_{n=1}^{N} H_n(t) S_n(t), & t \geq 1 \end{cases}$$

Hence V_0 is the initial value of the portfolio and, for $t \geq 1$, V_t is the time-t value of the portfolio before any transactions are made at that same time. Note that V is an adapted stochastic process (if you know the subset in $\mathscr{P}_t$, then you know $H(t)$, B_t, and $S_n(t)$, in which case you know V_t). Denote

$$\Delta S_n(t) = S_n(t) - S_n(t-1)$$

for the change in the value of the stochastic process S_n between times $t-1$ and t. Then $H_n(t)\Delta S_n(t)$ represents the one-period gain or loss due to the ownership of $H_n(t)$ units of security n between times $t-1$ and t. Similarly,

$$\sum_{u=1}^{t} H_N(u) \, \Delta S_n(u)$$

represents the cumulative gain or loss through time t due to the investment in security n. This sum is an example of what is called a (discrete time) *stochastic integral*, being the weighted sum of the values of one stochastic process (H_n), where the weights are given by the one-period changes of another stochastic process . Finally,

$$G_t \equiv \sum_{u=1}^{t} H_0(u)\Delta B_u + \sum_{n=1}^{N}\sum_{u=1}^{t} H_n(u)\Delta S_n(u), \quad t \geq 1$$

defines the *gains process* and represents the cumulative gain or loss through time t of the portfolio. Thus G is the stochastic integral of the trading strategy with respect to the price process. Note that $G = \{G_t; t = 1, \ldots, T\}$ is an adapted stochastic process.

Example 3.3 (continued) Suppose $B_t = (1+r)^t$, where $r \geq 0$ is a constant. Then for the value process we have $V_0 = H_0(1) + 5H_1(1)$,

$$V_1 = \begin{cases} (1+r)H_0(1) + 8H_1(1), & \omega = \omega_1, \omega_2 \\ (1+r)H_0(1) + 4H_1(1), & \omega = \omega_3, \omega_4 \end{cases}$$

and

$$V_2 = \begin{cases} (1+r)^2 H_0(2) + 9H_1(2), & \omega = \omega_1, \\ (1+r)^2 H_0(2) + 6H_1(2), & \omega = \omega_2, \omega_3 \\ (1+r)^2 H_0(2) + 3H_1(2), & \omega = \omega_4 \end{cases}$$

The gains process is given by

$$G_1 = \begin{cases} rH_0(1) + 3H_1(1), & \omega = \omega_1, \omega_2 \\ rH_0(1) - H_1(1), & \omega = \omega_3, \omega_4 \end{cases}$$

and

$$G_2 = \begin{cases} rH_0(1) + 3H_1(1) + r(1+r)H_0(2) + H_1(2), & \omega = \omega_1 \\ rH_0(1) + 3H_1(1) + r(1+r)H_0(2) - 2H_1(2), & \omega = \omega_2 \\ rH_0(1) - H_1(1) + r(1+r)H_0(2) + 2H_1(2), & \omega = \omega_3 \\ rH_0(1) - H_1(1) + r(1+r)H_0(2) - H_1(2), & \omega = \omega_4 \end{cases}$$

3.1.5   Self-Financing Trading Strategies

As mentioned earlier, for $t \geqslant 1$ the quantity V_t represents the time t value of the portfolio just before any transactions (that is, any changes of ownership positions) take place at that time. Meanwhile,

$$H_0(t+1)B_t + \sum_{n=1}^{N} H_n(t+1)S_n(t), \ t \geqslant 1$$

represents the time t value of the portfolio just after any time t transactions, that is, just before the portfolio is carried forward to time $t+1$. In general, these two portfolio values can be different, which means that at time t some money is either added to or withdrawn from the portfolio. However, for many applications money cannot be added to or withdrawn from the portfolio at times other than $t=0$ and $t=T$, and so this leads to the concept of self-financing trading strategies.

A trading strategy H is said to be *self-financing* if

$$(3.1) \qquad V_t = H_0(t+1)B_t + \sum_{n=1}^{N} H_n(t+1)S_n(t), \ t = 1, \dots, T-1.$$

In other words, the time t values of the portfolio just before and just after any time t transactions are equal. Intuitively, if no money is added to or withdrawn from the portfolio between times $t=0$ and $t=T$, then any change in the portfolio's value must be due to a gain or loss in the investments. Note this concept is not relevant to single period models. Moreover, one can show by some simple bookkeeping calculations that:

(3.2)   A trading strategy H is self-financing if and only if

$$V_t = V_0 + G_t, \ t = 1, 2, \dots, T.$$

Example 3.3 (continued)   For the trading strategy H to be self-financing, one must have at time $t = 1$

$$V_1 = (1+r)H_0(1) + 8H_1(1) = (1+r)H_0(2) + 8H_1(2)$$

in states ω_1 and ω_2 and

$$V_1 = (1+r)H_0(1) + 4H_1(1) = (1+r)H_0(2) + 4H_1(2)$$

in states ω_3 and ω_4. Equivalently, using $V_t = V_0 + G_t$ for $t = 1$ and $t = 2$ gives $V_1 = V_2 - [G_2 - G_1]$. Computing this for ω_1 yields

$$V_1 = (1+r)^2 H_0(2) + 9H_1(2) - [r(1+r)H_0(2) + H_1(2)]$$
$$= (1+r)H_0(2) + 8H_1(2)$$

which is the same as the self-financing equation (3.1). Similarly for ω_2. For ω_3 one computes

$$V_1 = (1+r)^2 H_0(2) + 6H_1(2) - [r(1+r)H_0(2) + 2H_1(2)]$$
$$= (1+r)H_0(2) + 4H_1(2)$$

which is also the same as earlier.

3.1.6   Discounted Prices

It is convenient to introduce discounted versions of some of the price processes that have been introduced above. For much of the financial theory that will be developed, what matters is the behavior of the security prices relative to each other, rather than their absolute behavior. Hence we will be interested in normalized versions of the security prices, obtained by dividing the prices of the various securities by the price of one of them. For this purpose it is convenient to select the bank account as the divisor, that is, as the *numeraire*.

The *discounted price process* $S_n^* = \{S_n^*(t); t = 0, 1, \ldots, T\}$ is defined by

$$S_n^*(t) \equiv S_n(t)/B_t, \ t = 0, \ 1, \ldots, T; \ n = 1, 2, \ldots, N$$

The *discounted value process* $V^* = \{V_n^*; t = 0, 1, \ldots, T\}$ is defined by

$$V_n^* \equiv \begin{cases} H_0(1) + \sum_{n=1}^{N} H_n(1)S_n^*(0), \ t = 0 \\ H_0(t) + \sum_{n=1}^{N} H_n(t)S_n^*(t), \ t = 1, \ldots, T \end{cases}$$

Finally, the *discounted gains process* $G^* = \{G_t^*; t = 1, 2, \ldots, T\}$ is defined by

$$G_t^* \equiv \sum_{n=1}^{N} \sum_{u=1}^{t} H_n(u) \, \Delta S_n^*(u), \ t = 1, \ldots, T$$

where the notation $\Delta S_n^*(u)$ means $S_n^*(u) - S_n^*(u-1)$, as should be guessed from the earlier definition of the (undiscounted) gains process. All of these are adapted, stochastic processes.

By carrying out some bookkeeping calculations it is straightforward to verify that

(3.3) $$V_t^* = V_t/B_t, \ t = 0, \ 1, \ldots, T$$

and that

(3.4)   A trading strategy H is self-financing if and only if

$$V_t^* = V_0^* + G_t^*, \text{ for } t = 1, 2, \ldots, T$$

Exercise 3.1 Verify (3.2).

Exercise 3.2 Verify (3.3).

Exercise 3.3 Verify (3.4).

3.2   Return and Dividend Processes

Given a price process $S_n, N = 1, \ldots, N$, suppose one defines a new process $R_n = \{R_n(t); \ t = 0, 1, \ldots, T\}$ by setting $R_n(0) = 0$ and, for all $t = 1, \ldots, T$,

(3.5) $$\Delta R_n(t) \equiv \begin{cases} \Delta S_n(t)/S_n(t-1), & S_n(t-1) > 0 \\ 0, & S_n(t-1) = 0 \end{cases}$$

This process R_n is called the *return process* corresponding to the price process S_n. The return process R_0 is defined in terms of the bank account process B in a similar manner, giving $\Delta R_0(t) = r_t$. These and other kinds of return processes are often useful for making various kinds of calculations.

Note that $\Delta R_n(t) \geqslant -1$, because the prices are non-negative. Moreover, $\Delta R_n(t) > -1$ for all t if and only if the price process S_n is strictly positive.

The equation defining R_n is the same as

(3.6) $$\Delta S_n(t) = S_n(t-1)\Delta R_n(t), \ t = 1, \ldots, T$$

which, in turn, is the same as

(3.7) $$S_n(t) = S_n(0) + \sum_{u=1}^{t} S_n(u-1) \, \Delta R_n(u), \ t = 1, \ldots, T$$

Still another equivalent equation is

(3.8) $$S_n(t) = S_n(0)\prod_{u-1}^{t}(1 + \Delta R_n(u)), \ t = 1, \ldots, T$$

These last two equations show that starting with a return process R_n satisfying $\Delta R_n > -1$ together with an initial price $S_n(0)$, one can define a strictly positive price process . Hence there is a one-to-one correspondence between positive price processes and pairs consisting of a positive initial price together with a return process having jumps bigger than minus one. This is a useful fact, because it is often easier to set up a securities market model by first specifying the return processes rather than by directly specifying the price processes.

3.2.1 Returns for Discounted Price Processes

The return processes corresponding to value processes, discounted price processes, and so forth can be defined in exactly the same way. Since $S_n^*(t) = S_n(t)/B_t$ for $t = 1, \ldots, T$, one may wonder how R_n^*, which denotes the return process corresponding to S_n^*, relates to R_n, the return process corresponding to the undiscounted price process. To find out, we can compute

$$
\begin{aligned}
\Delta S_n^*(t) &= S_n^*(t) - S_n^*(t-1) = S_n(t)/B_t - S_n^*(t-1) \\
&= \frac{S_n(t-1)[1 + \Delta R_n(t)]}{B_{t-1}[1 + \Delta R_0(t)]} - S_n^*(t-1) \\
&= S_n^*(t-1)\left[\frac{\Delta R_n(t) - \Delta R_0(t)}{1 + \Delta R_0(t)}\right]
\end{aligned}
$$

Since $\Delta S_n^*(t) = S_n^*(t-1)\Delta R_n^*(t)$ by definition, this implies

$$
\Delta R_n^*(t) = \frac{\Delta R_n(t) - \Delta R_0(t)}{1 + \Delta R_0(t)}
$$

This is consistent with

$$
\begin{aligned}
S_n^*(t) &= S_n^*(0) \prod_{u=1}^{t} (1 + \Delta R_n^*(u)) \\
&= S_n(0) \prod_{u=1}^{t} \left[\frac{1 + \Delta R_n(u)}{1 + \Delta R_0(u)}\right] = S_n(t)/B_t
\end{aligned}
$$

3.2.2 Returns for the Value and Gains Processes

Since $H_n(t)\Delta S_n(t) = H_n(t)S_n(t-1)\Delta R_n(t)$, it follows that the gains process satisfies

$$
\begin{aligned}
G_t &= \sum_{u=1}^{t} H_0(u)\, B_{u-1}\Delta R_0(u) + \sum_{n=1}^{N} \sum_{u=1}^{t} H_n(u)\, S_n(u-1)\, \Delta R_n(u) \\
&= \sum_{u=1}^{t} M_0(u)\, \Delta R_o(u) + \sum_{n=1}^{N} \sum_{u=1}^{t} M_n(u)\, \Delta R_n(u)
\end{aligned}
$$

where the quantity

$$
M_n(t) = \begin{cases} H_0(t)\, B_{t-1}, & n = 0 \\ H_n(t)\, S_n(t-1), & n = 1, 2, \ldots, N \end{cases}
$$

can be interpreted as the money invested in security n beginning at time $t-1$. In other words, $M \equiv \{M_0, M_1, \ldots, M_n\}$ is an alternative way to specify the trading strategy, and the preceding expression for G says that the gains process is equal to the stochastic integral of the trading strategy M with respect to the return process of the securities. Note that $M_n = \{M_n(t); t = 1, 2, \ldots, T\}$ is a predictable stochastic process.

Next, consider the return process, denoted R, corresponding to the value process V. Since

$$V_t = V_{t-1} + H_0(t)\Delta B_t + \sum_{n=1}^{N} H_n(t)\Delta S_n(t)$$

$$= V_{t-1} + M_0(t)\Delta R_0(t) + \sum_{n=1}^{N} M_n(t)\Delta R_n(t)$$

it follows that

$$\Delta R(t) = [V_t - V_{t-1}]/V_{t-1}$$

$$= \frac{M_0(t)}{V_{t-1}}\Delta R_0(t) + \sum_{n=1}^{N}\left[\frac{M_n(t)}{V_{t-1}}\right]\Delta R_n(t)$$

$$= \sum_{n=0}^{N} F_n(t)\Delta R_n(t)$$

where

$$F_n(t) \equiv M_n(t)/V_{t-1}, \quad n = 0, 1, \ldots, N$$

represents the fraction of the investor's wealth invested in security n at time $t-1$ and about to be carried forward to time t. The equation for R expresses the return process for the value process in terms of the return processes for the individual securities. Note that $F_n = \{F_n(t); t = 1, 2, \ldots, T\}$ is a predictable stochastic process. The quantity $F_n(t)$ can be negative for some n, t, and ω, but one always has $F_0(t) = 1 - F_1(t) - \ldots - F_N(t)$. Hence $F \equiv \{F_1, \ldots, F_N\}$ is still another form of the trading strategy.

In summary, the trading strategy can be expressed in three ways: as the number of units, H_n, invested in security n; as the amount of money, M_n, invested in security n; or as the fraction of wealth, F_n, invested in security n. In the latter case, if you also know the return process for each security, then you have a convenient, alternative expression for the value process, namely,

$$V_t = V_0 \prod_{u=1}^{t}[1 + \Delta R(u)] = V_0 \prod_{u=1}^{t}[1 + \sum_{n=0}^{N} F_n(u)\Delta R_n(u)]$$

So, starting with a trading strategy in the fractional form $F = \{F_1, \ldots, F_N\}$ together with the individual return processes R_0 and the initial value V_0, one can compute V_t as well as the trading strategy in the monetary form $M = \{M_0, M_1, \ldots, M_N\}$. Knowing, in addition, the initial prices B_0 and $S_n(0)$, one can compute the price processes as well as, finally, the trading strategy in unit form $H = \{H_0, H_1, \ldots, H_N\}$.

With $R^* = \{R^*(t); \, t = 0, 1, \ldots, T\}$ denoting the return process corresponding to the discounted value process V^*, it follows from the above results that

(3.9)
$$\Delta R^*(t) = \frac{\Delta R(t) - \Delta R_0(t)}{1 + \Delta R_0(t)}$$

Hence

$$V_t^* = V_0^* \prod_{u=1}^{t} [1 + \Delta R^*(u)] = V_0 \prod_{u=1}^{t} \left[\frac{1 + \Delta R(u)}{1 + \Delta R_0(u)} \right]$$

which is consistent with the fact that $V^* = V/B$.

3.2.3 Dividend Processes

Various kinds of securities, such as dividend-paying stocks, issue cash payments to the owners on a periodic basis. Up to this point, this feature has been ignored. It is of no interest for the single period model, because $S_n(1)$ represents the time $t = 1$ value of one unit of the security for the investor who made the purchase at time $t = 0$, and how this is divided up between a cash dividend and the time $t = 1$ value of a stock certificate, say, is of no consequence. For multiperiod models, however, it is often important to explicitly model any dividend payments. For example, the investor holding a stock over several periods may receive a cash dividend, and it is necessary to carefully model whether the investor reinvests the cash in the same stock, deposits the cash in the bank account, or uses the cash in another way.

There are two ways to incorporate dividend payments: implicitly and explicitly. With the implicit approach, $S_n(t)$ should be interpreted as the value of the investment where one unit of the security is purchased at time $t = 0$ and held indefinitely, and any dividends received are reinvested in the same security. For example, if a \$1 dividend is received at time $t = 1$, then the *ex-dividend* price at that time is $S_n(1) - 1$, which means the \$1 dividend was used to purchase $(S_n(1) - 1)^{-1}$ additional units of the security. But as time evolves further the bookkeeping becomes rather messy, as one tries to keep track of the true security price, the true position in the security, and so forth. Nevertheless, this implicit approach is sometimes convenient for addressing issues where the return process is what matters, because two securities having the same return process are (at least for some purposes) equivalent, even though one pays dividends and the other does not. In other words, the implicit approach is really one where you can work exclusively with return processes rather than a price process; in effect, each dividend-paying security is replaced by a security that does not pay any dividends but has exactly the same return process.

To see what the return process is for a dividend-paying security, and to describe the explicit approach, we call $D_n = \{D_n(t) : t = 0, \ldots, T\}$ the *dividend process* for security n, $n = 1, \ldots, N$, where $D_n(0) = 0$ and $\Delta D_n(t)$ represents the dividend per security unit paid at time t. Thus $D_n(t)$ represents the cumulative dividend payments associated with one unit of the security. Moreover, $S_n(t)$ represents the *ex-dividend* price of the security, that is, the price after any time t dividend payment. It will always be assumed that the dividend process is an adapted process. For securities paying dividends, the dividend processes should be specified as part of the data.

Now an investor owning one unit of security n at time $t - 1$ will earn a profit of $\Delta S_n(t) + \Delta D(t)$ over the ensuing period, so the corresponding one-period return is (assuming $S_n(t - 1) > 0$)

$$\Delta R_n(t) = \frac{\Delta S_n(t) + \Delta D_n(t)}{S_n(t - 1)}, \quad t = 1, \ldots, T; \; n = 1, \ldots, N$$

Thus knowing the price and dividend processes for a security, one can deduce the security's return process (of course, $R_n(0) = 0$), but not conversely. For a given return process, it is clear that there can exist an infinite number of price-dividend process pairs all having this same return process, with one of these pairs satisfying $D_n = 0$.

The discounted return process R_n^* for a dividend-paying security is defined by taking $R_n^*(0) = 0$ and

$$\Delta R_n(t) = \frac{\Delta S_n^*(t) + \Delta D_n(t)/B_t}{S_n^*(t - 1)}, \quad t = 1, \ldots, T; \; n = 1, \ldots, N$$

It is not difficult to verify that the earlier expression $\Delta R_n^*(t) = [\Delta R_n(t) - \Delta R_0(t)]/[1 + \Delta R_0(t)]$, derived for the case of no dividends, still holds.

In all that follows, a dividend-paying security will have its dividends modeled in this explicit fashion. Thus if no dividend process is specified, then it should be assumed the security does not pay any dividends.

Exercise 3.4   Show that in example 3.3 one has $R_1(1, \omega_1) = R_1(1, \omega_2) = 0.6$, $R_1(1, \omega_3) = R_1(1, \omega_4) = -0.2$, $R_1(2, \omega_1) = 0.725$, $R_1(2, \omega_2) = 0.35$, $R_1(2, \omega_3) = 0.3$ and $R_1(2, \omega_4) = -0.45$. What is the return process R_n^* corresponding to S_1^* in the case where the interest rate is the constant $r > 0$?

Exercise 3.5   Show that (3.5), (3.6), (3.7), and (3.8) are all equivalent when S_n is strictly positive. What if S_n can be zero?

Exercise 3.6   Verify relationship (3.9) in two different ways.

3.3   Conditional Expectation and Martingales

Just as with single period models, the multiperiod securities market model will have no arbitrage opportunities if and only if there exists a risk neutral probability measure. However, in the multiperiod situation the risk neutral probability measures are defined in terms of things called martingales, and these, in turn, are defined with conditional expectations. The purpose of this section will therefore be to introduce these two concepts from the world of probability theory.

In elementary probability theory, where, as we are assuming, the sample space Ω is finite, the conditional expectation of the discrete random variable Y given the event A is denoted $E[Y|A]$ and defined in terms of the conditional probability distribution $P\{Y = y|A\}$ by

$$E[Y|A] = \sum_y y\, P\{Y = y|A\}$$

Since $P\{Y = y|A\} = P\{Y = y, A\}/P\{A\}$ by Bayes's Law, it follows that

$$E[Y|A] = \sum_y y\, P\{Y(\omega) = y, A\}/P\{A\} = \sum_{\omega \in A} Y(\omega)\, P\{\omega\}/\{A\}$$

Hence in example 3.3, for instance, where $P\{\omega\} = 1/4$, for all $\omega \in \Omega$, one has $P\{S_2 = 9|S_1 = 8\} = P\{S_2 = 6|S_1 = 8\} = (1/4)/(1/4 + 1/4) = 1/2$, in which case $E[S_2|S_1 = 8] = 7.5$. Similarly, $E[S_2|S_1 = 4] = 4.5$.

When working with stochastic processes defined on a filtered probability space, it is often convenient to use $E[Y|\mathcal{F}]$ as a summary of all the conditional expectations of the form $E[Y|A]$ as the event A runs through the algebra $\mathcal{F}$. The idea is that $E[Y|\mathcal{F}]$ is defined by

$$E[Y|\mathcal{F}]\,1_A = E[Y|A], \text{ all } A \in \mathcal{P}$$

where $\mathcal{P}$ is the partition of Ω that corresponds to $\mathcal{F}$. Thus $E[Y|\mathcal{F}]$ will be a random variable that is measurable with respect to $\mathcal{F}$. In the case of example 3.3, for instance,

$$E[S_2|\mathcal{F}_1] = \begin{cases} 7.5, & \omega_1 \text{ and } \omega_2 \\ 4.5, & \omega_3 \text{ and } \omega_4 \end{cases}$$

Since $E[Y|\mathcal{F}]$ is a perfectly good random variable, we can compute its expectation:

$$E\left[E[Y|\mathcal{F}]\right] = E\left[\sum_{A \in \mathcal{P}} E[Y|A]\,1_A\right] = \sum_{A \in \mathcal{P}} P\{A\}\, E[Y|A]$$

$$= \sum_{A \in \mathcal{P}} P\{A\} \sum_{\omega \in A} Y(\omega)\, P\{\omega\}/P\{A\}$$

$$= \sum_{A \in \mathcal{P}} \sum_{\omega \in A} Y(\omega)\, P\{\omega\} = EY$$

A slight generalization of this is the following.

(3.10)   If $\mathcal{F}_1 \subset \mathcal{F}_2$, then $E\left[E[Y|\mathcal{F}_2]\,|\,\mathcal{F}_1\right] = E[Y|\mathcal{F}_1]$

In example 3.3, for instance, $E[E[S_2|\mathcal{F}_1]] = 7.5/2 + 4.5/2 = 6 = ES_2$.

If the random variable $X \in \mathcal{F}$, then one can write

(3.11) $$X = \sum_{A \in \mathcal{P}} x_A\,1_A,$$

where x_A is a scalar and $\mathscr{P}$ is the partition corresponding to $\mathscr{F}$. Hence

$$E[XY|\mathscr{F}] = \sum_{A \in \mathscr{P}} E[XY|A]\, 1_A = \sum_{A \in \mathscr{P}} E[x_A Y|A]\, 1_A$$

$$= \sum_{A \in \mathscr{P}} x_A E[Y|A]\, 1_A = X\, E[Y|\mathscr{F}]$$

In a similar fashion one can verify the following generalization.

(3.12)   Given random variables X_1, X_2, Y_1, and Y_2 with $X_1, X_2 \in \mathscr{F}$, one has
$E[X_1 Y_1 + X_2 Y_2|\mathscr{F}] = X_1 E[Y_1|\mathscr{F}] + X_2 E[Y_2|\mathscr{F}]$.

If Y is a constant, then clearly $E[Y|\mathscr{F}] = Y$. Taking $Y = 1$ and using (3.12), it follows that

(3.13)   If $X \in \mathscr{F}$ then $E[X|\mathscr{F}] = X$

In the case of example 3.3, for instance, $E[S_1 S_2|\mathscr{F}_1] = S_1 E[S_2|\mathscr{F}_1]$ and $E[S_1|\mathscr{F}_1] = S_1$.

Taking $A \in \mathscr{F}$ implies $1_A \in \mathscr{F}$, so $E[Y 1_A|\mathscr{F}] = 1_A E[Y|\mathscr{F}]$ by (3.12). Hence by (3.10) one has

$$E[1_A E[Y|\mathscr{F}]] = E[Y 1_A], \text{ all } A \in \mathscr{F}$$

It turns out this equation provides an alternative definition of $E[Y|\mathscr{F}]$, one that generalizes to probability spaces where Ω is not finite. In particular, suppose $X \in \mathscr{F}$ satisfies

(3.14) $E[1_A X] = E[Y 1_A], \text{ all } X \in \mathscr{F}$

Taking X as in (3.11), it follows that $E[1_A X] = x_A P\{A\}$ when $A \in \mathscr{P}$, the partition corresponding to $\mathscr{F}$. Meanwhile, taking the same $A \in \mathscr{P}$ one has

$$E[Y 1_A] = \sum_{\omega \in A} Y(\omega)P\{\omega\} = P\{A\}\sum_{\omega \in A} Y(\omega)P\{\omega\}/P\{A\} = P\{A\}E[Y|A]$$

Hence (3.14) implies

$$x_A = E[Y|A], \text{ all } A \in \mathscr{P}$$

which means $X = E[Y|\mathscr{F}]$. This characterization of $E[Y|\mathscr{F}]$ is summarized in the following.

(3.15)   Given an arbitrary random variable Y, the conditional expectation $E[Y|\mathscr{F}]$ is the unique random variable such that

(a) $E[Y|\mathscr{F}] \in \mathscr{F}$

(b) $E[E[Y|\mathscr{F}]1_A] = E[Y 1_A], \text{ all } A \in \mathscr{F}$

We now turn to the topic of martingales. We are given a filtered probability space together with an adapted stochastic process $Z = \{Z_t;\ t = 0, 1, \ldots, T\}$. The process Z is said to be a *martingale* if

$$E[Z_{t+s}|\mathscr{F}_t] = Z_t, \text{ all } s, t \geqslant 0$$

Example 3.4 Consider a coin with P(heads) $\equiv p$, where $0 < p < 1$. Let

$N_t \equiv$ number of heads after t independent coin flips,
$Z_t = N_t - pt$, and
$\mathcal{F}_t \equiv$ algebra corresponding to the observations of the first t coin flips.

It is easy to see that $E[N_t] = pt$. Moreover, Z is a martingale, because

$$
\begin{aligned}
E[Z_{t+s}|\mathcal{F}_t] &= E[N_{t+s} - p(t+s)|\mathcal{F}_t] \\
&= E[N_{t+s} - N_t + N_t|\mathcal{F}_t] - p(t+s) \\
&= E[N_{t+s} - N_t|\mathcal{F}_t] + E[N_t|\mathcal{F}_t] - pt - ps \\
&= E[N_s] + N_t - pt - ps \\
&= N_t - pt = Z_t
\end{aligned}
$$

Here we used the self-evident fact that coin flips $t+1, t+2, \ldots, t+s$ are independent of the first t flips, in which case the expected number of heads observed during flips $t+1, t+2, \ldots, t+s$, conditioned on the observations of the first t flips, is equal to the expected number of heads observed during s flips.

Martingales are often used as models of fair gambling games, where Z_t represents the gambler's stake after t plays of the game.

I conclude by mentioning two kinds of processes that are closely related to martingales. An adapted stochastic process $Z = \{Z_t; t = 0, 1, \ldots, T\}$ is said to be a *supermartingale* if

$$
E[Z_{t+s}|\mathcal{F}_t] \leqslant Z_t, \text{ all } s, t \geqslant 0
$$

Thus a supermartingale resembles a martingale, except that the conditional expectation of the future value can be less than as well as equal to the current value. All martingales are supermartingales, but not vice versa.

Finally, an adapted stochastic process $Z = \{Z_t; t = 0, 1, \ldots, T\}$ is said to be a *submartingale* if

$$
E[Z_{t+s}|\mathcal{F}_t] \geqslant Z_t, \text{ all } s, t \geqslant 0
$$

Thus Z is a submartingale if and only if $-Z$ is a supermartingale. Also, Z is a martingale if and only if it is both a submartingale and a supermartingale.

Exercise 3.7 Verify (3.10).

Exercise 3.8 Verify (3.12).

Exercise 3.9 With $X = \{X_t; t = 0, 1, \ldots, T\}$ an adapted stochastic process, show that the following are equivalent:

(a) X is a martingale.
(b) $X_t = E[X_T|\mathcal{F}_t]$, $t = 0, 1, \ldots, T - 1$.
(c) $E[\Delta X_{t+1}|\mathcal{F}_t] = 0$, $t = 0, 1, \ldots, T - 1$.

3.4   Economic Considerations

I now return to our securities market model and develop a relationship that is analogous to the one for single period models: there are no arbitrage opportunities if and only if there exists a risk neutral probability measure. This and most other economic concepts developed for single period models hold in a rather similar fashion for multiperiod models; really only the details are different.

An *arbitrage opportunity* in the case of a multiperiod securities market is some trading strategy H such that

(a) $V_0 = 0$,
(b) $V_T \geqslant 0$,
(c) $EV_T > 0$, and
(d) H is self-financing.

As with single period models, the existence of an arbitrage opportunity is not consistent with economic equilibrium. The presence of a possibility of turning zero dollars into a positive amount of dollars without any risk of losing money would beckon market forces that would disrupt the underlying structure of security prices.

In view of (3.3), it is immediate that

(3.16)   The self-financing trading strategy H is an arbitrage opportunity if and only if

(a) $V_0^* = 0$,
(b) $V_T^* \geqslant 0$, and
(c) $EV_T^* > 0$.

And thanks to (3.4), we also have that

(3.17)   The self-financing trading stragegy H is an arbitrage opportunity if and only if

(a) $G_T^* \geqslant 0$, and
(b) $EG_T^* > 0$.

Example 3.3 (continued)   If $B_t = 1$ for $t = 0$, 1, and 2, then there are no arbitrage opportunities. If the investor has any position at all in the risky asset at time $t = 1$, then there is always the possibility that the price will move in a losing direction. If any position is taken in the risky asset at time $t = 0$, then there is the possibility of 'being in the red' at time $t = 1$ with no guaranteed way of recovering in the next period.

On the other hand, suppose $B_t = (1 + r)^t$ with the scalar $r \geqslant 12.5$ per cent. Consider the trading strategy where you start with zero dollars and do nothing at time $t = 0$ or at time $t = 1$ if $S_1 = 4$, but if $S_1 = 8$ then at time $t = 1$ you sell short one share of the risky asset (i.e., $H_1(2) = -1$) and invest the $8 proceeds in the bank account (i.e., $H_0(2) = 8/(1 + r)$). Then at time $t = 2$ the value of the portfolio is

$$V_2 = \begin{cases} (1+r)^2 H_0(2) + 9H_1(2) = 8(1+r) - 9 \geqslant 0, & \omega = \omega_1 \\ (1+r)^2 H_0(2) + 6H_1(2) = 8(1+r) - 6 \geqslant 0, & \omega = \omega_2 \end{cases}$$

Hence this trading strategy is an arbitrage opportunity.

It turns out that, as with single period models, there are no arbitrage opportunities if and only if there exists a risk neutral probability measure. But while risk neutral probabilities are defined in terms of ordinary expectations for single period models, they are defined in terms of martingales for multiperiod models.

A *risk neutral probability measure* (also called a *martingale measure*) is a probability measure Q such that

1   $Q(\omega) > 0$ for all $\omega \in \Omega$, and
2   The discounted price process S_n^* is a martingale under Q for every $n = 1, 2, \ldots, N$.

In other words, in view of the definition of martingales, a risk neutral probability measure Q must satisfy

$$E_Q[S_n^*(t+s)|\mathcal{F}_t] = S_n^*(t), \ t, s \geqslant 0$$

that is,

(3.18) $$E_Q[B_t S_n(t+s)/B_{t+s}|\mathcal{F}_t] = S_n(t), \ t, s \geqslant 0$$

Example 3.3 (continued)   Suppose $B_t = (1+r)^t$ where $r \geqslant 0$ is a constant. We want to compute a martingale measure, if there is one. To do this, we can use (3.18) for different values of s and t, giving the following equations:

$t = 0, \ s = 1:$ $5(1+r) = 8[Q(\omega_1) + Q(\omega_2)] + 4[Q(\omega_3) + Q(\omega_4)]$

$t = 0, \ s = 2:$ $5(1+r)^2 = 9Q(\omega_1) + 6Q(\omega_2) + 6Q(\omega_3) + 3Q(\omega_4)$

$t = 1, \ s = 1:$ $8(1+r) = [9Q(\omega_1) + 6Q(\omega_2)]/[Q(\omega_1) + Q(\omega_2)]$

$t = 1, \ s = 1:$ $4(1+r) = [6Q(\omega_3) + 3Q(\omega_4)]/[Q(\omega_3) + Q(\omega_4)]$

Taking any three of these equations together with the equation $Q(\omega_1) + \ldots + Q(\omega_4) = 1$ allows one to solve for the four unknowns:

$$Q(\omega_1) = \left(\frac{1+5r}{4}\right)\left(\frac{2+8r}{3}\right) \quad Q(\omega_2) = \left(\frac{1+5r}{4}\right)\left(\frac{1-8r}{3}\right)$$

$$Q(\omega_3) = \left(\frac{3-5r}{4}\right)\left(\frac{1+4r}{3}\right) \quad Q(\omega_4) = \left(\frac{3-5r}{4}\right)\left(\frac{2-4r}{3}\right)$$

Note these are all strictly positive, and thus we have a valid probability measure, if $0 \leqslant r < 1/8$. On the other hand, if $r \geqslant 1/8$ then $Q(\omega_2)$ is not strictly positive, in which case there is no martingale measure.

If $r < 1/8$, then you cannot find any situation (that is, any time and state) where the discounted price next period can be strictly higher than the current discounted price unless there is a chance the discounted price next period is strictly lower. Nor can you find any situation where the discounted price next period can be strictly lower than the current discounted price unless there is a chance the discounted price next period is strictly higher. Hence in every situation there is a risk that a non-zero position in the risky security will lose money over the next period, and so there are no arbitrage opportunities.

On the other hand, if $r \geqslant 1/8$, then if $S_1 = 8$ at time $t = 1$ (which means the state is ω or ω_2), then $S_2^*(\omega_1) \leqslant S_1^*(\omega_1)$ and $S_2^*(\omega_2) < S_1^*(\omega_2)$. Here is a situation where the discounted price next period can be strictly lower than the present price without there being any risk that the discounted price next period can be strictly higher. Of course, now there is an arbitrage opportunity, as was described earlier.

We now come to the principal result of this section.

(3.19)   There are no arbitrage opportunities if and only if there exists a martingale measure Q.

A proof of this is similar to our proof of the analogous result for single period models. In order to explain one direction, namely why the existence of a martingale measure implies there are no arbitrage opportunities, we will first provide a useful result that is in general terms:

(3.20)   If Z is a martingale and H is a predictable process, then

$$G_t \equiv \sum_{u=1}^{t} H_u \, \Delta Z_u$$

is also a martingale.

This follows from some straightforward calculations using some properties of conditional expectations. Let $s, t \geqslant 0$ be arbitrary. Then

$$
\begin{aligned}
E[G_{t+s}|\mathcal{F}_t] &= E[G_{t+s} - G_t + G_t|\mathcal{F}_t] \\
&= E[H_{t+1}\Delta Z_{t+1} + \ldots + H_{t+s}\Delta Z_{t+s}|\mathcal{F}_t] + G_t \\
&= E[E[H_{t+1}\Delta Z_{t+1}|\mathcal{F}_t] \mid \mathcal{F}_t] \\
&\quad + E[E[H_{t+2}\Delta Z_{t+2}|\mathcal{F}_{t+1}] \mid \mathcal{F}_t] + \ldots \\
&\quad + E[E[H_{t+s}\Delta Z_{t+s}|\mathcal{F}_{t+s-1}] \mid \mathcal{F}_t] + G_t \\
&= E[H_{t+1}E[\Delta Z_{t+1}|\mathcal{F}_t] \mid \mathcal{F}_t] \\
&\quad + E[H_{t+2}E[\Delta Z_{t+2}|\mathcal{F}_{t+1}] \mid \mathcal{F}_t] + \ldots \\
&\quad + E[H_{t+s}E[\Delta Z_{t+s}|\mathcal{F}_{t+s-1} \mid \mathcal{F}_t] + G_t \\
&= E[H_{t+1} \cdot 0|\mathcal{F}_t] + \ldots + E[H_{t+s} \cdot 0|\mathcal{F}_t] + G_t \\
&= G_t
\end{aligned}
$$

where the next to last equality follows from the fact that Z is a martingale. Hence G is a martingale too.

It follows directly from (3.4) and (3.20) that we have the following result, which is of considerable practical importance:

(3.21) If Q is a martingale measure and H is a self-financing trading strategy, then V', the discounted value process corresponding to H, is a martingale under Q.

We can use (3.21) to quickly show that the existence of a martingale measure Q implies there cannot be any arbitrage opportunities. Suppose H is an arbitrary self-financing trading strategy with $V_T^* \geqslant 0$ and $EV_T^* > 0$. This implies $E_Q V_T^* > 0$. Since by (3.21) V^* is a martingale under Q, it follows that $V_0^* = E_Q V_T^* > 0$. Hence by (3.16) H cannot be an arbitrage opportunity, nor can any other trading strategies be arbitrage opportunities, by the arbitrary choice of H.

One can show the converse of (3.19) in several ways, such as by using an extension of the separating hyperplane theorem argument that was used for the case of single period models. However, it is much easier to build on what we already know for single period models, namely, the single-period result analogous to (3.19). In particular, knowing there are no arbitrage opportunities for the multiperiod model, one can construct one-period conditional probabilities that are compatible with risk neutrality. The martingale measure Q can then be computed from these conditional probabilities by multiplying them together in accordance with the information structure of the multiperiod model. In other words, the martingale measure for the multiperiod model is constructed by 'pasting together' various single period models.

To be more precise, there is one underlying single period model corresponding to each non-terminal node of the tree structure of the information submodel, that is, to each $A \in \mathscr{P}_t$ (the minimal partition corresponding to $\mathscr{F}_t$) for each $t < T$. The single period 'time 0' discounted price of risky security n is $S_n^*(t, \omega), \omega \in A$, which is constant on A. The corresponding single period 'sample space' consists of one state for each cell $A' \subseteq A$ that is a member of the partition $\mathscr{P}_{t+1}$ (that is, one state for each branch coming out of the node in the tree structure of the information submodel). Finally, the 'time 1' discounted prices for this single period model are given by the values of $S_n^*(t + 1, \omega)$ for $\omega \in A$.

If any underlying single period model has an arbitrage opportunity in the single period sense, then the multiperiod model must have an arbitrage opportunity in the multiperiod sense. To see this, suppose there exists an arbitrage opportunity $\hat{H}$ for the single period model corresponding to some $A \in \mathscr{P}_t$ for $t < T$. This means that the discounted gain $\hat{H}_1 \Delta S_1^*(t + 1) + \ldots + \hat{H}_N \Delta S_N^*(t + 1)$ is non-negative and not identical to zero on the event A. Now construct a multiperiod trading strategy H by taking

$$H_n(s, \omega) = \begin{cases} \hat{H}_n, & s = t+1, \omega \in A, n = 1,\ldots,N \\ -\hat{H}_1 S_1^*(t) - \ldots - \hat{H}_N S_N^*(t), & s = t+1, \omega \in A, n = 0 \\ \hat{H}_1 \Delta S_1^*(t+1) + \ldots + \hat{H}_N \Delta S_N^*(t+1), & s > t+1, \omega \in A, n = 0 \\ 0, & \text{otherwise} \end{cases}$$

Thus, as can be verified with a little work, H is the self-financing trading strategy which starts with zero money and does nothing unless the event A occurs at time t, in which case at time t the position $\hat{H}_n$ is taken in the nth risky security, while the position in the bank account is chosen in a self-financing manner. Subsequently, no position is taken in any of the risky securities; any non-zero value of the portfolio is reflected by a position in the bank account. If $\hat{H}$ is an arbitrage opportunity for the single period model, then this subsequent position in the bank account will, in fact, be non-negative for all $\omega \in \Omega$ and strictly positive for at least one $\omega \in A$. In particular, under H one will have $V_0^* = 0$, $V_T^* \geqslant 0$, and $V_T^*(\omega) > 0$ for at least one $\omega \in \Omega$, that is, H will be an arbitrage opportunity.

In other words, we see that

(3.22)   If the multiperiod model does not have any arbitrage opportunities, then none of the underlying single period models has any arbitrage opportunities in the single period sense.

Consequently, in view of what we know for single period models, corresponding to each underlying single period model is a risk neutral probability measure. For example, corresponding to each $A \in \mathscr{P}_t$ for $t < T$ is a probability measure, denoted $Q(t, A)$, on the single period sample space. This probability measure gives positive mass to each cell $A' \subseteq A$ in the partition $\mathscr{P}_{t+1}$, it sums to one over such cells, and it satisfies $E_{Q(t,A)} \Delta S_n^*(t+1) = 0$ for $n = 1, \ldots, N$.

Notice that $Q(t, A)$ gives rise to a probability for each branch in the information tree that emerges from the node corresponding to (t, A). These probabilities should be thought of as conditional risk neutral probabilities, given the event A at time t. Hence starting with a collection of risk neutral probability measures $Q(t, A)$ for all $A \in \mathscr{F}_t$ and $t < T$, one can construct a probability measure Q for the whole multiperiod model by proceeding in an obvious manner: $Q(\omega)$ is set equal to the product of the conditional probabilities along the path from the node at $t = 0$ to the node corresponding to (T, ω). Clearly $\sum_{\omega \in \Omega} Q(\omega) = 1$. Moreover, $Q(\omega) > 0$ for every $\omega \in \Omega$, because all the conditional risk neutral probabilities are strictly positive.

It remains to explain why the probability measure Q that has been constructed is actually a martingale measure. Since $E_{Q(t,A)} \Delta S_n^*(t+1) = 0$ for $n = 1, \ldots, N, A \in \mathscr{P}_t$ and $t < T$, it follows that

(3.23) $E_Q[\Delta S_n^*(t+1)|\mathscr{F}_t] = 0$ for n = 1, \ldots, N and t < T

Now take arbitrary $s, t, \geqslant 0$ and n:

$$
\begin{aligned}
E_Q[S_n^*(t+s)|\mathscr{F}_t] &= E_Q[\Delta S_n^*(t+s) + \ldots + \Delta S_n^*(t+1) + S_n^*(t)|\mathscr{F}_t] \\
&= E_Q[E_Q[\Delta S_n^*(t+s)|\mathscr{F}_{t+s-1}] \mid \mathscr{F}_t] + \ldots \\
&\quad + E_Q[E_Q[\Delta S_n^*(t+1)|\mathscr{F}_t] \mid \mathscr{F}_t] + S_n^*(t) \\
&= E_Q[0|\mathscr{F}_t] + \ldots + E_Q[0|\mathscr{F}_t] + S_n^*(t) \\
&= S_n^*(t)
\end{aligned}
$$

where the next to last equality follows from (3.23) (note this calculation demonstrates that, in general, an expression like (3.23) is equivalent to that used in the definition of a martingale). Hence S_n^* is a martingale under Q, and so Q is a risk neutral probability measure.

The preceding explanation of the fundamental principle (3.19) may be a bit abstract, but it becomes transparent if you look at the picture of an information tree for a simple multiperiod model.

Example 3.3 (continued)   Suppose $B_t = (1 + r)^t$ with r a constant, as before. Looking at the node corresponding to $t = 0$ (which has two branches emerging, corresponding to $\{\omega_1, \omega_2\}$ and $\{\omega_3, \omega_4\}$, respectively), one sees that the conditional probability measure $Q(0, \Omega)$ can be obtained by solving $5 = p8/(1 + r) + (1 - p)4/(1 + r)$. Thus p, the conditional probability associated with the $\{\omega_1, \omega_2\}$ branch, is $(1 + 5r)/4$, in which case the conditional probability associated with the other branch is $(3 - 5r)/4$. In a similar fashion, one analyzes the $(1, \{\omega_1, \omega_2\})$ node and finally the $(1, \{\omega_3, \omega_4\})$ node to obtain $(2 + 8r)/3$, $(1 - 8r)/3$, $(1 + 8r)/3$, and $(2 - 8r)/3$ for the conditional probabilities associated with the branches leading into the $(2, \omega_1)$, $(2, \omega_2)$, $(2, \omega_3)$, and $(2, \omega_4)$ nodes, respectively. Notice that all of these conditional probabilities are strictly positive when $0 \leqslant r < 1/8$, in accordance with our earlier observation that arbitrage opportunities will exist when $r \geqslant 1/8$. Moreover, notice these conditional probabilities are unique, that is, no other choices will yield risk neutral probabilities for the underlying single period models. Hence multiplying the conditional probabilities along the four paths leading to the four states in Ω, we quickly obtain the same martingale measure Q that was derived earlier in a different way. Indeed, we now recognize the earlier expressions for $Q(\omega)$ as being simply the products of the appropriate conditional probabilities.

The martingale measures can be defined in terms of return processes instead of price processes. We saw above that a strictly positive probability measure Q is a martingale measure if and only if (3.23) is satisfied. Since $\Delta S_n^*(t+1) = S_n^*(t)\Delta R_n^*(t+1)$, (3.23) is true if and only if $S_n^*(t)E_Q[\Delta R_n^*(t+1)|\mathscr{F}_t] = 0$ for all n and $t < T$. But $S_n^*(t) = 0$ implies $\Delta R_n^*(t+1) = 0$ by the definition of the return process, so this last statement is true if and only if:

$$
(3.24) \qquad E_Q[\Delta R_n^*(t+1)] = 0, \text{ all } n \text{ and } t < T
$$

that is, if and only if R_n^* is a martingale under Q for all n. In summary, we have

(3.25)   The strictly positive probability measure Q is a martingale measure if and only if R_n^* is a martingale under Q for $n = 1, \ldots, N$.

The corresponding requirement in terms of the (undiscounted) return process R_n is not so nice. It is not difficult to verify that

$$\Delta S_n^*(t+1) = S_n^*(t) \left(\frac{\Delta R_n(t+1) - \Delta R_0(t+1)}{1 + \Delta R_0(t+1)} \right)$$

so if all the price processes are strictly positive, then (3.23) is the same as

(3.26) $E_Q \left[\dfrac{\Delta R_n(t+1) - \Delta R_0(t+1)}{1 + \Delta R_0(t+1)} \bigg| \mathscr{F}_t \right] = 0$, all n and $t < T$

Of course, we could have known immediately that this is equivalent to (3.24), in view of the expression in section 3.2 for ΔR_n^* in terms of ΔR_n.

Now suppose some of the securities pay a dividend. To check whether there are any arbitrage opportunities, what really matters are the return processes of the securities, so principle (3.25) remains true. In other words, there are no arbitrage opportunities if and only if (3.24) (or (3.26)) holds, where now the return processes are defined in terms of dividend processes as in section 3.2: $\Delta R_n(t+1) = [\Delta S_n(t+1) + \Delta D_n(t+1)]/S_n(t)$ and $\Delta R_n^*(t+1) = [\Delta S_n^*(t+1) + \Delta D_n(t+1)/B_{t+1}]/S_n^*(t)$. Thus (3.24) can be rewritten as

(3.27) $E_Q[S_n^*(t+1) + \Delta D_n(t+1)/B_{t+1} | \mathscr{F}_t] = S_n^*(t)$, all n and t < T

This makes sense: if the investor purchases one unit of security n at time t, then the expected discounted value of this investment next period is equal to the discounted value of the time t position.

Using (3.27) and a fundamental property of conditional expectations, it is easy to see that

$$E_Q[S_n^*(t+2) + \Delta D_n(t+2)/B_{t+2} + \Delta D_n(t+1)/B_{t+1} | \mathscr{F}_t]$$
$$= E_Q[E_Q[S_n^*(t+2) + \Delta D_n(t+2)/B_{t+2} | \mathscr{F}_{t+1}]$$
$$+ \Delta D_n(t+1)/B_{t+1} | \mathscr{F}_t]$$
$$= E_Q[S_n^*(t+1) + \Delta D_n(t+1)/B_{t+1} | \mathscr{F}_t]$$
$$= S_n^*(t)$$

By a generalization of this argument, we therefore have:

(3.28)   If Q is a risk neutral probability measure, then for each risky security and every $t, s \geqslant 0$
$$S_n^*(t) = E_Q[\Delta D_n(t+1)/B_{t+1} + \ldots + \Delta D_n(t+s)/B_{t+s} | + S_n^*(t+s) \, \mathscr{F}_t]$$

Thus the time t discounted price equals the conditional expected value of the discounted dividend payments up through time $t+s$ plus the time $t+s$ discounted price.

Turning to another topic which is analogous to a notion introduced for single period models, a *linear pricing measure* is a non-negative vector $\pi = (\pi_1, \ldots, \pi_k)$ such that for every self-financing trading strategy H you have

$$V_0 = \sum_\omega \pi(\omega) \, V_T^*(\omega)$$

If Q is a risk neutral probability measure, then clearly it is also a linear pricing measure. Conversely, any strictly positive linear pricing measure π must be a risk neutral probability measure. To see this, first take any trading strategy with $H_1 = \ldots = H_N = 0$ to conclude $\pi_1 + \ldots + \pi_k = 1$. Next, fix arbitrary $n, t < T$, and some event $A \in \mathscr{F}_t = 1$, and consider the self-financing trading strategy which starts at time $t = 0$ with \$1 in the bank account and does no transactions unless event A occurs at time t, in which case all the money is transferred into a long position in security n for one period, after which it is immediately transferred back into the bank account, where it remains until time T. The bank account equals B_t at time t, so with security n having value $S_n(t)1_A$ (here 1_A denotes the indicator function of the event A, that is, $1_A(\omega) = 1$ if $\omega \in A$, whereas $1_A(\omega) = 0$ if $\omega \notin A$), this strategy entails a time t purchase of $B_t/S_n(t) = 1/S_n^*(t)$ units of security n if event A occurs. Since all the money is transferred back to the bank account at time $t + 1$, the discounted gain under this trading strategy will be

$$G_T^* = (1_A/S_n^*(t)) \, \Delta S_n^*(t+1) = 1_A \, \Delta R_n^*(t+1)$$

Now the trading strategy is self-financing, so (3.4) holds. Thus if π is a linear pricing measure, it follows that

$$\sum_\omega \pi(\omega) G_T^*(\omega) = 0$$

This is true for every $A \in \mathscr{F}_t$, so taking $Q(\omega) = \pi(\omega)$ we conclude by (3.24), (3.25), and our expression for G_T^* that Q is a risk neutral probability measure.

In summary, a vector π is a linear pricing measure if and only if it is a probability measure on Ω under which all the discounted price processes are martingales. This is the multiperiod generalization of principle (1.8).

As with single period models, the *law of one price* holds for a multiperiod model if there do not exist two trading strategies, say $\hat{H}$ and $\tilde{H}$, such that $\hat{V}_T(\omega) = \tilde{V}_T(\omega)$ for all $\omega \in \Omega$ but $\hat{V}_0 \neq \tilde{V}_0$. Clearly the existence of a linear pricing measure implies that the law of one price will hold.

Denote

$$\mathbb{W} = \{X \in \mathbb{R}^K : X = G^* \text{ for some trading strategy H}\}$$
$$\mathbb{W}^\perp = \{Y \in \mathbb{R}^K : X \cdot Y = 0 \text{ for all X} \in \mathbb{W}\}$$
$$\mathbb{A} = \{X \in \mathbb{R}^K : X \geqslant 0, \ X \neq 0\}$$
$$\mathbb{P} = \{X \in \mathbb{R}^K : X_1 + \ldots + X_K = 1, \ X \geqslant 0\} \text{ and}$$
$$\mathbb{P}^+ = \{X \in \mathbb{P} \ : X_1 > 0, \ldots, X_K > 0\}$$

Then just as with single period models, $\mathbb{P} \cap \mathbb{W}^{\perp}$ is the set of all the linear pricing measures and $\mathbb{M} \equiv \mathbb{P}^{+} \cap \mathbb{W}^{\perp}$ is the set of all risk neutral probability measures. Moreover, fundamental principle (3.19) is the same thing as saying $\mathbb{W} \cap \mathbb{A} = \emptyset$ if and only if $\mathbb{M} \neq \emptyset$. Notice that $\mathbb{M}$ is a convex set whose closure equals $\mathbb{P} \cap \mathbb{W}^{\perp}$.

Exercise 3.10   Consider a 2-period problem with $\Omega = \{\omega_1, \ldots, \omega_5\}$, $r = 0$, and one risky security:

ω	$S_0(\omega)$	$S_1(\omega)$	$S_2(\omega)$
ω_1	6	5	3
ω_2	6	5	4
ω_3	6	5	8
ω_4	6	7	6
ω_5	6	7	8

The filtration is the one generated by this risky security. Show that the set of all the martingale measures is

$$\mathbb{M} = \{Q \in \mathbb{R}^5 : Q_1 = q/2, Q_2 = (3 - 5q)/8, \ Q_3 = (1 + q)/8,$$
$$Q_4 = Q_5 = 1/4, 0 < q < 3/5\}$$

Show that $\mathbb{P} \cap \mathbb{W}^{\perp}$, the set of all the linear pricing measures, is equal to $\mathbb{M} \cup \{(0, 3/8, 1/8, 1/4, 1/4)\} \cup \{3/10, 0, 1/5, 1/4, 1/4)\}$.

Exercise 3.11   Let Q be a probability measure, such as a risk neutral probability measure, that is equivalent to P, set $X_T(\omega) = Q(\omega)/P(\omega)$, and let $X_t = E[X_T | \mathcal{F}_t]$ for $t = 0, 1, \ldots, T - 1$. Show that X is strictly positive with $X_0 = 1$. Let $\{Y_t; \ t = 0, 1, \ldots, T\}$ be a stochastic process. Show that Y is a martingale under Q if and only if the process $\{X_t Y_t; \ t = 0, 1, \ldots, T\}$ is a martingale under P. (Hint: use the abstract definition of conditional expectations).

Exercise 3.12   Use exercise 3.11 to show that if there exists a martingale measure, then there must exist a strictly positive, adapted, real-valued process $Z = \{Z_t; \ t = 0, 1, \ldots, T\}$ satisfying $Z_0 = 1$ and such that $B_t Z_t, S_1(t) Z_t, \ldots,$ and $S_N(t) Z_t$ are all martingales under P. Conversely, show that if there exists a process Z as indicated, then there must exist a martingale measure Q. Moreover, show how to compute Q from a specified Z. (Note: such a process Z is called a *state-price deflator*.)

3.5   The Binomial Model

The 'binomial model' is a simple yet very important model for the price of a single risky security. It is commonly used by practitioners, for example, to determine the price of various kinds of stock options.

Each period there are two possibilities: the security price either goes up by the factor u ($u > 1$) or it goes down by the factor d ($0 < d < 1$). The probability of an up move during a period is equal to the parameter p, and the moves over time are independent of each other. Hence the binomial model is related to the process N_t (introduced in example 3.4) representing the number of heads after t independent coin flips. The process N_t, in turn, is based upon what is called a *Bernoulli process*.

The stochastic process $\{X_t; t = 1, 2, \ldots\}$ is said to be a *Bernoulli process* with parameter p if the random variables $X_1, X_2, \ldots$ are independent and $P(X_t = 1) = 1 - P(X_t = 0) = p$ for all t. Hence one should think of a sequence of coin flips where the event $\{X_t = 1\}$ means that the outcome of flip number t is a 'head.' The underlying sample space Ω consists of all the sequences of the form

$$\omega = (0, 1, 0, 0, 1, 1, \ldots)$$

with each $\omega \in \Omega$ providing, in an obvious manner, a record of a possible sequence of flips.

Strictly speaking, the Bernoulli process features an infinite number of coinflips, so the vector ω has an infinite number of components and the sample space Ω has an infinite number of states. However, our securities market model features just a finite number T of periods, so for our purposes it suffices to consider a 'modified' Bernoulli process corresponding to only T coin flips. Now each state ω will have T components, each being either a 0 or a 1. There are 2^T vectors like this, and the sample space for our modified Bernoulli process will have exactly one of each. Whether standard or modified, $X_t(\omega)$ will take the value 1 or 0 as the tth component of $\omega \in \Omega$ is 1 or 0, respectively. Moreover, $\mathscr{F}_t$ will be the algebra corresponding to the observations of the first t coin flips, that is, $\mathscr{P}_t$ will be the partition consisting of 2^t cells, one for each possible sequence of t coin flips. And the probability measure is given by $P(\omega) = p^n(1 - p)^{T-n}$, where $\omega \in \Omega$ is any state corresponding to n 'heads' and T-n 'tails.'

The process $\{N_t; t = 1, 2, \ldots\}$ is defined in terms of the Bernoulli process (or the modified Bernoulli process) by setting

$$N_t(\omega) = X_1(\omega) + \ldots + X_t(\omega)$$

Hence the random variable N_t should be thought of as the number of heads in the first t coin flips (or as the number of up moves by the security during the first t periods). Since $E[X_t] = p$ and $\text{var}(X_t) = p(1 - p)$, it follows that, for any t,

$$E[N_t] = tp$$

and

$$\text{var}\,(N_t) = tp(1 - p)$$

Moreover, it is not difficult to show that

(3.29)   For all $t = 1, 2, \ldots$

$$P(N_t = n) = \binom{t}{n} p^n (1 - p)^{t-n}, \; n = 0, 1, \ldots, t.$$

This is called the *binomial probability distribution,* and

$$\binom{t}{n} = \frac{t!}{n!(t-n)!}$$

is called a *binomial coefficient.*

We are now ready to define the binomial security price model. This model features four parameters: p, d, u, and S_0, where $0 < p < 1, 0 < d < 1 < u$, and, of course, $S_0 > 0$. The time t price of the security is given simply by

$$S_t = S_0\, u^{N_t}\, d^{t-N_t}, \quad t = 1, 2, \ldots, T$$

Hence, as advertised, each period there are two possibilities: either with probability p the coin flip is heads and the price goes up by the factor u, or with probability $1 - p$ it is tails and the price goes down by the factor d. Moreover, in view of (3.29), the probability distribution of S_t is given by

$$(3.30) \qquad P(S_t = S_0 u^n d^{t-n}) = \binom{t}{n} p^n (1-p)^{t-n}, \; n = 0, 1, \ldots, t$$

With 2^T elements in the underlying sample space, the information tree terminates with 2^T nodes, as illustrated in figure 3.4. In particular, there are 2^T possible sample paths for the security price process. However, it is convenient to use a more compact diagram to illustrate the various possible sample paths. The event $\{S_t(\omega) = S_0 u^n d^{t-n}\}$ occurs if and only if exactly n out of the first t moves are 'up' moves; the order of these t moves does not matter. For example, $\{S_2(\omega) = S_0 ud\}$ if either the first move is an 'up' and

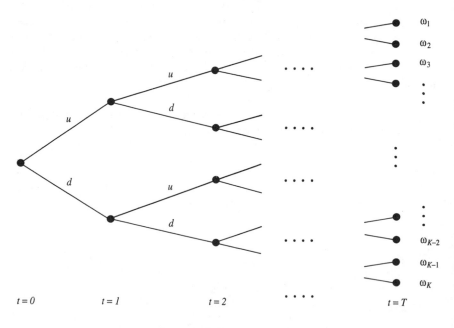

Figure 3.4   Information tree for the binomial model ($K = 2^T$)

the second is a 'down,' or vice versa. As you can see from (3.30), at time t the price process S_t can take one of only $t+1$ possible values, although there are 2^t possible sample paths of length t. Figure 3.5 shows a network where there is one node corresponding to each event of the form $\{S_t(\omega) = S_0 u^n d^{t-n}\}$. Note that the number of ways this event can occur is equal to the number of paths to this event from the beginning node, and this is equal to $\binom{t}{n}$. While the kind of network shown in figure 3.5 is convenient for many purposes, it should not be confused with the information structure network as in figure 3.4.

A desirable feature of the binomial security price model is that its return process is given simply by

$$(3.31) \qquad \Delta R_1(t) = u^{X_t} d^{1-X_t} - 1, \ t = 1, 2, \ldots, T$$

In other words, either $\Delta R_1 = u - 1$ with probability p or $\Delta R_1 = d - 1$ with probability $1 - p$. In particular, the value of the return process is independent of the current price of the security, a feature that is often desirable when modeling securities such as common stocks.

What about the martingale measure? Assuming the interest rate is constant so that $\Delta R_0(t) = r$ for all t, by (3.26) and (3.31) we must have

$$q \left[\frac{u - 1 - r}{1 + r} \right] + (1 - q) \left[\frac{d - 1 - r}{1 + r} \right] = 0$$

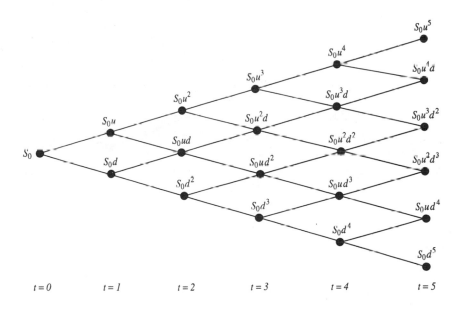

Figure 3.5 Lattice showing price process for the binomial model ($T = 5$)

where q is the conditional probability the next move is an 'up' move given the information $\mathscr{F}_t$ at any time t. Hence

$$q = \frac{1 + r - d}{u - d}$$

for all $\mathscr{F}_t$ and t. Since we need $q < 1$, we realize that there will exist a martingale measure if and only if $u > 1 + r$. In this case the martingale measure is given by

$$Q(\omega) = q^n (1 - q)^{T-n}$$

where $\omega \in \Omega$ is any state corresponding to n 'ups' and $T - n$ 'downs.' It follows that the probability distribution of S_t under the risk neutral probability measure is given for all t by

(3.32) $\qquad Q(S_t = S_0 u^n d^{t-n}) = \binom{t}{n} q^n (1 - q)^{t-n}, \; n = 0, 1, \ldots, t$

The binomial model lends itself to some useful computations, such as the probability distribution for the maximum value achieved by the security process during the T periods. We will derive this for the special case where $d = u^{-1}$, thereby leading to the simplification $S_t = S_0 u^{2N_t - t}$. Define

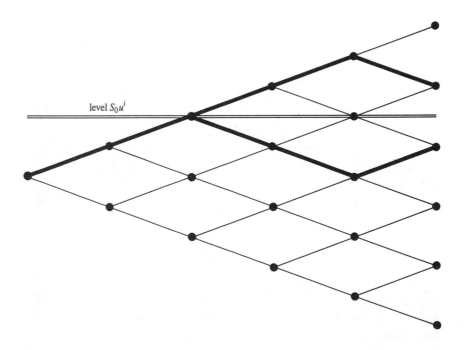

Figure 3.6   The reflection principle

$Y_T = \max\{S_t : t = 0, 1, \ldots, T\}$, and note this random variable takes the $T+1$ values S_0, S_0u, … S_0u^T. Our aim is to compute $P\{Y_T \geqslant S_0u^i\}$ for $i = 1, 2, \ldots, T$.

Fix i and notice that $S_t \geqslant S_0u^i$ if and only if $2N_t - t \geqslant i$, so $P\{Y_T \geqslant S_0u^i\}$ is the same as $P\{2N_t - t \geqslant i$ for some $t\}$. We shall compute this latter probability with something called the *reflection principle*, as illustrated in figure 3.6. The idea is to define the *first passage time* $\tau_i \equiv \min\{t : 2N_t - t = i\}$, where $\tau = \infty$ if $2N_t - t < i$ for all $t \leqslant T$, and consider all the sample paths for which $\tau_i \leqslant T$. There are three mutually exclusive events. If i equals one of the values T, $T - 2$, $T - 4, \ldots$, then it is possible to have $2N_T - T - i$, in which case, of course, $\tau_i \leqslant T$. Secondly, you can have $\tau_i < T$ and $2N_T - T > i$. Thirdly, you can have $\tau_i < T$ and $2N_T - T < i$. Hence

$$P\{Y_T \geqslant S_0u^i\} = P\{2N_t - t \geqslant i \text{ for some t}\}$$
$$= P\{event\ 1\} + P\{event\ 2\} + P\{event\ 3\}$$

This first probability is

$$P\{event\ 1\} = P\{N_t = (T + i)/2\} = \binom{T}{\frac{T+1}{2}} p^{(T+i)/2}(1 - p)^{(T-i)/2}$$

when $T + i$ is an even number, whereas $P\{event\ 1\} - 0$, otherwise. The second probability is easy, because if $2N_T - T > i$, then automatically $\tau_i < T$. Thus

$$P\{event\ 2\} = P\{N_T > (T + i)/2\} = \sum_{n=n^*}^{T} \binom{T}{n} p^n(1 - p)^{T-n}$$

where n^* denotes the smallest integer strictly greater than $(T + i)/2$ (this sum is taken to be zero if $n^* > T$).

Computing the third probability is more difficult, and this is where we use the reflection principle. The idea is that each sample path in event 2 is paired with a unique sample path in event 3, as illustrated in figure 3.6. The sample paths coincide up to time τ_i, and then each is the mirror image of the other across the level i. Hence the number of sample paths in the two events are equal, although the probabilities of the two events are not equal unless $p = 1/2$.

To finish the computation of $P\{event\ 3\}$ we need to do some book-keeping. Consider an arbitrary sample path from event 2, and suppose it is such that $N_T = n(\geqslant n^*)$. This sample path occurs with probability $p^N(1 - p)^{T-n}$ and there are $\binom{T}{n}$ sample paths with $N_T = n$. Now upon looking at figure 3.6 it becomes apparent that the 'partner' of this sample path terminates with $N_T = T + i - n$, a symmetric distance below the level $(T + i)/2$. The probability of this 'partner' sample path is $p^{T+i-n}(1 - p)^{n-i}$. Since there are $\binom{T}{n}$ sample paths in event 3 with $N_T - T + i - n$, it follows that

$$P\{\{event\ 3\} \cap \{N_T = T + i - n\}\} = \binom{T}{n} p^{T+i-n}(1 - p)^{n-i}$$

in which case

$$P\{event\ 3\} = \sum_{n=n^*}^{T} \binom{T}{n} p^{T+i-n}(1-p)^{n-i}$$

Hence we finally have

$$(3.33)\quad P\{Y_T \geqslant S_0 u^i\} = \binom{T}{\frac{T+i}{2}} p^{(T+i)/2}(1-p)^{(T-i)/2}$$

$$+ \sum_{n=n^*}^{T} \binom{T}{n} [p^n(1-p)^{T-n} + p^{T+i-n}(1-p)^{n-i}]$$

where the first term on the right hand side is zero when $T + i$ is an odd number and where n^* denotes the smallest integer strictly greater than $(T + i)/2$.

We now have, in principle, the probability distribution for the maximum security price during the T periods. More generally, these formulas can also be used for the maximum security price during the first t periods when $t < T$. Since the event $\{Y_t \geqslant S_0 u^i\}$ is the same as the event $\{T_i \leqslant t\}$, we also have the probability distribution for the first passage time to security price level $S_0 u^i$.

Similar formulas can be derived for the probability distributions of the minimum security price and the first passage times to price levels below S_0.

Exercise 3.13   Derive (3.29).

Exercise 3.14   For the case $T = 4$ and $d = 1/u$, compute the probability distributions of Y_T and τ_2.

3.6   Markov Models

This section will introduce a class of stochastic processes that share what is called the 'Markov property:' the future is independent of the past, given the present values of the process. Markov processes are important models of security prices, because they are often realistic representations of true prices and yet the Markov property leads to simplified computations.

Throughout this section the filtration $\mathbb{F} = \{\mathscr{F}_t;\ t = 0, 1, \ldots, T\}$ is generated by a stochastic process $X = \{X_t;\ t = 0, 1, \ldots, T\}$. This process takes values in some finite set E, called the *state space*. If $X_t = j \in E$, we shall say 'the process is in state j at time t.' The most common situation is for the state to be a scalar, but frequently it is more convenient for the state to be a vector. As usual, there is a sample space Ω and a probability measure P on it, and the information $\mathscr{F}_t$ should be thought of as the history of the present and past values of the process X.

The stochastic process X is said to be a *Markov chain* if

$$P\{X_{t+1} = j|\mathscr{F}_t\} = P\{X_{t+1} = j|X_t\}$$

for all $j \in E$ and all t. By elementary probability calculations, it follows that

(3.34) $P\{X_{t+s} = i|\mathscr{F}_t\} = P\{X_{t+s} = j|X_t\}$, all $s \geqslant 1$

Thus a Markov chain is a stochastic process where the only information useful for predicting future values is the current state; in other words, given the history of the process, the past values can be ignored as long as you know the present state.

The Markov chain X is said to be *stationary* or *time-homogeneous* if the conditional probabilities $P\{X_{t+1} = j|\mathscr{F}_t\}$ do not depend on time t. In this case it is convenient to define the *transition probabilities*

$$P(i,j) \equiv P\{X_{t+1} = j|X_t = i\}, \; i,j \in E$$

and to organize them into a *transition matrix*

$$P \equiv \left[P(i,j)\right]$$

Note this is a square matrix with the number of rows equal to the number of elements in the state space E. Moreover, the sum of the elements in each row of P equals one. It should be clear from the context whether P denotes the probability measure, a transition probability, or the transition matrix.

If the Markov chain is not stationary, then one can still talk about the transition probabilities, only now they depend on time: $P_t(i,j) \equiv P\{X_{t+1} = j|X_t = i\}$. In this more general case there is a distinct transition matrix for each point in time:

$$P_t \equiv \left[P_t(i,j)\right]$$

Example 3.5   The process $N = \{N_t; \; t = 1, \ldots, T\}$ studied in section 3.5 and representing the number of heads in t flips of a coin that lands 'head' with probability p is an example of a stationary Markov chain. For the state space it is convenient to take $\{0, 1, \ldots, T\}$, in which case the transition matrix is

$$P = \begin{pmatrix} 1-p & p & 0 & \cdots & 0 \\ 0 & 1-p & p & \cdots & 0 \\ \vdots & \vdots & \vdots & & \vdots \\ 0 & 0 & 0 & \cdots & 1 \end{pmatrix}$$

Since this Markov chain starts in state 0, it can only reach state T at the final time period T, and so the transition probabilities from state T do not really matter, except that they must add up to one. We arbitrarily took $P(T, T) = 1$, meaning that the Markov chain would remain in state T forever, even if it were to keep operating after time T.

A useful property of Markov chains is provided by the following:

(**3.35**)   If $Y = f(X_t, X_{t+1}, \ldots, X_T)$ for some function f, then

$$E[Y|\mathscr{F}_t] = E[Y|X_t]$$

This says the future and the past are conditionally independent, given the present.

Now suppose we have a securities market model where the discounted price process is a Markov chain. This means that $P\{S_{t+1}^* = j | \mathscr{F}_t\} = P\{S_{t+1}^* = j | S_t^*\}$ for all $j \in E$ and t. It is natural to wonder whether anything special can be said about the martingale measure, if there is one. In particular, one should ask whether the discounted security prices are Markov chains under the martingale measure. This is a non-trivial question, because a stochastic process may lose its Markov property when you change from one probability measure to an equivalent one. For example, you can make the third coin flip depend on the first coin flip just by changing the probability measure associated with the heads counting process N_t in example 3.5.

It turns out, however, that our question can be answered in the affirmative:

(**3.36**)   If there are no arbitrage opportunities, if the discounted price process S^* is a Markov chain under P, and if the filtration $\mathbb{F}$ is the one generated by S^*, then there exists a martingale measure Q under which S^* is a Markov chain.

To see this, suppose the Markov chain (under P) is stationary, and consider the construction of the martingale measure as developed in section 3.4. In particular, consider the conditional probabilities associated with the 'single period model' associated with an individual node of the information tree. If the corresponding, current state of the discounted price process S^* is s, then the conditional, risk neutral probabilities must be, of course, such that the expected value of S^* at the end of the period is equal to s. But there is a one-to-one correspondence between each branch leading out of this node and each transition probability $P(s, j)$ from state s that is strictly positive. In other words, $P(s, j) > 0$ if and only if j is a possible state for S^* at the end of the period. Hence choosing the risk neutral conditional probabilities for this node amounts to suitably choosing new transition probabilities $Q(s, j)$ from state s, making sure $Q(s, j) > 0$ if and only if $P(s, j) > 0$ for all j. By hypothesis, we know this choice can be made.

Now there may be many other nodes in the information tree where the corresponding, current state of S^* is s, but the same situation will exist. The single period models will all be identical, and so you can choose the same set of risk neutral transition probabilities $Q(s, j)$ for all these nodes.

In a similar manner, one chooses the risk neutral transition probabilities for all the other nodes in the information tree, making sure the probabilities are the same for all the nodes that share the same value for the current state of the discounted price process. Hence not only does this lead to the risk neutral probability measure Q as was derived in section 3.4, but these transition probabilities form a Markov transition matrix under which S^* is a Markov chain. Hence (3.36) is true when S^* is a stationary Markov chain under P, and this argument can be easily extended to cover the case where S^* is a Markov chain that is not stationary.

It follows from (3.35) and (3.36) that $E_Q[S_n^*(t+s)|\mathscr{F}_t] = E_Q[S_n^*(t+s)|S_t^*]$. Hence the standard relationship for Q to be a martingale measure can be written as

$$S_n^*(t) = E_Q[S_n^*(t+s)|S_t^*], \qquad \text{all } n, \ t, \text{ and } s$$

If the original price process S_t is a Markov chain under P and the bank account B_t is deterministic, then the discounted price process $S_t^* = S_t/B_t$ will also be a Markov chain. However, if the bank account process is stochastic, even a Markov chain, then the discounted price process will not necessarily be a Markov chain. In this case all is not lost; it might still be possible to take advantage of the Markov properties of the model.

One way to proceed when B_t is stochastic is to set up the securities market model with an underlying stochastic process X that is a stationary Markov chain under P and with the filtration being generated by this process. For example, X_t could be a vector of the current prices of all the relevant securities. In doing this, one would normally fix the initial state $X_0 = i_0$ and then let the sample space Ω be the set of all the possible sample paths of X. Then if $\omega \in \Omega$ corresponds to the sample path $(i_0, i_1, i_2, \ldots, i_T)$, one would take the probability measure to be such that $P\{\omega\} = P(i_0, i_1)P(i_1, i_2)$ $\ldots P(i_{T-1}, i_T)$.

Next, suppose for each t that f_t is a real valued function on the state space E such that the bank account process satisfies $B_t = f_t(X_t)$. If the risky security price processes are defined in a similar manner, then the discounted price processes can also be expressed as functions of the underlying Markov chain X, being the ratio of two such functions. Now none of these price process is necessarily a Markov chain; for example, the function f may give rise to the same price for two distinct states in E. However, we may re-do the argument for (3.36) and recover a useful result.

Again, we look at the single period model associated with each node of the information tree, only now associated with each node is the current state of the Markov chain X. We construct the conditional probabilities $Q(i, j)$ and the martingale measure Q as before, only now X will turn out to be a Markov chain under Q. Hence by (3.35) we will have for the resulting Q that $E_Q[S_n^*(t+s)|\mathscr{F}_t] = E_Q[S_n^*(t+s)|X_t]$, in which case the standard relationship for Q to be a martingale measure can be written as

$$S_n^*(t) = E_Q[S_n^*(t+s)|X_t], \qquad \text{all, } n, \ t, \text{ and } s$$

Example 3.5 (continued)   Taking $f_t(x) = S_0 u^x d^{t-x}$ we have for the binomial security price model of section 3.5 $S_t = f_t(N_t)$, where the head counting process N_t is a Markov chain, as discussed earlier. Actually, S_t is also a stationary Markov chain, even though f_t depends on t, because the future changes in the price process depend only on the future 'coin flips,' which are independent of time. If s is the state where $S_t = s$, then the transition probability $P(s,j) = p$ if $j = su$, $P(s,j) = 1 - p$ if $j = sd$, and $P(s,j) = 0$, otherwise. For general parameters u and d the state space is rather messy, as it can contain up to $(T+1)(T+2)/2$ distinct values, that is, the number of nodes in the network such as figure 3.4. However, in the important special case where $d = u^{-1}$, the state space has only $2T + 1$ distinct values, as can be seen by studying figure 3.5.

To demonstrate the preceding equations which the martingale measure Q must satisfy, we have $S_t^* = S_0 u^{N_t} d^{t-N_t}/(1+r)^t$ and

$$
\begin{aligned}
E_Q[S_{t+1}^*|S_t^*] &= E_Q[S_0 u^{X_{t+1}+N_t} d^{t+1-X_{t+1}-N_t}/(1+r)^{t+1}|S_t^*] \\
&= (S_t^*/(1+r))E_Q[u^{X_{t+1}} d^{1-X_{t+1}}|S_t^*] \\
&= (S_t^*/(1+r))E_Q[u^{X_{t+1}} d^{1-X_{t+1}}] \\
&= (S_t^*/(1+r))\left[\frac{1+r-d}{u-d}u + \frac{u-1-r}{u-d}d\right] = S_t^*
\end{aligned}
$$

Similarly, one verifies $E_Q[S_{t+1}^*|N_t] = S_t^*$.

A virtue of Markov chains is that it is straightforward to compute conditional probability distributions for the state of the Markov chain at a specified number of periods in the future. For example,

$$
\begin{aligned}
P\{X_2 = j|X_o = i\} &= \sum_{k \in E} P\{X_2 = j,\ X_1 = k|X_0 = i\} \\
&= \sum_{k \in E} P\{X_2 = j|\ X_1 = k,\ X_0 = i\}P\{X_1 = k|X_0 = i\} \\
&= \sum_{k \in E} P\{X_2 = j|X_1 = k\}P\{X_1 = k|X_0 = i\} \\
&= \sum_{k \in E} P_1(k,j)P_0(i,k)
\end{aligned}
$$

We recognize this last expression as the result of matrix multiplication. In other words, $P\{X_{t+2} = j|X_t = i\}$ will be equal to the ijth element of the matrix product $P_t P_{t+1}$. This pattern extends to any number of periods: $P\{X_{t+s} = j|X_t = i\}$ will be equal to the ijth element of the matrix product $P_t P_{t+1} \ldots P_{t+s-1}$. Of course, in the stationary case one simply has $P_t P_{t+1} \ldots P_{t+s-1} = P^s$.

Example 3.6 Consider the binomial security process model with $d = u^{-1}$; the price process S_t is a Markov chain with state space

$E = \{S_0 u^{-T}, S_0 u^{-T+1}, \ldots, S_0 u^{-1}, S_0, S_0 u, \ldots, S_0 u^{T-1}, S_0 u^T\}$. But suppose the conditional probability of an 'up' move varies with the state. In particular, suppose $P\{S_{t+1} = S_0 u^{i-1} | S_t = S_0 u^i\} = 1 - p_i$ and $P\{S_{t+1} = S_0 u^{i+1} | S_t = S_0 u^i\} = P_i$ for $2T - 1$ parameters $p_i, i = -T + 1, \ldots, -1, 0, 1, \ldots, T - 1$. (For example, the model builder could give price level S_0 a measure of stability by setting $p_i > 1/2$ for $i < 0$ and $p_i < 1/2$ for $i > 0$). Thus the transition matrix is

$$
\begin{bmatrix}
1 & 0 & 0 & & & & & & \\
1 - p_{-T+1} & 0 & p_{-T+1} & & & & & & \\
\cdot & & \cdot & \cdot & & & & & \\
& & 1 - p_{-1} & 0 & p_{-1} & & & & \\
& & & 1 - p_0 & 0 & p_0 & & & \\
& & & & 1 - p_1 & 0 & p_1 & & \\
& & & & & & \cdot & \cdot & \cdot \\
& & & & & & 1 - p_{T-1} & 0 & p_{T-1} \\
& & & & & & & 0 & 0 & 1
\end{bmatrix}
$$

and, for example, $P\{S_3 = S_0 u\} = (1 - p_0)p_{-1}p_0 + p_0(1 - p_1)p_0 + p_0 p_1(1 - p_2)$.

Exercise 3.15 Derive (3.35).

Exercise 3.16 Derive (3.34). (Hint: Use (3.35))

Exercise 3.17 Prove by mathematical induction for a stationary Markov chain X with transition matrix P that $P\{X_{t+s} = j | X_t + i\}$ is equal to the ijth element of the s-fold matrix product of P.

4 Options, Futures, and Other Derivatives

4.1 Contingent Claims

A *contingent claim* is a random variable X that represents the time T payoff from a 'seller' to a 'buyer.' This definition is essentially the same as for single period models, and it turns out that the basic ideas are very similar as well. However, much more can be said, primarily because the multiperiod setting leads to a number of rich examples, many of which see practical use in the financial industry.

In most instances the random variable X can be taken to be some function of an underlying security price, and so contingent claims are examples of what are called *derivative securities*. With a single period model, contingent claims are about the only kind of derivative security you can think of. But with several periods to work with it is possible to consider other kinds of derivative securities, that is, securities whose values depend on underlying securities but which cannot be modeled as a time T payoff X. Other kinds of derivatives will be discussed later in this chapter.

As with single period models, a contingent claim is like a contract or agreement between two parties. Since one party (the seller) promises to pay the other party (the buyer) the amount X at time T, the buyer will normally pay some money to the seller when they make their agreement, say at time $t < T$. The fundamental question to be addressed is: what is the appropriate value for this time t payment? In other words, what is the time t value of this contingent claim?

In general, the time T payoff X can be strictly negative for some states of the world $\omega \in \Omega$. This amounts to a payment by the buyer to the seller. In contrast, of considerable importance is the case where the buyer has the option at time T to proceed with the payment at that time. In this case, called a *European option*, the payment will naturally take place if and only if it is positive. Consequently, European options are the same things as non-negative contingent claims.

Example 4.1   Consider the simple model with $T = 2$ and $K = 4$ that was introduced as example 3.3 in chapter 3. The single risky security is as follows:

ω_k	$t = 0$	$t = 1$	$t = 2$
ω_1	$S_0 = 5$	$S_1 = 8$	$S_2 = 9$
ω_2	$S_0 = 5$	$S_1 = 8$	$S_2 = 6$
ω_3	$S_0 = 5$	$S_1 = 4$	$S_2 = 6$
ω_4	$S_0 = 5$	$S_1 = 4$	$S_2 = 3$

If $X = S_2 - 5$, the net profit at time $T = 2$ for purchasing one unit of the security for the price 5, then the payoff is negative in state ω_4. But if this is a European option, then one should take $X = \max \{S_2 - 5, 2\}$, that is, so $X(\omega)$ takes the values 4, 1, 1, and 0 in states ω_1, ω_2, ω_3, and ω_4, respectively. This European option is called a *call option* with exercise price 5. Similarly, $X = \max \{e - S_2, 0\}$ is a *put option* with exercise price e, that is, X is the option to sell one unit of the security for the price e at time $T = 2$.

Example 4.2   Suppose for the same securities market model as in example 4.1 that $X = \max \{[S_0 + S_1 + S_2]/3 - 5, 0\}$, so that $X(\omega)$ takes the values 7/3, 4/3, 0, and 0 in states ω_1, ω_2, ω_3, and ω_4, respectively. Now X is an example of what is called an *Asian* or *averaging* option. Options like this are used to hedge against rising prices for parties who need to buy fixed quantities of the security every period. Unlike put and call options, where the value of X depends only on the final value of the security, here the value of X depends on the whole history of the security.

Throughout this chapter it will be assumed that the securities market model is economically reasonable, that is, there exists a risk neutral probability measure Q. A contingent claim is said to be *marketable* or *attainable* if there exists a self-financing trading strategy such that $V_T(\omega) = X(\omega)$ for all $\omega \, \varepsilon \, \Omega$. The corresponding portfolio or trading strategy H is said to *replicate* or *generate* X. In the case of single period models, the time $t = 0$ value of a contingent claim was seen to be the expectation under a risk neutral probability measure of the discounted value of the claim. In the multiperiod case this conclusion generalizes slightly to:

(**4.1**)   *Risk neutral valuation principle*: The time t value of a marketable contingent claim X is equal to V_t, the time t value of the portfolio which replicates X. Moreover,

$$V_t^* = V_t/B_t = E_Q[X/B_T | \mathscr{F}_t], \quad t = 0, 1, \ldots, T$$

for all risk neutral probability measures Q.

The first statement in (4.1) is a consequence of the law of one price. Indeed (as will be discussed more fully below), if X could be purchased or sold at time t for an amount other than V_t, then one could exploit an arbitrage opportunity by taking suitable positions in this contingent claim and the other securities. Since $V_T = X$ if and only if $V_T^* = X/B_T$, the equation in (4.1) follows from the fact that V^* is a martingale under Q (see (3.21)).

Example 4.1 (continued)   Suppose $r = 0$ (see example 3.3) so $Q = (1/6, 1/12, 1/4, 1/2)$. If the call option with exercise price $e = 5$ is attainable, then its time $t = 0$ value must be

$$V_0 = E_Q[X] = \frac{1}{6}(4) + \frac{1}{12}(1) + \frac{1}{4}(1) + \frac{1}{2}(0) = 1$$

In states ω_1 and ω_2 we have

$$V_1 = E_Q[X|S_1 = 8] = \frac{2}{3}(4) + \frac{1}{3}(1) = 3$$

while in states ω_3 and ω_4 we have

$$V_1 = E_Q[X|S_1 = 4] = \frac{1}{3}(1) + \frac{2}{3}(0) = \frac{1}{3}$$

Similarly, the put with exercise price $e = 5$ pays off the amounts 0, 0, 0, and 2 in states ω_1 to ω_4, respectively, so $V_0 = 1$, $V_1 = 0$ in states ω_1 and ω_2, and $V_1 = 4/3$ in states ω_3 and ω_4.

It is important to be able to compute the trading strategy which generates a particular contingent claim. For one thing, this verifies that the contingent claim is indeed attainable. Moreover, even if you know the contingent claim is attainable, you may want to use the replicating trading strategy, perhaps to hedge a position in the contingent claim.

There are several good methods for computing replicating trading strategies. For the first method you already know the value process V for the replicating portfolio, and so you solve for the trading strategy H using the linear equations (one for each state) in the definition of the value process

$$V_t = H_0(t)B_t + \sum_{n=1}^{n} H_n(t)S_n(t)$$

and keeping in mind that H is predictable. This is illustrated in the following example:

Example 4.1 (continued)   For $t = 2$ we have

$$V_2(\omega_1) = 4 = H_0(2)(\omega_1)1 + H_1(2)(\omega_1)9$$
$$V_2(\omega_2) = 1 = H_0(2)(\omega_2)1 + H_1(2)(\omega_2)6$$
$$V_2(\omega_3) = 1 = H_0(2)(\omega_3)1 + H_1(2)(\omega_3)6$$
$$V_2(\omega_4) = 0 = H_0(2)(\omega_4)1 + H_1(2)(\omega_4)3$$

Since H is predictable we also have

$$H_0(2)(\omega_1)1 = H_0(2)(\omega_2) \quad H_0(2)(\omega_3)1 = H_0(2)(\omega_4)$$
$$H_1(2)(\omega_1)1 = H_1(2)(\omega_2) \quad H_1(2)(\omega_3)1 = H_1(2)(\omega_4)$$

Solving these equations yields $H_0(2) = -5$ and $H_1(2) = 1$ in states ω_1 and ω_2, whereas $H_0(2) = -1$ and $H_1(2) = 1/3$ in states ω_3 and ω_4. Meanwhile, for $t = 1$ we have

$$V_1(\omega) = 3 = H_0(1)(\omega)1 + H_1(1)(\omega)8, \quad \omega = \omega_1, \omega_2$$
$$V_1(\omega) = \frac{1}{3} = H_0(1)(\omega)1 + H_1(1)(\omega)4, \quad \omega = \omega_3, \omega_4$$
$$H_0(1)(\omega_1) = H_0(1)(\omega_2) = H_0(1)(\omega_3) = H_0(1)(\omega_4)$$
$$H_1(1)(\omega_1) = H_1(1)(\omega_2) = H_1(1)(\omega_3) = H_1(1)(\omega_4)$$

Solving these gives $H_0(1) = -7/3$ and $H_1(1) = 2/3$ for all ω.

For the second method for computing a replicating trading strategy, suppose all you know is X. You then work backwards in time, deriving V and H simultaneously. Since $V_T = X$, you first solve

$$X = H_0(T)B_T + \sum_{n=1}^{N} H_n(T)S_n(T)$$

for $H(T)$ as in the first method. Since H is self-financing, it follows that

$$V_{T-1} = H_0(T)B_{T-1} + \sum_{n=1}^{N} H_n(T)S_n(T-1)$$

so now you know V_{T-1}.

Next you solve

$$V_{T-1} = H_0(T-1)B_{T-1} + \sum_{n=1}^{N} H_n(T-1)S_n(T-1)$$

for $H(T-1)$ as in the first method, and then you compute V_{T-2}. You repeat this cycle working backwards in time until, finally, you compute V_0.

Example 4.1 (continued) Using this second method we first compute $H_0(2) = -5$ and $H_1(2) = 1$ for states ω_1 and ω_2, so $V_1 = -5(1) + 1(8) = 3$ in these same two states. Similarly, $H_0(2) = -1$ and $H_1(2) = 1/3$ in states ω_3 and ω_4, so $V_1 = -1(1) + (1/3)(4) = 1/3$ in these same two states. Next we use these values of V_1 to compute $H_0(1) = -7/3$ and $H_1(1) = 2/3$ for all ω. Finally, we see that $V_0 = (-7/3)(1) + (2/3)(5) = 1$ for all ω.

Still another method for computing a replicating strategy involves working with the discounted prices and the discounted value process. The self-financing equation $V_0^* + G_t^* = V_t^*$ is the same thing as

$$V_{t-1}^*(\omega) + \sum_{n=1}^{N} H_n(t)(\omega)\, \Delta S_n^*(t)(\omega) = V_t^*(\omega)$$

So if you know V_t^*, then you can use this system of equations together with the predictability requirement to solve for V_{t-1}^* along with the positions $H_1(t)\ldots, H_N(t)$. Hence you begin with $t = T$ and $V_T^* = X/B_T$ and you work backwards in time, computing the discounted value process V^* of the replicating portfolio as well as the replicating trading strategy's positions in all the risky securities. This gives $V = V^*B$. Finally, using the definition of either V or V^*, you compute H_0, the positions in the bank account. This is illustrated in the following example.

Example 4.2 (continued)   Assuming $r = 0$, the equations are

$$V_1^* + H_1(2)(1) = 7/3$$

and

$$V_1^* + H_1(2)(-2) = 4/3$$

in states ω_1 and ω_2, respectively. Hence $V_1^* = 2$ and $H_1(2) = 1/3$ in these same states. Similarly, the equations

$$V_1^* + H_1(2)(2) = 0$$

and

$$V_1^* + H_1(2)(-1) = 0$$

give $V_1^* = 0$ and $H_1(2) = 0$ in states ω_3 and ω_4.
For the second iteration we have

$$V_0^*(\omega) + H_1(1)(\omega)(3) = 2, \quad \omega = \omega_1,\ \omega_2$$

$$V_0^*(\omega) + H_1(1)(\omega)(-1) = 0, \quad \omega = \omega_3,\ \omega_4$$

Hence $V_0^* = 1/2$ and $H_1(1) = 1/2$ for all ω.
It remains to compute H_0. Using $H_0(1) = V_0^* - H_1(1)S_0$ we get $H_0(1) = -2$. Similarly, we get $H_0(2) = -2/3$ in states ω_1 and ω_2, and we get $H_0(2) = 0$ in states ω_3 and ω_4. Note that $E_Q[X] = (1/6)$ $(7/3) + (1/12)(4/3) = 1/2$, the same as the value of V_0^* that was already computed.

We now return to the earlier discussion of arbitrage pricing. If the actual traded price of a contingent claim differs from the value of the replicating portfolio, then one can find an arbitrage opportunity. To see this, let P_t denote the actual time t price of the contingent claim.

First suppose $P_t > V_t$. Then sell the contingent claim for P_t, collecting this amount. Simultaneously, begin the replicating trading strategy with an initial amount of capital equal to V_t. Invest the difference, $P_t - V_t$, at the bank account rate. At time T your liability on the contingent claim will be $P_T = X$, but this will coincide exactly with your replicating portfolio. One will precisely offset the other. Meanwhile, the investment in the bank account has become $(P_t - V_t)B_t/B_t > 0$, a sure profit.

On the other hand, if $P_t < V_t$, then you do the opposite of these transactions. You buy the contingent claim, follow the negative of the replicating trading strategy (thereby collecting V_t dollars), and invest the difference $V_t - P_t$ in the bank account. At time T your liability V_T is exactly offset by the value $P_T = X$ of the contingent claim. Meanwhile, you now have $(V_t - P_t)B_T/B_t > 0$ in the bank.

Turning to another topic, if the bank account process B is deterministic (see exercise 4.3) then a call option on a security is marketable if and only if the put option on the same security with the same exercise price is marketable. If they are both marketable, then one has the *put-call parity* relationship:

(4.2) $$p = c + e \, E_Q[1/B_T] - S_0$$

where c and p are the time $t = 0$ prices of the call and put options, respectively, both having the common exercise price e and the underlying security S. This is one in a number of examples where the price of the option of interest (in this case the put) can be expressed as a linear combination of the prices of one or more conventional calls, the price of the underlying security, and the 'forward' price $E_Q[1/B_T]$. Here is another example.

Example 4.3 Suppose the buyer acquires at time 0 an option which provides the right to choose at fixed time t, where $0 < t < T$, between a call option and a put option, both having the same exercise price e and expiring at time T. This is called a *chooser* option. If C_t and P_t denote their respective time t prices, then the option buyer will choose the call if and only if $C_t \geqslant P_t$, in which case the time T payoff will be

$$(S_T - e)^+ 1_{\{C_t \geqslant P_t\}} + (e - S_T)^+ 1_{\{C_t < P_t\}}$$

where 1_A, the indicator function of the event A, equals one if event A occurs and equals zero if it does not. We are interested in computing the time 0 value of this option with the risk neutral valuation principle (4.1).

Now by adding and subtracting the term $(S_T - e)^+ 1_{\{C_t < P_t\}}$, it follows that the time T payoff of the chooser option is equal to

$$(S_T - e)^+ + (e - S_T)1_{\{C_t < P_t\}}$$

Hence by risk neutral valuation, if this chooser option is marketable, then its time 0 price is equal to the price of the ordinary call option $(S_T - e)^+$ plus the quantity

(4.3) $$E_Q[(e - S_T)1_{\{C_t < P_t\}}/B_T]$$

Assuming the interest rate r is constant and the call option $(S_T - e)^+$ is marketable, expression (4.3) has a simple form. The put-call parity relationship (4.2) applies at time t, so the event $C_t < P_t$ is the same as the event $S_t < e(1+r)^{t-T}$. Hence

$$E_Q[(e-S_T)1_{\{C_t<P_t\}}/B_T] = E_Q[E_Q[(e-S_T)1_{\{C_t<P_t\}}/(1+r)^T|\mathscr{F}_t]]$$
$$= E_Q[1_{\{C_t<P_t\}}E_Q[(e-S_T)/(1+r)^T|\mathscr{F}_t]]$$
$$= E_Q[1_{\{C_t<P_t\}}(1+r)^{-t}\{e(1+r)^{t-T} - E_Q[S_T(1+r)^{t-T}|\mathscr{F}_t]\}]$$
$$= E_Q[1_{\{C_t<P_t\}}(1+r)^{-t}[e(1+r)^{t-T} - S_t]]$$
$$= E_Q[1_{\{S_t<e(1+r)^{t-T}\}}[e(1+r)^{t-T} - S_t]/(1+r)^t]$$

where the next to last equality uses the fact that the discounted price process $S^* = S/B$ is a martingale under Q. We recognize the final expression to be the time 0 price of an ordinary put option that has exercise price $e(1+r)^{t-T}$ and expires at time t. Hence under the indicated assumptions the time 0 price of the chooser option equals the price of a certain ordinary call plus the price of a certain ordinary put, with the latter expressable in terms of another call by the put-call parity relationship.

Example 4.1 (continued)   With interest rate $r = 0$ and exercise price $e = 5$, consider the chooser option where the buyer chooses between the put and call at time $t = 1$. By our earlier calculations for the ordinary put and call, the chooser option buyer will choose the call if $S_1 = 8$ and will choose the put if $S_1 = 4$. Hence the chooser option will pay off the amounts 4, 1, 0, and 2 in states ω_1 to ω_4, respectively, at time 2. The time 0 price of this chooser option is

$$V_0 = \frac{1}{6}(4) + \frac{1}{12}(1) + \frac{1}{4}(0) + \frac{1}{2}(2) = 1\frac{3}{4}$$

Meanwhile, the put with exercise price 5 that expires at time 1 will pay off the amount 0 if $S_1 = 8$ and the amount 1 if $S_1 = 4$, so its time 0 price is $\frac{1}{4}(0) + \frac{3}{4}(1) = \frac{3}{4}$. The time 0 price of the call that expires at time 2 was calculated earlier and found to be 1, so this illustrates that the price of the chooser option equals the price of this put plus the price of this call.

Of course, options can be defined in terms of two or more underlying securities. For example, given a function $g : \mathbb{R}^N \to \mathbb{R}^+$ one can take $X = g(S_1(T), \ldots, S_N(T))$. Then if you know the joint probability distribution of the random variables $S_1(T), \ldots S_N(T)$ under the martingale measure, it is easy to compute the time 0 value of this contingent claim. In particular, with

$$g(s_1, \ldots, s_N) = (a_1s_1 + \ldots + a_Ns_N - e)^+$$

for positive scalars $a_1, \ldots a_N$ you could have a call option on a stock index. Or with

$$g(s_1, \ldots, s_N) = \max\{s_1, \ldots, s_N, e\}$$

you would have a contingent claim delivering the best of N securities and the cash amount e.

Example 4.4 Suppose $K = 9$, $N = 2$, $T = 2$, $r = 0$, and the price processes and information structure are as displayed in figure 4.1. There is a unique risk neutral probability measure Q for this model; it is also displayed in figure 4.1. Now consider a call option with exercise price $e = 13$ on the time $T = 2$ value of the stock index $S_1(t) + S_2(t)$. In other words, this contingent claim $X = (S_1(2) + S_2(2) - 13)^+$ and is displayed in figure 4.1. As will be explained in section 4.4, X is marketable. Hence its time 0 price is easily computed to be $E_Q X = 11/12$.

Exercise 4.1 Consider the usual two-period model as in example 4.1 with $r = 0$. Compute the time $t = 0$ values and the replicating trading strategies for the following European options:

(a)   A call option with exercise price 7.
(b)   A put option with exercise price 7.
(c)   An Asian put option with exercise price 7.
(d)   A chooser option with exercise price 7 and decision time 1.

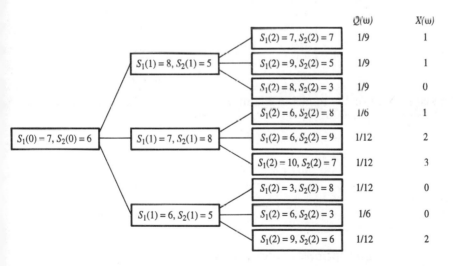

Figure 4.1   Data for example 4.4

Exercise 4.2 A *look-back* option is one where the payoff is based on the maximum (or perhaps the minimum) price of the underlying security during a recent time interval. Compute the time $t = 0$ value and the replicating strategy for the following look-back call option: $X = \max\{0, S_0 - 7, S_1 - 7, S_2 - 7\}$. As usual, work with the two period model of example 4.1 with $r = 0$.

Exercise 4.3 Consider a European put and a European call option on the same security S, where they have the same expiration date T and the same exercise price e.

(a) Show that (4.2) holds if both the put and call are marketable (Hint: use $(S_T - e)^+ - (e - S_T)^+ = S_T - e$ to show that the claim with time T payment equal to the constant e is also marketable).

(b) Show that if the bank account process B is deterministic, then the call option is marketable if and only if the corresponding put option is marketable (Hint: specify the trading strategy which replicates the constant payment e).

(c) Show that if the bank account process B is predictable but not deterministic, then it is possible for a call to be marketable even though the corresponding put as well as the claim with time T payment equal to the constant e are not marketable. Do this by considering the model with $T = 2$, $K = 6$, $N = 1$, $\mathscr{P}_1 = \{\{\omega_1, \omega_2\}, \{\omega_3, \omega_4\}, \{\omega_5, \omega_6\}\}$, $S_0 = 40$ options expiring at $T = 2$ with $e = 43\frac{48}{109}$, and prices as follows:

ω	$B_1(\omega)$	$S_1(\omega)$	$B_2(\omega)$	$S_2(\omega)$
ω_1	1.10	45	1.232	55
ω_2	1.10	45	1.232	40
ω_3	1.10	40	1.21	50
ω_4	1.10	40	1.21	35
ω_5	1.10	35	1.188	40
ω_6	1.10	35	1.188	30

Exercise 4.4 For the model in example 4.4, compute the time 0 price and the replicating portfolio for the following options:

(a) Call with $e = 13$ on the time 2 value of the index $S_1 + S_2$ (hint: we already know the price is 19/18).

(b) Put with $e = 13$ on the time 2 value of the index $S_1 + S_2$.

(c) An option to acquire the maximum of S_1, S_2, and 6.

(d) A call with $e = 6$ on $\max\{S_1(2), S_2(2)\}$.

(e) An Asian (i.e., averaging) call option with $e = 13$ on the index $S_1 + S_2$.

4.2　European Options Under the Binomial Model

The binomial model was introduced in section 3.4. It consists of a single risky security satisfying

$$S_t = S_0 u^{N_t} d^{t-N_t}, \quad t = 1, 2, \ldots, T$$

where $0 < d < 1 < u$ and $N = \{N_t; t = 1, \ldots, T\}$ is a binomial process with parameter p, $0 < p < 1$. Assuming the interest rate r is constant with $u > 1 + r$, there exists a martingale measure; it is given by

$$Q(\omega) = q^n (1-q)^{T-n}, \quad q = \frac{1+r-d}{u-d}$$

where $\omega \in \Omega$ is any state corresponding to n 'up moves' and $T - n$ 'down moves' by the risky security.

The probability distribution of S_t under the martingale measure is given by (3.32). Hence if a contingent claim is of the form

$$X = g(S_T)$$

for a specified real-valued function g, then the time $t = 0$ value of X is given by

(4.4) $$V_0 = (1+r)^{-T} E_Q\, g(S_T)$$

$$= (1+r)^{-T} \sum_{n=0}^{T} \binom{T}{n} q^n (1-q)^{T-n} g(S_0 u^n d^{T-n})$$

The binomial model is a good illustration of a useful principle: if the underlying securities are Markov chains, then you probably can work out explicitly the probability distribution for the time T values of the securities under the martingale measure, in which case you can compute explicit formulas for the values of contingent claims which are of the form $X = g(S_T)$.

Example 4.5 For a call option with exercise price e we have

$$g(s) = (s - e)^+ = \begin{cases} s - e, & s \geq e \\ 0, & s \leq ,e \end{cases}$$

Hence the time $t = 0$ price is

$$V_0 = (1+r)^{-T} \sum_{n=0}^{T} \binom{T}{n} q^n (1-q)^{T-n} \max\{0,\ S_0 u^n d^{T-n} - e\}$$

Note that

$$S_0 u^n d^{T-n} - e > 0 \Leftrightarrow (u/d)^n > e/(S_0 d^t)$$
$$\Leftrightarrow n\, log(u/d) > log(e/(S_0 d^T))$$
$$\Leftrightarrow n > \frac{log(e/(S_0 d^T))}{log(u/d)}$$

We define $\hat{n}$ to be the smallest non-negative integer n such that this strict inequality is satisfied.

Now if $\hat{n} > T$, then $S_0 u^n d^{T-n} \leq e$ for all $n \leq T$, in which case $V_0 = 0$. On the other hand, if $0 \leq \hat{n} \leq T$, then there is a chance the call option will finish in the money, in which case $V_0 > 0$. In particular,

$$V_0 = (1+r)^{-T} \sum_{n=0}^{\hat{n}-1} \binom{T}{n} q^n (1-q)^{T-n} (0)$$

$$+ (1+r)^{-T} \sum_{n=\hat{n}}^{T} \binom{T}{n} q^n (1-q)^{T-n} [S_0 u^n d^{T-n} - e]$$

$$= \frac{S_0}{(1+r)^T} \sum_{n=\hat{n}}^{T} \binom{T}{n} q^n (1-q)^{T-n} u^n d^{T-n}$$

$$- \frac{e}{(1+r)^T} \sum_{n=\hat{n}}^{T} \binom{T}{n} q^n (1-q)^{T-n}$$

$$= S_0 \sum_{n=\hat{n}}^{T} \binom{T}{n} \left[\frac{qu}{1+r}\right]^n \left[\frac{(1-q)d}{1+r}\right]^{T-n}$$

$$- \frac{e}{(1+r)^T} \sum_{n=\hat{n}}^{T} \binom{T}{n} q^n (1-q)^{T-n}$$

$$= S_0 \sum_{n=\hat{n}}^{T} \binom{T}{n} \hat{q}^n (1-\hat{q})^{T-n} - \frac{e}{(1+r)^T} \sum_{n=\hat{n}}^{T} \binom{T}{n} q^n (1-q)^{T-n}$$

where $\hat{q} \equiv qu/(1+r)$. It is left to the reader to use elementary algebra to verify that $1 - \hat{q} = (1-q)d/(1+r)$ and $0 < \hat{q} < 1$. Hence both terms in the formula for V_0 involve the sum of $T - \hat{n} + 1$ binomial probabilities.

Example 4.6   Consider a look-back call option $X = (Y_T - e)^+$, where $Y_T = \max \{S_t : t = 0, 1, \ldots, T\}$, as introduced in section 3.4. Assume $d = u^{-1}$, so that Y_T will take one of the $T + 1$ values $S_0, S_0 u, \ldots$, or $S_0 u^T$. Under the martingale measure, the probability $P\{Y_T > S_0 u^1\}$ is given for $i = 1, \ldots, T$ by formula (3.33), only with parameter q in place of p. Hence in principle we have the probability distribution of Y_T, and so it is straightforward to compute a formula for the time $t = 0$ price $(1+r)^{-T} E_Q (Y_T - e)^+$. Similar approaches will work for the look-back put option $X = (e - Y_T)^+$ as well as look-back puts and calls based on the minimum security price level reached before time T.

Example 4.7   *Knockout* options are ones which expire worthless if the price level ever hits a specified level, say k. For example, suppose $S_0 < k, e < k, X = (S_T - e)^+$ if the maximum price $Y_T < k$, and $X = 0$ if $Y_T \geqslant k$. The ideas developed in section 3.4 and applied in example 4.6 can be used to value this option.

Suppose $d = u^{-1}$ and i is such that $S_0 u^i = k$. As explained in section 3.4, we know, at least in principle, the probability distribution under the martingale measure of τ_i, the first passage time to security price level k. Note that τ_i takes one of the values $1, 2, \ldots, T$, or, if the security price never reaches the level k, infinity. Moreover, we know the conditional probability $Q\{S_T = S_0 u^j \mid \tau_i = t\}$ is the same as the conditional probability $Q\{S_{T-t} = S_0 u^{j-i} \mid S_0 = k\}$, where integer $j < i$. In other words, this conditional probability is the same as the probability that the price process which is at level k at time t will find itself exactly $i - j$ price levels lower after the remaining $T - t$ periods. Under the martingale measure, this conditional probability is

$$Q\{S_T = S_0 u^j \mid \tau_i = t\} = \binom{T-t}{n} q^n (1 - q)^{T-t-n}, \quad j < i$$

provided $n \equiv (T - t + j - i)/2$ is an integer (here n is the number of 'up moves' during the last $T - t$ periods so that the price moves from level k to level $S_0 u^j$). Hence we can compute the joint probability distribution

$$Q\{S_T = S_0 u^j, \tau_i = t\} = Q\{S_T = S_0 u^j \mid \tau_i = t\} \, Q\{\tau_i = t\}$$

for $j < i$ and $t = 1, \ldots, T$. Next we easily compute for $j < i$

$$Q\{S_T = S_0 u^j, \tau_i = \infty\} = Q\{S_T = S_0 u^j\} - \sum_{t-1}^{T} Q\{S_T = S_0 u^j, \tau_i = t\}$$

All these probabilities, of course, are under the martingale measure Q. Finally, we compute the price $(1 + r)^{-T} E_Q X$ of the knockout option by using $(1 + r)^{-T} \sum_{j<i} Q\{S_T = S_0 u^j, \tau_i = \infty\}(S_0 u^j - e)^+$.

The option in example 4.7 is also called an *up-and-out* call. You could also have a *down-and-out* call ($k < S_0, k < e$), an *up-and-out* put ($S_0 < k, e < k$), and a *down-and-out* put ($k < S_0, k < e$). With all these options you can compute the time 0 price with a similar approach, that is, by deriving the joint probability distribution under the martingale measure $Q\{S_T = S_0 u^j, \tau_i = \infty\}$.

Paired with each of these four knockout options are options that become activated if and only if the price level k is ever reached. For example, an *up-and-in* call ($S_0 < k$, $e < k$) expires worthless if the maximum price remains strictly less than k, whereas the expiration value is $(S_T - e)^+$ if the maximum security price during $[0, T]$ is greater than or equal to k. You also have *down-and-in* calls, *up-and-in* puts, and *down-and-in* puts. All eight of these options are called *barrier* options. Again, you can compute time 0 prices of these four 'in' options by deriving the joint probability distribution $Q\{S_T = S_0 u^j, \tau_i < \infty\}$. Or, if you already know the price of the paired knockout option, then you can use the fact that the time 0 price of an ordinary call (or put) is equal to the sum of the prices of the barrier options in a pairing. For example, the price of the up-and-in call option with parameters k and e is equal to the price of the European call option with exercise price e less the price of the up-and-out call option with parameters k and e. This is because the expiration value of the call option is equal to the expiration value of the up-and-in call plus the expiration value of the up-and-out call.

Exercise 4.5   Consider the European call option under the binomial model with $T = 2$, $e = 1000$, $u = 1.1$, $d = 0.9$, and $r = 1/100$. Compute the option price as a function of the initial stock price S_0 and draw a precise graph of this function.

Exercise 4.6   Suppose $S_0 = 80$, $T = 3$, $u = 1.5$, $d = 0.5$, and $r = 0.1$ are the parameters for the binomial model, and consider a call option with exercise price $e = 80$.

(a)   Draw a lattice (i.e., recombining network) for the model and label the nodes with the security's price S_t.
(b)   Compute q and $\hat{q}$.
(c)   Label each node with the corresponding option value.
(d)   Determine the replicating portfolio.

Exercise 4.7   Suppose $S_0 = 36$, $T = 2$, $u = 1.5$, $d = 2/3$, and $r = 0$ are the parameters for the binomial model. Compute the prices of the following barrier options by deriving the joint probability distribution $Q\{S_T, \tau\}$, where τ is the first passage time to the barrier k.

(a)   Up-and-in call with $k = 54$ and $e = 24$.
(b)   Up-and-out call with $k = 54$ and $e = 24$.
(c)   Up-and-in put with $k = 54$ and $e = 40$.
(d)   Up-and-out put with $k = 54$ and $e = 40$.
(e)   Down-and-in call with $k = 24$ and $e = 30$.
(f)   Down-and-out call with $k = 24$ and $e = 30$.
(g)   Down-and-in put with $k = 24$ and $e = 54$.
(h)   Down-and-out put with $k = 24$ and $e = 54$.

4.3   American Options

With European options, that is, with contingent claims, the payoff X can only occur at a specified date T, the expiration date. American options are similar, only now the payoff can occur at any time τ on or before the specified expiration date T.

As with European options, you should think of an American option as a contract between two parties, a buyer and a seller. Specified as data is a non-negative, adapted stochastic process $Y = \{Y_t; t = 0, 1 \ldots, T\}$. If they make an agreement at time t, then at that time the buyer pays the seller an amount Z_t equal to the time t value of this option. The buyer then has the right to exercise this option at any time τ, where $t \leqslant \tau \leqslant T$. If the option is exercised at time τ, then the seller pays Y_τ to the buyer. An American option can only be exercised once. If it is never exercised, then no payoff occurs. The key problem, of course, is to determine the time t value Z_t of this option, that is, the *value process* $Z = \{Z_t; t = 0, 1, \ldots, T\}$ for this American option Y.

Example 4.8 Setting $Y_t = (S_n(t) - e)^+$ gives rise to an *American call option* with exercise price e. Hence the buyer has the right to purchase one unit of security n for the amount e at any time on or before date T. Similarly, setting $Y - t = (e - S_n(t))^+$ leads to an *American put* which gives the option buyer the right to sell one unit of the security on or before time T for the price e.

If you buy an American option, then you can always postpone the exercise decision until time T, so the value Z_t of the American option Y is at least as large as the value V_t of the European option that has payoff $X = Y_T$. In addition, the possibility of being able to collect a desirable payoff at an earlier time tends to make American options more valuable than their European counterparts. Surprisingly, however, there are important situations where the two values coincide.

(4.5) Consider an American option $Y = \{Y_t; t = 0, 1, \ldots, T\}$ and the corresponding European option with time T payoff $X = Y_T$. Let V_t denote the time t value of this European option. If $V_t \geq Y_t$ for all t and $\omega \in \Omega$, then, for all t, V_t is equal to Z_t, the time t value of the American option, and it is optimal to wait until time T to exercise.

The reasoning is quite simple: if you bought the American option and $V_t \geq Y_t$, then exercising at time t would be foolish, because you can always guarantee yourself a time t payoff of V_t. For example, you could turn around and sell the corresponding European option for V_t, or you could go short the portfolio which replicates the corresponding European option. Since it is optimal to wait until time T to decide whether to exercise, the values of the two options must be the same.

Example 4.1 (continued) Suppose $Y_t = (S_t - 5)^+$, where S_t is the price process in example 4.1. Recall $r = 0$ and $T = 2$. The value process V_t for the corresponding European option $X = \max \{0, S_2 - 5\}$ was derived in section 4.1. Figure 4.2 displays on the information tree for this model the price process, the value process V, and the payoff process Y. Since $V_t \geq Y_t$ for all t, V is equal to the value process Z for the American option.

Alternatively, suppose the American option's payoff Y is as displayed in figure 4.3. The time 2 payoffs are the same as in the figure 4.2 example, but now the time 0 and 1 payoffs Y_t are greater (e.g., think of the American call option with $e = 4$, and suppose the stock pays a \$1 dividend between times 1 and 2). Hence the value process V_t for the European option $X = Y_2$ will be the same as in the figure 4.2

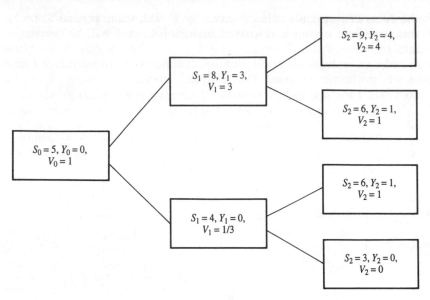

Figure 4.2   Values of American and European options are the same for example 4.1

example, but now the payoff process will not satisfy $V \geqslant Y$. In particular, $Y_1 > V_1$ when $S_1 = 8$, and now there is no reason to suppose

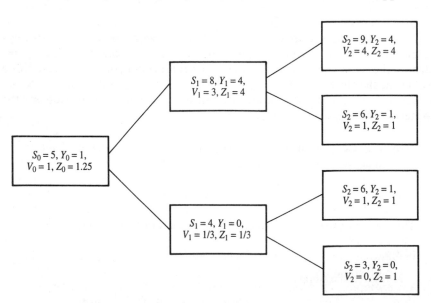

Figure 4.3   Values of American and European options are different for example 4.1

the American option's value is given by V. The value process Z for this American option is displayed in figure 4.3 and will be derived later.

In order to evaluate American options, it is necessary to introduce a new kind of stochastic process. The adapted stochastic process $Z = \{Z_t; t = 0, 1, \ldots, T\}$ is said to be a *supermartingale* (see section 3.3) if

$$E[Z_t \mid \mathcal{F}_s] \leqslant Z_s \qquad \text{all } 0 \leqslant s \leqslant t \leqslant T$$

Thus a supermartingale resembles a martingale, except that the conditional expected future value can be less than, instead of identical to, the current value. All martingales are supermartingales, but not vice versa. We know that the discounted value of a European option is a martingale under the risk neutral probability measure. It turns out that the discounted value of an American option is a supermartingale under the same measure.

It is necessary to introduce a second topic from the theory of stochastic processes. A *stopping time* is a random variable τ taking values in the set $\{0, 1, \ldots, T, \infty\}$ such that each event of the form $\{\tau = t\}, t \leqslant T$, is an element of the algebra $\mathcal{F}_t$. Thus you can evaluate whether the event $\{\tau = t\}$ occurs simply by examining $\mathcal{F}_t$, the information available at time t. For example, for a security with $S_0 = 10$, $\tau_1 \equiv \min\{t : S_t \geqslant 20\}$ is a stopping time, because you learn the event $\{\tau_1 = t\}$ by time t. However, the random variable $\tau_2 \equiv \max\{t : S_t \geqslant 20\}$ is not a stopping time, because you may not learn whether $\{\tau_2 = t\}$ until time T. Stopping times are allowed to take a value such as ∞ in order to provide for the possibility that the event of interest never occurs. For example, $\tau_1 = \infty$ if the event $\{S_t \geqslant 20\}$ does not occur by time T.

There are many stopping times associated with our security model's filtration. It is convenient to classify these stopping times by letting $\zeta(s, t)$ denote the set of (random variables which are) stopping times that take finite values in the closed interval $[s, t]$.

The process Z in what follows will turn out to be the value process for the American option Y.

(4.6) Suppose there exists a risk neutral probability measure Q and define the adapted stochastic process $Z = \{Z_t; T = 0, \ldots, T\}$ by

(4.7)
$$Z_t = \max_{\tau \in \zeta(t,T)} E_Q[Y_\tau B_t / B_\tau \mid \mathcal{F}_t].$$

Then the process Z/B is the smallest Q- supermartingale satisfying

(4.8)
$$Z_t \geqslant Y_t, \quad \text{all } t, \omega.$$

Moreover, the stopping time

(4.9)
$$\tau(t) \equiv \min\{s \geqslant t : Z_s = Y_s\}$$

maximizes the right hand side of (4.7) for $t = 0, 1, \ldots, T$.

In order to explain these principles, we will first describe a method for computing the process Z, a topic of importance in its own right. The computations will be done with dynamic programming, an algorithmic method of wide applicability. The idea in the case of American options is to work backwards in time, computing as you go the process Z. Note that (4.7) is clearly true for $t = T$, that is, $Z_T = Y_T$. Moreover, (4.9) holds for $t = T$.

Now the first iteration is to compute Z_{T-1} by taking

$$(\mathbf{4.10}) \qquad Z_{T-1} = \max\{Y_{T-1}, E_Q[Z_T B_{T-1}/B_T|\mathscr{F}_{T-t}]\}$$

noting for future reference that it will be optimal to take $\tau = T - 1$ if and only if $Z_{T-1} Y_{T-1}$. Now (4.7) can be rewritten for $t = T - 1$ as

$$Z_{T-1} = \max\{Y_{T-1}, E_Q[Y_T B_{T-1}/B_T|\mathscr{F}_{T-t}]\}$$

so comparing this with (4.10) we realize that Z_{T-1} given by (4.10) satisfies (4.7) for $t = T - 1$. Moreover, the stopping time that is spelled out in (4.9) for $T - 1$ is the one which maximizes the right hand side of (4.7) for $t = T - 1$.

Now suppose you have computed Z_t and you know that this satisfies (4.7) and that (4.9) for time t gives a stopping time which maximizes the right hand side of (4.7) for time t. Then Z_{t-1}, as given by

$$(\mathbf{4.11}) \qquad Z_{t-1} = \max\{Y_{T-1}, E_Q[Z_t B_{t-1}/B_t|\mathscr{F}_{t-t}]\}$$

will satisfy (4.7) for $t - 1$. To see this, note that (4.7) holds for time t, so with Z_{t-1} as has been computed we have

$$
\begin{aligned}
(\mathbf{4.12}) \quad Z_{t-1} &= \max\{Y_{t-1}, E_Q[\max_{\tau \in \zeta(t,T)} \{E_Q[Y_\tau B_t/B_\tau|\mathscr{F}_t]B_{t-1}/B_t|\mathscr{F}_{t-1}]\} \\
&\geq \max\{Y_{t-1}, E_Q[E_Q[Y_\tau B_t/B_\tau|\mathscr{F}_t]B_{t-1}/B_t|\mathscr{F}_{t-1}]\} \\
&= \max\{Y_{t-1}, E_Q[Y_\tau B_{t-1}/B_\tau|\mathscr{F}_{t-1}]\}
\end{aligned}
$$

for all $\tau \in \zeta(t, T)$. Hence Z_{t-1} as has been computed is greater than or equal to the right hand side of (4.7) for time $t - 1$. On the other hand, taking the stopping time in (4.9) for time t we see that (4.12) becomes an equality. It follows that Z_{t-1} as has been computed satisfies (4.7) for time t and that the stopping time given by (4.9) for time $t - 1$ is the one which maximizes the right hand side of (4.7) for time $t - 1$.

Hence by a mathematical induction argument we have described an algorithm for computing a process Z which satisfies (4.7), and we have verified that (4.9) gives the stopping times which achieve the maximum on the right hand side of (4.7). This algorithm is based on dynamic programming, which is simply the idea that if the optimal exercise strategy starting at time $t - 1$ calls for continuing at least one more period, then next period you will use the optimal exercise strategy starting at time t.

Example 4.1 (continued)   Starting with $Z_2 = Y_2$ we compute for states ω_1 and ω_2

$$E_Q[Z_2|\mathscr{F}_1] = E_Q[Y_2|\mathscr{F}_1] = \frac{2}{3}(4) + \frac{1}{3}(1) = 3$$

Hence $Z_1 = \max\{Y_1, E_Q[Z_2|\mathcal{F}_1]\} = \max\{4, 3\} = 4$ in these same states. Similarly, in states ω_3 and ω_4 we have $E_Q[Z_2|\mathcal{F}_1] = 1/3$ and $Z_1 = \max\{0, 1/3\} = 1/3$.

For the next dynamic programming iteration, that is, for time 0, we have

$$E_Q[Z_1|\mathcal{F}_0] = E_Q Z_1 = \frac{1}{4}(4) + \frac{3}{4}(1/3) = 1.25$$

in which case $Z_0 = \max\{Y_0, E_Q Z_1\} = \max\{1, 1.25\} = 1.25$. Note Z is displayed in figure 4.3.

Looking at (4.11) it is easy to see that $Z \geqslant Y$ and that $Z_t \geqslant E_Q[Z_{t+1}B_t/B_{t+1}|\mathcal{F}_t]$ for $t = 0, 1, \ldots, T-1$. It follows from this inequality that Z/B is a Q-supermartingale. Note that the value process $Z = Z/B$ (recall $B = 1$) in figure 4.3 for example 4.1 is indeed a Q-supermartingale.

Now suppose U is another process satisfying $U \geqslant Y$ and such that U/B is a Q-supermartingale. Then

(4.13) $\qquad U_{t-1} \geqslant \max\{Y_{t-1}, E_Q[U_t B_{t-1}/B_t|\mathcal{F}_{t-1}]\}, \quad t = 1, \ldots, T$

In particular, $U_T \geqslant Y_T = Z_T$, so taking (4.13) for $t = T$ we realize from (4.11) that $U_{t-1} \geqslant Z_{t-1}$. We can repeat this argument, working backwards in time, until we eventually obtain the conclusion that $U_0 \geqslant Z_0$. We thus conclude that Z/B is the smallest Q-supermartingale such that $Z \geqslant Y$. This completes the verification of principle (4.6).

Recall that the time t price of a European option X is given by $E_Q[XB_t/B_T|\mathcal{F}_t]$ provided X is marketable, whereas we are unable to pin down the price of X if it is not marketable. A similar situation exists for American options. If an American option Y is marketable (to be defined shortly), then its time t price is given by Z_t, as developed in (4.6). On the other hand, if Y is not marketable, then we are unable to specify its price.

The American option Y will be *marketable* or *attainable* if for each stopping time $\tau \leqslant T$ there exists a self-financing trading strategy such that the corresponding portfolio value V satisfies $V_\tau = Y_\tau$. In other words, Y will be marketable if one can *replicate* claims of the form Y_τ, and the trading strategy that corresponds to $V_\tau = Y_\tau$ is called a *replicating* or *hedging* trading strategy. This definition of marketability is stronger than necessary, since we really only need to worry about stopping times of the form (4.9). However, the approach taken here is simpler, and it is a property that can be checked without having to first compute the American option's value process Z.

Example 4.1 (continued) For the American option in figure 4.3 we will only check the stopping times of the form (4.9), that is

$$\tau(0) = \tau(1) = \begin{cases} 1, & \omega = \omega_1, \omega_2 \\ 2, & \omega = \omega_3, \omega_4 \end{cases}$$

and $\tau(2)(\omega) = 2$, *all* $\omega \in \Omega$. Now $Y_{\tau(2)} = Y_2$ is the same as the European call option X that we have been studying; we know X is marketable, so there exists a trading strategy such that $V_{\tau(t)} = Y_{\tau(t)}$ holds for $t = 2$.

For $\tau \equiv \tau(0) = \tau(1)$ we have

$$Y_\tau = \begin{cases} 4, & \omega = \omega_1, \omega_2 \\ 1, & \omega = \omega_3 \\ 0, & \omega = \omega_4 \end{cases}$$

To see if there is a trading strategy such that $V_{\tau(t)} = Y_{\tau(t)}$ is satisfied for $t = 0$ and 1, we work backwards in time, trying to compute the requisite trading strategy, beginning with the largest value of τ:

$$H_0(2) + 6\,H_1(2) = Y_2(\omega_3) = 1$$
$$H_0(2) + 3\,H_1(2) = Y_2(\omega_4) = 0$$

The solution exists and is $H_0(2) = -1$ and $H_1(2) = 1/3$ in states ω_3 and ω_4. Since the trading strategy must be self-financing, this implies $V_1 = 1/3$ in the same states.

The values of $H_0(2)$ and $H_1(2)$ for states ω_3 and ω_4 do not really matter, since $\tau = 1$ in these states. All that remains is to see if there are values of $H_0(1)$ and $H_1(1)$ satisfying

$$H_0(1) + 8\,H_1(1) = Y_1(\omega_1) = Y_1(\omega_2) = 4$$
$$H_0(1) + 4\,H_1(1) = V_1(\omega_3) = V_1(\omega_4) = 1/3$$

The solution exists and is $H_0(1) = -10/3$ and $H_1(1) = 11/12$. Thus there exists a trading strategy satisfying $V_{\tau(t)} = Y_{\tau(t)}$ for t equal to 0 and 1, in which case Y is a marketable American option. Notice that the time 0 value of the portfolio we just derived is $-10/3 + 5\,(11/12) = 5/4$, which is the same as the value of Z_0 for this American option that was computed earlier.

(4.14)   Suppose there exists a risk neutral probability measure Q, the process Z is as in (4.7), and the American option Y is marketable. Then Z is the value or price process for Y, and the optimal early exercise strategy $\tau(0)$ is given by (4.9).

To see that Z is the price process for Y, one can use an arbitrage argument similar to what was used for European options. Briefly, let p denote the time 0 price of Y, and suppose $p > Z_0$. Then one can sell the option for p dollars, undertake the trading strategy that replicates $Y_{\tau(0)}$ at a cost of Z_0, and invest the difference $p - Z_0$ in the bank account. Later, if the buyer exercises the option at time $t \leqslant \tau(0)$, you liquidate the portfolio, collecting Z_t dollars and paying the option buyer Y_t. Since $Z_t \geqslant Y_t$, these transactions at the exercise time will only add to your profit, thereby guaranteeing yourself a strictly positive profit overall.

On the other hand, suppose the option buyer does not exercise by time $t = \tau(0)$, where $\tau(0) < T$. Then you repeat this process, undertaking the trading strategy that replicates $Y_{\tau(t)}$ at a cost of $E_Q[Z_{t+1}B_t/B_{t+1}|\mathscr{F}_t]$, which is less than or equal to $Z_t = Y_t$ by the dynamic programming relationship (4.11). As before, if the option buyer exercises at some time $s \leqslant \tau(t)$, then the value of the portfolio will be enough to cover the payoff Y_s. If the buyer still has not exercised by time $\tau(t)$, then you repeat this process yet again, and so forth. The bottom line: you will always have enough money in your portfolio to cover the payoff, and your overall profit will be at least $p - Z_0 > 0$.

For the opposite case, suppose the time 0 price of the option satisfies $p < Z_0$. Then you buy the option for p dollars, you undertake the negative of the replicating trading strategy, thereby collecting Z_0 dollars, and you invest the difference $Z_0 - p$ in the bank account. Later you exercise the option at time $\tau(0)$, and you liquidate the replicating portfolio at the same time. Since $V_{\tau(0)} = Y_{\tau(0)}$, the amount you collect from the option seller is exactly equal to your liability on the portfolio. Meanwhile, you have $(Z_0 - p)B_{\tau(0)} > 0$ dollars in the bank account.

Hence if $p \neq Z_0$ there will exist an arbitrage opportunity, so Z_0 must be the time 0 price of the American option Y. Moreover, an optimal exercise strategy for the option buyer is given by (4.9), because any other strategy runs the risk of exercising when $Z_t(\omega) > Y_t(\omega)$, which means the option's buyer would foolishly sacrifice the amount $Z_t(\omega) - Y_t(\omega) > 0$. A similar argument will verify that Z_t is the time t price of this option and that (4.9) also gives the optimal exercise strategy starting at time t when $t > 0$.

We now turn to a new question: under what circumstances should the buyer of an American option never exercise early? Principle (4.6) gives one sufficient condition for $\tau = T$ to be the optimal exercise strategy. An adapted stochastic process $Z = \{Z_t; t = 0, 1, \ldots, T\}$ is said to be a *submartingale* (see section 3.3) if

$$E[Z_t|\mathscr{F}_s] \geqslant Z_s, \quad all \; 0 \leqslant s \leqslant t \leqslant T,$$

that is, if $-Z$ is a supermartingale. This definition permits one to state another sufficient condition.

(**4.15**) If Y is a marketable American option and Y/B is a Q-submartingale, then $\tau = T$ is always an optimal exercise strategy, and the price of this American option coincides with the price of the European option $X = Y_T$.

To understand this, we need something called the *optional sampling theorem*, which says that if Y/B is a Q-submartingale, then $E_Q[Y_\tau/B_\tau] \leqslant E_Q[Y_T/B_T]$ for all stopping times $\tau \leqslant T$. Hence by (4.7) with $t = 0$ we have $Z_0 = E_Q[Y_T/B_T]$, which we recognize as the price of the European option $X = Y_T$.

Principle (4.15) provides a condition that is sometimes convenient for checking whether the American and European options' values coincide. For example, we have the following.

(4.16)   In a world of non-negative interest rates and no dividends, an American call option written on an individual risky security should not be exercised early.

To see this it suffices to verify that $(S_t - e)^+/B_t = (S_t/B_t - e/B_t)^+$ is a Q-submartingale by showing for arbitrary $s, t \geqslant 0$ that

$$(S_{t+s}/B_{t+s} - e/B_{t+s})^+ \leqslant E_Q[\,(S_{t+s}/B_{t+s} - e/B_{t+s})^+|\mathcal{F}_t]$$

To begin with, we have

$$E_Q[\,(S_{t+s}/B_{t+s} - e/B_{t+s})^+|\mathcal{F}_t] \geqslant E_Q[\,(S_{t+s}/B_{t+s} - e/B_{t+s}|\mathcal{F}_t]$$

$$= E_Q[S_{t+s}/B_{t+s}|\mathcal{F}_t] - eE_Q[1/B_{t+s}|\mathcal{F}_t] = S_t/B_t - eE_Q[1/B_{t+s}|\mathcal{F}_t]$$

where the last equality is because S/B is a Q-martingale. But $B_{t+s} \geqslant B_t$, so $1/B_t \geqslant 1/B_{t+s}$ and thus

$$E_Q[\,(S_{t+s}/B_{t+s} - e/B_{t+s})^+|\mathcal{F}_t] \geqslant S_t/B_t - eE_Q[1/B_t|\mathcal{F}_t] = S_t/B_t - e/B_t$$

Finally, since $E_Q[\,(S_{t+s}/B_{t+s} - e/B_{t+s})^+|\mathcal{F}_t] \geqslant 0$, it follows that $E_Q[\,(S_{t+s}/B_{t+s} - e/B_{t+s})^+|\mathcal{F}_t] \geqslant \max\{0, S_t/B_t - e/B_t\}$, which is exactly what we wanted to show.

It should be emphasized that a crucial part of this verification of (4.16) is the requirement that the discounted security price S/B is a Q-martingale. If the risky security pays a dividend, then the discounted, ex-dividend price of this security is not necessarily a Q-martingale, in which case the American call option based on the ex-dividend price might be worth strictly more than the corresponding European option.

Exercise 4.8   For the model in example 4.1 with $r = 0$, what is the time 0 price of an American put that has exercise price $e = 6$? Is it optimal to exercise early? If so, when? And how do you hedge this option if you sell it at time 0?

Exercise 4.9   Consider the binomial stock price model with $T = 4$, $S_0 = 20$, $u = 1.2214$, and $d = 0.8187 = u^{-1}$. The interest rate is $r = 3.82\%$. What is the time 0 price of an American put that has exercise price $e = 18$? Is it optimal to exercise early? If so, when?

Exercise 4.10   Show that if $M = \{M_t; t = 0, \ldots, T\}$ is a supermartingale, then $E[M_\tau|\mathcal{F}_t] \leqslant M_t$ for all stopping times τ with $t \leqslant \tau \leqslant T$.

Exercise 4.11   Suppose the American option $Y_t = g(S_t)$, where g is a convex function with $g(0) = 0$. Let the interest rate be constant with $r \geqslant 0$. Show that $\tau = T$ is an optimal exercise strategy. (Hint: use (4.15) together with *Jensen's inequality*, which says that $g(E[X|\mathcal{F}]) \leqslant E[g(X)|\mathcal{F}]$ for any convex function g, any random variable X, and any algebra $\mathcal{F}$.)

Exercise 4.12   Suppose b is a positive constant and the interest rates are non-negative. Show that $-b/B_t$ is a Q-submartingale. If $M_1(t), \ldots, M_J(t)$ are

Q-submartingales and $m_1, \ldots, m_J$ are positive scalars, then show $m_1 M_1 + \ldots + m_J M_J$ is a Q-submartingale. Hence show for American options of the form

$$Y_t = m_0 S_t + m_1 (S_t - e_1)^+ + \ldots + m_J (S_t - e_J)^+ - b$$

where $m_1 \geqslant 0 \ldots, m_J \geqslant 0$, and $b \geqslant 0$ (but m_0 can be negative), that it is optimal to not exercise early.

4.4   Complete and Incomplete Markets

In order to price a contingent claim X you need to worry about whether it is marketable, that is, whether there exists a self-financing trading strategy such that $V_T = X$. In this regard, the situation is virtually the same as with single period models. This section will explain how the single period results generalize to multiperiod models and give special attention to the new issue of marketable American options. Throughout this section, of course, it will be assumed that there exists a risk neutral probability measure Q.

The model is said to be *complete* if every contingent claim is marketable; otherwise, the model is said to be *incomplete*. For single period models, we saw there were two characterizations of completeness: either (1.22), the number of independent vectors in a certain matrix, denoted A, equals the number of states in, or (1.24) the risk neutral probability measure is unique. Both characterizations generalize to multiperiod models, as can be seen by decomposing the multiperiod model into a network of single period models, as was done in section 3.3. In particular, think of the information tree corresponding to the multiperiod model, with one underlying single period model at each node of this network.

If the multiperiod model is complete, then for an arbitrary contingent claim X you can always work backwards in time, as was explained in section 4.1, to compute the trading strategy that generates X. This means the matrix A for each underlying single period model must have the requisite number of independent columns, or the computational procedure may fail. Thus every underlying single period model must be complete. Conversely, if every underlying single period model is complete, then the computational procedure for the multiperiod model will always succeed, and we have the following.

(4.17)   The multiperiod model is complete if and only if every underlying single period model is complete.

In particular, the multiperiod model is complete if and only if the A-matrix corresponding to every underlying single period model has the requisite number of independent columns. Now this generalization of (1.22) is a rather ugly and impractical characterization, so it will not be highlighted.

On the other hand, the generalization of (1.24) is rather nice. Every underlying single period model is complete if and only if each underlying single period model has a unique risk neutral 'conditional' probability measure. In view of the construction that was developed in section 3.3 of the risk neutral probability measure for the multiperiod model, every underlying single period model has a unique risk neutral 'conditional' probability measure if and only if the risk neutral probability measure for the multiperiod model is unique. Hence we have the following.

(4.18)   The multiperiod model is complete if and only if the risk neutral probability measure Q is unique.

Example 4.1 (continued)   This model is complete, because the risk neutral probability measure is unique.

Example 4.4 (continued)   This model is complete, because the risk neutral probability measure is unique.

Example 4.9 (continued)   The binomial model studied in section 4.2 is complete, because the risk neutral probability measure is unique.

In an incomplete model, therefore, there will exist at least two, and thus many, risk neutral probability measures. If X is an attainable contingent claim in an incomplete model, then its time 0 price will equal V_0 for the trading strategy which generates X. Since $V_0 = E_Q[X/B_T]$ for every risk neutral probability measure Q, we realize that for marketable contingent claims the quantity $E_Q[X/B_T]$ is constant over the risk neutral probability measures, that is, over all $Q \in \mathsf{M}$.

To show the converse, it suffices to suppose the contingent claim X is not attainable and then demonstrate that $E_Q[X/B_T]$ does not take the same value for all $Q \in \mathsf{M}$. The argument will only be sketched. Again, think of the network of underlying single period models, and suppose you are trying to compute the replicating trading strategy by working backwards in time. This procedure will break down at some single period model. As seen in section 1.5, this means there will exist at least two sets of risk neutral 'conditional' probabilities for this single period model giving different conditional expectations to X/B_T. It follows that there will exist at least two martingale measures Q giving different values to $E_Q[X/B_T]$.

In summary, we have the following generalization of (1.23), true for both complete and incomplete models.

(4.19)   The contingent claim X is attainable if and only if $E_Q[X/B_T]$ takes the same value for every $Q \in \mathsf{M}$.

Turning to American options, fortunately there is the following.

(4.20)   If the model is complete, then every American option is marketable.

To see this it suffices to take an arbitrary non-negative adapted process Y and an arbitrary stopping time τ and show that there exists a self-financing trading strategy such that $V_\tau = Y_\tau$. To do this we use a trick: we consider a trading strategy, say $\hat{H}$, which starts at time τ with the Y_τ dollars, all of which is put into and kept in the bank account until time T. Under such a strategy there will be $Y_\tau B_T / B_\tau$ dollars at time T. Meanwhile, since the model is complete, we know there exists a trading strategy, say H, which starts at time 0 and satisfies $V_T = Y_\tau B_T / B_\tau$. Since the time T values of the two portfolios are the same, we realize that the time τ values of the portfolios under H and $\hat{H}$ must coincide, that is, $V_\tau = \hat{V}_\tau = Y_\tau$. Hence H is the strategy we were seeking.

If the market is incomplete, then an arbitrary American option may or may not be marketable. In view of (4.19) and the preceding paragraph, we have the following.

(4.21) The American option Y is attainable if and only if, for each stopping time τ in (4.9), $E_Q[Y_\tau / B_\tau]$ takes the same value for all $Q \in \mathsf{M}$.

Unfortunately, this condition is not so easy to check in particular cases.

Example 4.10 Suppose $K = 5$, $N = 1$, $T = 2$, $r = 0$, the filtration $\mathcal{F}_t$ is generated by the price process S, and S is as shown:

ω	S_0	S_1	S_2	Q
ω_1	5	8	9	$q/4$
ω_2	5	8	7	$(2 - 3q)/4$
ω_3	5	8	6	$(2q - 1)/4$
ω_4	5	4	6	$1/4$
ω_5	5	4	3	$1/2$

The martingale measure Q was computed and is displayed in this table; here q is any scalar satisfying $1/2 < q < 2/3$. This model is not complete, because the martingale measure is not unique.

The contingent claim X is marketable if and only if

$$E_q X = [qX_1 + (2 - 3q)X_2 + (2q - 1)X_3 + X_4 + 2X_5]/4$$
$$= q[X_1 - 3X_2 + 2X_3]/4 + X_2/2 - X_3/4 + X_4/4 + X_5/2$$

is constant with respect to q, where here X_i denotes $X(\omega_i)$. Hence the contingent claim X is marketable if and only if

$$X_1 - 3X_2 + 2X_3 = 0$$

To check whether the American option Y is marketable, we certainly need to check whether this equation is satisfied with $X = Y_2$. In addition, we need to check whether, for relevant stopping times τ, $E_q Y_\tau$ is constant with respect to q. There are only two stopping times of interest: either $\tau_a \equiv 1_{\{S_1=8\}} + 2 \cdot 1_{\{S_1=4\}}$ or $\tau_b \equiv 2 \cdot 1_{\{S_1=8\}} + 1_{\{S_1=4\}}$. Applying (4.21), we compute

$$E_q Y_{\tau_a} = Y_1(\omega_1)/4 + Y_2(\omega_4)/4 + Y_2(\omega_5)/2$$

(recall Y is adapted, so $Y_1(\omega_1) = Y_1(\omega_2) = Y_1(\omega_3)$). This is clearly constant with respect to q. Similarly, we compute

$$E_q Y_{\tau_b} = Y_2(\omega_1)q/4 + Y_2(\omega_2)(2-3q)/4 + Y_2(\omega_3)(2q-1)/4 + 3Y_1(\omega_4)/4$$

$$= \frac{q}{4}[Y_2(\omega_1) - 3Y_2(\omega_2) + 2Y_2(\omega_3)] + Y_2(\omega_2)/2 - Y_2(\omega_3)/4 + 3Y_1(\omega_4)/4$$

The condition that this be constant with respect to q leads to the same requirement as before: the American option Y is marketable if and only if $X_1 - 3X_2 + 2X_3 = 0$ is satisfied with $X = Y_2$, that is, if and only if the European option $X = Y_2$ is marketable.

Exercise 4.13   Consider the model in example 4.10. For what values of the exercise price e is the call option marketable? For what values of e is the put option marketable?

4.5   Forward Prices and Cash Stream Valuation

Suppose you agree at time t to acquire a security at time τ, paying for it at time τ with an amount you negotiated at time t. Or suppose you want to purchase a cash stream of future receipts in exchange for your payment at time t. As will be discussed in this section, the prices of these derivative securities can be evaluated with arbitrage pricing theory.

Actually, these derivative securities can only be evaluated if they can be replicated with trading strategies, so for ease of exposition it will be assumed throughout this section that the securities market model is complete.

First consider a cash stream which consists of ΔD_s dollars received at time s, where $t < s \leqslant T$. This is just a time s contingent claim, so its time t value is $E_Q[\Delta D_s B_t / B_s | \mathscr{F}_t]$. If ΔD_s is deterministic (or even is $\mathscr{F}_t$ measurable), then this simplifies to $\Delta D_s E_Q[B_t / B_s | \mathscr{F}_t]$. If, in addition, the interest rate $r \geqslant 0$ is constant, then this simplifies further to $\Delta D_s(1+r)^{t-s}$. All these expressions are often called the time t *present value* of ΔD_s.

Next consider a cash stream $\Delta D_{t+1}, \ldots, \Delta D_\tau$. For example, these receipts may be the dividends associated with one unit of a security S. In view of the preceding paragraph, the time t present value of this cash stream is simply

$$\sum_{s=t+1}^{\tau} E_Q[\Delta D_s B_t / B_s | \mathscr{F}_t].$$

In the special case where this cash stream comes from the dividend process D associated with the security S, it follows from (3.22) that the time t present value of this cash stream is

$$S_t - E_Q[S_\tau B_t / B_\tau | \mathcal{F}_t].$$

These present value expressions are of fundamental importance in finance, especially when the interest rate is constant.

Sometimes two parties may each have a cash stream which, although featuring different receipts at various future times, have identical time t present values. In such a case, these two parties may find it advantageous to trade their cash streams. Such a transaction is called a *swap*. Swaps are also made when the time t present values of the two cash streams are different, simply by having one party pay the other at time t an amount equal to the difference between the two time t present values.

Turning to the subject of forward prices, suppose at time t you agree to purchase one unit of security S from a broker. No money or security units are exchanged at time t, but the agreement you made at time t stipulates that at the future time $\tau, t < \tau \leqslant T$, you will receive one unit of security S and you will pay your broker O_t dollars (note: the notation 'O_t' comes from *fOrward*). The question is: is there a correct value for the *forward price O_t*?

It should not come as a surprise to learn that the answer to this question is yes. The idea is to realize that holding the forward agreement plus O_t dollars at time τ is equivalent to holding one unit of security S at the same time. To be specific, in the first strategy you enter the forward agreement at time t, at the same time you replicate the contingent claim which pays O_t dollars at time τ, and at time τ you fulfill the forward agreement by paying O_t dollars and receiving the security. The time t cost of replicating O_t is simply the present value of O_t, that is,

$$E_Q[O_t B_t / B_\tau | \mathcal{F}_t] = O_t E_Q[B_t / B_\tau | \mathcal{F}_t].$$

The second strategy is worth S_τ at time τ, and its time t present value is simply S_t (by the definition of the martingale measure Q). But the first strategy is also worth S_τ at time τ, so by the law of one price the time t values of the two strategies must be equal, that is, $S_t = O_t E_Q[B_t / B_\tau | \mathcal{F}_t]$. In other words, we have the following.

(4.22) The time t forward price O_t of security S, which is received and paid for at time $\tau > t$ and which pays no dividends, is

$$O_t = \frac{S_t}{E_Q[B_t / B_\tau | \mathcal{F}_t]}$$

It is worth pointing out that this expression for the forward price is not necessarily true if the security S pays dividends. This is because (4.22) was derived by assuming S/B is a Q-martingale, an assumption that is false when the security pays a dividend. However, principle (4.22) can easily be generalized to the case of a dividend-paying security.

To derive a generalization, we need to concoct and then price the trading strategy which replicates the time τ contingent claim equal to S_τ. Here it is:

- At time t purchase one unit of the security by paying S_t.
- At time t borrow $E_Q[\Delta D_{t+1} B_t / B_{t+1} | \mathcal{F}_t]$ dollars by undertaking the negative of the trading strategy that replicates the time $t+1$ receipt ΔD_{t+1}. Then at time $t+1$ use the dividend payment ΔD_{t+1} to settle the liability under this strategy.

$$\vdots$$

- At time t borrow $E_Q[\Delta D_\tau B_t / B_\tau | \mathcal{F}_t]$ dollars by undertaking the negative of the trading strategy that replicates the time τ receipt ΔD_τ. Then at time τ use the dividend payment ΔD_τ to settle the liability under this strategy.

The time t value of this replicating portfolio must be

$$S_t - \sum_{s=t+1}^{\tau} E_Q[\Delta D_s B_t / B_s | \mathcal{F}_t]$$

Equating this with the time t present value of the time τ receipt O_t, we obtain the following conclusion.

(4.23)   The time t forward price O_t of security S, which is received and paid for at time $\tau > t$, and which has the dividend process D, is

$$O_t = \frac{S_t}{E_Q[B_t / B_\tau | \mathcal{F}_t]} - \sum_{s=t+1}^{\tau} \frac{E_Q[\Delta D_s B_t / B_s | \mathcal{F}_t]}{E_Q[B_t / B_\tau | \mathcal{F}_t]}$$

Sometimes forward prices are associated with assets which cannot be classified as securities because it is impossible to sell them short. For example, most agricultural commodities, such as live hogs, bushels of corn, and bales of cotton, cannot be sold short, perhaps because there is no market to borrow these physical goods from the farmers. Consequently, the usual arbitrage arguments break down, and one cannot be sure whether the discounted cash (or *spot*) prices of these assets are martingales under any probability measure.

For many such assets it is perfectly feasible to purchase them, provided you are willing to pay a *carrying cost* of c dollars per unit per period (perhaps this is an inventory storage charge). This is like a security that pays a dividend, only the dividend process satisfies $\Delta D_t = -c$ for all t.

Let A_t denote the time t cash price of this asset, $t = 0, 1, \ldots T$. An *arbitrage opportunity* associated with this asset can be defined just as with a security, except that one must add the stipulation that the position H_1 in this asset must be non-negative. Recalling the economic principles associated with ordinary securities, we realize that an arbitrage opportunity will exist with this asset if we can find some time t and some event $E \in \mathcal{F}_t$ such that

$$A_t(\omega)/B_t(\omega) \leqslant (A_{t+1}(\omega) - c)/B_{t+1}(\omega), \quad \text{all } \omega \in E$$

with this inequality being strict for at least one $\omega \in E$. If event E occurs, then we buy the asset with money borrowed from the bank, and next period we cash out with a net profit that is non-negative in all $\omega \in E$ and strictly positive for at least one such ω. It follows that if there exists a strictly positive probability measure Q such that

$$(4.24) \qquad A_t/B_t \geqslant E_Q[(A_{t+1} - c)/B_{t+1}|\mathscr{F}_t], \quad t = 0, 1, \ldots, T - 1.$$

then this kind of arbitrage opportunity cannot arise.

On the other hand, there is no economic mechanism to prevent inequality (4.24) from being strict for some ω and some t. If this asset $A = \{A_t; T = 0, 1 \ldots, T\}$ is actually a security, then a strict inequality by every strictly positive probability measure would signal an arbitrage opportunity, with the associated trading strategy entailing a short position in the security. But for our asset which cannot be sold short, a strict inequality in (4.24) is of no consequence, because a trading strategy involving a short position is inadmissible and thus not an arbitrage opportunity. Hence I have sketched out an explanation of the following.

> **(4.25)** If the market model includes an asset with cash price $A = \{A_t; T = 0, \ldots, T\}$ which cannot be sold short and which has carrying cost c per unit per period, then there are no arbitrage opportunities if and only if there exists a strictly positive probability measure Q such that all the discounted securities are Q-martingales and such that (4.24) is satisfied.

Now suppose there is a forward price O_t for this asset A, based upon payment at time τ. If this asset is actually a security, then by (4.23) we would have

$$(4.26) \qquad O_t = \frac{A_t}{E_Q[B_t/B_\tau|\mathscr{F}_t]} + c \sum_{s=t+1}^{\tau} \frac{E_Q[B_t/B_s|\mathscr{F}_t]}{E_Q[B_t/B_\tau|\mathscr{F}_t]}$$

However, if this asset cannot be sold short, then the law of one price does not hold. In particular, if the forward price O_t is strictly less than the right hand side of (4.26), then it would be desirable to buy the asset for time τ delivery at the forward price O_t while simultaneously following the negative of the trading strategy that replicates A_τ. But this cannot be done, because it is not possible to sell this asset short. There is no economic mechanism to prevent the forward price O_t from being strictly less than the right hand side of (4.26).

On the other hand, if the forward price O_t is strictly greater than the right hand side of (4.26), then it would be desirable to sell the asset for time τ delivery at the forward price O_t while simultaneously following the trading strategy that replicates A_τ. This can be done, so this is an arbitrage opportunity. This can be summarized as follows.

> **(4.27)** Suppose there is an asset with cash price $A = \{A_t; T = 0, 1 \ldots, T\}$ which cannot be sold short and which has carrying cost c per unit per period. The time t forward price O_t of this asset, which is received and paid for at time $\tau > t$, satisfies
>
> $$O_t \leqslant \frac{A_t}{E_Q[B_t/B_\tau|\mathscr{F}_t]} + c \sum_{s=t+1}^{\tau} \frac{E_Q[B_t/B_s|\mathscr{F}_t]}{E_Q[B_t/B_\tau|\mathscr{F}_t]}$$

Exercise 4.14   Consider a two-period model with $\Omega = \{\omega_1, \ldots, \omega_4\}$ and an asset with time 0 price $A_0 = 100$.

(a)   If the bank account process is deterministic according to $B_t = (1.05)^t$ for $t = 0, 1, 2$ and if the asset can be sold short, then what is the time 0 forward price O_0 of the asset for delivery at time 2?

(b)   If the bank account process is random with $B_t = (1.05)$, $B_2(\omega_1) = B_2(\omega_2) = 1.12$ and $B_2(\omega_3) = B_2(\omega_4) = 1.10$ and if the asset can be sold short, then what is the time 0 forward price O_0 for time 2 delivery of the asset?

(c)   If the bank account process is random as in part (b) and if the asset cannot be sold short, then what is the largest value for the time 0 price O_0 of the asset for time 2 delivery that is consistent with no-arbitrage?

(d)   Same as part (c), only now the asset has a carrying cost of $5 per period.

4.6   Futures

Futures prices closely resemble forward prices in that they both are based on the cash price of a security or asset at a fixed, future point in time. In particular, at time τ both the forward and futures prices for time τ delivery will equal the underlying cash price. However, there are subtle differences which can cause the two prices to be different.

Futures prices are associated with futures contracts which are traded on organized exchanges. For example, a speculator can purchase a contract for the delivery of 5000 bushels of wheat in July. The price is established at the time of the transaction, and then, as additional transactions occur between other buyers and sellers, the value of the speculator's purchased contract will fluctuate in accordance with the ensueing transaction prices. Moreover, the speculator can close out the position at any time before delivery by doing a reverse transaction at the exchange, thereby yielding a net profit based on the difference between the futures prices at the two transaction times. Hence, in the case of futures contracts, there may be arbitrage opportunities which can be 'cashed out' well before the scheduled delivery time.

In contrast, positions in forward contracts must be held until the time of actual delivery. This is because forward contracts are made between two specific individuals or parties, and the position held by one of these parties cannot be closed out before the delivery time by selling the position to a third party. Hence the only arbitrage opportunities that can be present are ones which, once a forward position is established, are held in constant fashion until the delivery time.

Just as with forwards, for every buyer of a futures contract there is a seller, that is, an individual who 'promises to deliver a specified quantity of the asset at a specified future point in time.' This phrase is in quotes, because usually the seller will close out his or her position before the delivery time, and some futures contracts are simply tied to the underlying cash price at the 'delivery' time, with no possibility for an actual delivery to occur.

An important feature of futures contracts is that buyers and sellers must deposit margin or collateral with the exchange. This is to make sure the buyer or seller does not walk away from a losing position. The amount of funds in the trader's margin account will fluctuate continuously in accordance with the fluctuations of subsequent futures prices. For example, if the futures price of a 5000 bushel July wheat contract goes down ten cents a bushel, then a buyer of this contract will have $500 removed from his or her margin account. In this fashion, cumulative net profits from futures transactions are continuously reflected until the positions are closed out.

Futures traders cannot borrow money and then put the resulting funds in their margin account in order to trade futures contracts. And the exchange will either ask for more funds or close out the trader's futures positions if the margin account becomes depleted. Hence futures traders always have positive wealth, and individuals with zero or negative wealth cannot trade futures contracts.

Futures traders may use securities as collateral in the margin account. For example, a trader could pledge funds earning interest in a bank account. Hence an individual with a security portfolio that has positive wealth can trade futures simply by using part or all of this portfolio as collateral for the margin requirement. This trader is thereby able to trade futures contracts without using any extra funds that are dedicated to the futures contracts. To buy a security you must come up with some cash, but you can buy a futures contract for free!

In order to make these ideas more precise and to see their consequences, we take our usual securities market model and superimpose one or more futures price processes. Let U_t (or $U_j(t)$, $j = 1, \ldots, J$) denote (the notation 'U' comes from *fUtures*) the time t futures price for a security or asset that is delivered at time $\tau \leqslant T$ (or τ_j, respectively). It may be appropriate to stipulate $U_j(\tau_j) = S_J(\tau_j)$ for $j = 1, \ldots, J$, but in some cases the futures market model may contain one or more futures price processes that are not tied to specific securities in this manner. For example, the securities could be stocks and U_t could be the futures price of May corn.

In addition to the usual strategies for trading the securities, let the predictable process $\hat{H}_t$ (or $\hat{H}_j(t)$) represent the position in the futures contract U (or U_j, respectively) held from time $t - 1$ to time t. Naturally, if the futures contract U_j expires at time $\tau_j < T$, then $\hat{H}_j(t) = 0$ is required for all $t > \tau_j$. The overall trading strategy will be a predictable, vector-valued process of the form $(H, \hat{H}) = (H_0, H_1, \ldots, H_N, \hat{H}_1, \ldots, \hat{H}_J)$.

At time t, just after any time t transactions, the value of a portfolio is the same as before when there are no futures contracts, namely,

$$H_0(t + 1)B_t + \sum_{n=1}^{N} H_n(t + 1)S_n(t)$$

However, the portfolio's value V_t just before any time t transactions will be different, for it will equal the money in the bank account and the securities (as with no futures) *plus* the net profit over the last period due to the futures trades. In other words,

$$V_t = H_0(t)B_n + \sum_{n=1}^{N} H_n(t)S_n(t) + \sum_{j=1}^{J} \hat{H}_j(t)\Delta U_j(t), \quad t > 0$$

We let

$$V_0 = H_0(1)B_0 + \sum_{n=1}^{N} H_n(t)S_0(t)$$

denote the usual time 0 value of the portfolio.

A trading strategy $(H, \hat{H})$ in our futures market model will be called *self-financing* if no money is consumed or added to the portfolio from an exogenous source between times 0 and T, that is, if

$$V_t = H_0(t+1)B_t + \sum_{n=1}^{N} H_n(t+1)S_0(t), \quad t = 1, \ldots, T-1$$

Our aim is to derive an explicit relationship for the futures price in terms of its underlying security. We can do this if it is assumed there are no arbitrage opportunities. Since futures traders must have positive wealth, we cannot proceed as with ordinary securities market models and define an arbitrage opportunity as a trading strategy that starts with $V_0 = 0$. But the idea will be the same; we will just shift the starting point to a positive level of initial wealth. A self-financing trading strategy in our futures market model will be called an *arbitrage opportunity* if

(a) $V_T \geqslant V_0 B_T$
(b) $V_T \neq V_0 B_T$

Thus an arbitrage opportunity will do no worse than putting all your money in the bank account, and there is the possibility that it will do strictly better.

Just as for ordinary securities market models, we can decompose the multiperiod futures market model into a network of single period models, with one single period model corresponding to each node in the information tree submodel of the filtration. It follows that an arbitrage opportunity will exist for the multiperiod model if and only if there exists an arbitrage opportunity for one or more of the underlying single period models. Hence we can learn about multiperiod futures markets by first studying single period futures markets.

We begin by comparing V_1 with $V_0(B_1/B_0)$:

$$V_1 = V_0(B_1/B_0) \Longleftrightarrow$$

$$H_0(1)B_1 + \sum_{n=1}^{N} H_n(1)S_n(1) + \sum_{j=1}^{J} \hat{H}_j(1)\Delta U_j(1)$$

$$\geqslant \left[H_0(1)B_0 + \sum_{n=1}^{N} H_n(1)S_n(0) \right](B_1/B_0) \longleftrightarrow$$

$$\sum_{n=1}^{N} H_n(1)S_n(1) + \sum_{j=1}^{J} \hat{H}_j(1)\Delta U_j(1) \geqslant B_1 \sum_{n=1}^{N} H_n(1)S_n(0)/B_0 \iff$$

$$\sum_{n=1}^{N} H_n(1)S_n^*(1) + \sum_{j=1}^{J} \hat{H}_j(1)\Delta U_j(1)/B_1 \geqslant \sum_{n=1}^{N} H_n(1)S_n^*(0) \iff$$

$$(4.28) \quad \sum_{n=1}^{N} H_n(1)\Delta S_n^*(1) + \sum_{j=1}^{J} \hat{H}_j(1)\Delta U_j(1)/B_1 \geqslant 0$$

Note the first inequality is strict for one or more states ω if and only if inequality (4.28) is strict. Thus $(H, \hat{H})$ is an arbitrage opportunity for this single period model if and only if (4.28) holds, with the inequality being strict for one or more $\omega \in \Omega$.

Looking at (4.28) we see that the quantity $\Delta U_j(1)/B_1$ plays the same kind of role as the quantity $\Delta S_n^*(1)$. Knowing what we do for conventional single period models, we conclude the following.

(4.29) There are no arbitrage opportunities in the single period futures market model if and only if there exists a strictly positive probability measure Q such that $S_n^*(0) = E_Q[S_n^*(1)]$, $n = 1, \ldots, N$ and that $U_j(0) = E_Q[U_j(1)/B_1]/E_Q [1/B_1]$, $j = 1, \ldots, J$. If the interest rate $r = (B_1 - B_0)/B_0$ is constant, then this last equation simplifies to $U_j(0) = E_Q U_j(1)$.

Now (4.29) can be viewed as a requirement for the risk neutral probability measure. Given the bank account, security, and futures prices, it gives the requirement which Q must satisfy for there to be no arbitrage opportunities. Notice the requirement that $U_j(\tau_J) = S_j(\tau_j)$ for some time τ_j was not used; we only used the futures exchange's trading rules. Hence (4.29) can be applied to situations where expiration times τ exceed one (or even to situations where a futures price is based on an asset that is not a security or on a security that is not part of the securities model).

Alternatively, one could start with an arbitrage free securities market model and wish to add futures prices based on these securities. In the case of the single period model, one would know Q (this comes from the original securities market model) and the fact that $U_j(1) = S_j(1)$, and so one would use (4.29) and the fact that $S_j(0) = E_Q[S_j(1)/B_1]$ to conclude

$$(4.30) \qquad\qquad U_j(0) = \frac{S_j(0)}{E_Q[1/B_1]}$$

Example 4.11 Consider the single period model with $N = 1$, $K = 2$, $S_0 = 5$, $S_1(\omega_1) = U_1(\omega_1) = 8$, $S_1(\omega_2) = U_1(\omega_2) = 4$, and the interest rate constant with $0 \leqslant r < 3/5$. The risk neutral probability measure is computed from $E_Q[\Delta S^*] = 0$ to be $Q(\omega_1) = (1 + 5r)/4$ and $Q(\omega_2) = (3 - 5r)/4$. Hence by (4.29) the futures market model is arbitrage free if and only if $U_0 = E_Q[S_1] = 5(1 + r) = 5B_1$. Of course, this is the same as (4.30) and is consistent with the fact that

$$(\mathbf{4.31}) \quad V_1 = H_0 B_1 + H_1 S_1 + \hat{H}\Delta U = (V_0 - 5H_1)B_1 + H_1 S_1 + \hat{H}\Delta U$$

$$= \begin{cases} V_0 B_1(\omega_1) + H_1(8 - 5B_1(\omega_1)) + \hat{H}\Delta U(\omega_1), & \omega = \omega_1 \\ V_0 B_1(\omega_2) + H_1(4 - 5B_1(\omega_2)) + \hat{H}\Delta U(\omega_2), & \omega = \omega_2 \end{cases}$$

$$= \begin{cases} V_0(1 + r) + H_1(3 - 5r) + \hat{H}(3 - 5r), & \omega = \omega_1 \\ V_0(1 + r) + H_1(-1 - 5r) + \hat{H}(-1 - 5r), & \omega = \omega_2 \end{cases}$$

The point here is that with $U_0 = 5(1 + r)$ there is no way to choose H_1 and $\hat{H}$ so as to make $V_1 \geqslant V_0(1 + r)$ and $V_1 \neq V_0(1 + r)$. On the other hand, with U_0 taking any other value, the vector ΔU will not be a scalar multiple of the vector $S_1 - S_0 B_1$, and one can choose H_1 and $\hat{H}$ so as to be an arbitrage opportunity.

More generally, if U_1 is arbitrary instead of being equal to S_1, then (4.29) implies $U_0 = U_1(\omega_1)(1 + 5r)/4 + U_1(\omega_2)(3 - 5r)/4$. A little algebra verifies that the vector ΔU_1 is a scalar multiple of the vector $S_1 - S_0 B_1$, which is consistent with no arbitrage.

Now return to the case where $U_1 = S_1$ and suppose the interest rate r is random. The formula $U_0 = E_Q[S_1]$ in (4.29) will not apply, and instead we must use the more general $U_0 = E_Q[S_1/B_1]/E_Q[1/B_1]$ or (4.30). For example, with $r(\omega_1) = 1/16$ and $r(\omega_2) = 1/8$, the risk neutral probability measure is computed to be $Q(\omega_1) = 221/608$ and $Q(\omega_2) = 387/608$. It follows from (4.30) that $U_0 = 5\ 35/69$, which is different than $E_Q S_1 = 5\ 69/152$. With $U_0 = 5\ 35/69$ one has $\Delta U(\omega_1) = 172/69$ and $\Delta U(\omega_2) = -104/69$, so the first part of (4.31) implies

$$V_1 = \begin{cases} \frac{17}{16}V_0 + \frac{43}{16}H_1 + \frac{172}{69}\hat{H}, & \omega = \omega_1 \\ \frac{9}{8}V_0 - \frac{26}{16}H_1 - \frac{104}{69}\hat{H}, & \omega = \omega_2 \end{cases}$$

Some more algebra verifies that the vector ΔU is a scalar multiple of $S_1 - S_0 B_1$, so there is no way of choosing H_1 and $\hat{H}$ so as to be an arbitrage opportunity. Similar results hold when B_1 is random and $U_1 \neq S_1$.

In the preceding example, when $U_1 = S_1$ the futures price U_0 came out equal to the forward price $O_0 = S_0/E_Q[1/B_1]$. Looking at (4.30) one sees that this will hold in all single period models, even if B_1 is random, when $U_1 = S_1$. This is not surprising, since in a single period model the trading strategies available for replicating mispriced forwards and futures are identical. But in a multiperiod setting only 'buy-and-hold' and 'short-and-hold' strategies can be used to replicate mispriced forwards, and so, as we shall see, the futures and forward prices can be different.

We are now ready to analyze the multiperiod futures market model. Consider the single period model associated with an arbitrary time t and event A in $\mathscr{P}_t$, the cell in the partition corresponding to $\mathscr{F}_t$. As stated earlier, the multiperiod futures market model has no arbitrage opportunities if and only if none of the underlying single period models has any arbitrage opportunities. Our arbitrary single period model has an arbitrage opportunity if and only if trading positions can be taken at time t such that $V_{t+1}1_A \geqslant 1_A V_t B_{t+1}/B_t$, with this inequality being strict for at least one $\omega \in A$. Proceeding in an analogous fashion through the implications that led to (4.28), we see that the single period model has an arbitrage opportunity if and only if

$$\sum_{n=1}^{N} H_n(t+1)\Delta S_n^*(t+1) + \sum_{j=1}^{J} \hat{H}_j(t+1)\Delta U_j(t+1)/B_{t+1} \geqslant 0, \text{ all } \omega \in A$$

with this inequality being strict for at least one $\omega \in A$. It follows as in (4.29) that this single period model has no arbitrage opportunities if and only if there is a conditional risk neutral probability measure $Q(t, A) > 0$ such that $E_{Q(t,A)}[\Delta S_n^*(t+1)] = 0$ for all n and $E_{Q(t,A)}[\Delta U_j(t+1)/B_{t+1}] = 0$ for all j. Finally, and just as with conventional, multiperiod securities markets models (see section 3.4), we can paste all the single period models together and conclude that the multiperiod futures market model has no arbitrage opportunities if and only if there exists a strictly positive probability measure Q such that each S_n^* is a Q-martingale and

(4.32) $\qquad E_Q[\Delta U_j(t+1)/B_{t+1}|\mathscr{F}_t] = 0, \quad \text{all } t \geqslant 0 \text{ and } j = 1, \ldots, J$

There is just one problem: condition (4.32) is rather distasteful, being unattractive and somewhat difficult to work with. It turns out that little will be lost and considerable simplification will be gained if it is assumed that the bank account process B is predictable (in the single period model, this is the same as requiring B_1 to be a constant), for then (4.32) reduces to the much nicer requirement that each (undiscounted) futures process is a martingale under Q. This is the approach we will take; the results are summarized in the following.

(4.33) Suppose the bank account process is predictable. Then there are no arbitrage opportunities in the multiperiod futures market model if and only if there exists a strictly positive probability measure Q such that each S_n^*, $n = 1, \ldots, N$, and each U_j, $j = 1, \ldots, J$, is a martingale under Q.

Now suppose U is the price of a futures contract based on the delivery of security S at time τ, so $U_\tau = S_\tau$. Then (4.33) implies $U_t = E_Q[S_\tau|\mathscr{F}_t]$ for all $t = 0, \ldots, \tau$. Meanwhile, consider the forward price O_t for delivery of the same security S at the same time τ. If this security pays no dividend, then (4.22) says

$$O_t = \frac{S_t}{E_Q[B_t/B_\tau|\mathscr{F}_t]} = \frac{E_Q[S_\tau B_t B_t/B_\tau|\mathscr{F}_t]}{E_Q[B_t/B_\tau|\mathscr{F}_t]} = \frac{E_Q[S_\tau/B_\tau|\mathscr{F}_t]}{E_Q[1/B_\tau|\mathscr{F}_t]}$$

Comparing this with $U_t = E_Q[S_\tau|\mathscr{F}_t]$, we realize the following.

(4.34) When the bank account process B is deterministic, the forward and futures prices for time τ delivery of the same security coincide, whereas if B is random (and predictable), then these forward and futures price processes can be different.

This same conclusion holds when the underlying security pays a dividend, as can be verified by using (4.23) and (3.28).

Example 4.1 (continued)   Suppose $B_1 = 1$ and

$$B_2(\omega) = \begin{cases} 17/16, & \omega = \omega_1, \omega_2 \\ 9/8, & \omega = \omega_3, \omega_4 \end{cases}$$

The unique probability measure such that S^* is a martingale is easily computed to be $Q(\omega_1) = 5/24$, $Q(\omega_2) = 1/24$, and $Q(\omega_3) = Q(\omega_4) = 3/8$. Hence for the futures price process U satisfying $U_2 = S_2$ one has $U_0 = E_Q[S_2] = 5\frac{1}{2}$ and

$$U_1 = E_Q[S_2|\mathscr{F}_1] = \begin{cases} 8\frac{1}{2}, & \omega = \omega_1, \omega_2 \\ 4\frac{1}{2} & \omega = \omega_3, \omega_4 \end{cases}$$

Meanwhile, the time 0 forward price for time 2 delivery of this security is given by $O_0 = S_0/E_Q[1/B_2] = 5/(46/51) = 5\ 25/46$.

Now turn to the topic of options on futures. For example, suppose contingent claim X is defined by $X = g(U_s)$ for some expiration date s satisfying $0 < s < \tau$. More generally, X is an $\mathscr{F}_s$ measurable random variable with s smaller than all the delivery times of the various futures contracts associated with the model. The objectives are to determine the price of this European option and to derive a trading strategy which replicates this option, that is, a self- financing trading strategy $(H, \hat{H})$ satisfying $V_s = X$, where, as above,

$$V_t = H_0(t)B_t + \sum_{n=1}^{N} H_n(t)S_n(t) + \sum_{j=1}^{J} \hat{H}_j(t)\Delta U_j(t), \quad t > 0$$

As usual, an option X will be called attainable or marketable if it can be replicated. And if X can be replicated by the trading strategy $(H, \hat{H})$, then the corresponding portfolio value V_t must be the time t price of X for all $t \leqslant s$.

In order to obtain nice results, from now on it will be assumed that the bank account process B is predictable and that there exists a risk neutral probability measure Q for this futures market model. It follows from this assumption and (4.33) that:

(4.35)   The discounted value process $V^* \equiv V/B$ is a Q-martingale.

Now X is attainable if and only if $X/B_s = V_s^*$ for some self-financing trading strategy, so just as with ordinary security market models (4.35) implies

(4.36)   If $X \in \mathscr{F}_s$ is an attainable contingent claim in the futures market model, then its time t price is $V_t = E_Q[XB_t/B_s|\mathscr{F}_t]$ for all $t \leqslant s$.

It is worth pointing out that results like (4.35) and (4.36) hold even if the bank account process B is not predictable, but you must be careful what you mean by the risk neutral probability measure in such a case.

This valuation formula for options on futures looks exactly the same as ordinary European options on securities, but there is a subtle difference. In practical applications it is common to work with a model consisting of the bank account and just one risky price process (chosen to be, of course, the price underlying the option). If this underlying risky price is a security, then the martingale measure Q will be such that the *discounted* risky price process is a martingale. On the other hand, if the underlying risky price is a futures price, then the martingale measure Q must be such that the *undiscounted* risky price process is a martingale. Thus starting with the same model for the risky price process, you can get two different prices for the same option on this price process, depending on whether it is a security or a futures price.

Example 4.12   Consider a futures market model that consists of a single risky security, namely, a futures price process U that is governed by the binomial model of section 3.5. In particular, for parameters $0 < d < 1 < u$ and $0 < p < 1$ and initial price U_0,

$$U_t = U_0 u^{N_t} d^{t-N_t} \quad t = 0, 1, \ldots$$

where N is a binomial process with parameter p. As usual, the interest rate $r \geqslant 0$ is constant.

The risk neutral probability measure is easy to obtain. We want U to be a martingale, so this is simply the same as before, only with the interest rate $r = 0$. In particular, the probability q of an 'up' move should be taken to be

$$q = \frac{1 - d}{u - d}$$

Everything else should be the same as before, even if the true interest rate r is strictly positive. In particular, formula (3.32) still holds for the probability distribution of U_t, except that we now use the new value of q.

Now consider the European call option $X = (U_s - e)^+$. To compute its time 0 price we proceed in exactly the same way as in section 4.2, only using the new value of q. In particular, we define $\hat{n}$ to be the smallest non-negative integer n such that

$$n > \frac{\log(e/(U_0 d^s))}{\log(u/d)}$$

If $\hat{n} > s$, then U_0 is so far out of the money that there is no chance of finishing in the money (that is, with $U_s > e$)), in which case the time 0 price of the option is $V_0 = 0$. On the other hand, if $\hat{n} \leqslant s$, then

$$V_0 = U_0 \sum_{n=\hat{n}}^{s} \binom{s}{n} \hat{q}^n (1 - \hat{q})^{s-n} - \frac{e}{(1+r)^s} \sum_{n=\hat{n}}^{s} \binom{s}{n} q^n (1 - q)^{s-n}$$

where $q = (1 - d)/(u - d)$ and $\hat{q} = qu/(1 + r) = (1 - d)u/[(u - d)(1 + r)]$. This formula has exactly the same form as for a call option on a security, only now $q \neq (1 + r - d)/(u - d)$.

Exercise 4.15   Verify that (4.34) holds when the underlying security pays a dividend.

---

5 Optimal Consumption and Investment Problems

5.1 Optimal Portfolios and Dynamic Programming

The purpose of this chapter is to study the multiperiod generalizations of the single period consumption and investment problems that were introduced in chapter 2. I begin by investigating the basic optimal portfolio problem, where the objective is to maximize the expected utility of time T wealth and where there is no consumption before time T.

A *utility function* $u : \mathbb{R} \times \Omega \to \mathbb{R}$ is specified, with $u(w, \omega)$ representing the utility of wealth w at time T when $\omega \in \Omega$ is the state of the world. It will be assumed that $w \to u(w, \omega)$ is differentiable, concave, and strictly increasing for each $\omega \in \Omega$. Usually u will be independent of ω.

An initial wealth v is specified. The investor can choose any self-financing trading strategy H consistent with this initial wealth. The measure of performance of any such H will be the expected utility of terminal wealth, that is,

$$Eu(V_T) = \sum_{\omega \in \Omega} P(\omega)\, u(V_T(\omega), \omega)$$

The investor is therefore interested in solving the following optimal portfolio problem:

(5.1)
$$\text{maximize } Eu(V_T)$$
$$\text{subject to } V_0 = v$$
$$H \in \mathbb{H}$$

where $\mathbb{H}$ denotes the set of all self-financing trading strategies.

Keeping in mind that trading strategies must be predictable, we see that (5.1) actually involves three kinds of constraints. But two of these three kinds can easily be set aside. Since $V_T = B_T V_T^*$ and $V_T^* = V_0^* + G_T^*$, it follows that (5.1) is equivalent to

(5.2)   maximize $Eu(B_T\{v + G_T^*\})$

subject to $(H_1, \dots, H_N) \in \mathbb{H}_p$

where $\mathbb{H}_p$ denotes the set of all predictable processes that take values in $\mathbb{R}^N$. Thus if $(\hat{H}_1, \dots, \hat{H}_N)$ is a solution of (5.2), then it is a simple matter to choose $\hat{H}_0$ so that $\hat{H} = (\hat{H}_0, \hat{H}_1, \dots, \hat{H}_N)$ is self-financing and $V_0 = v$, thereby giving an optimal solution of (5.1).

Problem (5.2) can be solved with several approaches. One is to use standard calculus and optimization theory, keeping in mind the predictability constraint.

Example 5.1   Suppose $T = 2, K = 4, N = 1$, the interest rate r is a constant satisfying $0 \leqslant r < 0.125$, the filtration is the one generated by the risky security, and the price process for the risky security and the probability measure are as follows:

ω	$S_0(\omega)$	$S_1(\omega)$	$S_2(\omega)$	$P(\omega)$
ω_1	5	8	9	1/4
ω_2	5	8	6	1/4
ω_3	5	4	6	1/4
ω_4	5	4	3	1/4

In addition, suppose the investor has an exponential utility function: $u(W) = 1 - \exp\{-w\}$. In view of the predictability requirement, the strategy H_1 for trading the risky security entails the specification of three scalar values: the position, denoted H^5, carried forward from time 0 when the price $S_0 = 5$, the position, denoted H^8, carried forward from time 1 when the price $S_1 = 8$, and the position, denoted H^4, carried forward from time 1 when the price $S_1 = 4$. Hence the objective function in (5.2) can be written as

$$Eu(B_2\{v + G_2^*\}) = 1 - E \exp\{-(1+r)^2[v + H_1(1)\Delta S_1^* + H_1(2)\Delta S_2^*]\}$$

$$= 1 - \frac{1}{4}\left(\exp\left\{-(1+r)^2\left[v + H^5\frac{3-5r}{1+r} + H^8\frac{1-8r}{(1+r)^2}\right]\right\}\right.$$

$$+ \exp\left\{-(1+r)^2\left[v + H^5\frac{3-5r}{1+r} + H^8\frac{-2-8r}{(1+r)^2}\right]\right\}$$

$$+ \exp\left\{-(1+r)^2\left[v + H^5\frac{-1-5r}{1+r} + H^4\frac{2-4r}{(1+r)^2}\right]\right\}$$

$$\left.+ \exp\left\{-(1+r)^2\left[v + H^5\frac{-1-5r}{1+r} + H^4\frac{-1-4r}{(1+r)^2}\right]\right\}\right)$$

Setting the partial derivative with respect to each of the three variables equal to zero leads to the following three equations:

(5.3)

$$\exp\left\{-(1+r)^2\left[v + H^5\frac{3-5r}{1+r} + H^8\frac{1-8r}{(1+r)^2}\right]\right\}$$
$$= \frac{2+8r}{1-8r}\exp\left\{-(1+r)^2\left[v + H^5\frac{3-5r}{1+r} + H^8\frac{-2-8r}{(1+r)^2}\right]\right\}$$

$$\exp\left\{(1+r)^2\left[v + H^5\frac{-1-5r}{1+r} + H^4\frac{2-4r}{(1+r)^2}\right]\right\}$$
$$= \frac{(3-5r)(1+4r)}{(1+5r)(1-8r)}\exp\left\{-(1+r)^2\left[v + H^5\frac{3-5r}{1+r} + H^8\frac{2-8r}{(1+r)^2}\right]\right\}$$

$$\exp\left\{-(1+r)^2\left[v + H^5\frac{-1-5r}{1+r} + H^4\frac{-1-4r}{(1+r)^2}\right]\right\}$$
$$= \frac{(3-5r)(2-4r)}{(1+5r)(1-8r)}\exp\left\{-(1+r)^2\left[v + H^5\frac{3-5r}{1+r} + H^8\frac{2-8r}{(1+r)^2}\right]\right\}$$

Taking logs, one obtains a system of three linear equations; from this the final solution is easily obtained:

$$H^5 = \frac{3\ln(3-5r) + (2-4r)\ln(2-4r) + (1+4r)\ln(1+4r)}{12(1+r)}$$
$$- \frac{3\ln(1+5r) + (2+8r)\ln(2+8r) + (1-8r)\ln(1-8r)}{12(1+r)}$$

$$H^8 = -\frac{1}{3}\ln\left(\frac{2+8r}{1-8r}\right) \qquad H^4 = \frac{1}{3}\ln\left(\frac{2-4r}{1+4r}\right)$$

It remains to compute H_0, the strategy for trading the bank account. Clearly $H_0(1) = v - 5H^5$. In states ω_1 and ω_2 the value of the portfolio will be $V_1 = (v - 5H^5)(1+r) + 8H^5$, so setting this equal to $H_0(2)(1+r) + 8H^8$ gives $H_0(2) = (v - 5H^5) + 8(H^5 - H^8)/(1+r)$. Similarly, one computes $H_0(2) = (v - 5H^5) + 8(H^5 - H^4)/(1+r)$ for states ω_3 and ω_4.

As seen in the case of single period models, if there exists an arbitrage opportunity, then there cannot exist an optimal solution to portfolio problems (5.1) or (5.2). In other words, if (5.1) or (5.2) has a solution, then there are no arbitrage opportunities, in which case there must exist a risk neutral probability measure. Indeed, principle (2.6) for single period models generalizes to the following:

(5.4) If (H,V) is a solution of the optimal portfolio problem (5.1) or (5.2), then a risk neutral probability measure is defined by

$$Q(\omega) = \frac{P(\omega)B_T u'(V_T(\omega),\omega)}{E[B_T u'(V_T)]}, \quad \omega \in \Omega$$

where u' denotes the partial derivative with respect to the first argument.

To see this, consider an arbitrary time t, arbitrary security n, and arbitrary event A in $\mathscr{P}_{t-1}$, the partition corresponding to $\mathscr{F}_{t-1}$. Corresponding to A is $H_n(t)1_A$, the position in security n that is carried forward from time $t-1$ when event A occurs. The first order necessary condition corresponding to this scalar-valued variable is

$$\sum_{\omega \in A} P(\omega)u'(B_T(\omega)\{v + G_T^*(\omega)\},\omega)B_T(\omega)\Delta S_n^*(t,\omega) = 0$$

This is true for all $A \in \mathscr{P}_{t-1}$, so

$$E[u'(B_T\{v + G_T^*\})B_T\Delta S_n^*(t)|\mathscr{F}_{t-1}] = 0$$

Hence $E_Q[\Delta S_n^*(t)|\mathscr{F}_{t-1}] = 0$ if Q is defined as in (5.4), since $V_T = B_T\{v + G_T^*\}$.

Example 5.1 (continued) The three equations in (5.3) correspond respectively to

$$u'(V_2(\omega_1)) = \frac{2+8r}{1-8r}u'(V_2(\omega_2))$$

$$u'(V_2(\omega_3)) = \frac{(3-5r)(1+4r)}{(1+5r)(1-8r)}u'(V_2(\omega_2))$$

$$u'(V_2(\omega_4)) = \frac{(3-5r)(2-4r)}{(1+5r)(1-8r)}u'(V_2(\omega_2))$$

Hence (5.4) implies

$$Q(\omega_1) = \frac{(1+5r)(2+8r)}{12} \qquad Q(\omega_2) = \frac{(1+5r)(1-8r)}{12}$$

$$Q(\omega_3) = \frac{(3-5r)(1+4r)}{12} \qquad Q(\omega_4) = \frac{(3-5r)(2-4r)}{12}$$

Conventional methods verify that this is the unique risk neutral probability measure.

It should be apparent that the approach illustrated in example 5.1 for computing the optimal trading strategy may be impractical for large problems. With N equations and N variables for each node of the underlying information tree, the resulting system of equations may be too large to solve.

But an alternative approach called dynamic programming may reduce these computational difficulties.

The dynamic programming idea was already introduced in connection with computing the value of American options. The idea is to realize that when faced with a sequence of decisions, the optimal decision to make now should be consistent with the intention to act optimally in all future periods. In other words, if you know the optimal strategy starting at time $t+1$, then the determination of the optimal strategy starting at time t can be reduced to one or more one-period problems. It follows that a multiperiod decision problem can be solved by solving a sequence of one-period problems. You work backwards in time, first computing the optimal decisions with one period to go, then computing the optimal decisions with two periods to go, and so forth.

In order to implement this procedure in the case of our optimal portfolio problem, it is necessary to keep track of the *optimal value process* $U_t(w), t = 0, \ldots, T$. Here $U_t(w)$ equals the maximum (over all self-financing trading strategies) expected utility of time T wealth given it is now time t, the time t wealth is w, and the time t history is $\mathscr{F}_t$. Hence $U_t(w)$ will be an $\mathscr{F}_t$ measurable random variable.

The value of $U_t(w)$ when $t = T$ is clear: it coincides with the utility function, that is,

$$U_T(w) = u(w, \omega)$$

It turns out that for $t < T$ the value of $U_t(w)$ satisfies the important *dynamic programming functional equation*:

$$(5.5) \qquad U_t(w) = \max_{H \in \mathscr{F}_t} \ E[U_{t+1}(B_{t+1}\{w/B_t + H \cdot \Delta S^*_{t+1}\})|\mathscr{F}_t]$$

Here H, the decision variable for period t, is an N-dimensional random variable that is required to be $\mathscr{F}_t$ measurable. The value of H that maximizes this expression will turn out to be the vector of optimal positions in the risky securities carried forward from time t, given the history $\mathscr{F}_t$. The notation $H \cdot \Delta S^*_{t+1}$ represents the inner product, that is, $H \cdot \Delta S^*_{t+1} = H_1 \Delta S^*_1(t+1) + \ldots + H_N \Delta S^*_N(t+1)$. This equals the discounted gain from time t to time $t+1$. Notice that the argument of U_{t+1} in (5.5) equals the time $t+1$ wealth if the time t wealth is w, H gives the positions in the risky securities, and $H_0(t+1)$, the position in the bank account, is chosen in a self-financing manner.

The dynamic programming equation (5.5) can be used to compute an optimal solution to the portfolio problem (5.1) or (5.2) by computing the optimal value functions $U_t(w)$ in a recursive manner. First compute $U_{T-1}(w)$, then compute $U_{T-2}(w)$, and so forth. Along the way keep track of the maximizing values of H, for these will form the components of the optimal trading strategy. When completed, $U_0(w)$ will equal the optimal value of the objective function in (5.1) or (5.2) given $w = v$. Thus the dynamic programming method provides a bonus: you have a solution for all possible values of the initial wealth $w = v$, not just a specific value.

Example 5.1 (continued)   Taking $t = 1$ and either ω_1 or ω_2, the right hand side of (5.5) becomes

$$\max_{h} E[1 - \exp(-(1 + r)^2\{w/(1 + r) + h\Delta S_2^*\})|S_1 = 8]$$

$$= \max_{h} (1 - \frac{1}{2}\exp\{-(1+r)w-(1-8r)h\} - \frac{1}{2}\exp\{-(1 + r)w + (2 + 8r)h\})$$

The decision variable h here is a scalar. Computing the derivative of this argument with respect to h and setting this equal to zero soon leads to the maximizing value of h, namely,

$$h = -\frac{1}{3}\ln\left(\frac{2 + 8r}{1 - 8r}\right)$$

Substituting this back into the right hand side of (5.5) yields

$$U_1(w) = 1 - \frac{1}{2}\exp\{-(1 + r)w\}\left\{\left(\frac{2 + 8r}{1 - 8r}\right)^{(1-8r)/3} + \left(\frac{2 + 8r}{1 - 8r}\right)^{-(2+8r)/3}\right\}$$

$$= 1 - \frac{3}{2}(2 + 8r)^{-(2+8r)/3}(1 - 8r)^{-(1-8r)/3}\exp\{-(1 + r)w\}$$

for ω_1 and ω_2.

In a similar fashion, taking $t = 1$ and either ω_3 or ω_4, the right hand side of (5.5) becomes

$$\max_{h} E[1 - \exp\left(-(1 + r)^2\{w/(1 + r) + h\Delta S_2^*\}\right)|S_1 = 4]$$

$$= \max_{h} (1 - \frac{1}{2}\exp\{-(1 + r)w - (2 - 4r)h\} - \frac{1}{2}\exp\{-(1 + r)w + (1 + 4r)h\})$$

so $\ln[(2 - 4r)/(1 + 4r)]/3$ is the maximizing value of h and

$$U_1(w) = 1 - \frac{1}{2}\exp\{-(1 + r)w\}\left\{\left(\frac{2 - 4r}{1 + 4r}\right)^{(1+4r)/3} + \left(\frac{2 - 4r}{1 + 4r}\right)^{-(2-4r)/3}\right\}$$

$$= 1 - \frac{3}{2}(2 - 4r)^{-(2-4r)/3}(1 + 4r)^{-(1+4r)/3}\exp\{-(1 + r)w\}$$

for ω_3 and ω_4.

We are now ready to do the dynamic programming iteration and compute $U_0(w)$. Denote

$$f(r, \omega) = \begin{cases} \frac{3}{2}(2+8r)^{-(2+8r)/3}(1-8r)^{-(1-8r)/3}, & \omega = \omega_1, \omega_2 \\ \frac{3}{2}(2-4r)^{-(2-4r)/3}(1+4r)^{-(1+4r)/3}, & \omega = \omega_3, \omega_4 \end{cases}$$

so $U_1(w)$ can be written concisely as

$$U_1(w) = 1 - f(r, \omega)\exp\{-(1+r)w\}$$

Equation (5.5) becomes

$$U_0(w) = \max_h E[1 - f(r, w)\exp\{-(1+r)[(1+r)\{w + h\Delta S_1^*\}]\}]$$

$$= \max_h (1 - \frac{1}{2}f(r, \omega_1)\exp\{-(1+r)^2 w - (1+r)(3-5r)h\}$$

$$- \frac{1}{2}f(r, \omega_3)\exp\{-(1+r)^2 w + (1+r)(1+5r)h\})$$

Setting the derivative with respect to h equal to zero, one is eventually led to the maximizing value of h:

$$h = \frac{3\ln(3-5r) + (2-4r)\ln(2-4r) + (1+4r)\ln(1+4r)}{12(1+r)}$$
$$- \frac{3\ln(1+5r) + (2+8r)\ln(2+8r) + (1-8r)\ln(1-8r)}{12(1+r)}$$

Substituting this back into the right hand side of (5.5) enables one to obtain an expression for $U_0(w)$. However, the algebraic details are excessive, so an actual formula will not be provided.

In summary, the dynamic programming approach can, in principle, be used to solve the optimal portfolio problem. It provides solutions for many cases where a conventional approach, based on the first-order necessary conditions, is inadequate. On the other hand, there are many practical situations where the computational difficulties are formidable, if not unsurmountable. Fortunately, the risk neutral computational approach, which is the subject of the next section, can often overcome these computational difficulties.

Exercise 5.1   Use dynamic programming to compute the optimal trading strategy as a function of the initial wealth v for the securities market in example 5.1. Use log utility, that is, $u(w) = \ln(w)$, and assume the interest rate r is an arbitrary constant. Compute the optimal objective value as a function of the parameters r and v. (Hints: try the special case $r = 0$ first; show the optimal time 0 position in the risky security is $(1+r)(1-5r)v/[(1+5r)(3-5r)]$.)

Exercise 5.2   Use dynamic programming to show that with exponential utility (that is, $u(w) = a - (b/c)\exp\{-cw\}$, where a, $b > 0$ and $c > 0$ are scalar parameters), with a general securities model, and with a predictable bank account process, that the optimal position in the securities is always independent of the current wealth. What happens if you drop the predictability requirement? Give a proof or use the security in example 5.1 to provide a counter-example.

Exercise 5.3   Suppose there is a single risky security that follows the binomial model with parameters $0 < d < 1 + r < u$ and $0 < p < 1$. The interest rate $r \geqslant 0$ is constant. The initial price S_0, the initial wealth v, and the time horizon T are arbitrary. Use dynamic programming to compute the optimal trading strategy for the following utility functions:

(a) $u(w) = 1 - \exp\{-w\}$ (Hint: show by induction that $U_t(w)$) is of the form $1 - k_t \exp\{-(1 + r)^{T-t} w\}$, where k_t is a constant.)
(b) $u(w) = \ln(w)$ (Hint: show by induction that $U_t(w)$ is of the form $\ln(w) + k_t$, where k_t is a constant.)

Exercise 5.4   For the model in example 5.1 with constant interest rate $r = 0$, compute the optimal trading strategy for the indicated utility function, using both the standard optimization approach (i.e., set the three partials equal to zero) and dynamic programming. Verify that your answers are the same.

(a) $u(w) = -w^{-1}$ (isoelastic utility)
(b) $u(w) = \beta w - \frac{1}{2} w^2$ (quadratic utility).

5.2   Optimal Portfolios and Martingale Methods

The risk neutral computational approach for solving multiperiod optimal portfolio problems is pretty much the same as for solving single period problems. Given problem (5.1) or (5.2), the first step is to identify $\mathbb{W}_v$, the set of all the *attainable wealths*. This is $\mathbb{W}_v = \{w \in \mathbb{R}^K : W = V_T$ for some self-financing H with $V_0 = v\}$, the set of all the time T contingent claims that can be generated by some self-financing trading strategy starting with initial wealth v. If the model is complete, this set is simply

$$(5.6) \qquad\qquad \mathbb{W}_v = \{W \in \mathbb{R}^K : E_Q[W/B_T] = v\}$$

If the model is not complete, then the specification of $\mathbb{W}_v$ is more complex and will be discussed in a later section.

The second step is to solve the subproblem:

$$(5.7) \qquad\qquad \text{maximize} \quad Eu(W)$$
$$\text{subject to} \quad W \in \mathbb{W}_v$$

If the model is complete, then this problem can be solved with a Lagrange multiplier technique, as will be explained in a moment. Finally, having obtained the optimal solution $\hat{W}$, say, the third step is to compute the trading strategy H which generates $\hat{W}$, doing this exactly as one would compute the trading strategy that replicates a contingent claim.

Throughout this section it will be assumed that the model is complete, so the only step requiring explanation is the second, solving subproblem (5.7). An efficient procedure will now be described, and examples will be provided.

Actually, the second step is very little different from what was done for single period models. In view of (5.6), we want to solve (5.7) by introducing the Lagrange multiplier λ and then solving

(5.8) $$\text{maximize} \quad Eu(W) - \lambda E_Q[W/B_T]$$

This is an unconstrained problem with the variable $W \in \mathbb{R}^K$. Introducing the state price density $L = Q/P$, the objective function in (5.8) can be rewritten as

$$E[u(W) - \lambda LW/B_T] = \sum_{\omega \in \Omega} P(\omega)[u(W(\omega)) \quad \lambda L(\omega)W(\omega)/B_T(\omega)]$$

If W maximizes this expression, then the necessary conditions must be satisfied, giving rise to one equation for each $\omega \in \Omega$:

$$u'(W(\omega)) = \lambda L(\omega)/B_T(\omega), \quad \text{all } \omega \in \Omega$$

(it is now being assumed that the utility function $u : \mathbb{R} \to \mathbb{R}$ is a function only of wealth, independent of the state $\omega \in \Omega$). This is equivalent to

(5.9) $$W(\omega) = I(\lambda L(\omega)/B_T(\omega)), \quad \text{all } \omega \in \Omega$$

where I denotes the inverse function corresponding to u'.

All that remains is to determine the correct value of λ. This is simply the value such that $v = E_Q[W/B_T]$ is satisfied when (5.9) is substituted for W. In other words, λ should be chosen to satisfy

(5.10) $$E_Q[I(\lambda L/B_T)/B_T] = v$$

The inverse function I is normally decreasing with a range that includes $(0, \infty)$, so normally a solution λ to (5.10) will exist for any $v > 0$. Hence the solution of subproblem (5.7) is really no different from what it was for single period models, except that now we discount by B_T rather than B_1. In view of the single period results in section 2.2, we immediately have the following examples.

Example 5.2 (exponential utility) The exponential utility function of example 2.2 can easily be generalized to be of the form $u(w) = a - bc \exp\{-w/c\}$, where a, b, and c are scalar parameters with $b > 0$ and $c > 0$. This gives the optimal attainable wealth

$$W = \frac{v + cE[(L/B_T)\ln(L/B_T)]}{E[L/B_T]} - c \ln(L/B_T)$$

and the optimal objective value

$$Eu(W) = a - bcE[L/B_T] \exp \left\{ \frac{-v/c - E[(L/B_T)\ln(L/B_T)]}{E[L/B_T]} \right\}$$

Example 5.3 (log utility)   If $u(w) = \ln(w)$, then the optimal attainable wealth is

$$W = vB_T/L$$

and the optimal objective value is

$$Eu(W) = \ln(v) - E[\ln(L/B_T)]$$

Example 5.4 (isoelastic utility)   If $u(w) = \gamma^{-1}w^\gamma$, where $-\infty < \gamma < 1$ and $\gamma \neq 0$, then the optimal attainable wealth is

$$W = \frac{v(L/B_T)^{-1/(1-\gamma)}}{E[(L/B_T)^{-\gamma/(1-\gamma)}]}$$

and the optimal objective value is

$$Eu(W) = \frac{v^\gamma}{\gamma}\left\{E\left[(L/B_T)^{-\gamma/(1-\gamma)}\right]\right\}^{1-\gamma}$$

Example 5.5 (quadratic utility)   This example builds on the results in section 2.4. If $u(w) = \beta w - w^2/2$ for parameter $\beta > 0$, then $I(i) = \beta - i$. Equation (5.9) becomes $W = \beta - \lambda L/B_T$. Solving equation (5.10) for λ and then substituting gives

$$W = \beta + \left[\frac{v - \beta E_Q[1/B_T]}{E_Q[L/B_T^2]}\right] L/B_T$$

for the optimal attainable wealth. Substituting this into the objective function eventually leads to

$$Eu(W) = \frac{\beta^2\left[E_Q[L/B_T^2] - \{E_Q[1/B_T]\}^2\right] - v^2 + 2\beta v E_Q[1/B_T]}{2E_Q[L/B_T^2]}$$

for the optimal objective value.

Example 5.1 and 5.2 (continued)   The risk neutral probability measure and the state price vector are easily computed to be as follows:

ω	$Q(\omega)$	$L(\omega) = Q(\omega)/P(\omega)$
ω_1	$(1 + 5r)(2 + 8r)/12$	$(1 + 5r)(2 + 8r)/3$
ω_2	$(1 + 5r)(1 - 8r)/12$	$(1 + 5r)(1 - 8r)/3$
ω_3	$(3 - 5r)(1 + 4r)/12$	$(3 - 5r)(1 + 4r)/3$
ω_4	$(3 - 5r)(2 - 4r)/12$	$(3 - 5r)(2 - 4r)/3$

We first compute $E[L/B_2] = E_Q[(1 + r)^{-2}] = (1 + r)^{-2}$,

$$E[(L/B_2)\ln(L/B_2)] = (1 + r)^{-2}E_Q[\ln(L)] - 2(1 + r)^{-2}\ln(1 + r)$$

and

$$E_0[\ln(L)] = \frac{1}{12}\Big(-12\ln(3) + 3(1+5r)\ln(1+5r) + 3(3-5r)\ln(3-5r)$$
$$+ (1+5r)(2+8r)\ln(2+8r) + (1+5r)(1-8r)\ln(1-8r)$$
$$+ (3-5r)(1+4r)\ln(1+4r) + (3-5r)(2-4r)\ln(2-4r)\Big)$$

Hence the optimal attainable wealth is

$$W(\omega) = v(1+r)^2 + E_Q[\ln(L)] + \ln(3)$$

$$+ \begin{cases} -\ln(1+5r) - \ln(2+8r), & \omega = \omega_1 \\ -\ln(1+5r) - \ln(1-8r), & \omega = \omega_2 \\ -\ln(3-5r) - \ln(1+4r), & \omega = \omega_3 \\ -\ln(3-5r) - \ln(2-4r), & \omega = \omega_4 \end{cases}$$

Solving the system

$$(1+r)^2 H_0(2) + 9H_1(2) = W(\omega_1)$$

$$(1+r)^2 H_0(2) + 6H_1(2) = W(\omega_2)$$

yields

$$H_1(2) = -\frac{1}{3}\ln\left(\frac{2+8r}{1-8r}\right)$$

and

$$H_0(2) = v + \frac{E_Q[\ln(L)] + \ln(3)}{(1+r)^2}$$
$$+ \frac{2\ln(2+8r) - \ln(1+5r) - 3\ln(1-8r)}{(1+r)^2}$$

in states ω_1 and ω_2. Similarly, solving the system

$$(1+r)^2 H_0(2) + 6H_1(2) = W(\omega_3)$$

$$(1+r)^2 H_0(2) + 3H_1(2) = W(\omega_4)$$

yields

$$H_1(2) = \frac{1}{3}\ln\left(\frac{2-4r}{1+4r}\right)$$

and

$$H_0(2) = v + \frac{E_Q[\ln(L)] + \ln(3)}{(1+r)^2}$$
$$+ \frac{\ln(1+4r) - \ln(3-5r) - 2\ln(2-4r)}{(1+r)^2}$$

in states ω_3 and ω_4.

Next, solving the system

$$(1+r)H_0(1) + 8H_1(1) = V_1(\omega_1) = (1+r)H_0(2,\omega_1) + 8H_1(2,\omega_1)$$
$$(1+r)H_0(1) + 4H_1(1) = V_1(\omega_3) = (1+r)H_0(2,\omega_3) + 4H_1(2,\omega_3)$$

yields the values of $H_0(1)$ and $H_1(1)$ (see the calculations in section 5.1). Finally,

$$Eu(W) = 1 - (1+r)^{-2}\exp\{-v(1+r)^2 - E_Q[\ln(L)] + 2\ln(1+r)\}$$

is the optimal objective value.

Example 5.6   Suppose there is a single risky security that is governed by the binomial model with general parameters r, p, u, and d, and suppose $u(w) = \ln(w)$. In view of section 3.5,

$$L(\omega) = \frac{Q(\omega)}{P(\omega)} = \left(\frac{q}{p}\right)^n \left(\frac{1-q}{1-p}\right)^{T-n}$$

where $q = (1+r-d)/(u-d)$ and n is the number of "up" moves by the risky security corresponding to state ω. Recall that N_T, the number of up moves during the T periods, is a binomial random variable having parameters T and p. With log utility, it follows from example 5.3 that

$$W = v(1+r)^T \left(\frac{p}{q}\right)^{N_T} \left(\frac{1-p}{1-q}\right)^{T-N_T}$$

is the optimal attainable wealth. Moreover, since $EN_T = pT$, the optimal objective value is

$$Eu(W) = \ln(v) + \ln(1+r)^T - E\ln(L)$$

$$= \ln(v) + T\ln(1+r) - E\left[\ln\left(\frac{q}{p}\right)^{N_T}\right] - E\left[\ln\left(\frac{1-q}{1-p}\right)^{T-N_T}\right]$$

$$= \ln(v) + T\ln(1+r) - pT\ln\left(\frac{q}{p}\right) - (1-p)T\ln\left(\frac{1-q}{1-p}\right)$$

Now for arbitrary $n < T$, suppose $N_{T-1} = n$ and consider the optimal positions in the bank account and risky security that should be carried forward from time $T - 1$. These are obtained by solving

$$(1+r)^T H_0(T) + S_{T-1} u H_1(T) = v(1+r)^T (p/q)^{n+1} (\{1-p\}/\{1-q\})^{T-n-1}$$
$$(1+r)^T H_0(T) + S_{T-1} d H_1(T) = v(1+r)^T (p/q)^n (\{1-p\}/\{1-q\})^{T-n}$$

thereby yielding

$$H_1(T) = \frac{v(1+r)^T (p/q)^n (\{1-p\}/\{1-q\})^{T-n-1} (p-q)}{S_{T-1}(u-d)q(1-q)}$$

and

$$H_0(T) = \frac{v(p/q)^n (\{1-p\}/\{1-q\})^{T-n-1} [u(1-p)q - d(1-q)p]}{(u-d)q(1-q)}$$

Since $V_{T-1} = (1+r)^{T-1} H_0(T) + S_{T-1} H_1(T)$, it follows with some algebra that

$$V_{T-1} = v(1+r)^{T-1} (p/q)^n (\{1-p\}/\{1-q\})^{T-n-1}$$

Now consider the fraction of money that is invested at time $T-1$ in the risky security. This is

(5.11) $$\frac{S_{T-1} H_1(T)}{V_{T-1}} = \frac{(1+r)(p-q)}{(u-d)q(1-q)}$$

Notice this is independent of n and T. Moreover, notice that V_{T-1} has the same form as $V_T = W$, so an induction argument can be used to show that the optimal trading strategy has a very simple form: at each time and in each state simply invest the fraction (5.11) of one's wealth in the risky asset.

Exercise 5.5 For the model in example 5.1 with constant interest rate r equal to a general parameter $0 \leqslant r < 0.125$ and with log utility $u(w) = \ln(w)$, compute the optimal attainable wealth, the optimal objective value, and the optimal trading strategy using the risk neutral computational approach.

Exercise 5.6 In the specific case of example 5.1 with $r = 0$, compute the optimal attainable wealth, the optimal objective value, and the optimal trading strategy under the utility function

(a) $u(w) = -w^{-1}$
(b) $u(w) = \beta w - w^2/2$.

Exercise 5.7 Suppose there is a single risky security that is governed by the binomial model over T periods with constant interest rate $r \geqslant 0$ and general values for the parameters $S_0, p, u,$ and d. Compute the optimal attainable wealth, the optimal objective value, and the optimal trading strategy under the exponential utility function $u(w) = -\exp(w)$. In particular, show that if time t node entails n "ups" and $t-n$ "downs," then under the optimal strategy the corresponding value of the portfolio is

$$v(1+r)^t + \frac{[qt-n]\ln(q/p) + [(1-q)t - (n-t)]\ln((1-q)/(1-p))}{(1+r)^{T-t}}$$

Exercise 5.8   For the binomial model as in exercise 5.7 and with the quadratic utility function $u(w) = \beta w - w^2/2$, show that the optimal attainable wealth is

$$W = \beta + \frac{(1+r)^T v - \beta}{[q^2/p + (1-q)^2/(1-p)]^T} \left(\frac{q}{p}\right)^n \left[\frac{1-q}{1-p}\right]^{T-n}$$

where n is the number of "up" moves in the corresponding sample path. Moreover, show that the optimal objective value is

$$Eu(W) = \beta^2/2 - \frac{[(1+r)^T v - \beta]^2}{2[q^2/p + (1-q)^2/(1-p)]^T}$$

Hint:

$$\sum_{n=0}^{T} \binom{T}{n} a^n b^{T-n} = (a+b)^T$$

Exercise 5.9   For the binomial model as in exercises 5.7 and 5.8 and with the isoelastic utility function $u(w) = \gamma^{-1} w^\gamma$, show that the optimal attainable wealth is

$$W = \frac{(1+r)^T v L^{-1/(1-\gamma)}}{\left[p\left(\frac{q}{p}\right)^{-\gamma/(1-\gamma)} + (1-p)\left(\frac{1-q}{1-p}\right)^{-\gamma/(1-\gamma)}\right]^T}$$

and the optimal objective value is

$$Eu(W) = \frac{1}{\gamma}\left[(1+r)^T v\right]^\gamma \left[p\left(\frac{q}{p}\right)^{-\gamma/(1-\gamma)} + (1-p)\left(\frac{1-q}{1-p}\right)^{-\gamma/(1-\gamma)}\right]^{T(1-\gamma)}$$

Hint: see exercise 5.8.

5.3   Consumption–Investment and Dynamic Programming

A *consumption process* $C = \{C_t; t = 0, \ldots, T\}$ is a non-negative, adapted stochastic process with C_t representing the amount of funds consumed by the investor at time t. A *consumption–investment plan* consists of a pair (C, H), where C is a consumption process and H is a trading strategy. A utility will be earned for the amount that is consumed in each period; naturally, the higher the consumption, the higher the utility. The investor seeks to choose the consumption–investment plan that maximizes the expected utility over the T periods. In particular, the investor faces a trade-off between consumption and investment, especially in the early periods. This section will explain how to solve this problem with dynamic programming.

Given the investor's initial wealth v, the consumption–investment plan (C, H) will be called *self-financing* if no money is added to or withdrawn from the portfolio between times 0 and T, other than the amounts that are consumed. As usual,

$$(5.12) \qquad V_t = H_0(t)B_t + \sum_{n=1}^{N} H_n(t)S_n(t), \quad t \geqslant 1$$

represents the value of the portfolio before any time t transactions. It will be assumed for $t \geqslant 1$ that V_t is also the value of the portfolio *before* any time t consumption. We let $V_0 = v$ denote the initial wealth. Thus to say (C, H) is self-financing means that

$$(5.13) \quad V_t = C_t + H_0(t+1)B_t + \sum_{n=1}^{N} H_n(t+1)S_n(t), \quad t = 0, \ldots, T-1$$

Given initial wealth v, the self-financing consumption–investment plan (C, H) is said to be *admissible* if $C_T \leqslant V_T$. Since C is a non-negative process, this implies $V_T \geqslant 0$.

The investor's consumption–investment problem is

$$(5.14) \qquad \text{maximize} \quad E\left[\sum_{t=0}^{T} \alpha^t u(C_t)\right]$$

$$\text{subject to:} \quad v = \text{initial wealth}$$

$$(C, H) \text{ is admissible}$$

Here $u : \mathbb{R} \to [-\infty, \infty]$ is a specified concave increasing utility function and α is a specified scalar parameter satisfying $0 < \alpha \leqslant 1$. Since the consumption process is required to be non-negative, without loss of generality it will be assumed that $u(w) = -\infty$ for all $w < 0$ (whereas, of course, $u(w) > -\infty$ for all $w > 0$).

To solve this problem with dynamic programming we will compute, working backwards in time in a recursive manner, the value function $u_t(w)$. This represents the maximum expected utility of consumption through time T, starting with wealth w and consumption at time t and given the time t history $\mathscr{F}_t$.

The value of u_T is easy to specify. Since the utility function u is increasing, the investor will want to consume all the wealth that is available in the final period. Thus $u_T = u$.

Starting at time $T - 1$ with wealth w, the investor is faced with a problem that is essentially equivalent to a series of the single period problems of section 2.3:

(5.15)   maximize $u(C_{T-1}) + E[\alpha u_T(W)|\mathscr{F}_{T-1}]$

subject to: $w = C_{T-1} + H_0(T)B_{T-1} + \sum_{n=1}^{N} H_n(T)S_n(T-1)$

$$W = H_0(T)B_T + \sum_{n=1}^{N} H_n(T)S_n(T)$$

$$H_n(T) \in \mathscr{F}_{T-1} \text{ for } n = 0, \ldots, N; \quad C_{T-1} \in \mathscr{F}_{T-1}$$

Notice the assumption that $u(w) = -\infty$ for all $w < 0$ will force the solution of (5.15) to satisfy $C_{T-1} \geqslant 0$ and $W \geqslant 0$.

Using the first constraint to solve for $H_0(T)$ and then substituting this in the second constraint, one eventually obtains

$$W = (w - C_{T-1})B_T/B_{T-1} + \sum_{n=1}^{N} H_n(T)[S_n(T) - B_T S_n(T-1)/B_{T-1}]$$

$$= (w - C_{T-1})B_T/B_{T-1} + B_T \sum_{n=1}^{N} H_n(T)\Delta S_n^*(T)$$

Hence (5.15) can be rewritten as

$$\max u(C_{T-1}) + \alpha E\left[u_T\left((w - C_{T-1})B_T/B_{T-1} + B_T \sum_{n=1}^{N} H_n(T)\Delta S_n^*(T)\right)\Big|\mathscr{F}_{T-1}\right]$$

subject to: $H_n(T) \in \mathscr{F}_{T-1}$ for $n = 1, \ldots, N$ and $C_{T-1} \in \mathscr{F}_{T-1}$

We now set $u_{T-1}(w)$ equal to this optimal objective value.

In general, having computed $u_t(w)$, the value function $u_{t-1}(w)$ is computed from the *dynamic programming functional equation*

(5.16) $u_{t-1}(w) = \max\left\{u(C_{t-1}) + \right.$

$$\left. \alpha E\left(u_t\left((w - C_{t-1})B_t/B_{t-1} + B_t \sum_{n=1}^{N} H_n(t)\Delta S_n^*(t)|\mathscr{F}_{t-1}\right)\right)\right\}$$

where the maximum is over all $H_n(t) \in \mathscr{F}_{t-1}$ for $n = 1, \ldots, N$ and $C_{t-1} \in \mathscr{F}_{t-1}$. The value function $u_0(v)$ will then be the optimal objective value for the original problem (5.14) or (5.15), and the maximizing values of C_{t-1} and $H_n(t)$ will be part of the optimal consumption–investment plan. The final component, H_0, will come from the self-financing equation.

Example 5.7   Consider the security model of example 5.1 with interest rate the constant $r \geqslant 0$ and utility function $u(w) = u_2(w) = \ln(w)$. The dynamic programming functional equation for $t = 2$ and for states ω_1 and ω_2 is

(5.17) $u_1(w) = \max\{\ln(c) + \dfrac{\alpha}{2} \ln[(w-c)(1+r) + (1-8r)h|$

$+ \dfrac{\alpha}{2} \ln[(w-c)(1+r) - (2+8r)h]\}$

Computing the partial derivatives of the argument with respect to c and h and then setting these equal to zero gives two equations; the solution is eventually found to be

$$c = \frac{w}{1+\alpha} \quad \text{and} \quad h = -\frac{1}{2}\frac{\alpha(1+r)(1+16r)w}{(1+\alpha)(2+8r)(1-8r)}$$

Note this means that if $S_1 = 8$ and the wealth at time 1 is w, then it is optimal to consume $w/(1+\alpha)$ right away and invest the balance by taking the (short) position h in the risky security and the (self-financing) position

$$H_0(2) = \frac{\alpha w/(1+\alpha) - 8h}{1+r}$$

in the bank account. Substituting these values of c and h back into the dynamic programming equation (5.17) eventually results in the time 1 value function for states ω_1 and ω_2:

$$u_1(w) = (1+\alpha)\ln(w) + f_8(\alpha, r)$$

where $f_8(\alpha, r)$ is a new function defined for convenience by

$$f_8(\alpha, r) = \alpha \ln\left(\frac{3\alpha(1+r)}{2(1+\alpha)(1-8r)}\right) + \frac{\alpha}{2}\ln\left(\frac{1-8r}{2+8r}\right) - \ln(1+\alpha)$$

Similarly, if $S_1 = 4$, then one computes the optimal time 1 consumption to be $c = w/(1+\alpha)$, the optimal position in the risky security:

$$h = \frac{1}{2}\frac{\alpha(1+r)(1-8r)w}{(1+\alpha)(2-4r)(1+4r)}$$

and the time 1 value function for states ω_3 and ω_4:

$$u_1(w) = (1+\alpha)\ln(w) + f_4(\alpha, r)$$

where $f_4(\alpha, r)$ is a new function defined for convenience by

$$f_4(\alpha, r) = \alpha \ln\left(\frac{3\alpha(1+r)}{2(1+\alpha)(1+4r)}\right) + \frac{\alpha}{2}\ln\left(\frac{1+4r}{2-4r}\right) - \ln(1+\alpha)$$

To summarize matters at this point,

$$u_1(w) = \begin{cases} (1+\alpha)\ln(w) + f_8(\alpha, r), & \omega = \omega_1, \omega_2 \\ (1+\alpha)\ln(w) + f_4(\alpha, r), & \omega = \omega_3, \omega_4 \end{cases}$$

and we are now in a position to use the dynamic programming equation (5.16) to recursively compute u_0:

$$u_0(w) = \max_{c,\,h} \left\{ \ln(c) + \frac{\alpha}{2}(1+\alpha)\ln[(w-c)(1+r) + (3-5r)h] \right.$$

$$\left. + \frac{\alpha}{2}f_8 + \frac{\alpha}{2}(1+\alpha)\ln[(w-c)(1+r) - (1+5r)h] + \frac{\alpha}{2}f_4 \right\}$$

Computing the partial derivatives and so forth eventually leads to

$$c = \frac{w}{1+\alpha+\alpha^2} \quad \text{and} \quad h = \frac{\alpha(1+\alpha)(1+r)(1-5r)w}{(1+\alpha+\alpha^2)(3-5r)(1+5r)}$$

in which case

$$u_0(w) = (1+\alpha+\alpha^2)\ln(w) - \ln(1+\alpha+\alpha^2) + \alpha(1+\alpha)\ln\left(\frac{2\alpha(1+\alpha)(1+r)}{(1+\alpha+\alpha^2)}\right)$$

$$- \frac{\alpha}{2}(1+\alpha)\ln[(1+5r)(3-5r)] + \frac{\alpha}{2}f_8(\alpha,r) + \frac{\alpha}{2}f_4(\alpha,r)$$

If you relax the assumption that $u(c) = -\infty$ for all $c \leqslant 0$, then the dynamic programming method can still be utilized to compute optimal consumption–investment plans, provided you explicitly worry about the constraint that the consumption process be non-negative. This may entail considerable extra work, as can be seen in the following example.

Example 5.8 Consider the security model of examples 5.1 and 5.7 with interest rate $r = 0$, $\alpha = 1$, and exponential utility function $u(c) = -\exp(-c)$. Since $u'(0) = 1$, in order to guard against negative consumption levels it is necessary to explicitly impose in the dynamic programming functional equation not only the constraint that the decision variable $c \geqslant 0$, but also constraints which guarantee that next period's wealth will be non-negative. For example, for states ω_1 and ω_2 and time $t = 1$ the dynamic programming equation should be

$$u_1(w) = \max_{\substack{c \geqslant 0 \\ w-c+h \geqslant 0 \\ w-c-2h \geqslant 0}} \left\{ -e^{-c} - \frac{1}{2}e^{-w+c-h} - \frac{1}{2}e^{-w+c+2h} \right\}$$

These three constraints define the feasible region, a triangular subset of $\mathbb{R}^2$ with vertices at $(c, h) = (0, -w)$, $(0, w/2)$, and $(w, 0)$.

We compute the maximizing values of the decision variables c and h by examining the partial derivatives. The partial derivative of the argument with respect to h is equal to zero if and only if $h = -\frac{1}{3}\ln2$. The partial derivative with respect to c is equal to zero if and only if

$$c = \frac{1}{2}\{w + \ln 2 - \ln[e^{-h} + e^{2h}]\}$$

Substituting $h = \frac{1}{3}\ln 2 - -0.231$, we see that the point $(c, h) = (0.0283 + w/2, -0.231)$ maximizes the argument over $\mathbb{R}^2$. This point will fall in the feasible region if and only if $w \geq 0.5186$, in which case, we see by substitution, $u_1(w) = -1.9442\, e^{-w/2}$.

If $w = 0.5186$, then the solution just discussed will make the constraint $w - c + h \geq 0$ tight. We therefore realize that the solution (c, h) must satisfy $c = w + h$ for all $w \leq 0.5186$. Substituting this equation, the objective function becomes $-e^{-w-h} - \frac{1}{2} - \frac{1}{2}e^{3h}$. The derivative of this equals zero if and only if $h = -w/4 - 0.1014$, in which case $c = 3w/4 - 0.1014$. But note that this gives $c \geq 0$ if and only if $w \geq 0.1352$. We therefore conclude that the optimal solution for all w satisfying $0.1352 \leq w \leq 0.5186$ is $(c, h) = (3w/4 - 0.1014, -w/4 - 0.1014)$, in which case, we see by substitution, $u_1(w) = -1.4756\, e^{-3w/4} - \frac{1}{2}$.

For $w = 0.1352$ this solution gives $c = 0$. We therefore realize that for all w satisfying $0 \leq w \leq 0.1352$ the optimal solution must be at the vertex of the triangle where $c = 0$ and $h = -w$, in which case $u_1(w) = -\frac{3}{2} - \frac{1}{2}e^{-3w}$

Needless to say, the computation of $u_1(w)$ for states ω_3 and ω_4 will be equally difficult (see exercise 5.13). Moreover, with the messy nature of $u_1(w)$, the computation of $u_0(w)$ will be even more difficult. Without taking this example further, it should be clear that the computational difficulties can become formidable when you relax the assumption that $u'(0) = \infty$.

Exercise 5.10   For the security model of example 5.1 with constant interest rate $r = 0$, utility parameter $\alpha = 1$, and isoelastic utility function $u(c) = -1/c$, use dynamic programming to compute the optimal consumption process and the optimal trading strategy.

Exercise 5.11   For a single security governed by the binomial model with parameters p, u, d, r, and T, with utility parameter $\alpha \leq 1$, and with log utility $u(c) = \ln(c)$, use dynamic programming to show that the optimal amount to consume at time t is

$$C_t = \frac{W_t}{1 + \alpha + \ldots + \alpha^{T-t}}$$

where W_t is the wealth available at that same time. Moreover, show that at every time t the optimal fraction of the invested funds which are put in the risky security is

$$\frac{S_t H_1(t+1)}{W_t - C_t} = \frac{(1+r)[pu + (1-p)d - (1+r)]}{(1+r-d)(u-1-r)}$$

Finally, show that the time t value function is of the form $u_t(w) = (1 + \alpha + \ldots + \alpha^{T-t})\ln(w)$ plus a constant.

Exercise 5.12   For a single security governed by the binomial model with parameters p, u, d, r, and T, with utility parameter $\alpha \leqslant 1$, and with isoelastic utility $u(c) = c^\gamma/\gamma$, use dynamic programming and an induction argument to show that the optimal amount to consume at time t is $C_t = k_t W_t$, where k_t is a positive constant that depends on t but is independent of the state ω. Show that at every time t the optimal fraction of the invested funds which are put in the risky security is

$$\frac{S_t H_1(t+1)}{W_t - C_t} =$$

$$\frac{(1+r)\left[(1-p)^{1/(\gamma-1)}(1+r-d)^{1/(\gamma-1)} - p^{1/(\gamma-1)}(u-1-r)^{1/(\gamma-1)}\right]}{(1-p)^{1/(\gamma-1)}(1+r-d)^{\gamma/(\gamma-1)} + p^{1/(\gamma-1)}(u-1-r)^{\gamma/(\gamma-1)}}$$

Finally, show that the time t value function is of the form $u_t(w) = \gamma_t w^\gamma$, where γ_t is a constant that depends on t but is independent of the state ω.

Exercise 5.13   For the situation in example 5.8, compute $u_1(w)$ and the corresponding maximizing values of c and h for states ω_3 and ω_4 and for all $w \geqslant 0$.

5.4   Consumption–Investment and Martingale Methods

As an alternative to dynamic programming, the risk neutral probability measure can be exploited to provide an efficient method for solving the consumption–investment problem (5.14), an approach that is a natural generalization of the one taken for single period models. Throughout this section it will be assumed that there exists a unique martingale measure Q, so the model is complete. A consumption process C will be called *attainable* if there exists a trading strategy H such that (C, H) is an admissible consumption–investment plan satisfying $C_T = V_T$ (implicit is a specified initial wealth V). In this case one says that H *replicates* or *generates* C.

The first step in the risk neutral computational approach is to characterize the set of all attainable consumption processes. The second step is to find the element of this set that maximizes expected utility, that is, the objective function in (5.14). Finally, one derives the self-financing trading strategy H that generates this optimal C.

We begin by observing the following:

(5.18)   Given an initial wealth $v \geqslant 0$, a consumption process C, and a self-financing trading strategy H, one has

$$V_t/B_t = v + G_t^* - \sum_{u=0}^{t-1} C_u/B_u, \qquad t = 1, \ldots, T$$

One can see this by an induction argument. The reader can use (5.13) to verify this is true for $t = 1$. For the induction step, suppose this equation holds for $t = s$. Now (5.13) implies

$$H_0(s+1) = V_s/B_s - C_s/B_s - \sum_{n=1}^{N} H_n(s+1)S_n^*(s)$$

so substituting this in (5.12) with $t = s + 1$ after dividing by B_{s+1} yields

$$V_{s+1}/B_{s+1} = V_s/B_s + \sum_{n=1}^{N} H_n(s+1)\Delta S_n^*(s+1) - C_s/B_s$$

The induction assumption that (5.18) holds for $t = s$ therefore finishes the argument that (5.18) holds for $t = s + 1$.

Relationship (5.18) will enable us to characterize the attainable consumption processes. If we define $M_t = v + G_t^*$, then M is a martingale under the risk neutral probability measure Q satisfying $M_0 = v$. Hence if (5.18) applies, then $M_t = V_t/B_t + C_0/B_0 + \ldots + C_{t-1}/B_{t-1}$ and

$$v = E_Q[V_t/B_t + C_0/B_0 + \ldots + C_{t-1}/B_{t-1}], \qquad t = 1, \ldots, T$$

If, in addition, $C_T = V_T$, then

(5.19)
$$v = E_Q[C_0/B_0 + \ldots + C_T/B_T]$$

In other words, equation (5.19) is a necessary condition for the consumption process C to be attainable. It turns out that (5.19) is also a sufficient condition, that is,

(5.20)   Given the initial wealth $v \geqslant 0$, the consumption process C is attainable if and only if (5.19) holds. If V_0 is the value of the portfolio which replicates C, then $V_0 \geqslant 0$.

To see why equation (5.19) is sufficient, observe that $X \equiv B_T[C_0/B_0 + \ldots + C_T/B_T]$ is an attainable contingent claim. Actually, X should be viewed as the composition of $T + 1$ attainable contingent claims, where the tth claim is the receipt of C_t dollars at time t, which are then deposited and held in the bank account until time T. Thus there are T self-financing trading strategies $H^1, \ldots, H^T$ that replicate the T contingent claims $C_1, \ldots, C_T$, respectively. Taking $H \equiv H^1 + \ldots + H^T$, it follows that H is a self-financing trading strategy such that (C, H) is an admissible consumption–investment plan with $C_T = V_T$.

For the second part of (5.20), we see from (5.18) that

$$V_t/B_t + \sum_{u=0}^{t-1} C_u/B_u = E_Q\left[V_T/B_T + \sum_{u=0}^{T-1} C_u/B_u \mid \mathscr{F}_t\right]$$

is a martingale under Q with time T value equal to

$$\sum_{u=0}^{T} C_u/B_u$$

Thus

$$V_t/B_t = E_Q\left[\sum_{u=t}^{T} C_u/B_u \mid \mathscr{F}_t\right]$$

must be non-negative for all t.

Assuming the utility function satisfies $u(c) = -\infty$ for all $c < 0$, then by (5.20) the optimal consumption–investment problem (5.14) is equivalent to the following:

(5.21)   maximize $E\left[\sum_{t=0}^{T} \alpha^t u(C_t)\right]$

subject to $E_Q[C_0/B_0 + \ldots + C_T/B_T] = v$

C is an adapted process

The assumption about the utility function will guarantee that the optimal solution is a non-negative stochastic process. In view of (5.20), the optimal solution will be an attainable consumption process whose objective value is greater than or equal to that for every other attainable consumption process. Hence with a solution C of (5.21), all that remains to obtain the solution of (5.14) is to derive the trading strategy that replicates C.

Problem (5.21) can be solved with a Lagrange multiplier in a fashion similar to the optimal portfolio problem of section 5.2. However, the situation here is a little more tricky because the decision variable is an adapted process, not just a random variable. The following result will play a crucial role.

(5.22) $E_Q\left[\sum_{t=0}^{T} C_t/B_t\right] = E\left[\sum_{t=0}^{T} C_t N_t\right]$

where N is the adapted stochastic process defined for all t by $N_t = E[L|\mathscr{F}_t]/B_t$.

Since $L = Q/P$, this result follows from a simple calculation:

$$E_Q\left[\sum_{t=0}^{T} C_t/B_t\right] = E\left[L\sum_{t=0}^{T} C_t/B_t\right]$$

$$= E\left[\sum_{t=0}^{T} E[C_t L/B_t|\mathscr{F}_t]\right] = E\left[\sum_{t=0}^{T} C_t N_t\right]$$

As a consequence, problem (5.21) can be rewritten as follows:

(5.23)   maximize $E\left[\sum_{t=0}^{T} \alpha^t u(C_t)\right]$

subject to $E\left[\sum_{t=0}^{T} C_t N_t\right] = v$

C is an adapted process.

Introducing a Lagrange multiplier λ, we now want to solve:

(5.24)
$$\text{maximize } E\left[\sum_{t=0}^{T} \alpha^t u(C_t) \quad \lambda \sum_{t=0}^{T} C_t N_t\right]$$

With suitable assumptions about the utility function u to ensure the optimal solution C will feature strictly positive consumption values (e.g., it suffices to require that the marginal utility $u'(c)$ converges to ∞ as c approaches 0 from above and that $u'(c)$ converges to 0 as c increases to ∞), the following first order necessary condition must be satisfied:

(5.25)
$$\alpha^t u'(C_t) = \lambda N_t, \quad \text{all} \quad \omega \in \Omega, \quad t = 0, \dots, T$$

Equivalently, if $I(\cdot)$ is the inverse of the marginal utility function $u'(\cdot)$, then we must have

(5.26)
$$C_t = I(\lambda N_t/\alpha^t), \quad \text{all} \quad \omega \in \Omega, \quad t = 0, \dots, T$$

All that remains is to establish the correct value of the Lagrange multiplier λ; this is simply the value such that the constraint in (5.23) is satisfied when (5.26) is substituted, that is, the correct value of λ is the unique solution of

(5.27)
$$E\left[\sum_{t=0}^{T} N_t I(\lambda N_t/\alpha^t)\right] = v$$

Example 5.9   With $u(c) = \ln(c)$ we have $u'(c) = c^{-1}$ and $I(i) = i^{-1}$, in which case $I(\lambda N_t/\alpha^t) = \alpha^t/(\lambda N_t)$. Equation (5.27) becomes

$$v = E\left[\sum_{t=0}^{T} N_t \alpha^t/(\lambda N_t)\right] - \frac{1}{\lambda}\sum_{t=0}^{T} \alpha^t$$

Thus

$$\lambda = \begin{cases} \frac{T+1}{v}, & \alpha = 1 \\ \frac{1-\alpha^{T+1}}{v(1-\alpha)}, & \alpha < 1 \end{cases}$$

It follows from (5.26) that the optimal solution is

$$C_t = \frac{\alpha^t}{\lambda N_t} = \begin{cases} \frac{v}{(T+1)N_t}, & \alpha = 1; \quad t = 0, \dots, T \\ \frac{\alpha^t v(1-\alpha)}{(1-\alpha^{T+1})N_t} & \alpha < 1; \quad t = 0, \dots, T \end{cases}$$

Thus, for instance, when $\alpha = 1$ the optimal objective value is $(T+1)$ $\ln\{v/(T+1)\} - E\ln(N_0) - \dots - E\ln(N_T)$.

Examples 5.1 and 5.9 (continued)   For the security model of example 5.1 with a constant interest rate $r \geq 0$, the stochastic process N is as follows:

ω	$P(\omega)$	$L(\omega)$	N_0	N_1	N_2
ω_1	$1/4$	$\frac{(1+5r)(2+8r)}{3}$	1	$\frac{1+5r}{2(1+r)}$	$\frac{L}{(1+r)^2}$
ω_2	$1/4$	$\frac{(1+5r)(1-8r)}{3}$	1	$\frac{1+5r}{2(1+r)}$	$\frac{L}{(1+r)^2}$
ω_3	$1/4$	$\frac{(3-5r)(1+4r)}{3}$	1	$\frac{(3-5r)}{2(1+r)}$	$\frac{L}{(1+r)^2}$
ω_4	$1/4$	$\frac{(3-5r)(2-4r)}{3}$	1	$\frac{3-5r}{2(1+r)}$	$\frac{L}{(1+r)^2}$

The optimal consumption process is $C_t = \alpha^t v / [(1 + \alpha + \alpha^2) N_t]$, so, in particular,

$$C_2 = V_2 = \frac{\alpha^2 v (1+r)^2}{(1+\alpha+\alpha^2)L}$$

Now by considering how to replicate the contingent claim V_2, we must have, in states ω_1 and ω_2, respectively,

$$(1+r)^2 H_0(2) + 9H_1(2) = \frac{\alpha^2 v(1+r)^2}{(1+\alpha+\alpha^2)L(\omega_1)}$$

and

$$(1+r)^2 H_0(2) + 6H_1(2) = \frac{\alpha^2 v(1+r)^2}{(1+\alpha+\alpha^2)L(\omega_2)}$$

Solving for $H_0(2)$ and $H_1(2)$ yields

$$H_1(2) = -\frac{\alpha^2 v(1+r)^2(1+16r)}{(1+\alpha+\alpha^2)(1+5r)(2+8r)(1-8r)}$$

and

$$H_0(2) = \frac{12\alpha^2 v(1+10r)}{(1+\alpha+\alpha^2)(1+5r)(2+8r)(1-8r)}$$

Hence the value of the portfolio just after time 1 consumption is

$$(1+r)H_0(2) + 8H_1(2) = \frac{4\alpha^2 v(1+r)(1+4r)}{(1+\alpha+\alpha^2)(1+5r)(2+8r)}$$

Adding C_1 to this gives

$$V_1 = \frac{2\alpha v(1+r)(1+\alpha)}{(1+\alpha+\alpha^2)(1+5r)}$$

for the value of the portfolio just before time 1 consumption in states ω_1 and ω_2.

In a similar fashion we compute

$$\Pi_1(2) - \frac{\alpha^2 v(1+r)^2(1-8r)}{(1+\alpha+\alpha^2)(3-5r)(1+4r)(2-4r)}$$

$$H_0(2) = \frac{36\alpha^2 vr}{(1+\alpha+\alpha^2)(3-5r)(1+4r)(2-4r)}$$

and

$$V_1 = \frac{2\alpha v(1+r)(1+\alpha)}{(1+\alpha+\alpha^2)(3-5r)}$$

in states ω_3 and ω_4.

Finally, we compute the trading strategy that will replicate V_1, giving

$$H_1(1) = \frac{\alpha(1+\alpha)(1+r)(1-5r)v}{(1+\alpha+\alpha^2)(1+5r)(3-5r)}$$

and

$$H_0(1) = \frac{2\alpha(1+\alpha)(-1+15r)v}{(1+\alpha+\alpha^2)(1+5r)(3-5r)}$$

Notice that $C_0 + H_0(1) + 5H_1(1) = v$, as required.

Exercise 5.14   Use the martingale approach to show that with the isoelastic utility function $u(c) = c^\gamma/\gamma, \gamma < 1, \gamma \neq 0$, the optimal consumption process is given by

$$C_t = \frac{v}{\Delta}\alpha^{t/(1-\gamma)}N_t^{1/(\gamma-1)}$$

and the optimal objective value is given by $v^\gamma \Delta^{1-\gamma}/\gamma$, where

$$\Delta = \sum_{t=0}^{T} \alpha^{t/(1-\gamma)} E\left[N_t^{\gamma/(\gamma-1)}\right]$$

Exercise 5.15   For the security model of example 5.1 with $\alpha \leqslant 1$, initial wealth v, constant interest rate $r \geqslant 0$, and isoelastic utility function $u(c) = c^\gamma/\gamma$, use the risk neutral computational approach to write algebraic formulas for the optimal consumption process C. Compute numerical values for this process as well as the optimal trading strategy in the special case $\gamma = -1$, $\alpha = 1$, and $r = 0$.

5.5   Maximum Utility From Consumption and Terminal Wealth

This section investigates the problem where utility is gained from both the consumption each period as well as the amount of money that is dedicated at time T for subsequent use. This is a modest generalization of the ordinary consumption–investment problem, where now only a portion C_T of the time T wealth V_T is consumed, leaving $V_T - C_T$ for future investment. This new situation is equivalent to the ordinary consumption–investment problem, except that the utility function for period T consumption is allowed to be different from the utility function for the other periods. Not surprisingly, it is easy to solve this generalized consumption–investment problem, using slight generalizations of either the dynamic programming or the risk neutral computational approaches.

Throughout this section it will be assumed that there exists a unique risk neutral probability measure Q, so the model is complete. Let $\mathscr{A}_v$ denote the set of all the admissible consumption–investment plans with initial wealth $V_0 = v$, so each $(C, H) \in \mathscr{A}_v$ is self-financing with C a non-negative, adapted process satisfying $C_T \leqslant V_T$.

For the generalized consumption–investment problem, two concave, increasing utility functions are specified: u_c measures the utility of consumption each period and satisfies $u_c(c) = -\infty$ for all $c < 0$ (for computational convenience we shall usually assume, in addition, $u_c'(c) \to \infty$ as $c \searrow 0$), while u_p measures the utility of the funds that are reserved at time T for the future, as in an ordinary optimal portfolio problem. The problem is to choose the $(C, H) \in \mathscr{A}_v$ which maximizes the expected total utility, which is

$$E\left[\sum_{t=0}^{T} \alpha^t u_c(C_t) + \alpha^T u_p(V_T - C_T)\right]$$

We are also interested in the corresponding *value function*, which keeps track of the optimal objective value as a function of the initial wealth v. This is denoted $J(v)$ and is given by

$$(\mathbf{5.28}) \qquad J(v) = \max_{(C, H) \in \mathscr{A}_v} E\left[\sum_{t=0}^{T} \alpha^t u_c(C_t) + \alpha^T u_p(V_T - C_T)\right]$$

With the dynamic programming approach we use (5.16), exactly the same recursive functional equation as with the ordinary consumption–investment problem, for $t = 1, \ldots, T$, namely

$$u_{t-1}(w) = \max_{C, H} \left\{ u_c(C) + \alpha E\left(u_t\left((w - C)B_t/B_{t-1}\right.\right.\right.$$
$$\left.\left.\left. + B_t \sum_{n=1}^{N} H_n \Delta S_n^*(t)\right) \middle| \mathscr{F}_{t-1}\right)\right\}$$

where the maximum is taken over all $H_n \in \mathscr{F}_{t-1}$ for $n = 1, \ldots, N$ and over all $C \in \mathscr{F}_{t-1}$. As usual, the function $u_t(w)$ is to be interpreted as the maximum expected discounted utility beginning at time t with wealth w, and so $u_0(w) = J(w)$. Moreover, after recursively computing the u_t functions, one obtains the optimal consumption–investment plan by taking the maximizing values of H and C, beginning with $t = 1$.

A crucial difference between the dynamic programming approach for the ordinary consumption–investment problem and the one here is the specification of the terminal utility function u_T. In the former case one simply takes $u_t(w) = u_c(w)$, because with wealth w at time T the obvious thing to do is to consume everything. But now in this situation one needs to optimally divide the wealth between immediate consumption and terminal investment, which means one should take

$$(5.29) \qquad u_T(w) = \max_{0 \leqslant c \leqslant w} \{u_c(c) + u_p(w - c)\}$$

Hence the dynamic programming approach for a problem featuring both consumption and terminal wealth is essentially the same as for an ordinary consumption–investment problem, except that the utility associated with time T consumption should be as in (5.29) instead of u_c.

Example 5.10 Suppose $u_c(c) = \ln(c)$ and $u_p(w) = w^\gamma/\gamma$ with $\gamma < 1$ and $\gamma \neq 0$, so $u_T(w) = \max\{\ln(c) + (w - c)^\gamma/\gamma\}$. A little calculus shows the maximizing c is a root of the equation $c = (w - c)^{1-\gamma}$. For instance, if $\gamma = -1$, then

$$c = w + 1/2 - \sqrt{w + 1/4} = [\sqrt{w + 1/4} - 1/2]^2$$

in which case

$$u_T(w) = 2\ln(\sqrt{w + 1/4} - 1/2) - \frac{1}{\sqrt{w + 1/4} - 1/2}$$

$$= 2u_c(g(w)) + u_p(g(w))$$

where g is the concave, increasing function $g(w) = \sqrt{w + 1/4} - 1/2$ with domain $[0, \infty)$.

Turning to the risk neutral computational approach, in view of (5.19) and (5.20) it should be clear that the following holds:

(5.30) Given the initial wealth $v \geqslant 0$ and the admissible consumption–investment plan (C, H), one has

$$v = E_Q[C_0/B_0 + \ldots + C_{T-1}/B_{T-1} + V_T/B_T]$$

Conversely, if this equation holds and if C is a consumption process with $C_T \leqslant V_T$, then there exists a trading strategy H such that (C, H) is an admissible consumption–investment plan with $v \geqslant 0$.

It follows that our optimization problem can be formulated as follows:

$$\text{maximize } E\left[\sum_{t=0}^{T} \alpha^t u_c(C_t) + \alpha^T u_p(V_T - C_T)\right]$$

$$\text{subject to } v = E_Q[C_0/B_0 + \ldots + C_{T-1}/B_{T-1} + V_T/B_T]$$

$$V_T \geqslant C_T, \ V_T \in \mathscr{F}_T$$

$$C \text{ is an adapted process}$$

Our assumption that $u_c'(c) \to \infty$ as $c \searrow 0$ will guarantee that the maximizing consumption process will satisfy $C_t > 0$ for all t. We will assume in addition that $u_p'(w) \to \infty$ as $w \searrow 0$, so that the constraint $V_T > C_T$ will automatically be satisfied by the optimal solution. In other words, with these assumptions about the utility functions it suffices to work with the following formulation of the optimization problem:

(5.31) $\qquad$ maximize $E\left[\displaystyle\sum_{t=0}^{T} \alpha^t u_c(C_t) + \alpha^T u_p(V_T - C_T)\right]$

$\qquad\qquad$ subject to $v = E_Q[C_0/B_0 + \ldots + C_{T-1}/B_{T-1} + V_T/B_T]$

$\qquad\qquad\qquad$ C is an adapted process

$\qquad\qquad\qquad$ $V_T \in \mathscr{F}_T$

The optimal solution will immediately give a consumption process with $C_t > 0$ for all t and with $C_T < V_T$. It follows from (5.30) that there exists a trading strategy H making (C, H) an admissible consumption–investment plan which must be the solution of the original optimization problem.

Problem (5.31) is solved with the same approach as was used with problem (5.21). We introduce the Lagrange multiplier λ and the adapted process N defined by $N_t = E[L|\mathscr{F}_t]/B_t$, thereby allowing us to rewrite (5.31) as

$$\text{maximize } E\left[\sum_{t=0}^{T} \alpha^t u_c(C_t) + \alpha^T u_p(V_T - C_T) - \lambda \sum_{t=0}^{T-1} C_t N_t - \lambda V_T N_T\right]$$

where the maximum is over stochastic processes C and random variables V_T. Differentiating with respect to each C_t and then V_T, we see that the following first order necessary conditions must be satisfied:

$$\alpha^t u_c'(C_t) = \lambda N_t, \qquad t = 0, \ldots, T-1$$
$$\alpha^T u_c'(C_T) = \alpha^T u_p'(V_T - C_T),$$
$$\alpha^T u_p'(V_T - C_T) = \lambda N_T$$

Introducing $I_c(\cdot)$, the inverse of the marginal utility function $u_c'(\cdot)$, as well as $I_p(\cdot)$, the inverse of the marginal utility function $u_p'(\cdot)$, it follows that the optimal solution must satisfy

(5.32) $\qquad$
$$C_t = I_c(\lambda N_t/\alpha^t), \qquad t = 0, \ldots, T,$$
$$V_T = I_c(\lambda N_T/\alpha^T) + I_p(\lambda N_T/\alpha^T)$$

for some positive value of the scalar λ. The correct value of λ is the one which satisfies the constraint in (5.31) upon substitution of (5.32), namely,

(5.33) $\qquad$
$$E\left[\sum_{t=0}^{T} I_c(\lambda N_t/\alpha^t)N_t + I_p(\lambda N_T/\alpha^T)N_T\right] = v$$

With this value of λ the optimal objective value is thus

$$J(v) = E\left[\sum_{t=0}^{T} \alpha^t u_c(I_c(\lambda N_t/\alpha^t)) + \alpha^T u_p(I_p(\lambda N_T/\alpha^T))\right]$$

Example 5.10 (continued)   Suppose $u_c(c) = \ln(c)$ and $u_p(w) = -1/w$, so $I_c(i) = 1/i$ and $I_p(i) = 1/\sqrt{i}$. Hence (5.33) becomes

$$\frac{1}{\lambda}\sum_{t=0}^{T} \alpha^t + \frac{1}{\sqrt{\lambda}}E\left[\sqrt{N_T \alpha^T}\right] = v$$

and so the correct value of λ can be obtained by solving a simple quadratic equation.

We can sharpen these results if the utility functions are sufficiently differentiable. Define $f : (0, \infty) \to (0, \infty)$ by

$$f(\lambda) = E\left[\sum_{t=0}^{T} I_c(\lambda N_t/\alpha^t)N_t + I_p(\lambda N_T/\alpha^T)N_T\right]$$

so equation (5.33) is the same thing as $f(\lambda) = v$. With minor assumptions about the utility functions, the function f will be continuous and strictly decreasing, in which case it will have an inverse function, which will be denoted g. Thus $f(\lambda) = v$ if and only if $\lambda = g(v)$. In particular, the expressions in (5.32) for the optimal solution become

$$C_t = I_c(g(v)N_t/\alpha^t), \qquad t = 0, \ldots, T$$
$$V_T = I_c(g(v)N_T/\alpha^T) + I_p(g(v)N_T/\alpha^T)$$

and the optimal objective value $J(v) = K(g(v))$, where we have introduced the function

$$K(\lambda) = E\left[\sum_{t=0}^{T} \alpha^t u_c(I_c(\lambda N_t/\alpha^t)) + \alpha^T u_p(I_p(\lambda N_T/\alpha^T))\right]$$

But

$$f'(\lambda) = E\left[\sum_{t=0}^{T} I'_c(\lambda N_t/\alpha^t)N_t^2/\alpha^t + I'_p(\lambda N_T/\alpha^T)N_T^2/\alpha^T\right]$$

so

$$K'(\lambda) = E\left[\sum_{t=0}^{T} \alpha^t u'_c(I_c(\lambda N_t/\alpha^t))\frac{d}{d\lambda}I_c(\lambda N_t/\alpha^t)\right.$$
$$\left. + \alpha^T u'_p(I_p(\lambda N_T/\alpha^T))\frac{d}{d\lambda}I_p(\lambda N_T/\alpha^T)\right]$$

$$= E\left[\sum_{t=0}^{T}\alpha^{t}(\lambda N_{t}/\alpha^{t})\frac{d}{d\lambda}I_{c}(\lambda N_{t}/\alpha^{t})+\alpha^{T}(\lambda N_{T}/\alpha^{T})\frac{d}{d\lambda}I_{p}(\lambda N_{T}/\alpha^{T})\right]$$

$$= E\left[\sum_{t=0}^{T}\alpha^{t}(\lambda N_{t}/\alpha^{t})^{2}I_{c}'(\lambda N_{t}/\alpha^{t})+\alpha^{T}(\lambda N_{T}/\alpha^{T})^{2}I_{p}'(\lambda N_{T}/\alpha^{T})\right]$$

$$= \lambda f'(\lambda)$$

It follows that
$$J'(v) = g(v)$$

because by standard rules of differential calculus
$$J'(v) = K'(g(v))g'(v) = g(v)f'(g(v))g'(v) = g(v)$$

Notice that the g function will be positive and strictly decreasing, so we conclude from these calculations that the value function J is strictly increasing and strictly concave.

Exercise 5.16   For a simple single period model with one security with $\Omega = \{\omega_1, \omega_2\}$, $S_0 = 4$, $S_1(\omega_1) = 5$, $S_1(\omega_2) = 3$, $\alpha = 1$ and constant interest rate $r = 0$, suppose the utility functions are as in example 5.10 with $\gamma = -1$. Moreover, suppose $P(\omega_1) = 2/3$. Compute the optimal consumption process and trading strategy for the generalized consumption–investment problem of this section using:

(a) the dynamic programming approach,
(b) the risk neutral computational approach.

Exercise 5.17   Show that the $g(v)$ functions corresponding to the isoelastic utility function $u(w) = \gamma^{-1}w^{\gamma}$ for general values of the parameter γ, where $-\infty < \gamma < 1$ and $\gamma \neq 0$, are given by

$$g_c(v) = v^{\gamma-1}\left(E\left[\sum_{t=0}^{T}N_t^{\gamma/(\gamma-1)}\alpha^{t/(1-\gamma)}\right]\right)^{1-\gamma}$$

and

$$g_p(v) = v^{\gamma-1}\left(E\left[L^{\gamma/(\gamma-1)}B_T^{\gamma/(1-\gamma)}\right]\right)^{1-\gamma}$$

for the ordinary consumption–investment and the ordinary optimal portfolio problems, respectively.

Exercise 5.18   Show that if $u_p(w) = \ln(w)$, then $g(v) = 1/v$ for an ordinary optimal portfolio problem with $u_c = 0$.

5.6   Optimal Portfolios With Constraints

The ideas in this section are, for the most part, straightforward generalizations of the single period concepts in section 2.5. A non-empty, closed, convex subset $\mathbb{K}$ of $\mathbb{R}^N$ is specified, and the trading strategy, when expressed as the N-vector representing the fractions of the wealth held in the risky securities, is required to be an element of $\mathbb{K}$ at each time t. Examples of $\mathbb{K}$ are given in section 2.5. This constrained, multiperiod problem can be solved with either dynamic programming or a risk neutral computational approach, as will now be discussed.

To be precise, *trading strategies* will be of the form $F = (F_1, \ldots, F_N)$, where each $F_n = \{F_n(t); t = 1, \ldots, T\}$ is a predictable stochastic process with $F_n(t) = H_n(t)S_n(t-1)/V_{t-1}$ representing the fraction of the time $t-1$ wealth that is invested at that time in security n and held until time t. Assuming the trading strategy is self-financing, it follows that $1 - F_1(t) - \ldots - F_N(t)$ is the fraction of time $t-1$ wealth that is invested in the bank account. In general, the value $F_n(t)$ can be less than zero or greater than one. However, with the specification of the constraint set $\mathbb{K}$, for a trading strategy to be *admissible* it is necessary that $F(t) \in \mathbb{K}$ for $t = 1, \ldots, T$. Let $\mathscr{A}$ denote the set of all such admissible trading strategies.

According to section 3.2, the time T value V_T of the portfolio can be expressed as

$$V_T = v \prod_{t=1}^{T} \left[1 + r_t + \sum_{n=1}^{N} F_n(t)\{\Delta R_n(t) - r_t\} \right]$$

where v is the initial wealth, $r_t = (B_t - B_{t-1})/B_{t-1}$ is the interest rate associated with the interval $[t-1, t]$, and $\Delta R_n(t) = R_n(t) - R_n(t-1)$ is the change in the return process associated with security n. With the specification of the utility function u and the initial wealth v, the constrained optimal portfolio problem is:

(5.34)
$$\text{maximize} \quad Eu(V_T)$$
$$\text{subject to} \quad F \in \mathscr{A}, \quad V_0 = v$$

The corresponding *value function* is

$$J(v) \equiv \sup_{F \in \mathscr{A}} Eu(V_T)$$

This problem can be solved with dynamic programming by using recursively the dynamic programming functional equation:

$$u_{t-1}(w) = \max_{F \in \mathbb{K}} E\left[u_t\left(w\left\{ 1 + r_t + \sum_{n=1}^{N} F\{\Delta R_n(t) - r_t\} \right\} \right) \middle| \mathscr{F}_{t-1} \right]$$

for $t = 1, 2, \ldots, T$ together with the boundary condition $u_T(w) = u(w)$. Thus $u_t(w)$ represents the maximum expected utility of terminal wealth when you start with initial wealth w at time t and the information available is $\mathscr{F}_t$. In particular, $J(v) = u_0(v)$. The dynamic programming approach is illustrated in the following example.

Example 5.11 Consider the two-period, single security model in example 5.1 with the interest rate $r_t = 0$. Some relevant data are:

ω	$P(\omega)$	$\Delta R_1(\omega)$	$\Delta R_2(\omega)$
ω_1	1/4	3/5	1/8
ω_2	1/4	3/5	-2/8
ω_3	1/4	-1/5	2/4
ω_4	1/4	-1/5	-1/4

Suppose the utility function $u(w) = \ln(w)$ and short selling of the risky security is prohibited, so $\mathbb{K} = [0, \infty)$. The dynamic programming equation for $t = 2$ and $\omega = \omega_1, \omega_2$ is

$$u_1(w) = \max_{F \geqslant 0} E[\ln(w\{1 + F\Delta R_2\}|S_1 = 8]$$

$$= \max_{F \geqslant 0} \left\{ \frac{1}{2}\ln[w(1 + F/8)] + \frac{1}{2}\ln[w(1 - F/4)]\right\}$$

The argument is a concave function with respect to F, and its derivative at $F = 0$ is negative, so the argument is maximized on $[0, \infty)$ at $F = 0$. Substituting this value gives $u_1(w) = \ln(w)$ for ω_1 and ω_2.

The dynamic programming equation for $t = 2$ and $\omega = \omega_3, \omega_4$ is

$$u_1(w) = \max_{F \geqslant 0} \left\{ \frac{1}{2}\ln[w(1 + F/2)] + \frac{1}{2}\ln[w(1 - F/4)] \right.$$

The argument here is concave with respect to F, but the derivative at $F = 0$ is positive, so the argument is maximized on $[0, \infty)$ where the derivative equals 0. This is easily computed to be $F = 1$, giving by substitution

$$u_1(w) = \ln(3) - \frac{3}{2}\ln(2) + \ln(w)$$

for ω_3 and ω_4.

The dynamic programming equation for $t = 1$ is

$$u_0(w) = \max_{F \geqslant 0} E[u_1(w\{1 + F\Delta R_1\}]$$

$$= \max_{F \geqslant 0} \left\{ \frac{1}{2}\ln[w(1 + 3F/5)] + \frac{1}{2}\left(\ln(3) - \frac{3}{2}\ln(2) + \ln[w(1 - F/5)]\right)\right\}$$

The maximizing value of F is found, as above, to be $F = 5/3$, and substitution gives the value function

$$u_0(v) = J(v) = \ln(v) + \frac{1}{4}\ln(2)$$

In summary, the optimal strategy is to invest $5v/3$ dollars in the risky security at time 0 (since $S_0 = 5$, this means one should buy $v/3$ units or shares), borrowing $2v/3$ dollars from the bank. If $S_1 = 8$, then at time 1 the portfolio will be worth $2v$ dollars; all of this should be held in the bank account until time 2, ending up with $2v$ dollars in both states ω_1 and ω_2. If $S_1 = 4$, then at time 1 the portfolio will be worth

2v/3 dollars. In this case it is optimal to invest exactly this sum in the risky security (that is, go long v/6 units), taking no position with the bank. Hence one will end up with v and $v/2$ dollars in states ω_3 and ω_4, respectively.

The risk neutral computational approach for the constrained, multiperiod problem is very similar to the approach for the single period problem, with one important exception: the scalar parameter v will now be a predictable stochastic process. As before, the *support function* $\delta(x) : \mathbb{R}^N \to \mathbb{R} \cup \{+\infty\}$ of $\mathbb{K}$ is convex and defined by

$$\delta(x) \equiv \sup_{F \in \mathbb{K}} \; (-Fx')$$

The *effective domain* of δ is the convex cone $\tilde{\mathbb{K}} \equiv \{x \in \mathbb{R}^N : \delta(x) < \infty\}$. It will be assumed that $\mathbb{K}$ is such that δ is continuous on $\tilde{\mathbb{K}}$. In addition, it will be assumed $0 \in \mathbb{K}$ so $\delta \geqslant 0$. Examples of δ and $\tilde{\mathbb{K}}$ are given in section 2.5.

We now introduce a predictable stochastic process $\kappa = \{\kappa(t); t = 1, \ldots, T\}$ which is required to satisfy $\kappa(t) \in \tilde{\mathbb{K}}$ for all $t \geqslant 1$. Thus $\kappa(t, \omega)$ will be an N-vector; its nth component will correspond to the nth risky security, as will be shown in a moment. Let $\mathcal{N}$ denote the set of all such processes κ.

We next define an auxiliary market $\mathcal{M}_\kappa$ for each $\kappa \in \mathcal{N}$ by modifying the return processes for the bank account and the risky securities according to

$$r_t \to r_t + \delta(\kappa(t)), \qquad\qquad t \geqslant 1$$
$$\Delta R_n(t) \to \Delta R_n(t) + \delta(\kappa(t)) + \kappa_n(t), \qquad n = 1, \ldots, N; t \geqslant 1$$

For each such market, let Q_κ denote a corresponding risk neutral probability measure, if one exists. Notice that the market $\mathcal{M}_0$ with $\kappa = 0$ is the same as the original market, since $\delta(0) = 0$. It will usually be the case that Q_κ exists and is unique, in which case a unique Q_κ will also exist for all $\kappa \in \mathcal{N}$ in some neighborhood of $\kappa = 0$, by the assumed continuity of $\delta(\cdot)$.

For the market $\mathcal{M}_\kappa$ and any trading strategy F, whether it is admissible or not, the time T value of the portfolio is

(5.35) $$V_T^\kappa = v \prod_{t=1}^T \left[1 + r_t + \delta(\kappa_t) + \sum_{n=1}^N F_n(t)\{\Delta R_n(t) + \kappa_n(t) - r_t\} \right]$$

$$= v \prod_{t=1}^T \left[1 + r_t + \sum_{n=1}^N F_n(t)\{\Delta R_n(t) - r_t\} + \delta(\kappa_t) + F(t)\kappa_t' \right]$$

where the scalar $F(t)\kappa_t'$ denotes the inner product of the row vector $F(t)$ with the column vector κ_t'.

For each $\kappa \in \mathcal{N}$ we shall be interested in the unconstrained optimal portfolio problem:

$$\text{maximize} \quad Eu(V_T^\kappa)$$
$$\text{subject to} \quad V_0 = v$$

In other words, this is the ordinary optimal portfolio problem for the market $\mathcal{M}_\kappa$. Let $J_\kappa(v)$ denote the corresponding optimal objective value.

Consider an arbitrary market $\mathcal{M}_\kappa$ with $\kappa \neq 0$. As with the single period case, if $F(t) \in \mathbb{K}$ for all t, then by the definition of $\delta(\cdot)$ one has $\delta(\kappa_t) + F(t)\kappa_t' \geq 0$ for all ω and t, in which case by (5.35) $V_T^\kappa \geq V_T^0$ for all $\omega \in \Omega$. On the other hand, if $F(t) \notin \mathbb{K}$ for some t, then $\delta(\kappa_t) + F(t)\kappa_t' \geq 0$ might not hold for all ω and t, in which case one might have $V_T^\kappa < V_T^0$ for some $\omega \in \Omega$. In particular, if $F(t) \notin \mathbb{K}$ for some t, then it is possible to have $Eu(V_T^\kappa) < Eu(V_T^0)$. For this reason, it is possible to have $J_\kappa(v) < J_0(v)$ for some $\kappa \in \mathcal{N}$, that is, the optimal objective value for the unconstrained problem in some of the auxiliary markets may be strictly less than the optimal objective value for the unconstrained problem in the original market.

Now for an arbitrary market $\mathcal{M}_\kappa$ with $\kappa \neq 0$, it is clear that $J_\kappa(v)$, the optimal objective value for the unconstrained problem, is greater than or equal to the optimal objective value for the constrained problem (because if you add constraints, then the optimal objective value, which is being maximized, will not increase).

Meanwhile, suppose $F(t)$ denotes the optimal trading strategy for the original constrained problem, which has optimal objective value $J(v)$. By (5.35) we have $V_T^0 \leq V_T^\kappa$, in which case $J(v) = Eu(V_T^0) \leq Eu(V_T^\kappa)$. But the right hand side of this inequality will be less than or equal to the optimal objective value for the constrained problem in the market $\mathcal{M}_\kappa$.

Putting together the inequalities of the two preceding paragraphs, we thus have

$$(\textbf{5.36}) \qquad\qquad J(v) \leq J_\kappa(v), \qquad \text{all} \quad \kappa \in \mathcal{N}$$

If this is an equality for some $\kappa \in \mathcal{N}$, then the optimal F corresponding to the right hand side is a candidate as the solution of the original constrained problem, because of the following generalization of principle (2.49):

> **(5.37)** Suppose for some $\hat{\kappa} \in \mathcal{N}$ that F, the optimal trading strategy for the unconstrained portfolio problem in the market $\mathcal{M}_{\hat{\kappa}}$, satisfies
>
> (a) $F \in \mathcal{A}$ (i.e.,$F(t) \in \mathbb{K}$ for all $t \geq 1$)
>
> (b) $\delta(\hat{\kappa}(t)) + F(t)\hat{\kappa}'(t) = 0, \qquad$ all $t \geq 1$
>
> Then F is optimal for the constrained problem in the original market $\mathcal{M}_0$ and $J(v) = J_{\hat{\kappa}}(v) \leq J_\kappa(v)$ for all $\kappa \in \mathcal{N}$.

To see this, note by expression (5.35) for V_T^κ that W, the attainable wealth under F in the market $\mathcal{M}_{\hat{\kappa}}$, is also the attainable wealth under F in the original market $\mathcal{M}_0$. Since F is feasible for the constrained problem, it follows that $Eu(w) \leq J(v)$. But $Eu(w) = J_{\hat{\kappa}}(v)$, so by (5.36) we must have $Eu(w) = J(v) = J_{\hat{\kappa}}(v) \leq J_\kappa(v)$ for all $\kappa \in \mathcal{N}$.

In summary, with the risk neutral computational approach you first solve the *dual problem*

$$\text{minimize } J_\kappa(v)$$
$$\kappa \in \mathcal{N}$$

If $\hat{\kappa}$ denotes the optimal solution, then the optimal trading strategy for the unconstrained problem in the market $\mathcal{M}_{\hat{\kappa}}$ will be the candidate for the solution of the constrained problem in the original market $\mathcal{M}_0$. All that remains is to verify that this strategy satisfies the two conditions in (5.37). Perhaps surprisingly, this procedure is usually efficient and successful; an explanation of why this is so is rather difficult and will not be given here.

Example 5.11 (continued)   For this single risky security, two-period model with the no short selling constraint $\mathbb{K} = [0, \infty)$, one has

$$\delta(X) = \begin{cases} 0, & x \geqslant 0 \\ \infty, & x < 0 \end{cases}$$

and $\tilde{\mathbb{K}} = [0, \infty)$. The set $\mathcal{N}$ of admissible predictable processes will be all κ of the form

$$\kappa_t(\omega) = \begin{cases} \kappa^5, & t = 1, \\ \kappa^8, & t = 2, \omega = \omega_1, \omega_2 \\ \kappa^4, & t = 2, \omega = \omega_3, \omega_4 \end{cases}$$

where κ^5, κ^8 and κ^4 are non-negative scalars. Since $\delta(x) = 0$ for all $x \in \tilde{\mathbb{K}}$, the interest rate process in the market $\mathcal{M}_\kappa$ is the same as the interest rate process in the market $\mathcal{M}_0$, which is taken to be $r_1 = r_2 = 0$. Hence the bank account process $B_t^\kappa = 1$ for all t and all $\kappa \in \mathcal{N}$.

The return process R_t^κ for the risky security will vary with $\kappa \in \mathcal{N}$. This is shown below, along with the risk neutral probability measure Q_κ and the state price density L_κ:

ω	$\Delta R_1^\kappa(\omega)$	$\Delta R_2^\kappa(\omega)$	$Q_\kappa(\omega)$	$L_\kappa(\omega)$
ω_1	$3/5 + \kappa^5$	$1/8 + \kappa^8$	$\frac{(1-5\kappa^5)(2-8\kappa^8)}{12}$	$\frac{(1-5\kappa^5)(2-8\kappa^8)}{3}$
ω_2	$3/5 + \kappa^5$	$-1/4 + \kappa^8$	$\frac{(1-5\kappa^5)(1+8\kappa^8)}{3}$	$\frac{(1-5\kappa^5)(1+8\kappa^8)}{3}$
ω_3	$-1/5 + \kappa^5$	$1/2 + \kappa^4$	$\frac{(3+5\kappa^5)(1-4\kappa^4)}{12}$	$\frac{(3+5\kappa^5)(1-4\kappa^4)}{3}$
ω_4	$-1/5 + \kappa^5$	$-1/4 + \kappa^4$	$\frac{(3+5\kappa^5)(2+4\kappa^4)}{12}$	$\frac{(3+5\kappa^5)(2+4\kappa^4)}{3}$

The optimal attainable wealth and the value function for the unconstrained problem in the market $\mathcal{M}_\kappa$ are given respectively by

$$W_\kappa = v/L_\kappa = \begin{cases} \frac{3v}{(1-5\kappa^5)(2-8\kappa^8)}, & \omega = \omega_1, \\[2mm] \frac{3v}{(1-5\kappa^5)(1+8\kappa^8)}, & \omega = \omega_2, \\[2mm] \frac{3v}{(3+5\kappa^5)(1-4\kappa^4)}, & \omega = \omega_3, \\[2mm] \frac{3v}{(3+5\kappa^5)(2+4\kappa^8)}, & \omega = \omega_4 \end{cases}$$

and

$$J_\kappa(v) = \ln(v) - E\ln(L_\kappa)$$

$$= \ln(v) - \frac{1}{4} \ln \left(\frac{(1 - 5\kappa^5)(2 - 8\kappa^8)}{3} \right) - \frac{1}{4} \ln \left(\frac{(1 - 5\kappa^5)(1 + 8\kappa^8)}{3} \right)$$

$$- \frac{1}{4} \ln \left(\frac{(3 + 5\kappa^5)(1 - 4\kappa^4)}{3} \right) - \frac{1}{4} \ln \left(\frac{(3 + 5\kappa^5)(2 + 4\kappa^4)}{3} \right)$$

Hence the dual problem is:

maximize $2\ln(1 - 5\kappa^5) + 2\ln(3 + 5\kappa^5) + \ln(2 - 8\kappa^8)$
$$+ \ln(1 + 8\kappa^8) + \ln(1 - 4\kappa^4) + \ln(2 + 4\kappa^4)$$

subject to $\quad \kappa^5 \geqslant 0, \quad \kappa^8 \geqslant 0, \quad \kappa^4 \geqslant 0$

The optimal solution of this is easily found to be

$$\kappa^5 = 0, \quad \kappa^8 = \frac{1}{16}, \quad \kappa^4 = 0$$

Substituting these values in the above expressions for W_κ and $J_\kappa(v)$ gives

$$W_\kappa = \begin{cases} 2v, & \omega = \omega_1, \omega_2 \\ v, & \omega = \omega_3 \\ v/2, & \omega = \omega_4 \end{cases}$$

and $J_\kappa(v) = \ln(v) + \ln(2)/4$ (Note these are the same values that were obtained with dynamic programming). The replicating trading strategy is $F_1 = 5/3; F_2 = 0$ if $\omega = \omega_1, \omega_2$; and $F_2 = 1$ if $\omega = \omega_3, \omega_4$. The two conditions in (5.36) are clearly satisfied, so this must be the optimal strategy for the constrained problem.

Exercise 5.19 For the security model in example 5.11 with $r = 0$ and log utility, suppose short selling is allowed but you cannot borrow money from the bank. Solve this optimal portfolio problem with:

(a) dynamic programming (Hint: show $u_0(v) = \ln(v) + \ln(6/5)$)
(b) the risk neutral computational approach (Hint: show the optimal solution of the dual problem is $\kappa(1) = -\frac{1}{15}$ and $\kappa(2) = 0$).

5.7 Optimal Consumption–Investment With Constraints

It is straightforward to take the optimal consumption/investment model of sections 5.3 and 5.4, add constraints on the admissible trading strategies, and solve the resulting problem with either dynamic programming or a risk neutral computational approach. Indeed, there is no problem extending these ideas to the model studied in section 5.5, where multiperiod consumption/investment is combined with terminal wealth. All this will be explained in this section.

As in section 5.6, the trading strategies are predictable and of the form $F = (F_1, \ldots, F_N)$, with $F_n(t)$ representing the fraction of the time $t - 1$ wealth that is invested at that time in security n and held until time t. A non-empty, closed, convex subset $\mathbb{K}$ of $\mathbb{R}^N$ is specified, and it is required that $F(t) \in \mathbb{K}$ for $t = 1, \ldots, T$. A consumption process $C = \{C_t; t = 0, \ldots, T\}$ is an adapted, non-negative stochastic process with C_t representing the amount of funds consumed by the investor at time t. A consumption–investment plan consists of a pair (C, F), where C is a consumption process and F is a trading strategy.

As usual, the consumption–investment plan (C, F) will be called self-financing if no money is added to or withdrawn from the portfolio between times 0 and T, other than the amounts that are consumed. With V_t denoting the value of the portfolio just before any time t transactions or consumption, for self-financing plans it means that

$$(5.38) \qquad V_t = (V_{t-1} - C_{t-1})\left[1 + r_t + \sum_{n=1}^{N} F_n(t)\{\Delta R_n(t) - r_t\}\right]$$

for $t = 1, \ldots, T$, where $r_t = (B_t - B_{t-1})/B_{t-1}$ is the interest rate associated with the interval $(t - 1, t)$ and $\Delta R_n(t) = R_n(t) - R_n(t - 1)$ is the change in the return process for security n. A consumption–investment plan will be called admissible if it is self financing and $V_T \geqslant C_T$. Since consumption processes are non-negative, this implies $V_T \geqslant 0$. Let $\mathscr{A}_v$ denote the set of all admissible consumption–investment plans with initial wealth v.

With the specification of the initial wealth v, the discount parameter satisfying $0 < \alpha \leqslant 1$, and the concave, increasing utility function u, the investor's consumption–investment problem is:

$$(5.39) \qquad \text{maximize } E\left[\sum_{t=0}^{T} \alpha^t u(C_t)\right]$$

$$\text{subject to: } (C, F) \in \mathscr{A}_v$$

The corresponding value function is

$$J(v) = \sup_{(C, F) \in \mathscr{A}_v} E\left[\sum_{t=0}^{T} \alpha^t u(C_t)\right]$$

Note that (5.39) is the same as problem formulation (5.14) in section 5.3, except that implicit is the added requirement that $F(t) \in \mathbb{K}$ for all t.

This problem can be solved by using recursively the dynamic programming functional equation

$$u_{t-1}(w) =$$

$$\max_{\substack{F \in \mathbb{K} \\ 0 \leqslant c \leqslant w}} \left\{ u(c) + \alpha E \left[u_t \left((w-c) \left\{ 1 + r_t + \sum_{n=1}^{N} F_n(t)\{\Delta R_n(t) - r_t\} \right\} \right) \middle| \mathscr{F}_{t-1} \right] \right\}$$

for $t = 1, 2, \ldots, T$ together with the boundary condition $u_T(w) = u(w)$. Thus $u_t(w)$ represents the maximum expected utility of consumption from time t onwards when you start with initial wealth w at time t and the information available is $\mathscr{F}_t$. Moreover, $J(v) = u_0(v)$. With the common assumption that $u'(0) = \infty$, the explicit constraint $0 \leqslant C$ can be eliminated, thereby simplifying the computations. The dynamic programming approach is illustrated in the following example.

Example 5.12 Consider the two-period, single security model in example 5.1 with interest rate $r_t = 0$, the same situation as in example 5.11. Suppose the utility function $u(c) = -c^{-1}$ and short selling of the risky security is prohibited, so $\mathbb{K} = [0, \infty)$. With $P(\omega_1) = \ldots = P(\omega_4) = 1/4$, the dynamic programming equation for $t = 2$ and $\omega = \omega_1, \omega_2$ is

$$u_1(w) = \max_{\substack{F \geqslant 0 \\ 0 \leqslant c \leqslant w}} \left\{ -\frac{1}{c} - \alpha E \left[\frac{1}{(w-c)(1 + F\Delta R_2)} \,\middle|\, S_1 = 8 \right] \right\}$$

$$= \max_{\substack{F \geqslant 0 \\ 0 \leqslant c \leqslant w}} \left\{ -\frac{1}{c} - \frac{\alpha}{2(w-c)(1 + F/8)} - \frac{\alpha}{2(w-c)(1 - F/4)} \right\}$$

Computing the partial derivative of the argument with respect to F and setting this equal to zero gives

$$F = \frac{8 - 8\sqrt{2}}{2 + \sqrt{2}} < 0$$

But this violates the short-selling constraint, so take $F = 0$ and substitute this into the above dynamic programming equation, giving

$$u_1(w) = \max_{0 \leqslant c \leqslant w} \left\{ -\frac{1}{c} - \frac{\alpha}{w-c} \right\}$$

Setting the derivative of the argument with respect to c equal to zero, one easily obtains $C = w/(1 + \sqrt{\alpha})$ for the optimal consumption quantity and

$$u_1(w) = -\frac{(1 + \sqrt{\alpha})^2}{w}, \qquad \omega = \omega_1, \omega_2$$

for the maximum expected utility.

For $t = 2$ and $\omega = \omega_3$, ω_4 the dynamic programming equation is

$$u_1(w) = \max_{\substack{F \geqslant 0 \\ 0 \leqslant c \leqslant w}} \left\{ -\frac{1}{c} - \frac{\alpha}{2(w-c)(1+F/2)} - \frac{\alpha}{2(w-c)(1-F/4)} \right\}$$

Setting to zero the partial derivative with respect to F leads to

$$F = \frac{4\sqrt{2} - 4}{2 + \sqrt{2}} > 0$$

which satisfies the short-selling constraint. Substituting this into the dynamic programming equation yields

$$u_1(w) = \max_{0 \leqslant c \leqslant w} \left\{ -\frac{1}{c} - \frac{\alpha(1 + \sqrt{2})^2}{6(w - c)} \right\}$$

Hence the optimal consumption quantity is $C = w/(1 + \sqrt{\alpha_1})$ and the maximum expected utility is

$$u_1(w) = -\frac{(1 + \sqrt{\alpha_1})^2}{w} \qquad \omega = \omega_3, \, \omega_4$$

where for convenience the new parameter

$$\alpha_1 = \frac{\alpha(1 + \sqrt{2})^2}{6}$$

has been introduced.

For $t = 1$ the dynamic programming equation is

$$u_0(w) = \max_{\substack{F \geqslant 0 \\ 0 \leqslant c \leqslant w}} \left\{ -\frac{1}{c} - \frac{\alpha(1 + \sqrt{\alpha})^2}{2(w-c)(1+3F/5)} - \frac{\alpha(1 + \sqrt{\alpha_1})^2}{2(w-c)(1-F/5)} \right\}$$

Setting the partial derivative of the argument with respect to F equal to zero leads to

$$F = \frac{5[\sqrt{3}(1 + \sqrt{\alpha}) - 1 - \sqrt{\alpha_1}]}{\sqrt{3}(1 + \sqrt{\alpha}) + 3 + 3\sqrt{\alpha_1}}$$

This is easily verified to be positive, so the short-selling constraint is satisfied. Substituting this back into the dynamic programming equation gives

$$u_0(w) = \max_{0 \leqslant c \leqslant w} \left\{ -\frac{1}{c} - \frac{\alpha_0}{w - c} \right\}$$

where for convenience the new parameter

$$\alpha_0 = \frac{\alpha}{8}\left[1 + \sqrt{\alpha} + \sqrt{3} + \sqrt{3\alpha_1}\right]^2$$

has been introduced. Hence $C = w/(1 + \sqrt{\alpha_0})$ is the optimal time-0 consumption quantity and

$$J(v) = u_0(v) = -\frac{(1 + \sqrt{\alpha_0})^2}{v}$$

is the value function for the original problem.

The risk neutral computational approach for the multiperiod consumption–investment problem is essentially the same as for the multiperiod optimal portfolio problem. The *support function* $\delta(x) : \mathbb{R}^N \to \mathbb{R} \cup \{+\infty\}$ of $-\mathbb{K}$ is defined by

$$\delta(x) \equiv \sup_{F \in \mathbb{K}} (-Fx)$$

the *effective domain* of which is the convex cone $\tilde{\mathbb{K}} \equiv \{x \in \mathbb{R}^N : \delta(x) < \infty\}$. It will be assumed that $\mathbb{K}$ is such that δ is continuous on $\tilde{\mathbb{K}}$ with $0 \in \mathbb{K}$.

Let $\mathcal{N}$ denote the set of all predictable stochastic processes $\kappa = \{\kappa(t) : t = 1, \ldots, T\}$ satisfying $\kappa(t) \in \tilde{\mathbb{K}}$ for all t. For each $\kappa \in \mathcal{N}$ one defines an auxiliary market $\mathcal{M}_\kappa$ by modifying the return processes for the bank account and the risky securities according to

$$r_t \to r_t + \delta(\kappa(t)) \qquad\qquad t \geqslant 1$$
$$\Delta R_n(t) \to \Delta R_n(t) + \delta(\kappa(t)) + \kappa_n(t) \qquad n = 1, \ldots, N; t \geqslant 1$$

For each such market, let Q_κ denote a corresponding risk neutral probability measure. It will usually be the case that $Q = Q_0$ exists and is unique, in which case a unique Q_κ will also exist for all $\kappa \in \mathcal{N}$ in some neighbourhood of $\kappa = 0$.

For the market $\mathcal{M}_\kappa$ and any self-financing consumption plan (C, F), whether it is admissible or not, the self-financing equation (5.38) becomes

(5.40)

$$V_t = (V_{t-1} - C_{t-1})\left[1 + r_t + \sum_{n=1}^{N} F_n(t)\{\Delta R_n(t) - r_T\} + \delta(\kappa_t) + F(t)\kappa_t'\right]$$

where the scalar $F(t)\kappa'(t)$ denotes the inner product of the row vector $F(t)$ with the column vector $\kappa'(t) = \kappa_t'$. Notice that the market $\mathcal{M}_0$ with $\kappa = 0$ is the same as the original market.

For each $\kappa \in \mathcal{N}$ we shall be interested in the unconstrained consumption–investment problem:

(5.41)   maximize $E\left[\sum_{t=0}^{T}\alpha^t u(C_t)\right]$

subject to : $V_0 = v, \quad V_T \geqslant C_T$

$V, \, C, \, F$ satisfy (5.40) for $t \geqslant 1$

In other words, this is the ordinary consumption–investment problem for the market $\mathcal{M}_\kappa$, with no special constraints on the values of F. Let $J_\kappa(v)$ denote the corresponding optimal objective value.

As we saw for constrained optimal portfolio problems in section 5.6,

(5.42) $J(v) \leqslant J_\kappa(v), \qquad$ all $\kappa \in \mathcal{N}$

that is, the optimal objective value for the original constrained problem is less than or equal to the optimal objective value for the unconstrained problem in market $\mathcal{M}_\kappa$, provided $\kappa \in \mathcal{N}$. This is because if (C, F) is feasible for (5.39), then (5.40) together with $\delta(\kappa_t) + F(t)\kappa_t' \geqslant 0$ imply (C, F) is also feasible for (5.41). Hence if (5.42) is an equality for some $\kappa \in \mathcal{N}$, then the optimal (C, F) corresponding to this v is a candidate for the solution of the original constrained problem, because of the following counterpart of (5.37) (which is true by exactly the same kind of logic):

(5.43)   Suppose for some $\hat{\kappa} \in \mathcal{N}$ that (C, F), the optimal consumption–investment plan for the unconstrained consumption–investment problem in the market $\mathcal{M}_{\hat{\kappa}}$, satisfies

(a) $(C, F) \in \mathcal{A}_\kappa$

(b) $\delta(\hat{\kappa}_t) + F(t)\hat{\kappa}_t' \geqslant 0, \quad$ all $t \geqslant 1$

Then (C, F) is optimal for the original constrained consumption–investment problem, and $J(v) = J_{\hat{\kappa}}(v) \leqslant J_\kappa(v)$ for all $\kappa \in \mathcal{N}$.

In summary, to solve the constrained consumption–investment problem with the risk neutral computational approach, you first solve the dual problem of minimizing the right hand side of (5.42) over $\kappa \in \mathcal{N}$. This will be illustrated in the following example.

Example 5.12 (continued)   Since $\mathbb{K} = [0, \infty)$ and the original markets are the same, the auxiliary markets $\mathcal{M}_\kappa$ will be the same as in example 5.11. In particular, the set $\mathcal{N}$, the notation for the processes κ, the return processes R^κ, and the risk neutral probability measures Q_κ are given in section 5.6.

In order to solve the unconstrained problem (5.41) for each $\kappa \in \mathcal{N}$, it is necessary to introduce for each κ the process N^κ corresponding to N of (5.22); this is given below (recall $B_t^\kappa = 1$ for all t):

ω	$N_0^v(\omega)$	$N_1^v(\omega)$	$N_2^v(\omega)$
ω_1	1	$(1 - 5\kappa^5)/2$	$(1 - 5\kappa^5)(2 - 8\kappa^8)/3$
ω_2	1	$(1 - 5\kappa^5)/2$	$(1 - 5\kappa^5)(1 + 8\kappa^8)/3$
ω_3	1	$(3 + 5\kappa^5)/2$	$(3 + 5\kappa^5)(1 - 4\kappa^4)/3$
ω_4	1	$(3 + 5\kappa^5)/2$	$(3 + 5\kappa^5)(2 + 4\kappa^4)/3$

By exercise 5.14, the optimal objective value for the unconstrained problem (5.41) is given by

$$J_\kappa(v) = -\frac{\Delta^2}{v}$$

where

$$\Delta = \sum_{t=0}^{2} \alpha^{t/2} E\left[\sqrt{N_t^\kappa}\right]$$

Hence the dual problem amounts to maximizing Δ^2 over all $\kappa \in \mathcal{N}$, that is, over all non-negative, predictable κ. With a little bit of work, the solution is found to be

$$\hat{\kappa}^5 = 0, \quad \hat{\kappa}^8 = \frac{1}{16}, \quad \hat{\kappa}^8 = 0$$

giving the corresponding value

$$\Delta = 1 + \frac{\sqrt{\alpha}}{2\sqrt{2}}\left[1 + \sqrt{3}\right] + \frac{\alpha}{4}\left[1 + 2\sqrt{2}\right]$$

Note that this value of Δ gives, after a little algebra, $J_{\hat{\kappa}}(v) = -(1 + \sqrt{\alpha_0})^2/v$, the same as the optimal objective value for the original constrained consumption–investment problem, as computed earlier with dynamic programming.

Since $N_1^\kappa(\omega_1) = N_1^\kappa(\omega_2) = 1/2$, $N_1^\kappa(\omega_3) = N_1^\kappa(\omega_4) = 3/2$, $N_2^\kappa(\omega_1) = N_2^\kappa(\omega_2) = 1/2$, $N_2^\kappa(\omega_3) = 1$ and $N_2^\kappa(\omega_4) = 2$, exercise 5.14 also gives $C_1(\omega_1) = C_1(\omega_2) = v\sqrt{2\alpha}/\Delta$, $C_1(\omega_3) = C_1(\omega_4) = v\sqrt{2\alpha/3}/\Delta$, $C_2(\omega_1) = C_2(\omega_2) = v\alpha\sqrt{2}/\Delta$, $C_2(\omega_3) = v\alpha/\Delta$, and $C_2(\omega_4) = v\alpha/(\Delta\sqrt{2})$.

To compute the replicating trading strategy, we begin by noting that $C_2(\omega_1) = C_2(\omega_2)$ implies $F_2(\omega_1) = F_2(\omega_2) = 0$ for the optimal fraction of the available funds that are invested in the risky security at time 1. It follows that

$$V_1(\omega) = C_1(\omega) + C_2(\omega) = \frac{v}{\Delta}\left[\alpha\sqrt{2} + \sqrt{2\alpha}\right], \qquad \omega = \omega_1, \omega_2$$

Next, solving

$$(V_1 - C_1)(1 + F/2) = v\alpha/\Delta$$
$$(V_1 - C_1)(1 - F/4) = v\alpha/(\Delta\sqrt{2})$$

gives

$$F_2(\omega_3) = F_2(\omega_4) - \frac{4(\sqrt{2}-1)}{2+\sqrt{2}}$$

and

$$V_1(\omega_3) = V_1(\omega_4) = \frac{v}{\Delta}\left[\frac{\alpha(2+\sqrt{2})}{3\sqrt{2}} + \frac{\sqrt{2\alpha}}{\sqrt{3}}\right]$$

Finally, solving

$$(V_0 - C_0)(1 + 3F/5) = \frac{v}{\Delta}\left[\alpha\sqrt{2} + \sqrt{2\alpha}\right]$$

$$(V_0 - C_0)(1 - F/5) = \frac{v}{\Delta}\left[\frac{\alpha(2+\sqrt{2})}{3\sqrt{2}} + \frac{\sqrt{2\alpha}}{\sqrt{3}}\right]$$

gives the same value for F_1 as was obtained with dynamic programming.

Needless to say, the preceding ideas can be combined with the ideas of section 5.6 to solve the section 5.5 kind of problem where there is utility from both consumption and terminal wealth. In particular, you can use either dynamic programming (see exercise 5.20) or the risk neutral computational approach that will now be explained.

With $\mathcal{A}_v$ the set of admissible consumption–investment plans with initial wealth v and F satisfying the constraint $\mathbb{K}$, we are interested in the value function

$$J(v) = \max_{(C, F) \in \mathcal{A}_v} E\left[\sum_{t=0}^{T} \alpha^t u_c(C_t) + \alpha^T u_p(V_T - C_T)\right]$$

where u_c and u_p are two specified utility functions, as in section 5.5. This is the same as (5.28), and this corresponds to exactly the same optimization problem as in section 5.5, only now the constraint $F(t) \in \mathbb{K}$ is implicit.

We now define the auxiliary markets $\mathcal{M}_\kappa$ exactly the same as for the constrained optimal portfolio problem of section 5.6 and as the constrained consumption–investment problem studied earlier in this section. The set $\mathcal{N}$ of predictable processes κ, the modified return processes, and so forth will depend on $\mathbb{K}$ and the original security model, but they will be independent of the utility functions and whether u_c or u_p equals zero.

Next, for each $\kappa \in \mathcal{N}$ we wish to consider the "unconstrained" optimization problem:

$$\text{maximize} \quad E\left[\sum_{t=0}^{T} \alpha^t u(C_t) + \alpha^T u_p(V_T - C_T)\right]$$

$$\text{subject to}: \quad V_0 = v, \quad V_T \geqslant C_T$$
$$V, C, F \text{ satisfy } (5.40) \text{ for } t \geqslant 1$$

This is the same as (5.41), only now there is the additional term associated with the utility of terminal wealth. In particular, this is the same as the optimization problem of section 5.5 for the market $\mathcal{M}_\kappa$, with no special constraints on the values of F. Thus $J_\kappa(v)$, the corresponding optimal objective value, can be computed with the methods of that section.

Finally, we solve the dual problem of minimizing $J_\kappa(v)$ over $\kappa \in \mathcal{N}$. If $\hat{\kappa} \in \mathcal{N}$ is the minimizing value and $(\hat{C}, \hat{F})$ is the corresponding optimal consumption–investment plan, then it only remains to check the two conditions in (5.43) in order to conclude that $(\hat{C}, \hat{F})$ is also the optimal solution for the original constrained optimization problem.

Example 5.13   Consider the two-period, single security model in example 5.1 with interest rate $r_t = 0$. This is the same situation as in examples 5.11 and 5.12, except now it is assumed that $u_c(c) = \ln(c)$ and $u_p(w) = \ln(w)$. The auxiliary markets $\mathcal{M}_\kappa$, including the processes N^κ, are the same as in example 5.12.

In view of section 5.5, the optimal solution for the unconstrained problem is of the form $C_t = \alpha^t/(\lambda N_t^\kappa)$ and $V_2 = 2\alpha^2/(\lambda N_2^\kappa)$, where the process N^κ depends on the underlying market $\mathcal{M}_\kappa$. Since $f(\lambda) = (1 + \alpha + 2\alpha^2)/\lambda$, it follows that $\lambda = g(v) = (1 + \alpha + 2\alpha^2)/v$ and

$$C_t = \frac{\alpha^t v}{(1 + \alpha + 2\alpha^2)N_t^\kappa} \qquad V_2 = \frac{2\alpha^2 v}{(1 + \alpha + 2\alpha^2)N_2^\kappa}$$

Moreover, since

$$K(\lambda) = -(1 + \alpha + 2\alpha^2)\ln\lambda + (\alpha + 4\alpha^2)\ln\alpha - \alpha E\ln N_1^\kappa - 2\alpha^2 E\ln N_2^\kappa$$

it follows from $J_\kappa(v) = K(g(v))$ that

$$J_\kappa(v) = (1 + \alpha + 2\alpha^2)\ln\left(\frac{v}{1 + \alpha + 2\alpha^2}\right) + (\alpha + 4\alpha^2)\ln\alpha$$
$$- \alpha E\ln N_1^\kappa - 2\alpha^2 E\ln N_2^\kappa$$

Now upon substituting N^κ (see example 5.12), it is apparent the dual problem amounts to maximizing

$$(\alpha/2 + \alpha^2)\left[\ln(1 - 5\kappa^5) + \ln(3 + 5\kappa^5)\right] - \alpha\ln(2) - 2\alpha^2\ln(3)$$
$$+ \frac{\alpha^2}{2}\left[\ln(2 - 8\kappa^8) + \ln(1 + 8\kappa^8) + \ln(1 - 4\kappa^4) + \ln(2 + 4\kappa^4)\right]$$

over non-negative values of the scalars κ^4, κ^5 and κ^8. The optimal solution is easily found to be $\kappa^4 = \kappa^5 = 0$, $\kappa^8 = 1/16$. The corresponding process N^κ is

$$N_1^\kappa(\omega) = \begin{cases} 1/2, & \omega_1, \omega_2 \\ 3/2, & \omega_3, \omega_4 \end{cases} \qquad N_2^\kappa(\omega) = \begin{cases} 1/2, & \omega_1, \omega_2 \\ 1, & \omega_3 \\ 2, & \omega_4 \end{cases}$$

in which case $C_0 - v/(1 + \alpha + 2\alpha^2)$,

$$C_1(\omega) = \begin{cases} \dfrac{2\alpha v}{1 + \alpha + 2\alpha^2}, & \omega_1, \omega_2 \\ \dfrac{2\alpha v/3}{1 + \alpha + 2\alpha^2}, & \omega_3, \omega_4 \end{cases} \qquad C_2(\omega) = \begin{cases} \dfrac{2\alpha^2 v}{1 + \alpha + 2\alpha^2}, & \omega_1, \omega_2 \\ \dfrac{\alpha^2 v}{1 + \alpha + 2\alpha^2}, & \omega_3 \\ \dfrac{\alpha^2 v/2}{1 + \alpha + 2\alpha^2}, & \omega_4 \end{cases}$$

and $V_2 = 2C_2$. After computing the replicating trading strategy F, one verifies that the two conditions in (5.43) are satisfied, which means this consumption–investment plan must be optimal for the constrained problem. The optimal objective value $J(v)$ is

$$(1 + \alpha + 2\alpha^2) \ln \left(\frac{v}{1 + \alpha + 2\alpha^2} \right) + (\alpha + 4\alpha^2)\ln\alpha + (\alpha + \alpha^2/2) \ln 2 - \frac{\alpha}{2} \ln 3$$

Exercise 5.20 Use dynamic programming to compute the optimal trading strategy F for the problem in example 5.13. Show that $F_1 = 5/3$, $F_2(\omega) = 0$ when $\omega = \omega_1, \omega_2$, and $F_2(\omega) = 1$ when $\omega = \omega_3, \omega_4$. Verify that you get the same value for $J(v)$ as in example 5.13.

5.8 Portfolio Optimization in Incomplete Markets

In view of section 2.6 and the themes of this chapter, there are three principal approaches to solving optimal portfolio and consumption–investment problems when the underlying securities market is incomplete: dynamic programming, the convex optimization approach using Lagrange multipliers as in sections 5.2 and 5.4, only with multiple constraints and multiple risk neutral probability measures, and an approach featuring augmented ficti-tious securities coupled with constraints on the trading strategies. These three approaches are straightforward extensions of principles studied earlier in this chapter, so the emphasis will be on the presentation of an example, with redundant explanations kept to a minimum.

The dynamic programming approach for incomplete markets is exactly the same as for complete markets. The computational requirements depend primarily on the number of periods, the number of nodes in the information tree, and the number of securities, but not on whether the market is com-plete. It is largely a matter of taste whether one chooses the trading strategy in terms of the units held of each security (i.e., H) or in terms of the fractions of wealth allocated among the securities (i.e., F).

Example 5.14 The incomplete securities market model is the same as example 4.10, namely, $K = 5$, $N = 1$, $r = 0$, the filtration $\mathscr{F}_t$ is gener-ated by the price process S, and the specifications of S, the underlying probability measure P, and the family of risk neutral probability measures Q are:

ω	S_0	S_1	S_2	$\Delta R(1)$	$\Delta R(2)$	P	Q
ω_1	5	8	9	3/5	1/8	1/5	$q/4$
ω_2	5	8	7	3/5	$-1/8$	1/5	$(2-3q)/4$
ω_3	5	8	6	3/5	$-1/4$	1/5	$(2q-1)/4$
ω_4	5	4	6	$-1/5$	1/2	1/5	1/4
ω_4	5	4	3	$-1/5$	$-1/4$	1/5	1/2

The parameter q here is any scalar satisfying $1/2 < q < 2/3$. The objective will be to maximize expected utility of terminal wealth given the log utility function $u(w) = \ln(w)$.

With trading strategies expressed as the fraction F of wealth held in the risky security, the dynamic programming functional equation is:

$$u_t(w) = \max_F \ E[u_{t+1}(w\{1 + F\Delta R(t+1)\})|\mathscr{F}_t]$$

Taking $u_2(w) = \ln(w)$ when $t = 1$ and $\omega = \omega_1$, ω_2 or ω_3 this is

$$u_t(w) = \max_F \ \frac{1}{3}[\ln(w\{1+F/8\}) + \ln(w\{1-F/8\}) + \ln(w\{1 - F/4\})]$$

Notice this utility function forces the time $t = 2$ wealth to be positive, so one has the implicit constraint $-8 < F < 4$. Computing the derivative of the argument with respect to F, the necessary condition leads to the quadratic equation $3F^2 - 8F - 64 = 0$. This equation has two roots, but only one falls in the interval $(-8, 4)$, so

$$F = \frac{4}{3}(1 - \sqrt{13}) \cong -3.4741$$

Substituting this back into the dynamic programming equation eventually leads to $u_1(w) = \ln(w) + k_8$, where for convenience I have introduced the scalar

$$k_8 = \frac{1}{3} \ln\left[\left(7 - \sqrt{13}\right)\left(5 + \sqrt{13}\right)\left(4 + 2\sqrt{13}\right)\right] - \ln 6 \cong 0.0703$$

In a similar fashion one computes for $t = 1$ and $\omega = \omega_4$ or ω_5 the optimal fraction $F = 1$ and $u_1(w) = \ln(w) + k_4$, where k_4 is another new scalar given by $k_4 = \ln(3) - (3/2)\ln(2) \cong 0.0589$.

Turning to the dynamic programming equation for $t = 0$, one has

$$u_0(w) = \max_F \ \left\{\frac{3}{5}[\ln(w\{1 + 3F/5\}) + k_8] + \frac{2}{5}[\ln(w\{1 - F/5\}) + k_4]\right\}$$

It follows in the usual manner that the optimal fraction is $F = 7/3$ and that the optimal value function $J(v) = u_0(v) = \ln(v) + k_5$ where

$$k_5 = \frac{1}{5}\ln(3) + \frac{12}{5}\ln(2) - \ln(5) + \frac{3}{5}k_8 + \frac{2}{5}k_4 \cong 0.3397$$

Starting with v dollars and implementing the optimal values of F that were just computed, one ends up with the terminal wealth

$$V_2 = \begin{cases} 2v(7 - \sqrt{13})/5, & \omega = \omega_1 \\ 2v(5 - \sqrt{13})/5, & \omega = \omega_2 \\ 4v(2 + \sqrt{13})/5, & \omega = \omega_3 \\ 4v/5, & \omega = \omega_4 \\ 2v/5, & \omega = \omega_5 \end{cases}$$

The second computational approach, which for convenience will be called the Lagrange multiplier approach, is essentially the same as for single period models (see section 2.6). One starts with the standard convex optimization problem (2.50), which now features two or more constraints. Each constraint corresponds to a risk neutral probability measure, and there are enough such risk neutral probability measures to form a "basis" for the set of all risk neutral probability measures. Since there will be one Lagrange multiplier corresponding to each constraint, the amount of computational work will go up, compared to a model for complete markets. This is because a system of equations (one equation for each constraint) will need to be solved to compute the correct value of these Lagrange multipliers.

Example 5.14 (continued) Two risk neutral probability measures suffice to comprise a basis for the set of risk neutral probability measures. Indeed, one can take, as I shall, the extreme points of the closure of this set, corresponding to the parameter values $q = 1/2$ and $q = 2/3$:

$$Q(1) = (1/8, \ 1/8, \ 0, \ 1/4, \ 1/2) \quad Q(2) = (1/6, \ 0, \ 1/12, \ 1/4, \ 1/2)$$

The corresponding state price vectors are:

$$L_1 = (5/8, \ 5/8, \ 0, \ 5/4, \ 5/2) \quad L_2 = (5/6, \ 0, \ 5/12, \ 5/4, \ 5/2)$$

The optimization problem we need to solve is:

$$\begin{aligned} \text{maximize} \quad & E[\ln(W)] \\ \text{subject to} \quad & E_{Q(1)}[W] = v \\ & E_{Q(2)}[W] - v \end{aligned}$$

Proceeding in the usual way, we introduce the Lagrange multipliers λ_1 and λ_2 and use the inverse of the marginal utility function to derive the following expression for the terminal (time $t = 2$) wealth:

$$W(\omega) = \frac{1}{\lambda_1 L_1(\omega) + \lambda_2 L_2(\omega)}$$

The correct values of the Lagrange multipliers are obtained by solving the system:

$$E_{Q(1)}\left[\frac{1}{\lambda_1 L_1 + \lambda_2 L_2}\right] = v$$

$$E_{Q(1)}\left[\frac{1}{\lambda_1 L_1 + \lambda_2 L_2}\right] = v$$

The solution is:

$$\lambda_1 = \frac{4}{v(5 + \sqrt{13})} \qquad \lambda_2 = \frac{3}{v(2 + \sqrt{13})}$$

Substitution in the above expression for $W(\omega)$ gives the same values as were computed earlier with dynamic programming.

The basic idea of the third approach is the same as with the single period model of section 2.6: first add one or more fictitious securities in such a way as to make the risk neutral probability measure unique. Then solve the portfolio optimization problem with the constraint that precludes trading in the fictitious securities.

To add the fictitious securities, a good approach is to work with return processes and the information tree, constructing the fictitious securities by proceeding from one node to the next. If the conditional risk neutral probabilities at a node are not unique, then add one or more (one-period) fictitious securities to that node so as to make these conditional probabilities unique. The analysis at any one node is equivalent to that for a single period problem.

As one proceeds through the tree, it may turn out that different nodes require the addition of different numbers of fictitious securities. In fact, some nodes may not require any. So after the initial pass through the network, note the maximum number of additional fictitious securities that are required. This becomes the number needed to add to the overall multiperiod problem. It is then necessary to go back to the nodes where less than this maximum number were defined and add some more (one-period) fictitious securities, as necessary, so as to bring the total number up to the maximum. In order to preserve the arbitrage-free property of the securities market, these additional (one-period) securities will need to be 'locally redundant,' that is, linear combinations of the (one-period) securities that are already specified at that same node. For convenience, these additional (one-period) securities that are defined in this 'topping-up' phase should be linear combinations of the original securities but not of any fictitious (one-period) securities that may have been defined during the initial pass through the information tree.

At this stage the same number of (one-period) fictitious securities will have been defined, in terms of their return processes, at each node of the information tree. There will also be a unique risk neutral conditional probability measure at each node. By specifying their time $t = 0$ values, the full specifications of all the (multiperiod) fictitious securities can now be synthesized. And the unique risk neutral probability measure for the overall multiperiod model can readily be computed.

Suppose there is a total of N securities, with the original ones indexed $n = 1, 2, \ldots, \hat{n}$ and the fictitious ones indexed $n = \hat{n} + 1, \ldots, N$. I would now like to introduce a constraint of the form

$$\mathbb{K} = \{F \in \mathbb{R}^N : F_{\hat{n}+1} = \ldots = F_N = 0\}$$

In view of section 5.6, this would imply taking

$$\delta(x) = \sup_{F \in \mathbb{K}} (-Fx') = \begin{cases} 0, & x_1 = \ldots = x_{\hat{n}} = 0 \\ \infty, & \text{otherwise} \end{cases}$$

$\tilde{\mathbb{K}} = \{x \in \mathbb{R}^N : x_1 = \ldots = x_{\hat{n}} = 0\}$, and $\mathcal{N}$ the set of all predictable processes κ satisfying $\kappa(t) \in \tilde{\mathbb{K}}$ for all t. Moreover, the return processes for the interest rate and original securities would remain unchanged in the auxiliary market $\mathcal{M}_\kappa$, while the return processes for the fictitious securities would be given by $\Delta R_n(t) + \kappa_n(t)$, where R_n is its return process in the original market.

However, this may lead to a complication. If you look at a node of the information tree where there are "locally redundant" fictitious securities, you may find that there does not exist a conditional risk neutral probability measure for that node in the auxiliary market $\mathcal{M}_\kappa$, because for non-zero κ the securities have ceased to be locally redundant. Indeed, arbitrage opportunities may now exist in every auxiliary market, which means the risk neutral computational procedure for solving the constrained optimization problem breaks down.

The way around this difficulty is to realize that there is no harm in trading a fictitious security if at a particular moment in time it is "locally redundant." In other words, if corresponding to a particular node in the information tree the one-period return for a fictitious security is a linear combination of the returns for the original securities, then we can relax the constraint which precludes trading in that security in that (one-period) circumstance. Hence the sets $\mathbb{K}$ and $\tilde{\mathbb{K}}$ should be defined for each node in the information tree, as these may vary across the network. The set $\mathbb{K}$ at a node should stipulate that $F_n = 0$ if and only if security n is fictitious but it is not "locally redundant" at that node. It follows that for $\mathcal{N}$ one should take all predictable processes κ such that $\kappa(t, \omega)$ is an element of the set $\mathbb{K}$ which corresponds to (t, ω).

As usual, an auxiliary market $\mathcal{M}_\kappa$ will be defined for each $\kappa \in \mathcal{N}$. The return processes for the interest rate and the original securities will remain the same, but in the auxiliary market $\mathcal{M}_\kappa$ the return process for fictitious security n will be given by $\Delta R_n(t) + \kappa_n(t)$, where R_n is its original return process. Now if fictitious security n is locally redundant at a node in the information tree, the corresponding value of $\kappa_n(t)$ will be zero, a unique conditional risk neutral probability measure will exist at that node, and the risk neutral computational approach for solving this constrained optimization problem can proceed without difficulty. This all will be illustrated in the following example.

Example 5.14 (continued)   We now need to let S_1 denote the original risky security. The conditional risk neutral probability measures for the nodes where $S_1(0) = 5$ and $S_1(1) = 4$ are unique, but this is not true for the node where $S_1(1) = 8$. There we need to add one fictitious security, which we denote security $n = 2$ and take $\Delta R_2(2, \omega_1) = 1/16$, $\Delta R_2(2, \omega_2) = 0$, and $\Delta R_2(2, \omega_3) = -3/16$. This results in the conditional risk neutral probability measure $(0.6, 0.2, 0.2)$, which is a special case of what exists with the original incomplete model. We take $\Delta R_2 = \Delta R_1$ at the other two nodes, so choosing $S_2(0) = 10$, the full specifications of fictitious security S_2 are listed below. The unique risk neutral probability measure Q is also provided.

ω	$S_2(0)$	$S_2(1)$	$S_2(2)$	$\Delta R_2(1)$	$\Delta R_2(2)$	Q
ω_1	10	16	17	3/5	1/16	0.15
ω_2	10	16	16	3/5	0	0.05
ω_3	10	16	13	3/5	-3/16	0.05
ω_4	10	8	12	-1/5	1/2	0.25
ω_5	10	8	6	-1/5	-1/4	0.50

There are no constraints at the nodes where $S_1(0) = 5$ and $S_1(1) = 4$, so there we take $\mathbb{K} = \{x \in \mathbb{R}^2\}$ and $\tilde{\mathbb{K}} = \{(0, 0)\}$. At the node where $S_1(1) = 8$ we want to preclude trading in fictitious security S_2 so there we have $\mathbb{K} = \{x \in \mathbb{R}^2 : F_2 = 0\}$ and $\tilde{\mathbb{K}} = \{x \in \mathbb{R}^2 : x_1 = 0\}$. Hence $\mathcal{N}$ consists of all the predictable processes κ of the form

$$\kappa(t, \omega) = \begin{cases} (0, \tilde{\kappa}), & t = 2, \quad \omega = \omega_1, \omega_2 \\ (0, 0), & \text{otherwise} \end{cases}$$

where $\tilde{\kappa}$ is a scalar.

The next step is to compute the risk neutral probability measure for the market $\mathcal{M}_\kappa$. We have

$$\Delta R_2^\kappa(2, \omega) = \begin{cases} 1/16 + \tilde{\kappa}, & \omega = \omega_1 \\ \tilde{\kappa}, & \omega = \omega_2 \\ -3/16 + \tilde{\kappa}, & \omega = \omega_3 \end{cases}$$

whereas $\Delta R_1^\kappa(2) = \Delta R_2(2)$ for all $\kappa \in \mathcal{N}$. Thus using the two equations $E_{Q_\kappa}[\Delta R_n^\kappa(2)|S_1(1) = 8]$ for $n = 1$ and 2 we solve for and obtain the conditional risk neutral probability measure at the node where $S_1(1) = 8$:

$$\left(\frac{3 + 16\tilde{\kappa}}{5}, \frac{1 - 48\tilde{\kappa}}{5}, \frac{1 + 32\tilde{\kappa}}{5} \right)$$

The conditional risk neutral probability measures at the other two nodes are the same as for the original market $\mathcal{M}_0$, so the risk neutral probability measure for the market $\mathcal{M}_\kappa$ must be:

$$\left(\frac{3+16\tilde{\kappa}}{20}, \frac{1-48\tilde{\kappa}}{20}, \frac{1+32\tilde{\kappa}}{20}, \frac{1}{4}, \frac{1}{2}\right)$$

The next step is to solve the dual problem of minimizing $J_\kappa(v)$ over $\kappa \in \mathcal{N}$. Since with log utility for unconstrained problems $J_\kappa(v) = \ln(v) - E\ln(Q_\kappa) + E\ln(P)$, this amounts to maximizing $E\ln(Q_\kappa)$ over $\tilde{\kappa} \in \mathbb{R}$. Writing this out and differentiating leads to the necessary condition:

$$\frac{16}{3+16\tilde{\kappa}} - \frac{48}{1-48\tilde{\kappa}} + \frac{32}{1+32\tilde{\kappa}} = 0$$

The solution is found to be

$$\tilde{v} = \frac{3\sqrt{13}-11}{16(7-\sqrt{13})}$$

With log utility for unconstrained problems the optimal terminal wealth is $V_2^\kappa - vP/Q_\kappa$, so substituting $\tilde{\kappa}$ one obtains the final result. This optimal terminal wealth for the constrained problem is equal to the optimal terminal wealth for the original incomplete market model, a terminal wealth that we computed earlier with two other approaches.

It should be clear that multiperiod consumption – investment problems for incomplete markets can also be solved with the same three approaches. The applications of these approaches are so similar to what has already been done that the details will be left to the reader.

Exercise 5.21   Solve the consumption – investment problem for the model in example 5.14, assuming log utility (i.e., $u(c) = \ln(c)$) and a discount parameter α taking a general non-negative value less than or equal to one. Derive the optimal trading strategy, the optimal consumption process, and the optimal value function $J(v)$. In particular, show that the optimal consumption quantity at time $t = 2$ is $2\alpha^2 vX(\omega)/[5(1+\alpha+\alpha^2)]$, where the random variable X is equal to $7 - \sqrt{13}$, $5 + \sqrt{13}$, $4 + 2\sqrt{13}$, 2, and 1 in states $\omega_1, \omega_2, \omega_3, \omega_4$, and ω_5, respectively.

(a)   Use the dynamic programming approach.
(b)   Use the Lagrange multiplier approach.
(c)   Use the fictitious securities approach.

6 Bonds and Interest Rate Derivatives

6.1 The Basic Term Structure Model

Although the securities market models discussed in the preceding chapters are very general in terms of the kinds of securities that can be modeled, the securities being modeled were usually thought of as equities such as common stocks. However, the case where fixed income securities such as bonds are included among the risky securities is so important that it will be the subject of this entire chapter. The securities market model for this situation is called a *term structure model*.

For a securities market model to be a term structure model, three things are required. First, it must be a multiperiod model. Second, the interest rate r must be a strictly positive, predictable process, so that the interest rate r_t for borrowing and lending over the period $(t-1, t]$ is known at time $t-1$. As usual, $B_0 = 1$ and $r_t = (B_t - B_{t-1})/B_{t-1}$ for $t = 1, \ldots, T$ so the assumption $r_t > 0$ means that the bank account B is strictly increasing in time. Since the term structure model will feature several interest rates, r will be called the *spot* interest rate as well as (although this is misleading, since r can be random) the *riskless* interest rate.

Thirdly, and most important, included among the risky securities is a collection of what are called *zero coupon* or *discount* bonds. Defined for each τ such that $1 \leqslant \tau \leqslant T$, the *zero coupon bond with maturity τ* is the security whose price at time τ is certain to be one. Its time-t price will be denoted Z_t^τ, so $Z^\tau = \{Z_t^\tau; 0 \leqslant t \leqslant \tau\}$ is an adapted process with $Z_\tau^\tau = 1$. The price of Z^τ is not defined for $t > \tau$.

The term structure model includes a zero coupon bond Z^τ for every τ satisfying $\tau = 1, \ldots, T$. Hence at each time t there is a collection $\{Z_t^{t+1}, Z_t^{t+2}, \ldots, Z_t^T\}$ of zero coupon bond prices. This collection is called the *term structure of zero coupon bond prices*.

The term structure model must be free of arbitrage opportunities, so there must exist a risk neutral probability measure Q under which the discounted prices of the zero coupon bonds are martingales. In other words, there must exist some probability measure Q with $Q(\omega) > 0$ for all $\omega \in \Omega$ such that, for every τ,

$$(6.1) \qquad Z_s^\tau = E_Q[B_s Z_t^\tau / B_t | \mathscr{F}_s], \qquad 0 \leqslant s \leqslant t \leqslant \tau$$

But $Z_\tau^\tau = 1$ and $B_t / B_s = (1 + r_{s+1}) \dots (1 + r_t)$, so taking $t = \tau$ we see that zero coupon bonds must satisfy the important relationship

$$(6.2) \quad Z_s^\tau = E_Q[B_s / B_\tau | \mathscr{F}_s] = E_Q[1 / \{(1 + r_{s+1}) \dots (1 + r_\tau)\} | \mathscr{F}_s], \ 0 \leqslant s \leqslant \tau$$

given any risk neutral probability measure Q. Since $r_t > 0$, this implies, for each fixed s and ω, that $\tau \to Z_s^\tau(\omega)$ is a strictly decreasing function with $Z_s^{s+1}(\omega) < 1$. Note that taking $\tau = s + 1$ in (6.2) gives

$$(6.3) \qquad\qquad r_{s+1} + 1 = 1 / Z_s^{s+1}, \qquad s = 0, 1, \dots, T - 1$$

With most kinds of securities market models it is customary to start with a probability space $(\Omega, \mathscr{F}, P, \mathbb{F})$ and then define the spot interest rate r and the risky securities with respect to the "real-world" probability measure P; this is because the future values of the risky securities are uncertain. Subsequently, a risk neutral probability measure Q is determined from these data. But with a term structure model, where future values of some key securities (i.e., the zero coupon bonds) are known with certainty, it is possible to take a different approach: first specify a probability space $(\Omega, \mathscr{F}, Q, \mathbb{F})$, letting Q be the risk neutral probability measure from the start, then specify the spot interest rate r, giving its probabilistic behavior with respect to Q, and finally use (6.2) to provide the specification of the zero coupon bond prices. Thus it is possible to construct a perfectly satisfactory term structure model without worrying about the probabilistic behavior of the spot interest rate and the zero coupon bond prices under a real-world probability measure.

Although this is a common approach, the reader should keep in mind that it is not immediately obvious whether there will exist a subjective probability measure P under which r and the zero coupon bond prices behave in a realistic or desirable manner. And it may be difficult to determine such a P, even if one is known to exist. This approach is illustrated in example 6.2, after first illustrating an alternative approach.

Example 6.1 With $T = 3$ and $\Omega = \{\omega_1, \omega_2, \dots, \omega_6\}$ suppose the time-1 partition is $\mathscr{P}_1 = \{\omega_1, \omega_2\} \cup \{\omega_3, \omega_4\} \cup \{\omega_5, \omega_6\}$ and the time-2 and time-3 partitions are $\mathscr{P}_2 = \mathscr{P}_3 = \{\omega_1\} \cup \dots \cup \{\omega_6\}$. The "real-world" probability measure P can be specified, but its values are not important. For the spot interest rate, let $r_1 = 0.06$,

$$r_2(\omega) = \begin{cases} 0.09, & \omega = \omega_1, \omega_2 \\ 0.06, & \omega = \omega_3, \omega_4 \\ 0.03, & \omega = \omega_5, \omega_6 \end{cases}$$

and

$$r_3(\omega) = \begin{cases} 0.10, & \omega = \omega_1 \\ 0.08, & \omega = \omega_2 \\ 0.07, & \omega = \omega_3 \\ 0.05, & \omega = \omega_4 \\ 0.04, & \omega = \omega_5 \\ 0.02, & \omega = \omega_6 \end{cases}$$

Next is the specification of the zero coupon bond price processes Z^1, Z^2, and Z^3. For this you cannot take arbitrary stochastic processes with $Z_t^\tau < 1$ for $t < \tau$ and with $Z_\tau^\tau = 1$; you must carefully respect equation (6.1) in order to preclude the introduction of arbitrage opportunities. Indeed, by equation (6.3) there is no flexibility in the choice of $Z_{\tau-1}^\tau$ for $\tau = 1, 2$, and 3; these values are presented in table 6.1.

Next, consider the specification of $Z_1^3(\omega_1) = Z_1^3(\omega_2)$. Taking $t = s + 1$ in (6.1) we have

(6.4) $Z_s^\tau = E_Q[(1 + r_{s+1})^{-1}Z_{s+1}^\tau | \mathscr{F}_s] = (1 + r_{s+1})^{-1}E_Q[Z_{s+1}^\tau | \mathscr{F}_s]$

Now we have flexibility in the choice of Z_s^τ for $s < \tau - 1$, coming from the freedom to choose the conditional, risk neutral probabilities. In particular, with two possibilities for the value of $Z_2^3(\omega)$ given the information at time 1, $Z_1^3(\omega)$ can be chosen to be any value such that $(1 + r_2)Z_1^3(\omega)$ is strictly between the maximum and minimum values that the zero coupon price can become next period. For example, since $Z_2^3(\omega_1) = (1.1)^{-1} = 0.9091$ and $Z_2^3(\omega_2) = (1.08)^{-1} = 0.9259$, it suffices for $Z_1^3(\omega_1)$ and $Z_1^3(\omega_2)$ to satisfy the constraints

$$0.9091 < 1.09Z_1^3(\omega_1) = 1.09Z_1^3(\omega_2) < 0.9259$$

We shall take $Z_1^3(\omega_1) = Z_1^3(\omega_2) = 0.840$. In a similar fashion, we must have

$$Z_2^3(\omega_3) = 0.9346 < 1.06Z_1^3(\omega_3) = 1.06Z_1^3(\omega_4) < Z_2^3(\omega_4) = 0.9524$$

and

$$Z_2^3(\omega_5) = 0.9615 < 1.03Z_1^3(\omega_5) = 1.03Z_1^3(\omega_6) < Z_2^3(\omega_6) = 0.9804$$

so we shall take $Z_1^3(\omega_3) = Z_1^3(\omega_4) = 0.890$ and $Z_1^3(\omega_5) = Z_1^3(\omega_6) = 0.940$.

Turning to the specification of Z_0^2 and Z_0^3, we see that the situation is somewhat more complicated because each zero coupon bond can become one of three instead of just two distinct values. Equation (6.4) must be satisfied by both Z^2 and Z^3:

$$1.06Z_0^2 = 0.9174p + 0.9434q + 0.9709(1 - p - q)$$

$$1.06Z_0^3 = 0.84p + 0.89q + 0.94(1 - p - q)$$

where $p = Q(\omega_1) + Q(\omega_2)$ and $q = Q(\omega_3) + Q(\omega_4)$. These equations coupled with the constraints $p > 0$, $q > 0$, and $p + q < 1$ give rise to three constraints on the pair (Z_0^2, Z_0^3). We shall simply take $p = q = 0.3$, thereby giving $Z_0^2 = 0.893$ and $Z_0^3 = 0.844$.

This completes the specification of the zero coupon bond processes and thus of the model; the details are presented in the table 6.1. Notice that Z^3 is not an increasing process.

Table 6.1   Data for example 6.1

ω	Z_0^1	Z_0^2	Z_1^2	Z_0^3	Z_1^3	Z_2^3	$Q(\omega)$
ω_1	0.9434	0.893	0.9174	0.844	0.84	0.9091	0.1839
ω_2	0.9434	0.893	0.9174	0.844	0.84	0.9259	0.1161
ω_3	0.9434	0.893	0.9434	0.844	0.89	0.9346	0.1517
ω_4	0.9434	0.893	0.9434	0.844	0.89	0.9524	0.1483
ω_5	0.9434	0.893	0.9709	0.844	0.94	0.9615	0.2582
ω_6	0.9434	0.893	0.9709	0.844	0.94	0.9804	0.1418

It remains to compute a risk neutral probability measure Q. This will be done by first computing the conditional risk neutral probabilities, using equation (6.4). We already have these for the first period: $Q(\omega_1) + Q(\omega_2) = Q(\omega_3) + Q(\omega_4) = 0.3$ and $Q(\omega_5) + Q(\omega_6) = 0.4$. For the second period, equation (6.4) with $s = 1$, $\tau = 3$, and $\omega = \omega_1$ or ω_2 gives $1.09(0.84) = \hat{q}(0.9091) + (1 - \hat{q})(0.9259)$, so $\hat{q} = Q(Z_2^3 = 0.9091 | Z_1^3 = 0.84) = 0.6131$. In a similar fashion, equation (6.4) gives $Q(Z_2^3 = 0.9346 | Z_1^3 = 0.89) = 0.5056$ and $Q(Z_2^3 = 0.9615 | Z_1^3 = 0.94) = 0.6455$. Taking appropriate products of these conditional probabilities yields the risk neutral probability measure, which is displayed in table 6.1. Note this is the unique risk neutral probability measure associated with this specification of the zero coupon bonds, so this model is complete.

Example 6.2   With $T = 3$, the sample space Ω, the filtration $\mathbb{F}$, and the spot interest rate r all the same as in example 6.1, we can jump directly to the specification of the risk neutral probability measure Q. Any strictly positive probability measure will do. We shall illustrate this by simply taking $Q(\omega_1) = \ldots = Q(\omega_6) = 1/6$.

This completes the specification of the model (unless you also want the real-world probability measure P). It remains to derive the zero coupon bond price processes by using equation (6.2) or (6.4). The values of $Z_{\tau-1}^\tau$ for $\tau = 1, 2$, and 3 will, of course, be the same as in example 6.1. Equation (6.4) with $s = 1$, $\tau = 3$, and $\omega = \omega_1$ or ω_2 is

$$Z_1^3(\omega_1) = Z_1^3(\omega_2) = \frac{1}{2}\frac{0.9091}{1.09} + \frac{1}{2}\frac{0.9259}{1.09} = 0.8417$$

Similarly, $Z_1^3(\omega_3) = Z_1^3(\omega_4) = 0.8901$ and $Z_1^3(\omega_5) = Z_1^3(\omega_6) = 0.9427$. Equation (6.3) with $s = 0$ and $\tau = 3$ is

$$Z_0^3 = \frac{1}{3}\frac{0.8417}{1.06} + \frac{1}{3}\frac{0.8901}{1.06} + \frac{1}{3}\frac{0.9427}{1.06} = 0.8410$$

Finally, equation (6.4) with $s = 0$ and $\tau = 2$ is

$$Z_0^3 = \frac{1}{3}\frac{0.9174}{1.06} + \frac{1}{3}\frac{0.9434}{1.06} + \frac{1}{3}\frac{0.9709}{1.06} = 0.8905$$

The details for this model are summarized as follows:

ω	Z_0^1	Z_0^2	Z_1^2	Z_0^3	Z_1^3	Z_2^3	$Q(\omega)$
ω_1	0.9434	0.8905	0.9174	0.8410	0.8417	0.9091	0.1667
ω_2	0.9434	0.8905	0.9174	0.8410	0.8417	0.9259	0.1667
ω_3	0.9434	0.8905	0.9434	0.8410	0.8901	0.9346	0.1667
ω_4	0.9434	0.8905	0.9434	0.8410	0.8901	0.9524	0.1667
ω_5	0.9434	0.8905	0.9709	0.8410	0.9427	0.9615	0.1667
ω_6	0.9434	0.8905	0.9709	0.8410	0.9427	0.9804	0.1667

Notice that here, in contrast with example 6.1, all the zero coupon bond price processes are increasing.

The approaches used to specify the models in examples 6.1 and 6.2 are easy to implement, but there is no direct control over all the prices and interest rates that are observable at time $t = 0$. For practical purposes, it is often important to have a model where these time $t = 0$ values are equal to prescribed quantities. This is feasible to achieve, simply by starting with these values and then using equations (6.1) to (6.4) to introduce arbitrage-free future values of the interest rates and zero coupon bond prices. The risk neutral probability measure is introduced simultaneously, as will now be illustrated.

Example 6.3   With $T = 3$, the sample space Ω, and the filtration $\mathbb{F}$ all the same as in examples 6.1 and 6.2, suppose the values $r_1 = 0.06$, $Z_0^1 = 0.9434$, $Z_0^2 = 0.89$, and $Z_0^3 = 0.84$ are observed at time $t = 0$. To introduce future values of r and of the prices of these zero coupon bonds, it suffices to use equations (6.3) and (6.4), moving forward one period at a time; the risk neutral conditional probabilities will be introduced simultaneously.

Starting with the arbitrary values $Z_1^2(\omega_1) = 0.91$, $Z_1^2(\omega_3) = 0.94$, $Z_1^2(\omega_5) = 0.97$, and $Q(Z_1^2 = 0.91) = 0.3$, it follows from equation (6.4) with $s = 0$ and $\tau = 2$ that $Q(Z_1^2 = 0.94) = 0.2867$ and $Q(Z_1^2 = 0.97) = 0.4133$. Equation (6.3) thus implies that r_2 takes the values 0.0989, 0.0638, and 0.0309 in states ω_1, ω_3 and ω_5, respectively.

Turning next to the specification of Z_1^3, we see that we can choose arbitrary values for two of the three possible values, say $Z_1^3(\omega_3) = 0.89$ and $Z_1^3(\omega_5) = 0.94$. This choice implies $Z_1^3(\omega_1) = 0.8223$, since equation (6.4) must be satisfied with $s = 0$ and $\tau = 3$.

The next step is to choose the values of Z_2^3, making sure equation (6.4) with $s = 0$ and $\tau = 3$ is satisfied for suitable values of the conditional, risk neutral probabilities. For instance, with $Z_2^3(\omega_1) = 0.90$ and $Z_2^3(\omega_2) = 0.92$, equation (6.4) gives $Q(Z_2^3 = 0.90 | Z_1^3 = 0.8223) = 0.185$. Similarly, the choice of $Z_2^3(\omega_3) = 0.94$, $Z_2^3(\omega_4) = 0.95$, $Z_2^3(\omega_5) = 0.96$, and $Z_2^3(\omega_6) = 0.98$ implies $Q(Z_2^3 = 0.94 | Z_1^3 = 0.89) = 0.32$ and $Q(Z_2^3 = 0.96 | Z_1^3 = 0.94) = 0.55$. Equation (6.3) stipulates the values of r_3. This model is summarized as follows:

ω	Z_1^2	Z_1^3	Z_2^3	r_2	r_3	Q
ω_1	0.91	0.8223	0.90	0.0989	0.1111	0.0555
ω_2	0.91	0.8223	0.92	0.0989	0.0870	0.2445
ω_3	0.94	0.89	0.94	0.0638	0.0638	0.0917
ω_4	0.94	0.89	0.95	0.0638	0.0526	0.1950
ω_5	0.97	0.94	0.96	0.0309	0.0417	0.2273
ω_6	0.97	0.94	0.98	0.0309	0.0204	0.1860

It remains to compute the risk neutral probability measure Q. This follows immediately from the conditional probabilities which have already been computed; the values of $Q(\omega)$ are shown above.

We now turn to a new topic, the *yield to maturity*. This is an adapted stochastic process, denoted $Y^\tau = \{Y_t^\tau; t = 0, \dots, \tau - 1\}$, that is uniquely associated with each zero coupon bond. The value Y_t^τ is defined to be the one-period interest rate such that a sum of money equal to the current price of the zero coupon bond, namely Z_t^τ, will become exactly $Z_\tau^\tau = 1$ at time τ when invested and compounded at this constant rate. In other words,

$$Z_t^\tau(1 + Y_t^\tau)^{\tau-t} = 1, \qquad 0 \leqslant t < \tau \leqslant T$$

which is the same as

$$(6.5) \qquad Z_t^\tau = (1 + Y_t^\tau)^{t-\tau}, \qquad 0 \leqslant t < \tau \leqslant T$$

as well as

$$(6.6) \qquad Y_t^\tau = [Z_t^\tau]^{1/t-\tau} - 1, \qquad 0 \leqslant t < \tau \leqslant T$$

Notice that $Y_t^{t+1} = r_{t+1}$, the current spot interest rate.

At each time t there is a collection $\{Y_t^{t+1}, \dots, Y_t^T\}$ of yields that is called the *term structure of interest rates* or the *yield curve*. In view of equations (6.5) and (6.6), knowledge of the term structure of interest rates is equivalent to knowledge of the term structure of zero coupon bond prices $\{Z_t^{t+1}, \dots, Z_t^T\}$.

Example 6.1 (continued)   Using equation (6.6), we quickly derive the following yields

ω	Y_0^1	Y_0^2	Y_0^3	Y_1^2	Y_1^3	Y_2^3
ω_1	0.06	0.0582	0.0582	0.09	0.0911	0.10
ω_2	0.06	0.0582	0.0582	0.09	0.0911	0.08
ω_3	0.06	0.0582	0.0582	0.06	0.0600	0.07
ω_4	0.06	0.0582	0.0582	0.06	0.0600	0.05
ω_5	0.06	0.0582	0.0582	0.03	0.0314	0.04
ω_6	0.06	0.0582	0.0582	0.03	0.0314	0.02

Notice the various kinds of term structures. The time $t = 0$ term structure is decreasing with respect to maturity, two of the time $t = 1$ term structures are increasing, and the third time $t = 1$ term structure is constant.

Another important concept pertaining to term structure models is that of *forward interest rates*. Suppose it is time s, and consider the forward price O_s of the τ-maturity zero coupon bond, delivered at time t, where $s \leqslant t \leqslant \tau$. In view of principle (4.22) and equation (6.2), this must be

$$O_s = \frac{Z_s^\tau}{E_Q[B_s/B_t \mid \mathscr{F}_s]} = \frac{Z_s^\tau}{Z_s^t}, \qquad 0 \leqslant s \leqslant t \leqslant \tau \leqslant T$$

This equation makes economic sense, since there are no arbitrage opportunities. In one case you buy the τ-maturity discount bond at time s and hold it until time τ. In the other case you make at time s a forward contract to take delivery of this same bond at time t and then hold it until it matures at time τ, financing the time t payment O_s by investing at time s exactly $O_s Z_s^t$ dollars in the t-maturity discount bond. In both cases you are sure to have \$1 at time τ, so the time s expenditures must be the same by the law of one price.

For the special case where $\tau = t + 1$,

(6.7)
$$O_s = \frac{Z_s^{t+1}}{Z_s^t}, \qquad 0 \leqslant s \leqslant t \leqslant T$$

must be the time-s forward price of a zero coupon bond that is delivered at time t and matures one period later. The yield, denoted $f(s, t)$, corresponding to forward price (6.7) must be

(6.8)
$$f(s, t) = \frac{Z_s^t}{Z_s^{t+1}} - 1$$

because Z_s^{t+1}/Z_s^t dollars invested at time t at the interest rate $f(s,t)$ will become one dollar at time $t + 1$. Note that $f(s, t) > 0$, because, as pointed out earlier, $t \to Z_s^t$ is a strictly decreasing function. Since the yield $f(s,t)$ is associated with a single period, it will be called the *forward spot interest rate* or, simply, the *forward interest rate*.

Taking $t = s$ in (6.8), we see from (6.3) that

$$f(s,s) = r_{s+1}, \qquad 0 \leqslant s < T$$

This is logically consistent, because if delivery occurs right away, then the forward and spot interest rates coincide. We also see from (6.8) that $f(s, t)$ is an $\mathscr{F}_s-$ measurable random variable for each $t \geqslant s$. Hence, for each fixed t, $s \to f(s, t)$ is an adapted stochastic process.

The collection $\{f(s, s), \dots, f(s, T - 1)\}$ is called the time-s *term structure of forward interest rates*. In view of equation (6.8), knowledge of the term structure of zero coupon bond prices gives you the term structure of forward interest rates. The converse is true, because $Z_s^s = 1$ and so you can use (6.8) to work out the remaining zero coupon bond prices in a recursive manner. Hence all three kinds of term structures are equivalent.

A useful relationship between the forward rates and the price of a discount bond is obtained from the identity

$$Z_s^\tau = \prod_{t=s+1}^{\tau} [Z_s^t / Z_s^{t-1}]$$

Substituting (6.8) yields

(6.9)
$$Z_s^\tau = \prod_{t=s+1}^{\tau} [1 + f(s, t - 1)]^{-1}$$

Compare this with equation (6.2).

Example 6.1 (continued)   Using equation (6.8), we quickly derive the following forward interest rates.

ω	$f(0,0)$	$f(0,1)$	$f(0,2)$	$f(1,1)$	$f(1,2)$	$f(2,2)$
ω_1	0.06	0.0564	0.0581	0.09	0.0921	0.10
ω_2	0.06	0.0564	0.0581	0.09	0.0921	0.08
ω_3	0.06	0.0564	0.0581	0.06	0.0600	0.07
ω_4	0.06	0.0564	0.0581	0.06	0.0600	0.05
ω_5	0.06	0.0564	0.0581	0.03	0.0329	0.04
ω_6	0.06	0.0564	0.0581	0.03	0.0329	0.02

This is consistent with equation (6.9), because, for example,

$$Z_0^2 = \frac{1}{(1.06)(1.0564)} = 0.893$$

Exercise 6.1   For a term structure model with $T = 5$, suppose the time $t = 0$ term structure is as indicated below. Derive the other two kinds of term structures.

(a)   The term structure of zero coupon bond prices is $Z_0^1 = 0.96$, $Z_0^2 = 0.915$, $Z_0^3 = 0.88$, $Z_0^4 = 0.837$, and $Z_0^5 = 0.80$.

(b)   The term structure of yields is $Y_0^1 = 4\%$, $Y_0^2 = 5\%$, $Y_0^3 = 6\%$, $Y_0^4 = 7\%$, and $Y_0^5 = 6.5\%$.

(c)   The term structure of forward interest rates is $f(0,0) = 4\%$, $f(0,1) = 6\%, f(0,2) = 5.5\%, f(0,3) = 5\%$, and $f(0,4) = 5\%$.

Exercise 6.2   For the same model as in example 6.2 except that $Q(\omega_i) = i/21$ for $i = 1, \ldots, 6$, compute all the zero coupon bond, yield, and forward rate processes. (Hint: show $Z_0^3 = 0.8604$)

6.2   Lattice, Markov Chain Models

Given an arbitrary filtration $\mathbb{F}$, it is usually difficult to specify the spot interest rate process r and other elements of the model so that the various interest rate and price processes will be realistic under a subjective probability measure P and, moreover, their time-0 values will be consistent with an arbitrary time-0 term structure. It is desirable to develop a class of simple models where these objectives are met.

An obvious candidate that comes to mind is an interest rate version of the binomial model studied in section 3.5. The idea would be to model the spot interest rate r just like the risky security in the binomial model, selecting a value q for the risk neutral conditional probability, and then the zero coupon bond prices would follow from equation (6.2). However, due to the fact this model involves only four parameters (namely, r_1, u, d, and q), there is no reason to expect the computed zero coupon bond prices to match an arbitrary term structure. This kind of model is too simple.

But all is not lost with the binomial model approach. A modest generalization will do the job. One retains the same submodel of the information structure as for the binomial model, namely, as portrayed in figure 3.4. But the spot interest rate process r will be generalized to the extent of being a Markov chain, along the lines of the risky security of example 3.6 in section 3.6. To be precise, let X denote a Markov chain with initial value $X_0 = 0$, with state space $E = \{0, 1, \ldots, T\}$, and with transition probabilities satisfying

$$P\{X_{t+1} = j | X_t = n\} > 0, \quad j = n+1 \text{ or } j = n,$$
$$P\{X_{t+1} = j | X_t = n\} = 0, \quad \text{otherwise}$$

for $t = 0, 1, \ldots, T - 1$. Hence X_t can be thought of as the cumulative number of heads after t tosses of a coin, but unlike the binomial process N_t studied in sections 3.5 and 3.6, the various coin flips are not necessarily independent or identically distributed. Instead, the probability that coin flip number $t + 1$ is a head depends, in general, on both t and the current value X_t.

Figure 6.1 shows a network with the nodes representing the states which X can possibly reach at each time t starting with X_0. The branches correspond

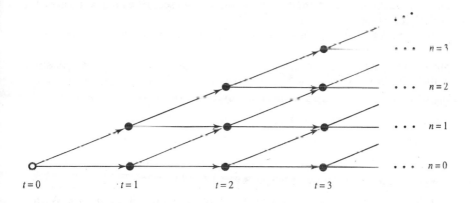

Figure 6.1.   State space for the Markov chain X

to positive transition probabilities. Needless to say, this picture is essentially the same as the lattice in figure 3.5 for the binomial model.

The Markov chain X is not stationary, because the transition probabilities can vary with respect to t. However, upon defining a new stochastic process by setting $\hat{X}_t = (X_t, t)$, it is apparent that $\hat{X}$ is also a Markov chain that is, in fact, stationary. Indeed, the nodes in figure 6.1 correspond to its possible states, each of the form (n, t), and the branches correspond to its positive Markov transition probabilities. This "stationary" perspective will be more convenient for the term structure model that is being developed.

Now suppose there are functions $\rho_t : \{0, 1, \ldots, t\} \to (0, \infty)$ for $t = 0, 1, \ldots, T - 1$. Usually, each such function is strictly increasing on its domain, but this is not crucial. We can define the spot interest rate process r by setting

$$r_{t+1}(\omega) = \rho_t(X_t(\omega)), \quad t = 0, 1 \ldots, T - 1$$

The Markov chain X can be interpreted as an exogenous "factor" with the property that knowledge of it implies knowledge of the spot interest rate r. Knowing that $X_t = n$ at time t, say, you not only know that $r_{t+1} - \rho_t(n)$, but you also know that at time $t + 1$ the spot interest rate r_{t+2} will be either $\rho_{t+1}(n)$ or $\rho_{t+1}(n + 1)$. In particular, if each function ρ_t is strictly increasing on its domain, then knowledge of r_{t+1} is equivalent to knowledge of X_t, and the spot interest rate process is itself a Markov chain. This is the usual case.

Of course, explicit knowledge of the functions ρ_t is not necessary; they were introduced primarily as a device to link this term structure model with the discussion in section 3.6 about Markov chains, especially example 3.5. To develop the term structure model one can proceed directly from the state space representation as displayed in figure 6.1 to the specification of the spot interest rate process r_t, simply by specifying its value at each node of the lattice. Let $r_{t+1}(n)$ denote the value associated with state (n,t) for $n = 0, 1 \ldots, t$ and $t = 0, 1, \ldots T - 1$. Even if $r_{t+1}(n_1) = r_{t+1}(n_2)$, say, the understanding is that at time t the agents in this securities market know the underlying state $\hat{X}_t = (n, t)$.

To complete the specification of the term structure model it suffices to specify the conditional risk neutral transition probabilities for the process $\hat{X}$. Since only two kinds of transitions from state $\hat{X}_t = (n, t)$ are possible, namely, to either state $(n + 1, t)$ or state (n, t), it is convenient to introduce the notation

$$q(n, t) = Q\{\hat{X}_{t+1} = (n + 1, t + 1)| \hat{X}_t = (n, t)\}$$

for $n = 0, 1, \ldots, t$ and $t = 0, 1, \ldots, T - 1$. Note, for example, that

$$Q\{r_{t+2} = r_{t+2}(n) \mid \hat{X}_t = (n, t)\} = 1 - q(n, t)$$

The complete specification of the Markov chain term structure model can now be neatly displayed with the lattice diagram shown in figure 6.2. With T time periods, there are $1 + 2 + \ldots + T = T(T + 1)/2$ nodes in this lattice, not counting the terminal nodes at time T. Thus there is a total of $T(T + 1)$ parameters to be specified in this model, one value of r and one value of q for each node.

What about the prices of the zero coupon bonds? In view of equation (6.2) and the Markov property, we have that

$$Z_t^{\tau} = E_Q[1/\{(1 + r_{t+1}) \ldots (1 + r_{\tau})\}| \mathscr{F}_t]$$
$$= E_Q[1/\{(1 + r_{t+1}) \ldots (1 + r_{\tau})\}|X_t]$$

In words, the price of a zero coupon bond depends on the state of the underlying factor X_t, but otherwise it is independent of the history of prices and interest rates. As with the spot interest rate, the value of Z_t^{τ} can be expressed as some function of X_t. Equivalently, the process Z^{τ} is fully

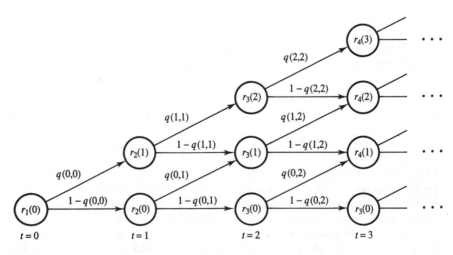

Figure 6.2   The Markov chain term structure model

specified by knowing its value at each node of the lattice in figure 6.2. We shall take this latter approach and let $Z_t^\tau(n)$ denote the value of Z_t^τ at the node corresponding to $X_t = n$.

It is useful to have a formula for $Z_t^\tau(n)$ in terms of the spot interest rate and conditional risk neutral probabilities. We can derive one from equation (6.4), which now can be rewritten as

$$(6.10) \qquad Z_t^\tau(n) = \frac{1}{1 + r_{t+1}(n)} \left[q(n, t) Z_{t+1}^\tau(n+1) + [1 - q(n, t)] Z_{t+1}^\tau(n) \right]$$

Denote

$$\delta(n, t, 1) = \frac{q(n, t)}{1 + r_{t+1}(n)} \quad \text{and} \quad \delta(n, t, 0) = \frac{1 - q(n, t)}{1 + r_{t+1}(n)}$$

so that (6.10) can be simplified to become

$$Z_t^\tau(n) = \sum_{i=0}^{1} \delta(n, t, i) \, Z_{t+1}^\tau(n + i)$$

Since $Z_\tau^\tau = 1$, a backwards induction argument on t can be used with this equation to show for $t = 0, \dots, \tau$ and $n = 0, \dots, t$ that

$$(6.11) \qquad Z_t^\tau(n) = \sum_{i_1=0}^{1} \delta(n, t, i_1) \sum_{i_2=0}^{1} \delta(n + i_1, t + 1, i_2) \cdots$$

$$\cdots \sum_{i_{\tau-t}=0}^{1} \delta(n + i_1 + \dots + i_{\tau-t-1}, \tau - 1, i_{\tau-1})$$

In particular, the time-0 prices of the zero coupon bonds are given by

$$(6.12) \qquad Z_0^\tau = \sum_{i_1=0}^{1} \delta(0, 0, i_1) \sum_{i_2=0}^{1} \delta(i_1, 1, i_2) \cdots$$

$$\cdots \sum_{i_\tau=0}^{1} \delta(i_1 + \dots + i_{\tau-1}, \tau - 1, i_\tau)$$

As mentioned at the beginning of this section, it is desirable for the term structure model to be consistent with the observed, time-0 term structure of zero coupon bond prices. In principle, equation (6.12) can be used to choose the parameters of the model in a consistent manner. But there are two problems with this. First, equation (6.12) is difficult to work with for the purpose of solving for parameters on the right hand side. Secondly, our general Markov term structure model entails $T(T + 1)$ parameters, whereas the observed time-0 term structure together with (6.12) give only T equations in the $T(T + 1)$ unknowns. We still have a great many degrees of freedom in the choice of the parameters.

This matter will be resolved by making further simplifications in the model. The idea is to reduce the effective number of parameters by making assumptions about the spot interest rate and/or the conditional risk neutral probabilities. The aim is to obtain a system of equations which is feasible to solve for unique values of the parameters.

The usual simplification is to make some assumption about the "volatilities," which are taken to be either the ratios $r_{t+1}(n+1)/r_{t+1}(n)$ or the ratios $[1 + r_{t+1}(n+1)]/[1 + r_{t+1}(n)]$. These two approaches are examined in the following two examples.

Example 6.4   Assume the conditional risk neutral probabilities are independent of n, that is,

$$q(n, t) = q(t), \quad 0 \leqslant n \leqslant t < T$$

These T numbers $q(0), \ldots, q(T-1)$, and thus all the conditional risk neutral probabilities, are specified. In addition, T numbers $c(0), \ldots, c(T-1)$ are also specified, and it is required that (the first equality here is just (6.3))

$$(6.13) \qquad \frac{Z_t^{t+1}(n+1)}{Z_t^{t+1}(n)} = \frac{1 + r_{t+1}(n)}{1 + r_{t+1}(n+1)} = c(t), \quad 0 \leqslant n \leqslant t < T$$

The number $c(t)$ can be interpreted as a measure of the volatility of the time-t spot interest rate, a measure which is independent of n. Using (6.13) recursively gives

$$(6.14) \quad Z_{\tau-1}^{\tau}(n+i) = Z_{\tau-1}^{\tau}(n)c^i(\tau-1), \quad 0 \leqslant n \leqslant n+i \leqslant \tau-1 < T$$

In particular,

$$(6.15) \qquad Z_{\tau-1}^{\tau}(i) = Z_{\tau-1}^{\tau}(0)c^i(\tau-1), \quad 0 \leqslant i \leqslant \tau-1 < T$$

Since $Z_{\tau-1}^{\tau}(n) = 1/[1 + r_\tau(n)]$, this says that knowing $r_t(0)$ you can deduce $r_t(n)$ for all $n \geqslant 1$. Hence this model will be fully specified if we can choose the T numbers $r_0(0), \ldots, r_{T-1}(0)$ (equivalently, $Z_0(0), Z_1(0), \ldots, Z_{T-1}(0)$) to be consistent with the T observed zero coupon bond prices $Z_0^1, \ldots, Z_0^T$.

To show how to do this, use will be made of the following equation:

$$(6.16) \qquad Z_t^{\tau}(n) = \prod_{j=t}^{\tau-1} g(j, \tau-1)Z_j^{j+1}(n), \qquad n = 0, 1, \ldots, t$$

where $g(s, s) \equiv 1$ and

$$g(j, s) \quad \equiv 1 - q(j) + q(j)c(j+1) \ldots c(s), \quad j = 0, 1, \ldots, s-1$$

Equation (6.16) can be verified with a backwards induction argument on t, beginning with $t = \tau - 1$, for which it is clearly true. Assuming (6.16) is true for $t + 1$, equation (6.10) gives

$$Z_t^\tau(n) = Z_t^{t+1}(n)\left[q(t)Z_{t+1}^\tau(n+1) + [1 \quad q(t)]Z_{t+1}^\tau(n)\right]$$

$$= Z_t^{t+1}(n)\left[q(t) \prod_{j=t+1}^{\tau-1} g(j, \tau-1) Z_j^{j+1}(n+1)\right.$$

$$+ \{1 - q(t)\} \prod_{k=t+1}^{\tau-1} g(k, \tau-1) Z_k^{k+1}(n)\right]$$

$$= Z_t^{t+1}(n)\left[q(t) \prod_{j=t+1}^{\tau-1} g(j, \tau-1) Z_j^{j+1}(n)c(j)\right.$$

$$+ \{1 - q(t)\} \prod_{k=t+1}^{\tau-1} g(k, t-1)Z_k^{k+1}(n)\right]$$

where the last equality uses (6.14). Hence

$$Z_t^\tau(n) = Z_t^{t+1}(n)\left[q(t) \prod_{j=t+1}^{\tau-1} c(j) + 1 - q(t)\right] \prod_{j=t+1}^{\tau-1} g(j, \tau-1)Z_j^{j+1}(n)$$

$$= Z_t^{t+1}(n)g(t, \tau-1) \prod_{j=t+1}^{\tau-1} g(j, \tau \quad 1) Z_j^{j+1}(n)$$

and equation (6.16) is verified.

It follows from (6.16) that

$$\frac{Z_0^{t+1}(0)}{Z_0^t(0)} = \frac{\prod_{j=0}^t g(j, t)Z_j^{j+1}(0)}{\prod_{j=0}^{t-1} g(j, t-1)Z_j^{j+1}(0)} = \frac{Z_t^{t+1}(0) \prod_{j=0}^{t-1} g(j, t)}{\prod_{j=0}^{t-2} g(j, t-1)}$$

where the second equality uses $g(t, t) = g(t-1, t-1) = 1$. Hence this and (6.15) give the key result for $0 \leqslant n \leqslant t < T$:

$$(6.17) \qquad Z_t^{t+1}(n) = \frac{Z_0^{t+1}(0)}{Z_0^t(0)}[c(t)]^n \frac{\prod_{j=0}^{t-2} g(j, t-1)}{\prod_{j=0}^{t-1} g(j, t)}$$

The right hand side of (6.17) is completely known, coming from either the specified numbers $q(t)$ and $c(t)$ or the time-0 term structure of zero coupon bond prices. Hence $r_{t+1}(n) = 1/Z_t^{t+1}(n) - 1$ is known for all n and t.

The numbers $c(t)$ are normally in the vicinity of 1, which means the spot interest rate does not change too much from one period to the next. Indeed, these numbers must be selected with care in order to keep the interest rates from becoming negative or unreasonably large. If, for instance, $c(t) = 1$, then by (6.14) $Z_t^{t+1}(n)$ is independent of n. This also implies $g(j, t) = g(j, t-1)$, so (6.17) becomes $Z_t^{t+1}(n) = Z_0^{t+1}(0)/Z_0^t(0)$, that is, one period zero coupon bond prices at time t do not depend on the state n but only on the initial term structure.

This model can be generalized to allow the risk neutral conditional probabilities $q(t)$ to depend on the state n. In the opposite direction, an important special case is obtained by taking $q(t) = q$ and $c(t) = 1/k$ for all t, where q and k are specified positive scalars with $q < 1$. Then for $j < s$ the function g becomes

$$g(j,s) = 1 - q + qk^{j-s} \equiv \frac{1}{h(s-j)}$$

where the new function h is defined in an obvious manner. In this case (6.17) becomes simply $Z_t^{t+1}(n) = Z_0^{t+1}(0)k^{-n}h(t)/Z_0^t(0)$.

Example 6.5   Assume $q(n,t) = 0.5$ for all n and t, so

$$\delta(n,t,1) = \delta(n,t,0) = \frac{0.5}{1 + r_{t+1}(n)} = 0.5Z_t^{t+1}(n)$$

Equation (6.12) simplifies to become

(6.18) $$Z_0^\tau = \left(\frac{1}{2}\right)^{\tau-1} Z_0^1(0) \sum_{i_1=0}^{1} Z_1^2(i_1) \sum_{i_2=0}^{1} Z_2^3(i_1 + i_2) \ldots$$

$$\ldots \sum_{i_{\tau-1}=0}^{1} Z_{\tau-1}^\tau(i_1 + \ldots + i_{\tau-1})$$

It remains to specify the $T(T+1)/2$ values of the spot interest rate. They will be chosen to be consistent with the T time-0 zero coupon bond prices as well as $T(T-1)/2$ specified spot rate volatilities, giving a total of $T(T+1)/2$ constraints.

The spot rate volatility is defined to be

(6.19) $$\sigma_t(n) \equiv \frac{1}{2} \ln\left(\frac{r_{t+2}(n+1)}{r_{t+2}(n)}\right), \quad 0 \leqslant n \leqslant t \leqslant T-1$$

Thus if you know r_{t+1} or $Z_t^{t+1}(n)$ for one value of n, you know both for all $n = 0, \ldots, t$, just like example 6.4. For instance, $r_{t+2}(n+1) = r_{t+2}(0)\exp\{2[\sigma_t(0) + \ldots + \sigma_t(n)]\}$. Using this idea, equation (6.18), and the time 0 term structure, you can work out all the values of the spot interest rate by moving forward in time in a recursive manner. Beginning with $\tau = 2$ in (6.18) and $t = 0$ in (6.19), you solve for the two unknowns $r_2(0)$ and $r_2(1)$. In general, knowing $Z_{t-1}^t(n)$ and $r_t(n)$ for all $0 \leqslant n < t < \tau$, you use $\tau - 1$ versions of (6.19) with $t = \tau - 2$ together with (6.18) to solve for the τ unknowns $r_\tau(0), \ldots, r_\tau(\tau-1)$.

An alternative perspective is to view the spot interest rate process r as being governed by the stochastic difference equation

(6.20) $$\Delta r_{t+1} = \mu(t, r_t) + \sigma(t, r_t)N_t,$$

where $\mu : \mathbb{R}^2 \to \mathbb{R}$ and $\sigma : \mathbb{R}^2 \to \mathbb{R}_+$ are specified functions, $\{N_t\}$ is a sequence of independent and identically distributed random variables with $Q(N_t = 1) = Q(N_t = -1) = 0.5$, and, as usual, $\Delta r_{t+1} = r_{t+1} - r_t$. This stochastic difference equation formulation is appealing, because under the risk neutral probability measure Q the conditional expected change in the spot rate is $\mu(t, r_t)$ and the conditional variance of the change in the spot rate is $\sigma^2(t, r_t)$.

Given a spot interest rate process r defined on a binary lattice, it is easy to come up with consistent functions for μ and σ. For example, knowing $r_t(n)$, $r_{t+1}(n)$, and $r_{t+1}(n + 1)$, the stochastic difference equation gives

$$r_{t+1}(n + 1) - r_t(n) = \mu(t, r_t(n)) + \sigma(t, r_t(n))$$

and

$$r_{t+1}(n) - r_t(n) = \mu(t, r_t(n)) - \sigma(t, r_t(n))$$

in which case one must have

$$\mu(t, r_t(n)) = \frac{r_{t+1}(n + 1) + r_{t+1}(n) - 2r_t(n)}{2}$$

and

$$\sigma(t, r_t(n)) = \frac{r_{t+1}(n + 1) - r_{t+1}(n)}{2}$$

More useful is to start with a stochastic difference equation for r and then derive a binomial lattice formulation. For example, suppose

(6.21) $$\Delta r_{t+1} = \phi(t) - a r_t + \sigma(t) N_t,$$

where a is a scalar satisfying $0 < a < 1$ and ϕ and σ are positive functions with domain $\mathbb{R}$. This formulation is appealing, because it says the interest rate tends to decrease if $r_t > \phi(t)/a$, otherwise the interest rate tends to increase. However, the function σ must satisfy a certain constraint in order for this process to be consistent with a binomial lattice formulation. In particular, an *up-down* move (that is, $N_t = 1$ and $N_{t+1} = -1$) must arrive at the same value for the spot interest rate as a *down-up* move (that is, $N_t = -1$ and $N_{t+1} = 1$). In other words, we must have

$$r_{t+2} = \phi(t + 1) + (1 - a)\phi(t) + (1 - a)^2 r_t + (1 - a)\sigma(t) - \sigma(t + 1)$$

$$= \phi(t + 1) + (1 - a)\phi(t) + (1 - a)^2 r_t - (1 - a)\sigma(t) + \sigma(t + 1)$$

for all t. A necessary and sufficient (assuming $\sigma > 0$) condition for this to be true is that $\sigma(t + 1) = (1 - a)\sigma(t) = (1 - a)^t \sigma(1)$. Hence the adaptation of this stochastic difference equation formulation to a binomial lattice leads to a severe restriction on the "volatility" functions σ.

This restriction on the volatility function can be ameliorated by working with a trinomial lattice. The idea here is that from one period to the next the spot interest rate moves to one of three possible values: "up," "middle," or "down." Moreover, various paths recombine: up-down = middle-middle = down-up, up-middle = middle-up, and middle-down = down-middle. Thus there will be three nodes after one period, five nodes after two periods, and, in general, $2t + 1$ nodes after t periods.

The stochastic difference equation for r has the same form as (6.20), only now the random variables $\{N_t\}$ are independent but satisfy $Q(N_t = 1) = Q(N_t = -1) = q(t)$ and $Q(N_t = 0) = 1 - 2q(t)$, where $0 < q(t) < 1/2$. Hence (see exercise 6.7) the conditional mean and variance of the change in the spot interest rate are $\mu(t, r_t)$ and $2q(t)\sigma^2(t, r_t)$, respectively.

Now consider again the special case (6.21), only with $\{N_t\}$ as in the preceding paragraph. This formulation is compatible with a trinomial lattice if and only if (see exercise 6.8) $\sigma(t + 1) = (1 - a)\sigma(t) = (1 - a)^t\sigma(1)$, the same condition as before. In this case, the conditional variance of the change of the spot interest rate is $2q(t)(1 - a)^{2t-2}\sigma(1)$. Hence flexibility in the choice of the probabilities $q(t)$ give the model builder some room to match the conditional variances with desired values. For instance, these variances can be made constant by taking $q(t) = 0.5(1 - a)^{2-2t}$, provided these probabilities satisfy $0 < q(t) < 1/2$.

Exercise 6.3 Show for example 6.4 that if $m_t^{-1} \leqslant [c(t)]^t \leqslant m_t$ for some number $m_t > 1$, then

$$\frac{Z_0^{t+1}(0)}{m_t Z_0^t(0)} \leqslant Z_t^{t+1}(n) \leqslant \frac{m_t Z_0^{t+1}(0)}{Z_0^t(0)}$$

Use this fact to show how the c's can be selected to ensure the spot interest rate remains between specified upper and lower bounds.

Exercise 6.4 Show for the special case of example 6.4 with $q(t) = q$ and $c(t) = 1/k$ that starting with arbitrary values of q, k, and the initial term structure, it is possible to obtain negative interest rates.

Exercise 6.5 For the model in example 6.4, show that

(a) $Z_t^\tau(n) = Z_t^\tau(0)\prod_{j=0}^{\tau-1} c^n(j)$, $n \leqslant t < \tau$

(b) $Z_t^\tau(n) = [Z_0^\tau(0)/Z_0^t(0)] \left[\prod_{j=t}^{\tau-1} c^n(j)\right] \left[\prod_{j=0}^{t-1} \frac{g(j,t-1)}{g(j,\tau-1)}\right]$, $n \leqslant t < \tau$

(c) $f(t, \tau, n) = [Z_0^\tau(0)/Z_0^{\tau+1}(0)] \left[c^{-n}(\tau)\right] \left[\prod_{j=0}^{t-1} \frac{g(j,\tau)}{g(j,\tau-1)}\right]$, $n \leqslant t < \tau$

where $f(t, \tau, n)$ denotes the forward spot rate corresponding to state n at time t.

Exercise 6.6 Example 6.5 can be generalized to allow for arbitrary conditional probabilities with $0 < q(n, t) < 1$, in which case the volatilities are defined by

$$\sigma_t(n) = \ln \{r_{t+2}(n + 1)/r_{t+2}(n)\}\sqrt{q(n, t)[1 - q(n, t)]}$$

For an arbitrary term structure of discount bond prices with $Z_0^1 > Z_0^2 > \ldots > Z_0^T$ and for arbitrary volatilities with $\sigma_t(n) > 0$, show by induction that there exists a unique and strictly positive spot interest rate process r such that the model is consistent with these quantities and free of arbitrage.

Exercise 6.7 Suppose the spot interest rate r is governed by the stochastic difference equation (6.20) with $Q(N_t = 1) = Q(N_t = -1) = q(t)$ and $Q(N_t = 0) = 1 - 2q(t)$, where $0 < q(t) < 1/2$. Verify that the conditional mean and variance of the change in the spot interest rate are $\mu(t, r_t)$ and $2q(t)\sigma^2(t, r_t)$, respectively.

Exercise 6.8 Suppose the spot interest rate r is governed by the stochastic difference equation (6.21) with $Q(N_t = 1) = Q(N_t = -1) = q(t)$ and $Q(N_t = 0) = 1 - 2q(t)$, where $0 < q(t) < 1/2$. Assuming $\sigma(t) > 0$, verify that this formulation is compatible with a trinomial lattice if and only if $\sigma(t + 1) = (1 - a)\sigma(t) = (1 - a)^t \sigma(1)$.

Exercise 6.9 Suppose the spot interest rate is governed by stochastic difference equation (6.20) with the volatility function of the form $\sigma(t, r) = \sqrt{r}\, \sigma(t)$ for some positive function σ on $\mathbb{R}$. Under what restrictions on μ and σ will this formulation be compatible with:

(a)   a binomial lattice?
(b)   a trinomial lattice?

6.3   Yield Curve Models

In the preceding two sections, the construction of term structure models emphasized the role of the spot interest rate process $r = \{r_t; t \geq 1\}$. The idea was to first specify the probability space and the filtration, to then specify the process r (usually it is taken to be a Markov chain), and to finally use equations like (6.2) to specify the zero coupon bond processes. This is an easy approach to implement, providing a variety of arbitrage-free term structure models. However, this approach has a disadvantage: it is difficult to model the behavior of yields and zero coupon bond prices at different maturities. For example, the model builder may be concerned with the volatility of the zero coupon bond that matures in period 10. Or the model builder may be particularly interested in the spread between short and long term interest rates. Features like these cannot be modeled explicitly with the spot interest rate approach.

An alternative approach, called the *yield curve* or *whole yield* approach, is to build the model by regarding the whole term structure as the state of a stochastic process. After specifying the probability space and the filtration submodel of the information flow, you directly specify how the whole term structure evolves in time. This can be done by working with either the term structure of yields, the term structure of zero coupon bond prices, or the term structure of forward spot rates. Whatever the choice, after one term structure process is specified, the other two as well as the spot interest rate processes follow from the equations in section 6.1. Moreover, the term structure process is usually taken to be a Markov chain, and one can work with either the real-world or the risk neutral probability measure.

A disadvantage of the yield curve approach is that worrying about arbitrage opportunities can make its development and implementation more difficult than with the spot interest rate approach. Combining equations (6.3) and (6.4) gives

(6.22) $$Z_s^\tau = Z_s^{s+1} E_Q[Z_{s+1}^\tau | \mathscr{F}_s], \ 0 \leqslant s < \tau \leqslant T$$

For the absence of arbitrage opportunities, it is necessary and sufficient that there exists a probability measure Q (the risk neutral probability measure) such that this equation is satisfied for all indicated s and τ. But as illustrated in the following example, an arbitrary selection of the term structure process may not satisfy (6.22) for any probability measure.

Example 6.6   Suppose $T = 3$, $K = 8$, and the information submodel is a binomial tree (but not a lattice). The time 0 zero coupon bond prices are taken to be $Z_0^1 = 0.95$, $Z_0^2 = 0.90$, and $Z_0^3 = 0.85$. In the case of an "up" move, the time 1 discount bond prices are taken to be $Z_1^2 = 0.94$ and $Z_1^3 = 0.89$, whereas in the case of a "down" move the time 1 discount bond prices are taken to be $Z_1^2 = 0.96$ and $Z_1^3 = 0.91$. Let q denote the risk neutral conditional probability of an "up" move between times 0 and 1. Equation (6.22) for $\tau = 2$ implies $q = 0.6316$, whereas equation (6.22) for $\tau = 3$ implies $q = 0.7632$. But there is no probability measure Q under which (6.22) is satisfied for both $\tau = 2$ and $\tau = 3$. Hence there must exist an arbitrage opportunity.

To produce an arbitrage opportunity, let H_i denote the units purchased at time 0 of the zero coupon bond that matures after i periods, $i = 1, 2$, and 3. The initial cost of this portfolio is $V_0 = 0.95H_1 + 0.9 H_2 + 0.85H_3$; for an arbitrage opportunity we want $V_0 = 0$, implying, for instance, $H_2 = -(19/18) H_1 - (17/18) H_3$. After an up move the time 1 value of the portfolio will be

$$V_1 = H_1 + 0.94 \, H_2 + 0.89 \, H_3 = 0.0078 \, H_1 + 0.0022 \, H_3$$

whereas after a down move the value will be

$$V_1 = H_1 + 0.96 \, H_2 + 0.91 \, H_3 = -0.0133 \, H_1 + 0.0033 \, H_3$$

Thus any trading strategy which makes the right hand sides of both values of V_1 strictly positive will be an arbitrage opportunity. For instance, one could take $H_1 = 0$ and $H_3 = 18$, in which case $H_2 = -17$.

The problem illustrated by example 6.6 was that the model was over-specified, making it impossible for (6.22) to be satisfied. To circumvent this difficulty, the trick is to specify just enough of the risk neutral probability measure Q and the term structure process values so that (6.22) (or one of its equivalents) can be used to uniquely specify the balance of the model This will be illustrated by working with a binary tree submodel of the information, where the risk neutral conditional probability of an "up" move from a node will always be denoted by q (the actual value can possibly vary from one node to another). The objective here is to explain how to achieve a satisfactory specification of the term structure process of zero coupon bond prices. Later, an alternative, more efficient approach will be presented, where the constructed process is the term structure of forward spot rates.

Suppose the term structure $\{Z_s^{s+1}, Z_s^{s+2}, \dots, Z_s^T\}$ of zero coupon bond prices at a time s node of the information tree has been specified. This can be any collection of $T - s$ numbers satisfying $1 > Z_s^{s+1} > Z_s^{s+2} > \dots > Z_s^T > 0$. The objective, to be carried out in two steps, is to specify the time $S + 1$ values of these zero coupon bond prices at the two "downstream" nodes. This two-step process can be replicated at the other nodes in the information tree, thereby completing the specification of the term structure process.

The first step is to set the time $s + 1$ zero coupon bond prices in the event of an up move. These will be $T - s - 1$ arbitrary numbers denoted $Z_{s+1}^{s+2}(u)\ Z_{s+1}^{s+3}(u) \dots Z_{s+1}^T(u)$ and satisfying

$$(6.23) \qquad 1 > Z_{s+1}^{s+2}(u) > Z_{s+1}^{s+3}(u) > \dots > Z_{s+1}^T(u) > 0$$

It is here that the model builder can incorporate desirable features, such as the manner in which the term structure shifts from one time period to the next

The second and final step is to use equation (6.22) to specify the $T - s - 1$ zero coupon bond prices, denoted $Z_{s+1}^{s+2}(d),\ Z_{s+1}^{s+3}(d), \dots Z_{s+1}^T(d)$, in the event of a "down" move. Solving for $Z_{s+1}^T(d)$, (6.22) gives

$$(6.24) \qquad Z_{s+1}^T(d) = \frac{Z_s^T / Z_s^{s+1} - q Z_{s+1}^T(u)}{1 - q}, \quad \tau = s + 2, \dots, T$$

Hence this completes the specification of the term structure process at the two downstream nodes, except for one possible problem: there is no guarantee that the term structure of zero coupon bond prices will be "legitimate," satisfying the inequalities

$$(6.25) \qquad 1 > Z_{s+1}^{s+2}(d) > Z_{s+1}^{s+3}(d) > \dots > Z_{s+1}^T(d) > 0$$

In view of (6.24), it is not sufficient for the zero prices after an up move to merely satisfy the inequalities in (6.23); they must satisfy some additional constraints.

Equation (6.24) says that $Z_{s+1}^T(d) > 0$ if and only if

$$(6.26) \qquad Z_{s+1}^T(u) < \frac{Z_s^T}{q Z_s^{s+1}}$$

This is easy to satisfy, since the right hand side is sure to be strictly positive.

Equation (6.24) says that $1 > Z_{s+1}^{s+2}(d)$ if and only if

(6.27)
$$Z_{s+1}^{s+2}(u) > \frac{Z_s^{s+2}}{qZ_s^{s+1}} - \frac{1-q}{q}$$

This also is easy to satisfy, since an easy computation shows that the right hand side is sure to be strictly less than one.

Finally, the remaining inequalities in (6.25) are

$$Z_{s+1}^{\tau}(d) > Z_{s+1}^{\tau+1}(d), \quad \tau = s+2, \ldots, T-1$$

Equation (6.24) says that these inequalities are satisfied if and only if

(6.28)
$$Z_{s+1}^{\tau}(u) - Z_{s+1}^{\tau+1}(u) < \frac{Z_s^{\tau} - Z_s^{\tau+1}}{qZ_s^{s+1}}, \quad \tau = s+2, \ldots, T-1$$

Given arbitrary values of $q, Z_s^{s+1}, \ldots,$ and Z_s^T with $q \in (0, 1)$ and $1 > Z_s^{s+1} > \ldots > Z_s^T > 0$, it is possible to choose $Z_{s+1}^{s+2}(u), \ldots, Z_{s+1}^T(u)$ so as to satisfy (6.28) as well as (6.23), (6.26), and (6.27) (see exercise 6.10). Similarly, given arbitrary values of $Z_s^{s+1}, \ldots,$ and Z_s^T with $1 > Z_s^{s+1} > \ldots > Z_s^T > 0$ and arbitrary values of $Z_{s+1}^{s+2}(u), \ldots, Z_{s+1}^T(u)$ satisfying (6.23), it is possible to choose q close enough to 0 so that (6.28) will be satisfied. Hence with a little bit of flexibility, it is always possible to specify legitimate term structures of zero coupon bond prices at both downstream nodes. Moreover, since equation (6.22) was utilized, the absence of arbitrage opportunities is ensured.

Example 6.7   Suppose $Z_s^{s+1} = \delta^i$ and $Z_{s+1}^{s+1+i}(u) = \theta^i$ for $i = 1, 2, \ldots$ and two numbers $\delta, \theta \in (0, 1)$. The numbers δ and T are fixed; there is some flexibility in the choice of q and θ. Inequality (6.26) is the same as

(6.29)
$$q \, \theta^{T-s-1} < \delta^{T-s-1}$$

whereas inequality (6.27) is the same as

(6.30)
$$1 - q + q\,\theta > \delta$$

Moreover, the inequalities in (6.28) are the same as

(6.31)
$$q(1 - \theta)\theta^{\tau-s-1} < (1 - \delta)\delta^{\tau-s-1}, \quad \tau = s+2, \ldots, T-1$$

Now suppose $\theta = \delta + \varepsilon$ for some $\varepsilon > 0$. Inequality (6.29) will be true provided $q < (\delta/\theta)^{T-s-1}$, so reasonable values of q can be accommodated if ε is small enough. Inequality (6.30) is automatically true, because $1 - q + q\theta > 1 - q + q\delta > (1 - q)\delta + q\delta > \delta$. Inequality (6.31) is true for all $\tau \leqslant T - 1$ if and only if it is true for $\tau = T - 1$, so our final requirement on q and ε is

$$q < \frac{(1 - \delta)}{(1 - \delta - \varepsilon)} \left(\frac{\delta}{\delta + \varepsilon} \right)^{T-s-2}$$

a requirement that is usually easy to achieve with reasonable values of q and ε.'

Constructing the term structures of zero coupon bond prices at each node of a binary tree can be tricky, because you need to worry about constraints of the form (6.25). It is often easier to work with term structures of forward spot rates, because instead of constraints like (6.25) you only need to make sure the forward spot rates at each node are positive (of course, in both cases you must also worry about the no-arbitrage conditions).

To see how to construct a forward spot rate yield curve model, suppose a term structure $\{f(s,s),\ldots,f(s,T-1)\}$ of (non-negative) forward spot rates has been specified at a time s node of the binary information tree. Let q be the conditional risk neutral probability of an "up" move to the time $(s+1)$ node where the term structure $\{f_u(s+1,s+1),\ldots,f_u(s+1,T-1)\}$ has also been specified. The objective is to use the no-arbitrage conditions to produce the term structure $\{f_d(s+1,s+1),\ldots,f_d(s+1,T-1)\}$ at the time $(s+1)$ "down" node.

Using equation (6.9) to substitute for Z in equation (6.22), one obtains the no-arbitrage condition

$$(6.32) \quad \prod_{t=s+2}^{\tau} [1+f(s,t-1)]^{-1}$$

$$= E_Q \left[\prod_{t=s+2}^{\tau} [1+f(s+1,t-1)]^{-1} \Big| \mathscr{F}_s \right], \quad \tau = s+2,\ldots,T$$

We can use these $T-s-1$ equations to solve for the $T-s-1$ variables $f_d(s+1,s+1),\ldots,f_d(s+1,T-1)$. Denote $g(s,t) \equiv [1+f(s,t)]^{-1}$, $g_u(s,t) \equiv [1+f_u(s,t)]^{-1}$, and $g_d(s,t) \equiv [1+f_d(s,t)]^{-1}$. Then (6.32) can be rewritten as

$$\prod_{t=s+2}^{\tau} g(s,t-1) = q \prod_{t=s+2}^{\tau} g_u(s+1,t-1) + (1-q) \prod_{t=s+2}^{\tau} g_d(s+1,t-1)$$

in which case

$$(6.33) \quad g_d(s+1,\tau-1)$$

$$= \frac{\displaystyle\prod_{t=s+2}^{\tau} g(s,t-1) - q \prod_{t=s+2}^{\tau} g_u(s+1,t-1)}{\displaystyle(1-q) \prod_{t=s+2}^{\tau} g_d(s+1,t-1)}, \quad \tau = s+2,\ldots,T$$

Hence the g_d's can be computed recursively, starting with $\tau = s+2$ (the denominator is just $1-q$ in this case), then $\tau = s+3$, and so forth. Given arbitrary values of q, the f's, and the f_u's, there is no guarantee that all the f_d's will turn out positive. However, given arbitrary values of the f's and some flexibility in the choice of q and the f_u's, it is always possible to obtain non-negative f_d's.

Exercise 6.10   Verify the statement made just after (6.28): given arbitrary values of q, $Z_s^{s+1}, \ldots,$ and Z_s^T with $q \in (0,1)$ and $1 > Z_s^{s+1} > \ldots > Z_s^T > 0$, it is possible to choose $Z_{s+1}^{s+2}(u), \ldots, Z_{s+1}^T$ so as to satisfy (6.28) as well as (6.23), (6.26), and (6.27).

Exercise 6.11   In example 6.7, suppose $s = 0$, $\delta = 0.95$, and $T = 8$. What values of $\theta > 0.95$ are admissible if $q = 0.5$? What values of q are admissible if $\theta = 0.96$? Compute $Z_1^\tau(d)$, $\tau = 2, \ldots, T$, for the case where $q = 0.5$ and $\theta = 0.96$.

Exercise 6.12   Suppose $s = 0$, $q = 0.5$, $T = 5$, $f(0,0) = 0.05$, $f(0,1) = 0.06$, $f(0,2) = 0.07$, $f(0,3) = 0.06$, and $f(0,4) = 0.05$. Moreover, suppose $f_u(1,t) = f(0,t) + 0.01$ for all $t \geqslant 1$. Use (6.33) to verify that $f_d(1,1) = 0.0502$, $f_d(1,2) = 0.0603$, $f_d(1,3) = 0.0505$, and $f_d(1,4) = 0.0407$.

Exercise 6.13   Suppose positive values of $f(s,s), \ldots, f(s, T-1)$ are fixed. For the cases listed below, explain whether it is always possible to produce positive values of $f_d(s+1, s+1), \ldots, f_d(s+1, T-1)$ satisfying (6.33). If yes, give a proof. If no, give a counter-example.

(a) $q \in (0,1)$ and positive values of $f_u(s+1, s+1), \ldots, f_u(s+1, T-1)$ are all fixed, arbitrary numbers.

(b) $q \in (0,1)$ is a fixed number, but there is flexibility in the choice of the positive numbers $f_u(s+1, s+1), \ldots, f_u(s+1, T-1)$.

(c)   The positive numbers $f_u(s+1, s+1), \ldots, f_u(s+1, T-1)$ are fixed, but there is flexibility in the choice of $q \in (0,1)$.

6.4   Forward Risk Adjusted Probability Measures

In order to facilitate computations for interest rate derivatives. this section will introduce and describe the properties of a new probability measure. In particular, a new and quite useful formula will be developed for the price of a contingent claim. First, however, are some preliminary results from probability theory.

Throughout this section fix the time $\tau \leqslant T$ and consider a strictly positive random variable $M_\tau \in \mathscr{F}_\tau$ satisfying $E_Q[M_\tau] = 1$. For the time being, Q here is an arbitrary probability measure, although shortly we shall take Q to be the risk neutral probability measure.

Define a new probability measure, denoted P_τ, by setting

$$P_\tau(\omega) \equiv M_\tau(\omega) Q(\omega), \text{ all } \omega \in \Omega$$

Note that P_τ is indeed a legitimate probability measure, because $P_\tau(\omega) > 0$ for all ω and the assumption $E_Q[M_\tau] = 1$ implies $P_\tau(\Omega) = 1$. Let E_τ denote the expectation operator corresponding to P_τ.

Next, define a martingale $M = \{M_t; t = 0, \ldots, \tau\}$ by setting

$$M_t \equiv E_Q[M_\tau | \mathscr{F}_t], \ t = 0, 1, \ldots, \tau.$$

Notice that $M_0 = E_Q[M_\tau] = 1$ and that M is a martingale with respect to Q but not necessarily with respect to P_τ. This martingale plays a role in the following technical result, which relates conditional expectation under the two probability measures.

(6.34)   If X is a random variable, then $E_\tau[M_t X|\mathcal{F}_t] = E_Q[M_\tau X|\mathcal{F}_t]$ for $t = 0, 1, \ldots, \tau$.

Clearly (6.34) is true for $X \in \mathcal{F}_t$, for then the equation is simply $M_t X = X E_Q[M_\tau|\mathcal{F}_t]$. It is also easily seen to be true for $t = 0$, for then $M_0 = 1$ and we have

$$E_\tau[X] = \sum_\omega X(\omega) P_\tau(\omega) = \sum_\omega X(\omega) M_\tau(\omega) Q(\omega) = E_Q[M_\tau X]$$

For the general case, it suffices to consider arbitrary $A \in \mathcal{P}_t$, an event in the partition of Ω corresponding to $\mathcal{F}_t$, and show that

(6.35) $$E_\tau[M_t X|A] = E_Q[M_\tau X|A]$$

For the left hand side we have

$$E_\tau[M_t X|A] = \frac{\sum_{\omega \in A} X(\omega) M_t(\omega) P_\tau(\omega)}{\sum_{\omega \in A} P_\tau(\omega)} = \frac{\sum_{\omega \in A} X(\omega) M_t(\omega) M_\tau(\omega) Q(\omega)}{\sum_{\omega \in A} M_\tau(\omega) Q(\omega)}$$

But M_t is constant on A and given by

$$M_t(\omega) = E_Q[M_t|A] = \sum_{\hat{\omega} \in A} M_\tau(\hat{\omega}) Q(\hat{\omega})/Q(A), \text{ all } \omega \in A$$

so substituting this in the expression for $E_\tau[M_t X|A]$ yields

$$E_\tau[M_t X|A] = \frac{\sum_{\omega \in A} X(\omega) M_\tau(\omega) Q(\omega)}{Q(A)} = E_Q[M_\tau X|A]$$

This completes the verification of (6.35) and thus (6.34).

We are now in a position to explain a fundamental relationship in probability theory:

(6.36)   The stochastic process $YM = \{Y_t M_t; t = 0, \ldots, \tau\}$ is a martingale under Q if and only if the stochastic process $Y = \{Y_t; t = 0, \ldots, \tau\}$ is a martingale under P_τ.

To see this, note that YM is a martingale under Q if and only if $Y_t M_t = E_Q[Y_\tau M_\tau|\mathcal{F}_t]$ for all t. Now using (6.34) with $X = Y_\tau$, we see the latter is true if and only if $Y_t M_t = E_\tau[M_t Y_\tau|\mathcal{F}_t]$ for all t. But $E_\tau[M_t Y_\tau|\mathcal{F}_t] = M_t E_\tau[Y_\tau|\mathcal{F}_t]$, so the latter is the same as $Y_t = E_\tau[Y_\tau|\mathcal{F}_t]$ for all t, that is, Y is a martingale under P_τ.

With these preliminaries out of the way, we are ready to return to our term structure model. Let the stochastic process $\pi = \{\pi_t : 0 \leqslant t \leqslant s\}$ represent the price of an asset such as a stock, a zero coupon bond, or a contingent claim, where $\tau \leqslant s \leqslant T$. Set $Y_t = \pi_t/Z_t^\tau$ and recall from principle (4.22) that Y_t

represents the time-t *forward price* for delivery of the asset at time τ. Using our standard notation for forward prices, we therefore will sometimes write O_t for $Y_t = \pi_t / Z_t^\tau$.

Next, let Q be the risk neutral probability measure and set $M_\tau = [B_\tau Z_0^\tau]^{-1}$. Note that $M_\tau(\omega) > 0$ and $E_Q[M_\tau] = (1/Z_0^\tau) E_Q[1/B_\tau] = 1$ (because $Z_0^\tau = E_Q[1/B_\tau]$). Hence we can proceed as above and define the Q-martingale

$$M_t = E_Q[M_\tau | \mathscr{F}_t] = \frac{1}{Z_0^\tau} E_Q[1/B_\tau | \mathscr{F}_t] = \frac{Z_t^\tau}{Z_0^\tau B_t}$$

where the last equality follows from the risk neutral formula (6.1) for Z_t^τ. We also define the *forward risk adjusted probability measure* (also called the τ *forward probability measure*):

$$P_\tau(\omega) = M_\tau(\omega) Q(\omega) = \frac{Q(\omega)}{Z_0^\tau B_\tau(\omega)}$$

Now observe that $Y_t M_t = O_t M_t = (\pi_t / Z_t^\tau)(Z_t^\tau / [Z_0^\tau B_t]) = \pi_t / [Z_0^\tau B_t]$, so the process YM represents the discounted price of the asset divided by the constant Z_0^τ. This is a martingale under the risk neutral probability measure Q, so by (6.36) we have the following important result:

(**6.37**)   Under the forward risk adjusted probability measure P_τ, the time-t forward price O_t for delivery of an asset at time τ is a martingale.

Principle (6.37) is important because it leads to a new and useful formula for the price of a derivative security. Let $\pi_\tau \in \mathscr{F}_\tau$ be the time $-\tau$ price of a security; for instance, π_τ is the time $-\tau$ payoff of a contingent claim. But the time $-\tau$ forward price O_τ for time $-\tau$ delivery of this security is $O_\tau = \pi_\tau$, so (6.37) implies

$$O_t = \pi_t / Z_t^\tau = E_\tau[O_\tau | \mathscr{F}_t] = E_\tau[\pi_\tau | \mathscr{F}_t], \quad t \leqslant \tau$$

Multiplying through by Z_t^τ yields the following:

(**6.38**)   If π_t is the time-t price of a security, then

$$\pi_t = Z_t^\tau E_\tau[\pi_\tau | \mathscr{F}_t], \quad t \leqslant \tau$$

The traditional risk neutral formula $\pi_t = B_t E_Q[\pi_\tau / B_\tau | \mathscr{F}_t]$ is convenient when the spot interest rate is constant or deterministic, for then the time$-\tau$ value B_τ of the bank account process is deterministic and this formula simplifies to $\pi_t = (B_t / B_\tau) E_Q[\pi_\tau | \mathscr{F}_t]$. Hence for derivative pricing all you need is the conditional distribution of π_τ under the risk neutral probability measure. But for interest rate models and other situations where the spot interest rate r is stochastic, the bank account value B_τ does not factor outside the conditional expectation, and so to apply the traditional formula you need the conditional *joint* distribution of (π_τ, B_τ) under the risk neutral probability measure. In practice, this may be difficult to obtain. On the other hand, even with stochastic interest rates, to apply the formula in (6.38), all you need is the conditional distribution of π_τ under the forward risk adjusted probability measure corresponding to time$-\tau$.

Example 6.1 (continued) For $\tau = 3$ we first compute $M_3(\omega) = [Z_0^3 B_3(\omega)]^{-1} = [0.844\{1 + r_1(\omega)\}\{1 + r_2(\omega)\{1 + r_3(\omega)\}]^{-1}$. Then using the risk neutral probabilities we compute the forward risk adjusted probability measure $P_3(\omega) = M_3(\omega)Q(\omega)$. These numbers are given below, along with the earlier values of the martingale M, which are computed using $M_t = E_Q[M_3|\mathscr{F}_t]$.

ω	B_3	M_0	M_1	M_2	M_3	P_3
ω_1	1.2709	1.0	0.939	0.9323	0.9323	0.1714
ω_2	1.2478	1.0	0.939	0.9495	0.9495	0.1102
ω_3	1.2023	1.0	0.995	0.9855	0.9855	0.1495
ω_4	1.1798	1.0	0.995	1.0043	1.0043	0.1489
ω_5	1.1355	1.0	1.051	1.0434	1.0434	0.2694
ω_6	1.1136	1.0	1.051	1.0640	1.0640	0.1509

To illustrate the application of formula (6.38), consider the contingent claim X with time-3 payoff $X(\omega_i) = i, i = 1, \ldots, 6$. The computation of π_2 is easy, because $\pi_2 = Z_2^3 E_3[X|\mathscr{F}_2] = Z_2^3 X$. Thus $\pi_2(\omega_6) = Z_2^3(\omega_6)X(\omega_6) = 0.9804(6) = 5.8824$, and similarly $\pi_2(\omega_i) = 0.9091, 1.8518, 2.8038, 3.8096$ and 4.8075 for $i = 1, \ldots, 5$, respectively.

For $\pi_1 = Z_1^3 E_3[X|\mathscr{F}_1]$ we need the conditional probability distribution, but this is easily computed from P_3. For example,

$$E_3[X|\{\omega_1, \omega_2\}] = 1 P_3(\omega = \omega_1|\{\omega_1, \omega_2\}) + 2 P_3(\omega = \omega_2|\{\omega_1, \omega_2\})$$
$$= \frac{P_3(\omega_1)}{P_3(\omega_1) + P_3(\omega_2)} + 2 \frac{P_3(\omega_2)}{P_3(\omega_1) + P_3(\omega_2)}$$
$$= 0.6087 + 2(0.3913) = 1.3913$$

so $\pi_1(\omega_1) = \pi_1(\omega_2) = Z_1^3(\omega_1)E_3[X|\{\omega_1, \omega_2\}] = 0.84(1.3913) = 1.1687$. Similarly, $\pi_1(\omega_3) = \pi_1(\omega_4) = 3.1141$ and $\pi_1(\omega_5) = \pi_1(\omega_6) = 5.0375$.

To complete the computation of the process π, we have $\pi_0 = Z_0^3 E_3[X|\mathscr{F}_0] = 0.844 E_3[X]$, so we simply use the probability measure P_3 itself and compute $\pi_0 = 3.113$.

Finally, using $O_t = \pi_t/Z_t^3$ we immediately have the forward price process: $O_0 = 3.6884$, $O_1(\omega_1) = O_1(\omega_2) = 1.3913$, $O_1(\omega_3) = O_1(\omega_4) = 3.4990$, $O_1(\omega_5) = O_1(\omega_6) = 5.3590$, and $O_2(\omega_i) = O_3(\omega_i) = i$ for $i = 1, \ldots, 6$. Using $o_t = E_3[o_3|\mathscr{F}_t]$ and the conditional probabilities corresponding to P_3, it is straightforward to verify that the process O is indeed a martingale under P_3.

Example 6.2 (continued) In order to prepare for the computation of some derivatives having known time-2 payoffs, we are interested in the corresponding forward risk adjusted probability measure P_2. With $M_2 = [Z_0^2 B_2]^{-1} = [0.8905(1 + r_1)(1 + r_2)]^{-1}$ and $Q(\omega) = 1/6$ for all ω, the quantities of interest are:

ω	B_2	M_2	P_2
ω_1	1.1554	0.9719	0.1620
ω_2	1.1554	0.9719	0.1620
ω_3	1.1236	0.9994	0.1666
ω_4	1.1236	0.9994	0.1666
ω_5	1.0918	1.0285	0.1714
ω_6	1.0918	1.0285	0.1714

Computing forward risk adjusted probability measures for lattice-type interest rate models is not much easier than it is for general models. This is because although the spot interest rate process r is a path-independent Markov chain, with each node of the lattice corresponding to a value of the spot rate at a point in time, the bank account process B is not path-independent. The different paths leading up to a node will correspond to different sequences of spot rates and thus to different bank account values. In general, for a binomial lattice, B_t will take one of 2^{t-1} values, whereas there will only be $t + 1$ nodes for time t. Hence when computing the forward risk adjusted probability measure, the lattice loses most of its simplifying advantages. The computations required for a lattice model are not much easier than for a general model having about the same number of states ω. In particular, there are no simple formulas for the forward risk adjusted probability measures associated with the binomial lattice models of section 6.2.

Exercise 6.14   For example 6.1, verify with detailed calculations that:

(a) M is a martingale under Q with $E_Q[M_3] = 1$.
(b)   The computed price process π satisfies (6.38) for all t and ω.
(c)   The computed price process π satisfies the traditional risk neutral valuation formula for all t and ω.
(d)   The computed forward price process O is a martingale under P_3.

Exercise 6.15   For example 6.1, suppose a derivative security has time-3 price $\pi_3(\omega_i) = \max \{i - 3, 0\}, i = 1, \ldots, 6$. Compute the time-0 price π_0.

Exercise 6.16   For example 6.2, suppose there is an asset with time-2 prices $\pi_2(\omega_1) = \pi_2(\omega_2) = 7$, $\pi_2(\omega_3) = \pi_2(\omega_4) = 9$, and $\pi_2(\omega_5) = \pi_2(\omega_6) = -1$. Show that $\pi_0 = 4.3848$, and compute π_1.

Exercise 6.17   For example 6.2, specify the Q-martingale M and the forward risk adjusted probability measure P_3 corresponding to $\tau = 3$.

Exercise 6.18   With the process M as in (6.36), show that the process $X = \{X_t; t = 0, \ldots, \tau\}$ is a martingale under P_τ, where $X_t(\omega) = 1/M_t(\omega)$, all ω and t.

Exercise 6.19   If $X = 1_A$ is the time$-\tau$ payoff of a contingent claim, where $A \in \mathscr{F}_\tau$, then show its time-0 price is $\pi_0 = Z_0^\tau P_\tau(A)$.

6.5 Coupon Bonds and Bond Options

Consider a European call option on the zero coupon bond Z^s having time-τ payoff:

$$X = (Z^s_\tau - K)^+, \quad 0 \leqslant \tau < s \leqslant T$$

Our aim is to compute the time-t price π_t of X for $t < \tau$. Using (6.38), this is given by

(6.39) $$\pi_t = Z^\tau_t E_\tau[(Z^s_\tau - K)^+ \mid \mathcal{F}_t], \quad t \leqslant \tau$$

where E_τ denotes expectation with respect to the forward risk adjusted probability measure P_τ. Hence we first need the conditional probability distribution of Z^s_τ under P_τ, and then we can compute the conditional expectation.

Alternatively, of course, we can use the customary risk neutral valuation formula:

(6.40) $$\pi_t = B_t E_Q[(Z^s_\tau - K)^+ / B_\tau \mid \mathcal{F}_t], \quad t \leqslant \tau$$

The specific circumstances will dictate which approach will be the easiest from the computational standpoint.

> **Example 6.2 (continued)** For a general model such as this, the forward risk adjusted approach is often the best, especially if one is planning to value more than one derivative having the same payoff time. Suppose $K = 0.95$, $t = 0$, $\tau = 2$, and $s = 3$. Then (6.39) gives
>
> $$\pi_0 = 0.8905 E_2[(Z^3_2 - 0.95)^+]$$
> $$= 0.8905\{0.1666(0.0024) + 0.1714(0.0115) + 0.1714(0.0304)\}$$
> $$= 0.0068$$
>
> Alternatively, using (6.40) we have
>
> $$\pi_0 = E_Q[(Z^3_2 - 0.95)^+ / B_2]$$
> $$= 0.1667(0.0024)/1.1236 + 0.1667(0.0115)/1.0918$$
> $$+ 0.1667(0.0304)/1.0918$$
> $$= 0.0068$$

It was remarked at the end of section 6.4 that lattice models of interest rates offer no simple formulas for forward risk adjusted probability measures because the bank account process is path dependent. For the same reason, the same remark holds true in regard to the use of the risk neutral formula (6.40): there are no simple formulas for the price of contingent claims such as our call option on a bond when the underlying model is a lattice model as in section 6.2.

A coupon bond is just a linear combination of zero coupon bonds. To see this, suppose a coupon bond is scheduled to pay C_n dollars at time t_n for $n = 1, \ldots, N$, where $t < t_1 < \ldots < t_N$. By either the risk neutral valuation formula (6.1) or the forward risk adjusted formula (6.38), the time-t price of the contingent claim which pays C_n at time t_n is precisely $Z_t^{t_n} C_n$. Moreover, the price of the cash flow is just the sum of the price of each component, so with β_t denoting the time-t price of this bond, we have

$$\beta_t = \sum_{n=1}^{N} Z_t^{t_n} C_n$$

In words, the price of the coupon bond is equal to the expected discounted value of the cash flow, where expectation is with respect to the risk neutral probability measure.

Example 6.1 (continued)   Suppose $C_1 = 7$, $t_1 = 2$, $C_2 = 107$, and $t_2 = 3$. Then $\beta_0 = 7Z_0^2 + 107Z_0^3 = 96.559$ and

$$\beta_1(\omega) = 7Z_1^2 + 107Z_1^3 = \begin{cases} 96.302, & \omega = \omega_1, \omega_2 \\ 101.834, & \omega = \omega_3, \omega_4 \\ 107.376, & \omega = \omega_5, \omega_6 \end{cases}$$

Now suppose we have a European call option on this coupon bond. The time-τ payoff, where $t < \tau < t_1$, is, as usual, $X = (\beta_\tau - K)^+$. For the time-t price, we can use (6.1), giving

$$(6.41) \qquad \pi_t = B_t E_Q\left[\left(\sum_{n=1}^{N} Z_\tau^{t_n} C_n - K\right)^+ / B_\tau | \mathscr{F}_t\right]$$

Or we can use (6.38), giving

$$(6.42) \qquad \pi_t = Z_t^\tau E_\tau\left[\left(\sum_{n=1}^{N} Z_\tau^{t_n} C_n - K\right)^+ | \mathscr{F}_t\right]$$

There are rarely any computational shortcuts with either the forward risk adjusted or the risk neutral approach.

Example 6.1 (continued) Suppose we have a call option on the coupon bond with exercise price $K = 100$ and exercise date $\tau = 1$. Equation (6.41) gives for the time-0 price

$$\pi_0 = (0.1517 + 0.1483)(1.834/1.06) + (0.2582 + 0.1418)(7.376/1.06)$$
$$= 3.3025$$

Exercise 6.20   Let c and p denote the time-0 prices of a European call and a put, respectively, both having the same exercise date τ, the same exercise price K, and the same underlying, namely, a zero coupon bond with maturity date $s > t$. Show that the following put-call parity relationship holds: $c - p = Z_0^s - KZ_0^\tau$. Compute p in the case of example 6.2 when $K = 0.95$, $\tau = 2$, and $s = 3$. Verify the put-call parity relationship for this particular put and the corresponding call.

Exercise 6.21 For example 6.1, compute the time 0 prices of the European put and call having exercise price $K = 0.95$, exercise date $\tau = 2$, and underlying Z^3. Verify the corresponding put-call parity relationship.

Exercise 6.22 For example 6.2, compute the time-0 and time-1 prices of the coupon bond which pays 8 dollars at time 2 and 108 dollars at time 3. Compute the time-0 prices of the European put and call on this bond, where the exercise price is $K = 102$ and the exercise date is $\tau = 1$.

6.6 Swaps and Swaptions

Swaps are agreements between two parties where the first pays a floating rate to the second, while the second pays a fixed rate to the first, with both payments being based on a common principal amount. The payments are made each period during an interval of time. The floating rate payment is based on the spot rate r, with the value actually used being either the one for the period just ended (the swap is *settled in arrears*) or the one for the period about to begin (the swap is *settled in advance*).

With ordinary swaps the initial floating rate payment is based on the spot rate when the agreement is made; this is true whether it is settled in arrears or in advance. There are also *forward start* swaps where the initial payments are based on a spot rate that is subsequent to the one which exists when the agreement is reached.

The value of a swap is just the expected present value of the net cash flow, so the value to one party is the negative of the value to the opposite party. With a *payer* swap the value is from the perspective of the party who pays the fixed rate and receives the floating rate. A *receiver* swap is the opposite.

This section will focus on a payer forward start swap on principal 1 settled each period in arrears, leaving other cases for the reader. The fixed interest rate is denoted K. With the initial floating rate payment based on r_τ, the party will pay K dollars and receive r_τ dollars at time τ. Similar payments will occur each period through time-s, so the time-t value of this payer forward start swap is

$$(6.43) \qquad r_t = E_Q\left[\sum_{u=\tau}^{s} \frac{B_t}{B_u}(r_u - K)\Big|\mathcal{F}_t\right], \qquad t < \tau \leqslant s \leqslant T$$

It turns out there is a simple and useful formula for π_t. Since $Z_{u-1}^u = (1 + r_u)^{-1}$, this value equals

$$\pi_t = E_Q \left[\sum_{u=\tau}^{s} \frac{B_t}{B_u} \left(\frac{1}{Z_{u-1}^u} - (1+K) \right) \Big| \mathscr{F}_t \right]$$

$$= E_Q \left[\sum_{u=\tau}^{s} \left(\frac{B_t}{B_u Z_{u-1}^u} \right) \Big| \mathscr{F}_t \right] - (1+K) E_Q \left[\sum_{u=\tau}^{s} \frac{B_t}{B_u} \Big| \mathscr{F}_t \right]$$

$$= \sum_{u=\tau}^{s} E_Q \left[\frac{B_t}{B_u Z_{u-1}^u} \Big| \mathscr{F}_t \right] - (1+K) \sum_{u=\tau}^{s} Z_t^u$$

where the last equality uses equation (6.2). Now using $Z_{u-1}^u = (1+r_u)^{-1} = B_{u-1}/B_u$ again, one obtains

$$\pi_t = \sum_{u=\tau}^{s} E_Q \left[\frac{B_t}{B_{u-1}} \Big| \mathscr{F}_t \right] - (1+K) \sum_{u=\tau}^{s} Z_t^u$$

$$= \sum_{u=\tau}^{s} Z_t^{u-1} - (1+K) \sum_{u=\tau}^{s} Z_t^u$$

$$= Z_t^{\tau-1} - K \sum_{u=\tau}^{s-1} Z_t^u - (1+K) Z_t^s$$

$$= Z_t^{\tau-1} - \sum_{u=\tau}^{s} C_u Z_t^u$$

where the cash flow variables $C_u = K$ for $u = \tau, \ldots, s-1$ and $C_s = 1 + K$ have been introduced. Thus the price of the forward swap is given by a simple present value calculation. In particular, in the case of an ordinary swap, for which $\tau = t + 1$, the time-t price is

(6.44)
$$\pi_t = 1 - \sum_{u=t+1}^{s} C_u Z_t^u$$

This should be interpreted as one minus the time-t price of a coupon paying bond, a bond having face value one and coupon rate K.

The *forward swap rate* κ is that value of the fixed rate K which makes the time-t value of the forward swap zero, that is,

$$\kappa = \kappa(t, \tau, s) \equiv \frac{Z_t^{\tau-1} - Z_t^s}{Z_t^\tau + \ldots + Z_t^s}$$

The (ordinary) *swap rate* is simply the special case when $\tau = t + 1$, that is, $\kappa(t, t+1, s)$

Example 6.1 (continued) With $K = 0.06$, $t = 0$, $\tau = 1$, and $s = 3$, the time-0 price of the payer swap is

$$\pi_0 = Z_0^0 - KZ_0^1 - KZ_0^2 - (1+K)Z_0^3$$
$$= 1 - 0.06(0.9434) - 0.06(0.893) - 1.06(0.844)$$
$$= -0.0049$$

in which case the price of the receiver swap is 0.0049. The swap rate is

$$\kappa = \frac{Z_0^0 - Z_0^3}{Z_0^1 + Z_0^2 + Z_0^3} = \frac{1}{0.9434} \frac{0.844}{+ 0.893 + 0.844} = 0.0582$$

A *payer swaption* is like a European call on the time $\tau - 1$ value of the corresponding payer forward start swap, where the exercise date is $\tau - 1$ and the exercise price is zero. A *receiver swaption* is defined in a similar manner with respect to the receiver swap. The payer and receiver swaptions thus have respective time-t prices $(t < \tau)$

$$E_Q\left[\frac{B_t}{B_{\tau-1}}\left(E_Q\left[\sum_{u=\tau}^{s}\frac{B_{\tau-1}}{B_u}(r_u - K)\bigg|\mathscr{F}_{\tau-1}\right]\right)^+\bigg|\mathscr{F}_t\right]$$

and

$$E_Q\left[\frac{B_t}{B_{\tau-1}}\left(E_Q\left[\sum_{u=\tau}^{s}\frac{B_{\tau-1}}{B_u}(K - r_u)\bigg|\mathscr{F}_{\tau-1}\right]\right)^+\bigg|\mathscr{F}_t\right]$$

Note the payer swaption price minus the receiver swaption price equals

$$E_Q\left[\frac{B_t}{B_{\tau-1}}E_Q\left[\sum_{u=\tau}^{s}\frac{B_{\tau-1}}{B_u}(r_u - K)\bigg|\mathscr{F}_{\tau-1}\right]\bigg|\mathscr{F}_t\right]$$

$$= E_Q\left[\frac{B_t}{B_{\tau-1}}\sum_{u=\tau}^{s}\frac{B_{\tau-1}}{B_u}(r_u - K)\bigg|\mathscr{Y}_t\right] = E_Q\left[\sum_{u=\tau}^{s}\frac{B_t}{B_u}(r_u - K)\bigg|\mathscr{F}_t\right]$$

which is the time-t price of a forward start swap. Thus the following parity relationship holds:

(6.45) payer swaption $-$ receiver swaption $=$ forward swap

In view of equation (6.44), the time-$(\tau - 1)$ price of the payer swap is given by

$$\pi_{\tau-1} = 1 - \sum_{u=\tau}^{s} C_u Z_{\tau-1}^u$$

so another expression for the time-t price of the payer swaption is

$$E_Q\left[\frac{B_t}{B_{\tau-1}}\left(1 - \sum_{u=\tau}^{s} C_u Z_{\tau-1}^u\right)^+\bigg|\mathscr{F}_t\right]$$

This provides another interpretation:

(6.46) A payer swaption is the same as a put option on a coupon bond, where the exercise date is $\tau - 1$ and the exercise price is one. This coupon bond has face value one and coupon rate K.

Similarly, receiver swaptions can be interpreted as call options on coupon bonds.

Still another interpretation can be obtained:

(6.47)   A payer (receiver) swaption is like a portfolio of call (respectively, put) options on the swap rate $\kappa(\tau - 1, \tau, s)$.

To be precise, suppose for each time $u = \tau, \tau + 1, \ldots, s$, there is a call option with time-u payoff $[\kappa(\tau - 1, \tau, s) - K]^+$. To see that this portfolio is like a payer swaption, consider its time-$(\tau - 1)$ value, namely

$$E_Q\left[\sum_{u=\tau}^{s} \frac{B_{\tau-1}}{B_u}[\kappa(\tau - 1, \tau, s) - K]^+ \bigg| \mathscr{F}_{\tau-1}\right]$$

It follows that the time-t value of this portfolio is

$$E_Q\left[\frac{B_t}{B_{\tau-1}} E_Q\left[\sum_{u=\tau}^{s} \frac{B_{\tau-1}}{B_u}[\kappa(\tau - 1, \tau, s) - K]^+ \bigg| \mathscr{F}_{\tau-1}\right] \bigg| \mathscr{F}_t\right]$$

$$= E_Q\left[\frac{B_t}{B_{\tau-1}}[\kappa(\tau - 1, \tau, s) - K]^+ E_Q\left[\sum_{u=\tau}^{s} \frac{B_{\tau-1}}{B_u} \bigg| \mathscr{F}_{\tau-1}\right] \bigg| \mathscr{F}_t\right]$$

$$= E_Q\left[\frac{B_t}{B_{\tau-1}}[\kappa(\tau - 1, \tau, s) - K]^+ \sum_{u=\tau}^{s} Z_{\tau-1}^u \bigg| \mathscr{F}_t\right]$$

But $\kappa(\tau - 1, \tau, s)[Z_{\tau-1}^\tau + \ldots + Z_{\tau-1}^s] = Z_{\tau-1}^{\tau-1} - Z_{\tau-1}^s$ by the definition of the swap rate, so substituting this in the preceding expression yields

$$E_Q\left[\frac{B_t}{B_{\tau-1}}\left(1 - Z_{\tau-1}^s - K\sum_{u=\tau}^{s} Z_{\tau-1}^u\right)^+ \sum_{u=\tau}^{s} Z_{\tau-1}^u \bigg| \mathscr{F}_t\right]$$

$$= E_Q\left[\frac{B_t}{B_{\tau-1}}\left(1 - \sum_{u=\tau}^{s} C_u Z_{\tau-1}^u\right)^+ \sum_{u=\tau}^{s} Z_{\tau-1}^u \bigg| \mathscr{F}_t\right]$$

which is recognized to be the time-t price of the payer swaption by (6.46).

Example 6.4   With $K = 0.06, t = 1, \tau = 2$, and $s = 3$, the time-t price of the payer swap is

$$\pi_1 = 1 - KZ_1^2 - (1 + K)Z_1^3$$

$$= \begin{cases} 1 - 0.06(0.9174) - 1.06(0.8417) = & 0.0528, \quad \omega = \omega_1, \omega_2 \\ 1 - 0.06(0.9434) - 1.06(0.8901) = & -0.0001, \quad \omega = \omega_3, \omega_4 \\ 1 - 0.06(0.9709) - 1.06(0.9427) = & -0.0576, \quad \omega = \omega_5, \omega_6 \end{cases}$$

The time-0 price of the payer swaption is

$$E_Q\left[\frac{B_0}{B_1}(\pi_1)^+\right] = (0.1667 + 0.1667)\left[\frac{1}{1.06}0.528\right] = 0.0166$$

The time-0 price of the receiver swaption is

$$E_Q\left[\frac{B_0}{B_1}(-\pi_1)^+\right] = 2(0.1667)\frac{0.0001}{1.06} + 2(0.1667)\frac{0.576}{1.06} = 0.0181$$

Note that the time-0 price of the forward start swap is

$$\frac{0.1667 + 0.1667}{1.06}\,[0.0528 - 0.0001 - 0.0576] = -0.0015$$

so, indeed, the parity relationship (6.45) is satisfied.
To verify interpretation (6.47), note that we have

$$\kappa = \kappa(\tau - 1, \tau, s) = \kappa(1,2,3) = \frac{Z_1^1 - Z_1^3}{Z_1^2 + Z_1^3}$$

$$= \begin{cases} \frac{1-0.8417}{0.9174+0.8417} = 0.09, & \omega = \omega_1, \omega_2 \\ \frac{1-0.8901}{0.9434+0.8901} = 0.06, & \omega = \omega_3, \omega_4 \\ \frac{1-0.9427}{0.9709+0.9427} = 0.03, & \omega = \omega_5, \omega_6 \end{cases}$$

so

$$(\kappa - K)^+ = (\kappa - 0.06)^+ = \begin{cases} 0.03, & \omega = \omega_1, \omega_2 \\ 0, & \text{otherwise} \end{cases}$$

The portfolio of interest has two options, one paying off at time $t = 2$, the other paying off at $t = 3$. Each pays 0.03 dollars in the event $A \equiv \{\omega_1, \omega_2\}$ but pays zero otherwise. The time-0 present value of this cash flow is

$$E_Q\left[\frac{0.03}{B_2}1_A\right] + E_Q\left[\frac{0.03}{B_3}1_A\right]$$

$$= \frac{2(0.1667)(0.03)}{1.06(1.09)} + \frac{0.1667(0.03)}{1.06(1.09)(1.1)} + \frac{0.1667(0.03)}{1.06(1.09)(1.08)} = 0.0166$$

which equals the time-0 price of the payer swaption, in accordance with (6.47).

Exercise 6.23   For the model in example 6.2 with $K = 0.06$, $\tau = 1$, and $s = 3$, compute the time-0 prices of the payer and receiver swaps, and compute the swap rate at $t = 0$.

Exercise 6.24   For the model in example 6.1 with $K = 0.06$, $\tau = 2$, and $s = 3$

(a)   Compute the time-1 prices of the payer swap.
(b)   Compute the time-0 price of the payer forward start swap.
(c)   Compute the time-0 price of the payer swaption.

(d) Compute the time-0 price of the receiver swaption, and verify parity relationship (6.45).
(e) Compute the swap rate $\kappa(1, 2, 3)$.
(f) Verify (6.47) by specifying the appropriate option portfolio and computing its time-0 value.

Exercise 6.25   Show that the time-t price of a payer forward start swap *settled in advance* is

$$\pi_t = E_Q\left[\sum_{u=\tau}^{s} \frac{B_t}{B_{u-1}} (r_u - K) \middle| \mathscr{F}_t\right], \quad t < \tau \leqslant s \leqslant T$$

6.7   Caps and Floors

A *caplet* is a European call option on the spot interest rate r at a fixed point in time. As with swaps, caplets can be settled in arrears or in advance. In the former case, the time-τ payoff of a caplet is simply $(r_\tau - K)^+$, where K is the specified strike or exercise price. For $t \leqslant \tau$ the time-t price of this caplet is

$$\pi_t = B_t E_Q[(r_\tau - K)^+ / B_\tau | \mathscr{F}_t] = Z_t^\tau E_\tau[(r_\tau - K)^+ | \mathscr{F}_t]$$

A *cap* is a strip of caplets, all having a common exercise price and with one for each time period in an interval of time. In general, some caplets in the cap will pay off and others will not, depending on whether the spot rate exceeds the strike. As with swaps, there are both ordinary and forward start caps, depending on whether the initial caplet corresponds to the current spot rate. The time-t price of a forward start cap settled in arrears is

$$(6.48) \qquad \pi_t = B_t \sum_{u=\tau}^{s} E_Q[(r_u - K)^+ / B_u | \mathscr{F}_t], \quad t < \tau \leqslant s \leqslant T$$

The time-t price of an ordinary cap is given by the same formula with $\tau = t + 1$.

Example 6.1 (continued)   Suppose the exercise price $K = 0.06$ and consider an ordinary cap settled in arrears. The payoff of the $\tau = 1$ caplet is identical to zero, so its time-0 price is zero. The payoff of the $\tau = 2$ caplet is

$$(r_2(\omega) - 0.06)^+ = \begin{cases} 0.03, & \omega = \omega_1, \omega_2 \\ 0, & \text{otherwise} \end{cases}$$

so its time-0 price is

$$E_Q[(r_2 - 0.06)^+ / B_2] = (0.1839 + 0.1161)\frac{0.03}{(1.06)(1.09)} = 0.0078$$

The payoff of the $\tau = 3$ caplet is

$$(r_3(\omega) - 0.06)^+ = \begin{cases} 0.04, & \omega = \omega_1 \\ 0.02, & \omega = \omega_2 \\ 0.01, & \omega = \omega_3 \\ 0, & \text{otherwise} \end{cases}$$

so its time-0 price is

$$E_Q[(r_3 - 0.06)^+/B_3] = \frac{0.1839(0.04)}{1.06(1.09)(1.1)} + \frac{0.1161(0.02)}{1.06(1.09)(1.08)}$$
$$+ \frac{0.1517(0.01)}{1.06(1.06)(1.07)} = 0.0091$$

Thus the time-0 price of the corresponding cap with $\tau = 1$ and $s = 3$ is $0.0078 + 0.0091 = 0.0169$.

Floorlets are defined in the same manner as caplets, only they are put options on the spot rate. Similarly, *floors* are strips of floorlets and thus are analogous to caps. In particular, the time-t price of a forward start floor settled in arrears is

(6.49) $$\pi_t = B_t \sum_{u=\tau}^{s} E_Q[(K - r_u)^+/B_u|\mathcal{F}_t], \quad t < \tau \leqslant s \leqslant T$$

Comparing this with (6.43) and (6.48) immediately gives the following parity relationship:

(6.50) The price of a cap minus the price of a floor equals the price of a swap.

Example 6.1 (continued) Consider the floor that is settled in arrears with $K = 0.06$, $\tau = 1$, and $s = 3$. Since $r_1 = 0.06$, the $\tau = 1$ floorlet has time-0 price equal to zero. The $\tau = 2$ floorlet has time-0 price

$$E_Q[(0.06 - r_2)^+/B_2] = (0.2582 + 0.1418)\frac{0.03}{(1.06)(1.03)} = 0.011$$

The $\tau = 3$ floorlet has time-0 price

$$\frac{0.1483(.01)}{1.06(1.06)(1.05)} + \frac{0.2582(.02)}{1.06(1.03)(1.04)} + \frac{0.1418(.04)}{1.06(1.03)(1.02)} = 0.0108$$

Thus the time-0 price of the floor is $0.011 + 0.0108 = 0.0218$. Note this is consistent with parity relationship (6.50), because the price of the corresponding cap is 0.0169, whereas (see section 6.6) -0.0049 is the price of the corresponding swap.

A *caption* is a put or call option whose underlying security is a forward cap. A *floortion* is a put or call option whose underlying security is a forward floor. These are examples of what are called *compound options*, that is, options whose underlying securities are themselves options.

Normally the exercise date of the caption or floortion is prior to the time associated with the initial caplet or floorlet in the underlying. Moreover, the strike of the caption or floortion is generally not the same as the strike of the cap or floor.

The computation of the price of a caption or floortion is best viewed as a two-step procedure. First you compute the probability distribution of the caption or floortion payoff under either the risk neutral or the forward risk adjusted probability measure. In other words, you first compute the probability distribution of the contingent claim. Then you compute in a standard way the price of this contingent claim. This is illustrated in the following example.

Example 6.1 (continued)   First consider a forward start cap with $K = 0.06, \tau = 2$ and $s = 3$. The $\tau = 2$ caplet has time-1 price

$$B_1 E_Q[(r_2 - 0.06)^+ / B_2 | \mathcal{F}_1] = \begin{cases} 1(0.03)/1.09 = 0.0275, & \omega = \omega_1, \omega_2 \\ 0, & \text{otherwise} \end{cases}$$

The $\tau = 3$ caplet has time-1 price

$$B_1 E_Q[(r_3 - 0.06)^+ / B_3 | \mathcal{F}_1]$$

$$= \begin{cases} \frac{0.613(0.04)}{1.09(1.1)} + \frac{0.387(0.02)}{1.09(1.08)} = 0.0271, & \omega = \omega_1, \omega_2 \\ \frac{0.5057(0.01)}{1.06(1.07)} = 0.0045, & \omega = \omega_3, \omega_4 \\ 0, & \omega = \omega_5, \omega_6 \end{cases}$$

where 0.613 equals the conditional probability $Q(\omega_1 | \{\omega_1, \omega_2\})$, and so forth. Thus the time-1 price of this forward start cap is

$$\pi_1 = \begin{cases} 0.0275 + 0.0271 = 0.0546, & \omega = \omega_1, \omega_2 \\ 0.0045, & \omega = \omega_3, \omega_4 \\ 0, & \omega = \omega_5, \omega_6 \end{cases}$$

Notice that the time-0 price of this cap is

$$\pi_0 = E_Q[\pi_1 / B_1] = \frac{0.3(0.0546)}{1.06} + \frac{0.3(0.0045)}{1.06} = 0.0168$$

as was computed earlier in a different manner.

Now consider a caption, in particular, a put on this cap with strike 0.02 and exercise date $\tau = 1$. Its time-1 payoff is

$$(0.02 - \pi_1)^+ = \begin{cases} 0, & \omega = \omega_1, \omega_2 \\ 0.0155, & \omega = \omega_3, \omega_4 \\ 0.02, & \omega = \omega_5, \omega_6 \end{cases}$$

in which case the time-0 price of the caption is

$$E_Q[(0.02 - \pi_1)^+/B_1] = \frac{0.3(0.0155)}{1.06} + \frac{0.4(0.02)}{1.06} = 0.0119$$

Similarly, the time-0 price of the caption which is a call having the same strike and exercise date is

$$E_Q[(\pi_1 - 0.02)^+/B_1] = \frac{0.3(0.0346)}{1.06} = 0.0098$$

Exercise 6.26 Consider the model in example 6.2.

(a) Compute the time-0 and time-1 prices of the forward start cap that is settled in arrears with $K = 0.06, \tau = 2$, and $s = 3$.
(b) Compute the time-0 and time-1 prices of the forward start floor that is settled in arrears with the same parameters.
(c) Verify that the time-0 prices in (a) and (b) satisfy the parity relationship (6.50).
(d) Compute the time-0 prices of the put and call captions, where the underlying is as in (a), the strike is 0.01, and the exercise date is $\tau = 1$.
(e) Compute the time-0 prices of the put and call floortions, where the underlying is as in (b), the strike is 0.01, and the exercise date is $\tau = 1$.

7 Models With Infinite Sample Spaces

7.1   Finite Horizon Models

The fundamental theorem of asset pricing says that there are no arbitrage opportunities if and only if there exists a risk neutral probability measure. In earlier chapters this principle was shown true for single and multiperiod models under the critical assumption that the underlying sample space Ω has a finite number of elements. This assumption is crucial, because it enables one to apply simple results of linear programming or, more generally, to use simple versions of the separating hyperplane theorem for problems posed in terms of finite dimensional spaces. But when the sample space Ω has a countably infinite or an uncountably infinite number of elements, the space of random variables representing terminal wealth will be a space of infinite dimension. There are certainly separating hyperplane theorems for these infinite dimensional settings, but a straightforward application of such a theorem will break down owing to technical complications. A more delicate analysis is required.

It turns out the fundamental theorem of asset pricing remains true in the case of infinite sample spaces Ω provided the number T of trading periods is finite. The purpose of this section is to establish this result. As will be seen in the following section, however, the theorem breaks down when the number T of trading periods is infinite.

Some results in this chapter are more technical than much of the earlier chapters. To begin with, in progressing to an infinite sample space it is necessary to generalize the concept of the filtration that is used as the information submodel. Recall that a collection $\mathscr{F}$ of subsets of Ω is called an *algebra* on Ω if

1   $\Omega \in \mathscr{F}$
2   $F \in \mathscr{F} \Rightarrow F^c = \Omega \backslash F \in \mathscr{F}$
3   F and $G \in \mathscr{F} \Rightarrow F \cup G \in \mathscr{F}$.

The collection $\mathscr{F}$ is called a σ-*algebra* on Ω if, in addition

4   $F_1, F_2, \ldots \in \mathscr{F} \Rightarrow \bigcup_{n=1}^{\infty} F_n \in \mathscr{F}$.

In words, (4) says that countable unions of subsets in $\mathscr{F}$ are also in $\mathscr{F}$. If Ω is finite, then (4) is superfluous, because Ω has only finitely many subsets. But if Ω has infinitely many subsets then (3) does not imply (4). Condition (4) is necessary for what needs to be done.

Our aim is to use σ-algebras as models for the information that is known to the investors at the various points in time. Recall that algebras were used for this purpose in the finite sample space context. Moreover, recall that when Ω is finite, algebras on Ω are equivalent to partitions of Ω, and this led to a very intuitive interpretation of algebras as models of the information known to the investors. Unfortunately, the analogous result does not hold for σ-algebras on Ω when Ω has an infinite number of elements. Recall from chapter 3 that for $A \subset \Omega$ to be an element of the partition $\mathscr{P}$ corresponding to $\mathscr{F}$, one must have $A \in \mathscr{F}$ as well as $\{B \in \mathscr{F}, A \neq B, \text{ and } B \subset A\}$ $\Rightarrow B = \emptyset$. But applying this requirement to infinite sample spaces produces silly, worthless results. For instance, if $\Omega = [0,1]$ and $\mathscr{F}$ includes all the open intervals of the form (a, b), where a and b are rational numbers, then this requirement implies the corresponding partition includes all the rational numbers of the unit interval as distinct elements.

Nevertheless, we will use σ-algebras to model the information known to the economic agents at individual points in time. The economic intuition to justify this approach is dubious, since the partition interpretation was abandoned. We must soldier on, being content with the view that σ-algebras are natural extensions of the concept that made good sense when Ω was finite.

As with the case of a finite sample space, the information flow in the securities market will be modeled by a *filtration* $\mathbb{F} = \{\mathscr{F}_t; t = 0, 1, \ldots T\}$, where $\{\mathscr{F}_t\}$ is an increasing sequence of σ-algebras. In particular, $\mathscr{F}_{t-1} \subseteq \mathscr{F}_t$ for $t = 1, \ldots, T$, because the investors learn as time goes on. The probability measure P is such that the probability $P(A)$ is well defined for each $A \in \mathscr{F}_T$.

The random variable X is said to be *measurable* with respect to the σ-algebra $\mathscr{F}$ if, for every real number x, the subset $\{\omega \in \Omega : X(\omega) \leqslant x\}$ is an element of the σ-algebra $\mathscr{F}$. In this case one writes $X \in \mathscr{F}$. The stochastic process $X = \{X_t; t = 0, \ldots, T\}$ is said to be *adapted* if $X_t \in \mathscr{F}_t$ for all t. The stochastic process $H = \{H_t; t = 1, \ldots, T\}$ is said to be *predictable* if $H_t \in \mathscr{F}_{t-1}$ for all t.

At this point it is convenient to introduce a new and rather technical concept. When speaking about equations, inequalities, and the like involving random variables, it is often appropriate to include the phrase *almost surely*. This means that the equation or whatever holds for all $\omega \in \Omega$ except, possibly, for some $\omega \in A$, where A is some event in $\mathscr{F}_T$ such that $P(A) = 0$. In other words, although the relationship in question might not hold for all $\omega \in \Omega$, the only exceptions are inconsequential and can be ignored. *Almost surely* is often abbreviated *a.s.*

The rest of the securities market model is largely the same as before. There is a *bank account* process $B = \{B_t; t = 0, 1, \ldots, T\}$, an adapted, non-decreasing stochastic process with $B_o = 1$. There are N *risky security* processes $S_n = \{S_n(t); t = 0, 1, \ldots, T\}$, where S_n is a non-negative, adapted stochastic process for each $n = 1, 2, \ldots, N$. And there are N *discounted price processes* $S_n^* = \{S_n^*(t); t = 0, 1, \ldots, T\}$, where $S_n^*(t) \equiv S_n(t)/B_t$ for all t.

We are now ready to tackle the fundamental theorem of asset pricing. This will be done after first presenting a preliminary result which is so technical that its explanation will be omitted.[1] Here Y and Z are each random variables taking values in $\mathbb{R}^N$, $\| Y \|$ denotes the Euclidean norm of the vector Y, and $Z \cdot Y$ denotes the inner product of the vectors Y and Z.

(7.1)   Suppose $\mathscr{G}$ and $\mathscr{H}$ are two σ-algebras with $\mathscr{G} \subseteq \mathscr{H} \subseteq \mathscr{F}_T$. Let $Y \in \mathscr{H}$ be such that

(7.2) $\{Z \in \mathscr{G} \text{ and } Z \cdot Y \geqslant 0 \text{ a.s.}\} \Rightarrow \{Z \cdot Y = 0 \text{ a.s.}\}$

Then there exists a scalar-valued random variable $D \in \mathscr{H}$ such that:

(7.3) $0 < D \leqslant 1, \text{a.s.}$

(7.4) $E[D \| Y \|] < \infty, \text{ and}$

(7.5) $E[YD|\mathscr{G}] = 0$

In words, (7.2) says that the only random variables $Z \in \mathscr{G}$ satisfying the inequality actually satisfy the equality. Shortly it will be seen that this is the same as saying there are no one-period arbitrage opportunities. The random variable D will play the role of a state price density and will be used in the construction of the risk neutral probability measure.

The trading strategy H, the value process V, the discounted value process V^*, and the discounted gains process G^* are defined in exactly the same manner as in the case of a finite sample space Ω (see section 3.1). Moreover, arbitrage opportunities are also defined the same way: the self-financing trading strategy H is an *arbitrage opportunity* if (1) $V_0 = 0$, (2) $V_T \geqslant 0$, and (3) $E[V_T] > 0$. Just as with (3.17), an equivalent condition for H to be an arbitrage opportunity is for the discounted gains process to satisfy $G_T^* \geqslant 0$ and $E[G_T^*] > 0$.

In view of this latter characterization of arbitrage opportunities, it is not surprising that the absence of arbitrage opportunities implies a condition that resembles (7.2). To prepare for this, let $S^* = \{S_t^*; t = 0, \ldots, T\}$ denote the $\mathbb{R}^N$-valued process whose nth component is S_n^*, the discounted price process for the nth risky security, $n = 1, \ldots, N$. There should not be any confusion about whether the subscripts here represent time t or security n. It is convenient to denote $\Delta S_t^* = S_t^* - S_{t-1}^*$, a $\mathbb{R}^N$-valued random variable.

(7.6)   If there are no arbitrage opportunities, then for all $t \in \{1, 2, \ldots, T\}$ and all $\mathbb{R}^N$-valued random variables Z,

(7.7) $\{Z \in \mathscr{F}_{t-1} \text{ and } Z \cdot \Delta S_t^* \geqslant 0 \text{ a.s.}\} \Rightarrow \{Z \cdot \Delta S_t^* = 0 \text{ a.s.}\}$

Principle (7.6) can be verified by contradiction, because if there exists some t and some $Z = (Z_1, \ldots, Z_N) \in \mathscr{F}_{t-1}$ such that $Z \cdot \Delta S_t^* \geq 0$ a.s. and $P(Z \cdot \Delta S_t^* > 0) > 0$, then one can construct an arbitrage opportunity, as will now be shown.

Let $A \in \mathscr{F}_{t-1}$ denote the set $\{\omega \in \Omega : P(Z \cdot \Delta S_t^* > 0 | \mathscr{F}_{t-1})(\omega) > 0\}$, and note that $P(A) > 0$ by assumption. The arbitrage opportunity H is obtained by taking $H_n(s)(\omega) = 0$ for all $s < t$, all $\omega \in \Omega$, and $n = 0, 1, \ldots, N$; by taking

$$H_n(t)(\omega) = \begin{cases} Z_n(\omega), & \omega \in A, n = 1, \ldots, N \\ -Z \cdot S_{t-1}^*(\omega), & \omega \in A, n = 0 \\ 0, & \omega \in A^C \end{cases}$$

and by taking

$$H_n(s)(\omega) = \begin{cases} V_t(\omega), & n = 0 \text{ and } \omega \in A \\ 0, & \text{otherwise} \end{cases}$$

for $s = t+1, \ldots, T$. Clearly H is predictable and $V_0 = 0$. It is left for the reader to verify that H is self-financing (exercise 7.1). This strategy takes the time-t wealth V_t and holds it in the bank account, so $V_T \geq 0$ if $V_t \geq 0$. But $V_t(\omega) = Z \cdot \Delta S_t^*(\omega) > 0$ if $\omega \in A$, whereas $V_t(\omega) = 0$, otherwise, so indeed $V_T \geq 0$. Moreover, $E[V_T] > 0$ if $E[V_t] > 0$. But

$$E[V_t] = E[1_A Z \cdot \Delta S_t^*] = E[1_A E[Z \cdot \Delta S_t^* | \mathscr{F}_{t-1}]] > 0$$

so all this implies H is an arbitrage opportunity, which is a contradiction.

Principles (7.1) and (7.6) can now be used to show that the absence of arbitrage opportunities implies the existence of a risk neutral probability measure. A *risk neutral probability measure* is defined in the same way as in the case of a finite sample space; it is a probability measure Q, equivalent to P, under which the discounted price of each risky security is a martingale. By *equivalent*, one means that for each event $A \in \mathscr{F}_T$ the probability $P(A) = 0$ if and only if $Q(A) = 0$. In words, there is agreement between the two probability measures about which events can and cannot happen.

To see why no arbitrage implies the existence of a risk neutral probability measure Q, I will indicate how to construct this measure. Begin by setting $\mathscr{F}_{T+1} = \mathscr{F}_T$, $S_{T+1}^* = S_T^*$, $D_{T+1} = 1$, and $Y_{T+1} = 0$. The scalar-valued random variables $D_1, \ldots, D_T$ and the $\mathbb{R}^N$-valued random variables $Y_1, \ldots, Y_T$ are now defined recursively, backwards in time. For example, suppose $D_{t+1}, \ldots, D_T$ and $Y_{t+1}, \ldots, Y_T$ have been defined such that

(7.8) D_k is $\mathscr{F}_k$ measurable, $t + 1 \leq k \leq T + 1$

(7.9) $Y_k = \Delta S_k^* E[D_{k+1} \ldots D_{T+1} | \mathscr{F}_k]$ a.s., $t + 1 \leq k \leq T$

(7.10) $0 < D_k \leq 1$ a.s., $t + 1 \leq k \leq T + 1$

(7.11) $E[D_K \| Y_k \|] < \infty$, $t + 1 \leq k \leq T$, and

(7.12) $E[Y_k D_k | \mathscr{F}_{k-1}] = 0$ a.s., $t + 1 \leq k \leq T$

Now use principle (7.1) with $\mathscr{G} = \mathscr{F}_{t-1}, \mathscr{H} = \mathscr{F}_t$, and $Y = Y_t$, where Y_t is as in (7.9) with $k = t$. Note that $Y_t \in \mathscr{F}_t$. Moreover, because of (7.6), property (7.2) holds. Thus by (7.1) there exists a scalar-valued random variable D_t such that equations (7.8), (7.10), (7.11), and (7.12) all hold with $k = t$.

Having specified $D_1, \ldots, D_T$, the next step is to define a few more items. Set

$$D_0 \equiv \frac{1}{1 + \|S_0^*\|} \quad \text{and} \quad D \equiv D_0 D_1 \ldots D_T$$

Note that $0 < D \leqslant 1$ a.s. In addition, define what will turn out to be the risk neutral probability measure by taking

$$Q(A) \equiv \frac{P(D1_A)}{E[D]}, \quad \text{all events } A \in \mathscr{F}_T$$

that is,

$$E_Q[X] \equiv \frac{E[DX]}{E[D]}, \quad \text{all random variables } X \in \mathscr{F}_T$$

Clearly Q is a probability measure that is equivalent to P. It remains to show that the discounted risky security prices are martingales under Q. There are two parts to this. The first is to show the usual conditional expected value relationship. The other is to show that the discounted risky price process is *integrable* under Q, that is, to show that various expected values of this process are well-defined and finite.

To verify Q-integrability, we have

$$E_Q\left[\|S_0^*\|\right] = \frac{1}{E[D]} E\left[D\|S_0^*\|\right] = \frac{1}{E[D]} E\left[D_0 D_1 \ldots D_T \|S_0^*\|\right]$$

$$\leqslant \frac{1}{E[D]} E\left[D_0 \|S_0^*\|\right] \leqslant \frac{1}{E[D]} < \infty$$

We also have

$$E_Q\left[\|S_t^* - S_{t-1}^*\|\right] = \frac{1}{E[D]} E\left[D\|S_t^* - S_{t-1}^*\|\right]$$

$$= \frac{1}{E[D]} E\left[D_0 \ldots D_t \|S_t^* - S_{t-1}^*\| D_{t+1} \ldots D_T\right]$$

$$= \frac{1}{E[D]} E\left[D_0 \ldots D_t \|S_t^* - S_{t-1}^*\| E\left[D_{t+1} \ldots D_T | \mathscr{F}_t\right]\right]$$

$$= \frac{1}{E[D]} E\left[D_0 \ldots D_t \|Y_t\|\right]$$

$$\leqslant \frac{1}{E[D]} E\left[D_t \|Y_t\|\right]$$

But this last expression is finite by (7.11), so S^* is Q-integrable.

It remains to show $E_Q[S_t^*|\mathscr{F}_{t-1}] = S_{t-1}^*$ for all t, that is, to show $E_Q[\Delta S_t^*|\mathscr{F}_{t-1}] = 0$ for all t. We have

$$E_Q[\Delta S_t^*|\mathscr{F}_{t-1}] = \frac{1}{E[D]} E[D\Delta S_t^*|\mathscr{F}_{t-1}]$$

$$= \frac{1}{E[D]} E[D_0 \dots D_{t-1}D_t(\Delta S_t^*)D_{t+1}\dots D_T|\mathscr{F}_{t-1}]$$

$$= \frac{D_0 \dots D_{t-1}}{E[D]} E[D_t(\Delta S_t^*)E[D_{t+1}\dots D_T|\mathscr{F}_T]|\mathscr{F}_{t-1}]$$

$$= \frac{D_0 \dots D_{t-1}}{E[D]} E[D_t Y_t|\mathscr{F}_{t-1}]$$

But this last expression equals 0 by (7.12), so S^* is indeed a martingale under Q.

In summary, if there are no arbitrage opportunities, then there exists a risk neutral probability measure. The converse is immediate, by the same argument as used for the finite sample space case. Hence we have established that the following is true even if the sample space Ω has infinitely many elements:

(7.13) *Fundamental Theorem of Asset Pricing* Suppose the number of trading periods T is finite. Then there are no arbitrage opportunities if and only if there exists a risk neutral probability measure.

Exercise 7.1 The statement was made that the arbitrage opportunity constructed in the explanation of (7.6) is a self-financing trading strategy. Verify this assertion.

Exercise 7.2 Suppose there is a single security S with $\Delta S_t = \exp\{\sigma W_t + \mu\}$, where $\{W_t\}$ is a sequence of independent standard normal random variables and where μ and σ are positive constants. In addition, suppose the spot interest rate is the constant $r \geq 0$. Derive a risk neutral probability measure, first for the case $T = 1$, then for the general case $T < \infty$.

7.2 Infinite Horizon Models

Finite horizon models with infinite sample spaces are not much different from finite horizon models with finite sample spaces, because the fundamental theorem of asset pricing holds in both cases. But this theorem is not quite true when there is an infinite number of trading periods, and there are also significant modeling issues associated with admissibility of trading strategies. This section will examine these and related matters.

First of all, what is meant by an infinite horizon model? For finite horizon models it was tacitly assumed that the time index t keeps track of both the number of periods as well as the elapsed time by some unit of measure such as months or years. This implies the time periods are of equal durations, such as one year. Retaining this set-up for an infinite horizon problem leads to the choice $T = \infty$, meaning there is a (countably) infinite number of trading periods, all with the same length.

There is an alternative approach, however, that is useful for some purposes: there is a finite planning horizon, but there is also a (countably) infinite number of trading periods before the planning horizon. Here, of course, the various periods have different lengths, as measured by clock time. For instance, with a planning horizon of one year, period t would last for $(1/2)^t$ years, $t = 1, 2, \ldots$ Either way (and, admittedly, the terminology is not entirely consistent), the defining feature of *infinite horizon models* is the (countably) infinite number of trading periods; whether the planning horizon measured in clock time is finite and whether all the periods are of the same length of clock time are unimportant issues for the purposes of this section. Throughout, one should think of t as the counter for the number of periods, thereby suggesting $T = \infty$.

Building the security price processes for the infinite horizon model presents no great difficulties. Needless to say, the sample space Ω will necessarily be infinite. With the specification of the probability space $(\Omega, \mathscr{F}, P)$, the filtration model of the information, $\mathbb{F} = \{\mathscr{F}_t; t = 0, 1, \ldots\}$, will be a collection of σ-algebras with $\mathscr{F}_t \subseteq \mathscr{F}_{t+1} \subseteq \ldots \subseteq \mathscr{F}$ for all t. The security price processes will then be, as usual, non-negative, adapted stochastic processes.

When it comes to the specification of the trading strategies, however, we quickly encounter a complication. As usual, we will want to require the trading strategies to be predictable stochastic processes, for this will enable the investors to use all the past and present available information without being able to look into the future. But without additional restrictions, the opportunity to trade infinitely many times will allow investors to make arbitrage profits, even with perfectly reasonable stock price models. This will be illustrated in the following example, which deals with the very simple binomial stock price model.

Example 7.1   Consider a simple binomial stock price model where the "up" factor $u = 1.1$,, the "down" factor $d = 0.9$, and the riskless interest rate $r = 0$. The objective here is to describe an arbitrage opportunity where you start with zero dollars and you are certain to end up with \$1. The probability of an up-move is strictly between 0 and 1; the exact value is unimportant. But note there is a risk neutral probability measure for this model; it is the one consistent with equal conditional probabilities for up and down moves over one period.

The idea will be to use a 'doubling' strategy where you start out at time $t = 0$ borrowing \$10, say, investing all of this in the stock. If the stock goes up in the first period, then your investment becomes \$11, so you repay your \$10 loan and you take the remaining \$1 and run. On the other hand, if the stock goes down, then your stock investment becomes worth \$9; since you owe \$10, this puts you \$1 in debt. You can "recover" by borrowing enough money to double the initial $10 investment in the stock. In particular, you borrow an additional $11, raising the total loan to $21 and making the total investment in the stock equal to $20. If the stock goes up over the second period, then your stock investment becomes $22, so you repay your $21 loan and you take the remaining $1 and run. But if the stock goes down, then your stock investment becomes $18, leaving you $3 in debt, requiring you to "double-up" at least one more time.

In general, if there is at least one up move during the first t periods, then you will have realized your desired $1 profit and you will have terminated all borrowing and trading by time t. On the other hand, if the stock goes down each of the first t periods, then after t periods you will be $1 - 2^t$ in debt, you will owe $11(2)^{t-1} - 1$ on your loan, and your current investment in the stock will be worth $9(2)^{t-1}$ (check: $1 - 2^t = 9(2)^{t-1} - [11(2)^{t-1} - 1]$). In this latter case then at time t you will borrow an additional $11(2)^{t-1}$ dollars to increase your stock investment to $10(2)^t$ dollars and keep on going.

Now if there is only a finite number T of periods, then with a positive probability the stock will have gone down every period and you will have ended up $1 - 2^T$ dollars in debt, in which case this would not be an arbitrage opportunity. But with an infinite number of trading periods, the probability of always going down and thus ending up in debt is equal to zero. In other words, under the doubling strategy the probability of ending up with $1 as your final wealth is equal to one. This is an arbitrage opportunity.

So what is the problem? Is our notion of an arbitrage opportunity improper for the case of an infinite horizon model? It is questionable to talk about being sure of having a positive wealth infinitely far out in the future when you run the risk of being in debt at every finite time, but keep in mind that the infinite horizon model can be associated with a planning horizon of finite clock time, with an infinite number of trading periods of varying length. With this latter perspective we would be referring to a positive wealth at a finite distance in the future. Our notion of arbitrage opportunities is not the problem.

The problem with example 7.1 is that the specified trading strategy is unrealistic. In the first place, there is no lower bound on the amount the investor could be in debt (this could be $1 - 2^t$ after t periods), nor is there an upper bound on the amount (which could be $11(2)^{t-1} - 1$ dollars after t periods) of the loan. Furthermore, there is no upper bound on the shares of stock that the investor might need to own (the dollars invested grow without bound as the price per share drops, so the number of shares owned will grow without bound as well). These situations are unrealistic from the modeling and economic points of view.

It is reasonable to make an assumption that would rule out these unrealistic situations. For example, one could stipulate that the trading strategies (i.e., the number of shares long or short) are bounded. Or one could stipulate that there is a lower bound on the wealth of the investor. Assumptions like these will rule out the doubling strategies that produce arbitrage opportunities. This is the approach I will take.

I now return to the fundamental theorem of asset pricing, which says there exists a risk neutral probability measure if and only if there are no arbitrage opportunities. In order to discuss this, and in view of the preceding discussion, it is necessary to give a careful definition about arbitrage opportunities in the case of an infinite horizon model (the definition of the risk neutral probability measure is no different than in the finite horizon case). A predictable trading strategy H will be said to be *admissible* if there exists a scalar $m < \infty$ such that the time-t wealth $V_t \geq -m$ for all t (this inequality holds with probability one; note admissibility rules out doubling strategies). The admissible, self-financing trading strategy H is said to be an *arbitrage opportunity* if (recall $V_t^* = V_t/B_t$ is the time-t discounted value of the portfolio):

1   $V_0 = V_0^* = 0$
2   There exists a random variable $V^* \in \mathscr{F}$ such that $V_t^* \to V^*$ as $t \to \infty$
    (that is, $P(V_t^* \to V^*) = 1$)
3   $V^* \geq 0$
4   $E[V^*] > 0$

Thus (1), (3), and (4) are the same as in the finite horizon case, except that here they involve the discounted wealth V^* after an infinite number of trading periods, with V^* given in (2).

It is now easy to explain the following:

 (7.14) If there exists a risk neutral probability measure Q, then there are no arbitrage opportunities.

To see this, suppose H is an admissible trading strategy with V^* as in (2) and with $V_0^* = 0$. Then just as in the finite horizon case, $t \to V_t^*$ is a martingale under Q, so $E_Q[V_t^*] = V_0^* = 0$ for all t. It follows from Fatou's Lemma (a technical convergence theorem for sequences of random variables) that $E_Q[V^*] \leq 0$, so V^* cannot satisfy both (3) and (4). Thus H cannot be an arbitrage opportunity.

Unfortunately, the converse of (7.14), which together with (7.14) would comprise the Fundamental Theorem of Asset Pricing, is not true for general infinite horizon models. This will be illustrated with the following example.

Example 7.2 Consider a securities market model with one risky security S, $r = 0$, and a countable sample space $\Omega = \{1, 2 \ldots\}$. Set $S_0 = 1$ and, for all $t \geq 1$ and all $\omega \in \Omega$, set

$$S_t(\omega) = \begin{cases} (1/2)^t & t < \omega \\ (\omega^2 + 2\omega + 2)(1/2)^\omega, & t \geq \omega \end{cases}$$

This means that in state ω the price falls by 50 per cent per period for $\omega - 1$ consecutive periods, from time $\omega - 1$ to time ω the price increases by $(\omega^2 + 2\omega)(1/2)^\omega$, and from then on the price is constant. In other words,

$$\Delta S_t(\omega) = S_t(\omega) - S_{t-1}(\omega) = \begin{cases} -(1/2)^t, & t < \omega \\ (\omega^2 + 2\omega)(1/2)^\omega, & t = \omega \\ 0, & t > \omega \end{cases}$$

Let H_t denote the number of shares of the risky security held from time $t - 1$ to time t. Given the nature of the price process, nothing is lost be restricting attention to trading strategies where $\{H_t\}$ is a sequence of real numbers. In order to avoid doubling strategies, it will also be assumed that the sequences $\{H_t\}$ are bounded. Of course, the trading strategies must be self-financing. Hence the admissible trading strategies are fully described by the initial wealth V_0 and the bounded sequence $\{H_t\}$ of real numbers.

If $t < \omega$, then during period t the portfolio loses $(1/2)^t H_t$ in value, whereas if $t = \omega$, then the portfolio gains $(\omega^2 + 2\omega)(1/2)^\omega H_t$. Of course, if $t > \omega$, then the portfolio remains constant in value, even though the value of H_t might be non-zero. Hence the time t value of the portfolio under admissible trading strategy $(V_0, \{H_t\})$ is

$$V_t(\omega) = \begin{cases} V_0 - \sum_{s=1}^{t}(1/2)^s H_s & t < \omega \\ V_0 - \sum_{s=1}^{\omega-1}(1/2)^s H_s + (\omega^2 + 2\omega)(1/2)^\omega H_\omega, & t \geqslant \omega \end{cases}$$

It is easy to verify that the value process V is bounded below, since the sequence H_t is required to be bounded.

The absence of arbitrage in this market follows from three factors: the date of the price increase is unpredictable; the price will be arbitrarily low even after the increase if ω is sufficiently large; and only bounded trading strategies are allowed. Recall the definition of an arbitrage opportunity as well as the fact that $V_t = V_t^*$ since $r = 0$. If $V_0 = 0$ and $\{H_t\}$ is such that $V_t \to V$ with $V(\omega) \geqslant 0$ for all ω, then

$$(7.15) \qquad -\sum_{t=1}^{\omega-1}(1/2)^t H_t + (\omega^2 + 2\omega)(1/2)^\omega H_\omega \geqslant 0, \quad \text{all } \omega \in \Omega$$

Now suppose for some integer k and some $\varepsilon > 0$ that

$$(7.16) \qquad \sum_{t=1}^{k}(1/2)^t H_t > \varepsilon$$

It follows easily by induction, using (7.15), that

$$(\omega^2 + 2\omega)(1/2)^\omega H_\omega > \varepsilon, \quad \text{all } \omega > k$$

But this cannot be true because $\{H_t\}$ is bounded, so there does not exist any integer k and $\varepsilon > 0$ such that (7.16) is true. In other words, it must be that

(7.17) $$\sum_{t=1}^{k} (1/2)^t H_t \leqslant 0, \quad \text{all } k \geqslant 1$$

Taking $\omega = 1$ in (7.15) and $k = 1$ in (7.17), it follows that $H_1 = 0$. More generally, if $H_1 = H_2 = \ldots = H_{k-1} = 0$, then (7.15) and (7.17) imply $H_k = 0$. Thus, by induction, our candidate for an arbitrage opportunity satisfies $H_t = 0$ for all t. There cannot exist any arbitrage opportunities.

To show there cannot exist any risk neutral probability measures Q, consider what the risk neutral conditional probabilities must be. Let q_{t-1} denote the risk neutral conditional probability of an "up" move from time $t - 1$ to time t. The corresponding conditional expectation of ΔS_t must be zero, that is,

$$q_{t-1}(t^2 + 2t)(1/2)^t + (1 - q_{t-1})[-1/2)^t] = 0. \quad \text{all } t \geqslant 1$$

This implies

(7.18) $$q_{t-1} = (t+1)^{-2}, \quad \text{all } t \geqslant 1$$

Another induction argument shows that the unconditional risk neutral probability $Q(\omega \geqslant t)$ must therefore equal $(t+1)/(2t)$, which, it should be noted, converges to $1/2$ as $t \to \infty$. But for this to be a valid probability measure, it must be that

$$\lim_{t \to \infty} Q(\omega \geqslant t) = 0$$

whereas here this limit equals 1.2. Thus there are no probability measures under which the price process S is a martingale.

While example 7.2 is a discouraging result, it is not the end of the world. In the first place, while some might argue that the security model is a reasonable one from the economic point of view, others would argue that it is not. Modest variations on the definition of an arbitrage opportunity could lead to the identification of undesirable trading strategies.[2] These variations can become very technical, so they will not be pursued here. In the second place, we had to work quite hard to come up with an example like this. Such examples are rare. In practice, risk neutral probability measures invariably exist for realistic models of securities markets, even if there is an infinite number of trading periods.

Exercise 7.3 Show in detail that (7.15) and (7.16) imply $(\omega^2 + 2\omega)(1/2)^\omega H_\omega > \varepsilon$ for all $\omega > k$.

Exercise 7.4   Show in detail that (7.15) and (7.17) imply $H_t = 0$ for all $t = 0$.

Exercise 7.5   Show in detail that (7.18) implies $Q(\omega \geqslant t) = (t+1)/(2t)$.

NOTES

1 This result and much of the subsequent development is based on Dalang, Morton and Willinger (1990). See also Schachermayer (1992).
2 See Schachermayer (1994) for a comprehensive, advanced study of this subject.

Appendix:
Linear Programming

Linear programs are optimization problems where there is a linear objective function in one or more variables and there is also a number of linear constraints. Linear programs have many useful applications, such as the scheduling of transportation systems, the control of production and inventory systems, and the optimal allocation of scarce resources. The study of linear programs is a primary topic in the subject of operations research. Many useful books have been written on the subject, ranging from the classical book by Dantzig (1963), through the excellent treatments by Simonnard (1966), Murty (1976) and Chvatal (1980), and up to the recent text by Sierksma (1996). The purpose of this appendix is to briefly summarize the aspects of linear programming that are utilized for the theory of securities markets in this book.

A typical linear program is of the form

(A.1)
$$minimize \quad c'X$$
$$subject \ to \quad AX \geqslant b$$
$$X \geqslant 0$$

where the decision variables comprise the non-negative column vector $X \in \mathbb{R}^n$ and the data consist of the column vector $c \in \mathbb{R}^n$, the column vector $b \in \mathbb{R}^m$, and the $m \times n$ matrix $A = (a_{ij})$. The feasible region, that is $\{X \in \mathbb{R}^n : AX \geqslant b, X \geqslant 0\}$, is either empty or a convex subset of $\mathbb{R}^n$, being the intersection of $m \times n$ half-spaces. Moreover, the feasible region, if it is non-empty, will have a number of *corners*, *vertices*, or *extreme points*, that is, feasible points which cannot be expressed as convex combinations of other feasible points. Since the objective function is linear, if an optimal solution exists, then at least one extreme point will be optimal.

Linear programs are solved by using one of two kinds of algorithms. The *simplex algorithm* and its variations proceed from one extreme point to another in a systematic fashion until the optimal extreme point is reached. The *ellipsoid method* ignores the extreme points but rather focuses on solving a certain system of inequalities; it enjoys the theoretical property of having a computational time that is bounded above by a fixed polynomial in the size of the data. Both kinds of algorithms are readily available in the form of commercial computer code.

There are several variations to the form in (A.1): the objective function can be maximized, some of the m constraints can be equalities and/or reverse inequalities, and some of the variables can be unrestricted in sign. However, all such variations can be transformed to the *standard form* (A.1). For instance, maximizing $c'x$ is the same as minimizing $-c'x$, and the constraint $\sum_j a_{ij} X_j \leqslant b_i$ is the same as $\sum_j (-a_{ij}) X_j \geqslant -b_i$. Also, the constraint $\sum_j a_{ij} X_j = b_i$ is the same as the pair of constraints $\sum_i a_{ij} X_j \leqslant b_i$ and $\sum_i a_{ij} X_j \geqslant b_i$. Finally, if the variable X_j is unrestricted in sign, then it is equivalent to replace it everywhere in the problem by the difference, say $U_j - V_j$, of two non-negative variables.

Every linear program (LP) is paired with its *dual*. For instance, the dual of the LP in standard form (A.1) is

(A.2)
$$\text{minimize} \quad Y'b$$
$$\text{subject to} \quad A'Y \leqslant c$$
$$Y \geqslant 0$$

where $Y \in \mathbb{R}^m$ is a column vector of variables. Using the transformations in the preceding paragraph, it is straightforward to show that the dual of (A.2) is the original LP (A.1) (see exercise A.1). This principle is true for any of the variations discussed in the preceding paragraph; in general, with the convention of calling the original LP the *primal*, one says that 'the dual of the dual is the primal.'

It is worthwhile spending a minute considering the duals of the different variations discussed above. First note that the m primal constraints are in one-to-one correspondence with the dual variables. Similarly, the n primal variables are in one-to-one correspondence with the dual constraints. To establish the dual of an arbitrary LP, one begins by making sure that if the primal objective function is to be minimized, then there are no "less than or equal to" (that is, "$\leqslant$") constraints. Similarly, if the primal objective function is to be maximized, then there must not be any "greater than or equal to" (that is, "$\geqslant$") constraints.

Next, as in going between (A.1) and (A.2), if the primal is "maximization" then the dual is "minimization," and vice versa. The data in the primal objective function becomes the data in the dual right hand side, and vice versa. If the data in the left hand side of the primal constraints is organized in the matrix A, then the corresponding dual matrix becomes the transpose A' (keep in mind that $(AX)' = X'A'$). Moreover, if a primal variable is required to be non-negative, then the corresponding dual constraint is an inequality ("$\leqslant$" if the dual objective function is to be maximized; "$\geqslant$" otherwise). Furthermore, if a primal constraint is an inequality, then the corresponding dual variable is required to be non-negative.

Now for the variations. If a primal variable is unrestricted in sign, then the corresponding dual constraint is an equality (see exercise A.2). And if a primal constraint is an equality, then the corresponding dual variable is unrestricted in sign (see exercise A.3).

Every linear program can be classified into one of three categories, as indicated in the following:

(**A.3**)   Given an arbitrary linear program, either

    (a)   it has a finite optimal solution,

    (b)   the optimal solution is unbounded, or

    (c)   the feasible region is empty.

For example, minimizing X_1 with respect to the non-negative variables X_1 and X_2 is an example of (a), whereas changing this to a maximization problem gives an example of (b). Adding the constraint $X_1 + X_2 \leqslant -7$ gives an example of (c).

There is a logical relationship between the category for a linear program and the category of its dual. Suppose X is feasible for (A.1) and Y is feasible for (A.2). Multiplying the primal constraints on the left by the row vector Y' gives $Y'AX \geqslant Y'b$. Meanwhile, the dual constraints are the same as $Y'A \leqslant c'$, so multiplying this on the right by the column vector X gives $Y'AX \leqslant c'X$. Combining these inequalities give $c'X \geqslant Y'b$. Since X and Y are arbitrary feasible points, some logical conclusions are:

(**A.4**)   If a linear program is in category (A.3a), then its dual cannot be in category (A.3b). Moreover, if a linear program is in category (A.3b), then its dual must be in category (A.3c).

If a linear program is in category (A.3a), then can its dual be in (A.3c)? The answer is no:

(**A.5**)   If a linear program is in category (A.3a), then so is its dual.

Before proving this result, it should be mentioned that it is possible for a linear program as well as its dual to both be in category (A.3c) (see exercise A.4). Thus if a linear program is in category (A.3c), it follows that its dual is in either category (A.3b) or (A.3c), but it cannot be in (A.3a).

In order to verify (A.5), use will be made of Farkas's Lemma, which is derived from the separating hyperplane theorem. Although this lemma was already stated for exercise 1.11, it will be repeated here for convenience:

(**A.6**)   Given the matrix D and the row vector d, either there exists a column vector v such that $Dv \leqslant 0$ and the scalar dv is strictly positive or there exists a non- negative row vector w such that $wD = d$, but not both.

To apply this lemma, take for D the matrix consisting of $n + m$ rows and $m + 1$ columns with (A', c) comprising the first n rows and $(-I, 0)$ comprising the last m rows, where I is the $m \times m$ identity matrix. Set d equal to the $m + 1$-dimensional row vector $(0, \ldots 0, 1)$. It is left to the reader (exercise A.5) to show that (A.2) is feasible if and only if there exists some v such that $Dv \leqslant 0$ and dv is strictly positive.

We now prove (A.5) by assuming linear program (A.1) is in category (A.3a) while LP (A.2) is in category (A.3c) and then deriving a contradiction.

By the preceding paragraph and (A.6), if LP (A.2) is in category (A.3c), then there exists a non-negative row vector $w = (w_1, w_2)$ such that $wD = d$, where w_1 has n components and w_2 has m components. Writing this equation explicitly yields two equations, one of which is $w_1 c = -1$. The other equation is $w_1 A' - w_2 = 0$, which is really the same as $A w_1' \geq 0$. So the infeasibility of (A.2) implies the existence of a w_1 such that $A w_1' \geq 0$ and $w_1 c = -1$.

Now let X be a feasible solution to the primal LP (A.1) and consider the point $X + \lambda w_1$, where λ is any non-negative scalar. Clearly $X + \lambda w_1$ is non-negative for all non-negative values of λ. Moreover, $A(X + \lambda w_1) \geq b$, so, in fact, $X + \lambda w_1$ is primal feasible for all non-negative λ. The objective function is $c(X + \lambda w_1) = cX - \lambda$, so letting λ increase to infinity it is apparent that the objective function decreases to minus infinity. This contradicts our assumption that the primal LP (A.1) is in category (A.3a).

It turns out that the conclusion of (A.5) can be strengthened. The proof of the following result is similar to the proof of (A.5), and so it will be left to the reader (see exercise A.6).

(A.7)   The duality theorem: If a linear program is in category (A.3a), then so is its dual, and the respective optimal values of the objective functions are equal to each other.

Exercise A.1   Use the transformations 'maximizing cX is the same as minimizing $-cX$' and so forth to prove that (A.1) is the dual of the dual of (A.1).

Exercise A.2   Use the aforementioned transformations and the duality between (A.1) and (A.2) to show that if a primal variable is unrestricted in sign, then the corresponding dual constraint is an equality.

Exercise A.3   Use the aforementioned transformations and the duality between (A.1) and (A.2) to show that if a primal constraint is an equality, then the corresponding dual variable is unrestricted in sign.

Exercise A.4   Show that neither the linear program

$$\text{minimize} \quad X_1 - 2X_2$$
$$\text{subject to} \quad X_1 - X_2 \geq -1$$
$$-X_1 + X_2 \geq 2$$
$$X_1 \geq 0, \ X_2 \geq 0$$

nor its dual have feasible solutions.

Exercise A.5   With D and d defined as in the proof of (A.5), show that there is no v such that $Dv \leq 0$ and that dv is strictly positive if and only if LP (A.2) is infeasible. In other words, show there exists some v such that $Dv \leq 0$ and dv is strictly positive if and only if LP (A.2) is feasible.

Exercise A.6   Prove the duality theorem (A.7). Hint: if it is false, then there cannot be any solutions to $AX \geq b$, $Y'A \leq c$, $X \geq 0$, $Y \geq 0$, and $c'X \leq Y'b$.

Bibliography

Bartle, Robert G. and Sherbert, Donald R. 1992: *Introduction to Real Analysis*, Wiley, New York.

Bazaraa, M. S. 1993: *Nonlinear Programming*, Wiley, New York.

Berberian, Sterling K. 1994: *A First Course in Real Analysis*, Springer, New York.

Bertsekas, Dimitri P. 1976: *Dynamic Programming and Stochastic Control*, Academic Press, New York.

Brown, William C. 1988: *A Second Course in Linear Algebra*, Wiley, New York.

—— 1991: *Matrices and Vector Spaces*, Marcel Dekker, New York.

Chiang, Alpha C. 1974: *Fundamental Methods of Mathematical Economics*, McGraw Hill, New York.

Chvatal, V. 1980: *Linear Programming*, W.H. Freeman & Co., New York.

Cinlar, Erhan, 1975: *Introduction to Stochastic Processes*, Prentice-Hall, Englewood Cliffs, NJ.

Cox, John C. and Rubenstein, Mark 1985: *Options Markets*, Prentice-Hall, Englewood Cliffs, NJ.

Dalang, R., Morton, A. and Willinger, W., 1990: "Equivalent martingale measures and no-arbitrage in stochastic securities market models", *Stochastics and Stochastic Reports*, 29, pp. 185–201.

Dantzig, G. B. 1963: *Linear Programming and Extensions*, Princeton University Press, Princeton, NJ.

Denardo, Eric V. 1982: *Dynamic Programming: Models and Applications*, Prentice-Hall, Englewood Cliffs, NJ.

Dixit, Avinash K. 1990: *Optimization in Economic Theory*, Oxford University Press, Oxford.

Dixit, Avinash K. and Pindyck, Robert S. 1994: *Investment Under Uncertainty*, Princeton University Press, Princeton, NJ.

Doob, J. L. 1953: *Stochastic Processes*, Wiley, New York.

Dothan, Michael U. 1990: *Prices in Financial Markets*, Oxford University Press, Oxford.

Duffie, Darrell 1988: *Security Markets: Stochastic Models*, Academic Press, New York.

—— 1992: *Dynamic Asset Pricing Theory*, Princeton University Press, Princeton, NJ.

Durrett, Richard 1991: *Probability: Theory and Examples*, Wadsworth & Brooks, Pacific Grove, CA.

Eatwell, John, Milgate, Murray and Newman, Peter 1989: *The New Palgrave: Finance*, W. W. Norton, New York.

Feller, William 1968: *An Introduction to Probability Theory and Its Applications*, Vol.1, 3rd edn., Wiley, New York.

—— 1971: *An Introduction to Probability Theory and Its Applications*, Vol. 2, 2nd edn. Wiley, New York.

Freedman, D. 1971: *Markov Chains*, Springer, New York.

Gantmacher, F. R. 1959: *The Theory of Matrices*, 2 vols, Chelsea, New York.

Harrison, J. Michael and Pliska, Stanley, R. 1981: "Martingales and stochastic integrals in the theory of continuous trading," *Stochastic Processes and Their Applications*, 11, pp. 215–60.

Hayhurst, George 1987: *Mathematical Programming Applications*, Macmillan, New York.

Hoel, P., Port, S. and Stone, C. 1972: *Introduction to Stochastic Processes*, Houghton Mifflin, Boston.

Huang, Chi-fu and Litzenberger, Robert H. 1988: *Foundations for Financial Economics*, North-Holland, New York.

Hull, John 1993: *Options, Futures, and Other Derivative Securities*, Prentice Hall, Englewood Cliffs, NJ.

Ingersoll, Jr., Jonathan E. 1987: *Theory of Financial Decision Making*, Rowman & Littlefield, Totowa, NJ.

Jarrow, Robert A. 1988: *Finance Theory*, Prentice-Hall, Englewood Cliffs, NJ.

Jarrow, Robert and Turnbull, Stuart 1996: *Derivative Securities*, South-Western College Publishing, Cincinnati.

Jeter, Melvyn W. 1986: *Mathematical Programming: An Introduction to Optimization*, Marcel Dekker, New York.

Karatzas, Ioannis 1989: "Optimization Problems in the Theory of Continuous Trading," *SIAM J. Control and Optimization*, 27, pp. 1221–59.

Karlin, Samuel and Taylor, Howard M. 1975: *A First Course in Stochastic Processes*, Academic Press, New York.

—— 1981: *A Second Course in Stochastic Processes*, Academic Press, New York.

Karr, Alan F. 1993: *Probability*, Springer, New York.

Mangasarian, Olvi L. 1969: *Nonlinear Programming*, McGraw-Hill, New York.

Markowitz, Harry 1990: *Mean-Variance Analysis in Portfolio Choice and Capital Markets*, Blackwell, Oxford.

Merton, Robert C. 1990: *Continuous-Time Finance*, Blackwell, Oxford.

Mikusinski, Jan and Mikusinski, Piotr 1993: *An Introduction to Real Analysis: From Number to Integral*, Wiley, New York.

Murty, Katta G. 1976: *Linear and Combinatorial Programming*, Wiley, New York.

Neveu, J. 1975: *Discrete-parameter Martingales*, North-Holland, Amsterdam.

Olkin, Ingram, Gleser, Leon J. and Derman, Cyrus 1980: *Probability Models and Applications*, Macmillan, New York

Ostaszewski, Adam 1993: *Mathematics in Economics: Models and Methods*, Blackwell, Oxford.

Parzen, Emanuel 1967: *Stochastic Processes*, Holden-Day, San Francisco.

Pitman, Jim 1993: *Probability*, Springer, New York.

Pliska, Stanley R. 1982: "A discrete time stochastic decision model," in *Advances in Filtering and Optimal Stochastic Control*, (edited by W. H. Fleming and L. G. Gorostiza; Lecture Notes in Control and Information Sciences, 42), Springer-Verlag, New York, pp. 290–304.

—— 1986: "A stochastic calculus model of continuous trading: optimal portfolios," *Math. Operations Research*, 11, pp. 371–84.

Puterman, Martin L. 1994: *Markov Decision Processes: Discrete Stochastic Dynamic Programming*, Wiley, New York.

Revuz, D. 1984: *Markov Chains*, North-Holland, Amsterdam.

Roman, Steven 1992: *Advanced Linear Algebra*, Springer, New York.

Ross, Sheldon M. 1976: *A First Course in Probability*, Macmillan, New York.

—— 1985: *Introduction to Probability Models*, Academic Press, New York.

Schachermayer, W., 1992: "A Hilbert space proof of the fundamental theorem of asset pricing in finite discrete time", *Insurance: Mathematics and Economics*, 11, pp. 1–9.

—— 1994: "Martingale measures for discrete-time processes with infinite horizon", *Mathematical Finance*, 4, pp. 25–56.

Sierksma, Gerard 1996: *Linear and Integer Programming: Theory and Practice*, Marcel Dekker, New York.

Simonnard, Michel 1966: *Linear Programming*, Prentice-Hall, Englewood Cliffs, NJ.

Strang, Gilbert 1988: *Linear Algebra and Its Applications*, Harcourt, Brace, and Jovanovich, San Diego.

Taylor, Howard M. and Karlin, Samuel 1984: *An Introduction to Stochastic Modeling*, Academic Press, New York.

Whittle, Peter 1982: *Optimization Over Time: Dynamic Programming and Stochastic Control*, Vol. 1, Wiley, New York.

—— 1983: *Optimization Over Time: Dynamic Programming and Stochastic Control*, Vol. 2, Wiley, New York.

Williams, David 1991: *Probability with Martingales*, Cambridge University Press, Cambridge.

Wilmott, Paul, Dewynne, Jeff and Howison, Sam 1993: *Option Pricing: Mathematical Models and Computation*, Oxford Financial Press, Oxford.

Index